Garlic
Garlic
Garlic

Other Books by Linda & Fred Griffith

The New American Farm Cookbook
The Best of the Midwest
Cooking Under Cover
Onions, Onions, Onions

Garlic
Garlic
Garlic

Exceptional Recipes for the
World's Most Indispensable Ingredient

Linda & Fred Griffith

Illustrations by Michael Halbert

Houghton Mifflin Company

Boston · New York

1998

Library of Congress Cataloging-in-Publication Data

Griffith, Linda.
Garlic, garlic, garlic : exceptional recipes for the world's most indispensable ingredient /
Linda and Fred Griffith ; illustrations by Michael Halbert
p. cm.
Includes index.
ISBN 0-395-89254-6
1. Cookery (Garlic) 2. Garlic. I. Griffith, Fred. II. Title.
TX819.G3G74 1998
641.6'526—dc21   98-28213   CIP

Designed by Susan McClellan and Eugenie Delaney

Printed in the United States of America

QUM 10 9 8 7 6 5 4 3 2 1

To our ever-growing family, the next generation

Madison Newman Myers

Forrest Jennings Drucker

Mackenzie Weller Hanauer Myers

Sydney Tate Drucker

Amanda Kim Myers

Alexandra Dove Castillo-Griffith

Paige Nicole Myers

May they always grow good garlic and enjoy good health.

CONTENTS

Thanks

G O, TRIBE! The summer of 1994 saw the opening of Cleveland's Jacobs Field—a truly glorious baseball park. Since that time, we have found that a good baseball game, played in the heart of our fair city, is the best form of relaxation when recipe testing and book writing make us weary. So we applaud the Cleveland Indians for bringing us so much pleasure—as well as a few tears. With their help we have published our last three books.

Throughout our writing careers we have found that farmers never refuse a request for help. When Cleveland's winter was its darkest and coldest, when even the California Late garlic was sprouting, Bob Zimmerman and Wendy Douglas of Bobba-Mike's Garlic Farm dug into their personal stash, providing us with superlative garlic for recipe testing. And now, since our urban yard has room for only about 100 plants, they have even designated a plot at their farm to be planted with seed cloves of our choosing. Thanks to Dan Donnarummo for introducing us to them.

Our enthusiasm for old varieties of hardneck garlic was awakened after reading Chester Aaron and Ron Engeland, Filaree Farm's chronicler. We thank Chester not only for his hospitality but for the garlic that was planted in our garden just after October's full moon. To Maya Watershine Woods and Tom Cloud, thanks for graciously welcoming us to Filaree Farm, for allowing us to quote liberally from *Growing Great Garlic* and for supplying us with a host of exquisite Russian and Georgian varieties. And thanks, too, to retired garlic farmer Horace Shaw for his enthusiastic assistance.

We found everyone in Gilroy, California, to be warm, welcoming and helpful. Without Patti Hale, however, we would never have seen the real story of her employer, Gilroy Foods, and the Gilroy Garlic Festival. Much of the garlic consumed in this country, California Early and California Late, comes from Don Christopher's Christopher Ranch, and even more than that is processed at Gilroy Foods. Thanks to Louie and Judy Bonino and Phil and Katherine Foster for welcoming us to their farms.

Robison Ranch's Jim and Jane Robison were graciously hospitable and provided heavenly shallots, Walla Walla onions and of course garlic. And we thank our seafood guru, Jon Rowley, and the people at Taylor United, whose Mediterranean mussels are the best.

Our friend Sanford Herskovitz, Mr. Brisket,

continues to nurture us with sage advice. Wine maven Donald Patz has again read our recipes and made wine suggestions, while his Patz and Hall wines helped sustain us. For additional wine counsel, we thank retailers Mario Vitale and Bob Fishman and distributors Sandra Jordan Earl and George Hammer.

Thanks to our special consultants: The Wine and Food Library's Jan and Dan Longone, John Swensen, Cornelius O'Donnell, Shirley Corriher, Jean Anderson and Sally Iannone for good counsel. Thanks to Dr. Philipp Simon for his quick responses to our e-mail queries. And to Art Form's Patti and Michael Artino, who kept our organic garden rich with herbs. Thanks also to organic farmers Adele Sraub from The Farmer Is Adele and Silver Creek Farm's Mollie and Ted Bartlett. Nick Journey of Boston's Steve Connolly Seafood got us the best seafood in the world. Richard Bauschard, AIA, showed us how much information there is about garlic on the Internet, and our computer gurus, Carolyn Javitch and Jack Smith, taught us how to access all of it. And Elfie Tran, who represents the Southwestern France Tourist Board, happily gathered information regarding her region's awesome garlic celebrations.

Our tasters have shown great courage, consuming mind-boggling amounts of garlic in a single meal: Deborah and David Klausner, Brenda and Evan Turner, Russell Trusso, Mario Vitale, Ann Sethness and Jack Smith, Sandy and Bob Lontkowski, Frances and Sanford Herskovitz, Carol and Bob Gross, Marlene and Mike Rosen, Sandy and Peter Earl, Dinny and Ronnie Bell, Dorie and Merv Sopher, Wes and Meg Gerlosky, Peter (our resident ethnobotanist) and Wilma Gail, Bob Zimmerman and Wendy Douglas, Linda's mother, Gert LeVine and Diann and John Yambor. We keep you vampire free.

More appreciation to Russell Vernon and his celebrated West Point Market; Ray Gallucci of Gust Gallucci, Cleveland's splendid Italian grocery; Bill Carroll, Nick Sharkey and Sandra Badgett of Ford Motor Company; Karen Preston of Leading Hotels of the World; and many friends at Continental Airlines, especially those who didn't complain about the sacks of garlic we stored overhead. Jake Kelly, of JFK Enterprises, Westlake, Ohio, turned us on to liquid garlic spray. Thanks also to QVC's Bob Bowersox and Paula Piercy, to food stylist Aliza Green, and to Le Creuset, one of the world's greatest cookware makers, and to Lauren Peck, marketing communicator extraordinaire.

Deepest thanks to Rux Martin and Barry Estabrook, who gave us this opportunity to work with the brilliant Fran McCullough, who challenged us and sharpened this book with her editing, and, of course, to our enthusiastic agent, Judith Weber. And last, but far from least, more thanks to: Michael Halbert for his smashing cover and illustrations; Susan McClellan for another grand design; Dolores Simon for meticulous copyediting and Jessica Sherman, Jacinta Monniere and Lori Galvin-Frost, whose attention to details keep us looking good.

We couldn't have traveled as we did without our friend Cindy Glazer, who gave tender loving care to Sanford and Frannie and the multitude of cats—Pooh Bear, Ginger Peachy, Smoky, Chile Willie, and Chuck.

And last, but not least, love and thanks to our biggest fans, our children: Tracy and Rob Myers, Janean and Andrew Myers, Barbara Griffith and Rob Bialic, Gwen and Barry Drucker, Rose and Wally Griffith.

Introduction

Our subtitle says it all: we cannot imagine cooking without garlic. That's not to say that we incorporate it into everything we make. But we happily admit that we are two of its biggest fans.

For us, garlic is the indispensable ingredient, nearly as vital as salt. But we have to tell the truth. We grew up *without* garlic.

Fred's father used tons of onions in his southern West Virginia restaurant, but he never used fresh garlic. Whatever garlic there was came granulated or powdered in jars. Compared to onions, garlic was expensive. And perhaps for some of his customers it was "low class"—an oxymoronic double whammy that for years kept a big percentage of the American population from enjoying this remarkable allium.

While Linda's New England youth was full of earthy, intense foods, she has no recollection of her mother or grandmother ever using fresh garlic in their tzimmes or cholent or chicken fricassee.

Social obligations in her early married life took Linda into the kitchen. Her first guide was the 1960 *Ladies' Home Journal Cookbook*. There were 23 Italian pasta dishes, but only nine called for garlic—and not much of it! The *Journal Cookbook* didn't want to offend readers. Here's one of its "Cooktips," quoted in full: "If you want a mild garlic flavor, put a clove of it into soup, stew, or sauce on a toothpick and remove before serving. The toothpick makes it much easier to remove." Hardly enough to get a vampire's attention, let alone keep him at bay.

America's resistance to garlic (or at least indifference to it) goes back to the earliest days. "Garlicks, tho' used by the French, are better adapted to the uses of medicine than cookery." Thus did Amelia Simmons, in the first American cookbook, over 200 years ago, give short shrift to our subject. Looking through a vast collection of antique American cookbooks, we found very few garlic references. The earliest actual recipe was for "pokemely," or cucumber pickles. J. B. Bordley, in his 1799 *Essays and Notes on Husbandry*, called for garlic, along with dill, mustard and horseradish. Lydia Marie Child in *The American Frugal Housewife* of 1833 also has a recipe for pickles in which she calls for "onions or garlic."

We could find no record of a passion for garlic back then. Sarah Josepha Hale in *Early American Cookery* of 1841 makes no mention of garlic. In *The American Kitchen Magazine* of January 1898, Mrs. Lincoln in her column passes along a chili recipe sent to her by a man in the Southwest. It calls for "two doses of garlic," as though it were a physic.

There are 3,455 recipes in *"Oscar" of the Waldorf's Cook Book*, written by Oscar Tschirky and published in 1896. It became the standard for the better American cooks in the early part of this century, but we found only one garlic recipe, for extract of garlic—cloves marinated in wine.

Americans seem to have inherited this garlic aversion from the English. In 1939, Drummond and Wilbraham brought out *The Englishman's Food: A History of Five Centuries of the English Diet*. Not a solitary mention of garlic in its 480 pages.

English writer Ernest Oldmeadow took his countrymen to task in 1943 for their unwillingness to give garlic a fair shake. "English travelers of the Superior Person type have made garlic a chief count in their indictment of the rude foreigner. 'Reeking of oil and garlic' was a stock phrase in their writings."

Oldmeadow says that John Ruskin considered alliums to be one of the strongest of class barriers. Samuel Johnson said garlic causes an ill wind behind and ditch diggers smell of it. Garlic was just not something that people with good taste enjoyed.

But we shouldn't blame it all on the English.

Elisabeth Luard, in her book *The Old World Kitchen*, quotes this advice for garlic lovers from a French epicure: "Enjoy your garlic at home parties only, maybe for lunch in the country; but in town, only for supper, so that everybody has a good night's sleep ahead to eliminate the fragrance which could be unbearable to others. Garlic has to be restrained to private pleasure."

And we can throw a little blame at, of all people, the Italians for garlic's bad times in the marketplace. Pellegrino Artusi's *The Art of Eating Well* may be the ultimate Italian cookbook. Originally published in 1891, it is now in its 111th printing. Artusi, who liked garlic, used it in only a few of his recipes, and he put the blame on his ancestors, the ancient Romans, who, he said, "left garlic to the down and out, while King Alfonse of Castile abhorred it to the point that he would punish anybody who dared appear at court with its odor on his breath."

W HEN WE WERE JUST STARTING TO become serious cooks, most of what we read about French and Italian cooking was filtered through the sensibilities of American writers. Heaven knows Craig Claiborne had been around and knew European kitchens. But in his landmark 1961 *New York Times Cook Book*, there were only two garlic dishes in the index out of perhaps 1,500 recipes. Garlic did pop up from time to time in recipes, but there would be no garlic orgy. Also in 1961,

Julia Child started teaching Americans about French food, with recipes that often used garlic, and sometimes a lot of it. But Julia would often pull her punches for her American viewers and readers by making the garlic optional.

Perhaps it was the social critic Russell Lynes who started to break down the class barriers that kept people away from garlic. After World War II, he wrote about the differences between highbrow, middlebrow and lowbrow Americans. In one famous passage, he noted that the highbrow person would make a dinner salad of simple greens with a dressing of olive oil and vinegar, tossed in an unwashed wooden salad bowl that had been *rubbed with a peeled clove of garlic.* (The lowbrow person would have green Jell-O with grated carrots in it and the middlebrow a chunk of head lettuce with mayo.) That set many of us on an immediate quest for wooden salad bowls and garlic cloves.

No one did more to free garlic from its American exile than James Beard. While there wasn't a lot of garlic in his early books, one recipe in *How to Eat Better for Less Money,* written with Sam Aaron in 1954, started us on the path to culinary liberation. It was also a recipe that Beard loved to demonstrate on television, because it always caused a stir. Garlic, he insisted, "is something that no good cook can be without." And he gave us a version of the ancient Provençal recipe of cooking an old chicken with 40 cloves of garlic in a casserole sealed with dough.

"When garlic is cooked a long time," Beard wrote, "most of its powerful pungency evaporates and only the essence of the flavor remains. For this reason it is perfectly feasible to use in a dish what would seem to most people like an inordinate quantity of garlic."

CELEBRATED ANTIQUARIAN and food historian Jan Longone used to be a successful caterer. She remembers how Beard's 40-clove chicken caught the attention of food lovers. She started making it for her clients, and soon garlic-hungry people would bring their empty casseroles to her kitchen. She would fill the dish with chicken legs and the garlic cloves, seal the lid with a flour and water paste, and send it home with the appropriate instructions for the oven.

At the great Paris restaurant Taillevent, we watched as a waiter brought such a pastry-sealed casserole to a table nearby. He chipped away at the dough until he was able to lift off the lid, revealing a pale chicken, head, feet and all, in a heavenly fragrant mist of garlic and other herbs.

He dismantled the chicken and put the boned breast meat on a simple plate, spooned on the rich, garlicky sauce, and presented it to the diners. He took the rest of the chicken away and brought it back later, boned and scattered on a salad of greens. James Beard would have been thrilled with this presentation.

No CONTEMPORARY American restaurant has had as much influence on the way we think about food in this country as Chez Panisse in Berkeley, California. Since 1971, the restaurant's founder, Alice Waters, has influenced our culinary world view with her cooking, her writing and her aesthetic judgments. The name of the restaurant comes from the work of the novelist Marcel Pagnol, who wrote so appraisingly about the garlic-rich culture and cuisine of Provence. From the beginning, garlic was an important player at Chez Panisse. Waters taught us how good a whole roasted head of garlic could be—squeezed out of its hull and spread like butter on a toothsome chunk of bread. And long before the proliferation of fairground garlic gatherings across the country, she was having her own Chez Panisse garlic festival every year on Bastille Day.

Other restaurateurs have done likewise. JoAnn Clevenger, who has been the proprietor of the small but enormously successful Upperline Restaurant in New Orleans since 1983, had used garlic for years. She had also used milk, cream, butter, sausages, well-marbled meats, rich sauces—all key elements in a great cooking tradition. It distressed her to read time and again that such things were bad for you. But when garlic was hailed as therapeutic and health-giving, she decided to celebrate. At last, here was something that couldn't hurt you, that could actually be good for you. So in April of 1988, JoAnn decided to have a garlic festival in her restaurant. Lucky diners had the choice of fresh Gulf fish with pecans and roasted garlic sauce, chicken with garlic polenta, roast duck with red wine garlic sauce, heavily garlicked filet of beef, and, for dessert, roast garlic spice cake with rum butter cream. Dangerous richness was tempered by a built-in antidote—a lot of garlic. At the bottom of the first garlic festival menu, Clevenger quotes Waverley Root: "Seasoners are the poetry of food, and its music, too. What is garlic? The tuba."

The festival continues, and Clevenger now devotes two months, June and July, to celebrating the pleasures of garlic.

Paul Bertolli, a Chez Panisse alumnus, celebrates garlic at his Oakland restaurant, Oliveto. And of course there are a dozen high-profile festivals where all kinds of garlic, garlic braids and wreaths, garlic equipment, garlic art, garlic salsas and sauces, garlic pills, freshly cooked foods loaded with garlic and even garlic ice cream are sold.

IN OUR OWN HOME, garlic just crept up on us. Linda bought her first garlic press in 1962 and it still works. We used to warn dinner guests that there was garlic in the food. On our trips abroad we'd often smuggle home a nice braid of French or Italian garlic, quadruple-plastic-wrapped in our suitcase.

But as much garlic as we used over those

years, for us garlic was garlic; we didn't know that there were many different varieties. And it wasn't until we started researching this book that we found out just how different these varieties can be—how different, for example, an Armenian garlic can be from one grown in Italy. We learned the difference between the popular softneck garlics that comprise most of the California crop, and the world of temperamental "designer" garlics that have become the province of the small boutique growers because of their complex flavors.

Today garlic is fashionable; almost everyone likes it. Good garlic growers become famous. More and more people are looking for something other than the conventional California softnecks, and they happily pay ten times as much for an exotic hardneck variety in a specialty market. In the past quarter of a century the use of garlic in America has quadrupled.

And of course the people who champion garlic's health benefits have made it popular with millions who might otherwise never have used it.

THE GARLIC REVOLUTION is in full swing, and the signs are everywhere. As we move along, we'll take note of some of the memorable people we've encountered. We'll visit a few farms, big and small, go to a festival or two, watch a million pounds of garlic get dehydrated, find out why the alternative medicine movement is infatuated with garlic, why vampires fear it, and why Shakespeare never had a good thing to say about it.

Now let us cook.

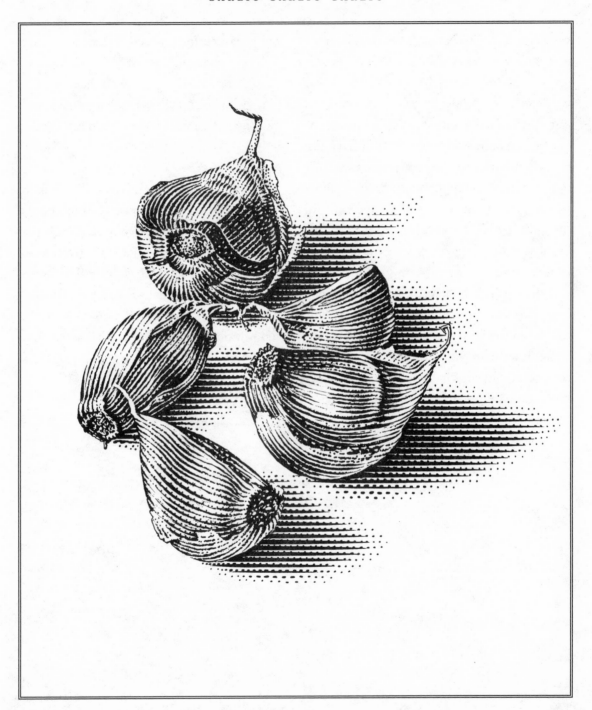

Garlic in the Kitchen

EVERY COOK KNOWS that if you take a knife to a good onion there will be a price to pay: you will weep. While the power to burn is not quite as pronounced in a clove of garlic, it's still there. A few minutes of chopping, mincing or crushing a batch of garlic cloves will prove the point. All alliums have the same power; they contain sulfur compounds that can cause discomfort, if not grief, in the kitchen. Not all garlic varieties are equal in this regard; some are as fierce as the most powerful storage onion while others barely make you blink.

The sharper edges of raw garlic are less apparent in the company of other aggressive ingredients, such as vinegar and tomatoes. The sulfur compounds that cause the sharpness disappear with cooking, and what is left from that remarkable reaction delights the taste buds and makes the food that garlic flavors better and tastier and healthier to eat.

Fresh Garlic

IF YOU GROW GARLIC, you know that there is nothing quite as wonderful as the flavor of brand-new garlic, just harvested and dried for a week or so. But most people do not grow their own.

Fresh garlic has the best flavor in the first few months after its harvest. Since most garlic grown in the United States is harvested during July and August, that makes late summer and fall prime garlic time.

Properly stored, California softneck varieties, the kind you are most likely to find in your supermarket, may last into early March, whereas the "designer" hardneck varieties lose their best flavors by late January and February. When those little green sprouts appear, you know your garlic is beginning to show signs of deterioration. Just remove that sprout and you'll still have a decent-tasting clove.

When *all* of the California garlic is sprouting, we know the end is in sight for garlic harvested the preceding summer. That's when we look for varieties coming in from Mexico and South America, most of them softnecks. Those with streaky red skins usually have a richer flavor, but there are really no hard and fast rules. Many imported garlics are reboxed when they enter the country, so often there's no way to tell the country of origin by the time they appear in the supermarkets.

HARDNECK GARLIC

VARIETIES OF FRESH GARLIC

From the cook's standpoint, there are two basic kinds of garlic—softneck and hardneck. Feel the top of the whole head. If there is no hard stick in the center, you have a softneck. The flexible top of the softneck makes it the variety most often used for garlic braids. (Hardnecks can be braided, but the tops must be soaked first to soften them.)

Hardneck garlics, the ones with the little stick in the middle, are more difficult to grow and more perishable, but they bring a wider range of flavors to the table. And many varieties have very large cloves, as well as more colorful skins.

Most of what we buy in supermarkets all over the country is softneck garlic from California, called California Early and California Late. The Early has a larger bulb, with somewhat larger cloves. These are the easiest varieties of garlic to grow in large quantities, and they also have the longest shelf life of all varieties. Their skin is usually white or silvery. If you scout local greenmarkets, however, you will probably find some outstanding designer garlics with more interesting flavors.

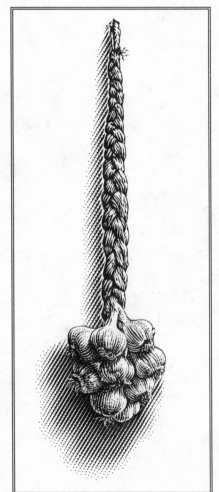

DESIGNER GARLIC VARIETIES

More expensive because they are more difficult to grow, designer garlics boast a wide variety of flavors, and they often have exotic names and histories to match. Many come from the countries in the southern part of the former Soviet Union. That's the region where the earliest garlics grew. Some of these have red or red-striped skins, others have mottled blue skins. Some are beige, others are quite white. Underneath the skins, the flesh is generally white. Sometimes, however, it will be almost tan, like old ivory.

The flavors of these varieties are amazingly varied. As with fine wine, garlic can be described in many ways. Different people will experience somewhat different flavors from the same clove. Cooking any garlic changes the flavor dramatically but rarely ruins it. Some garlics have a very hot but simultaneously sweet and

SOFTNECK GARLIC

A Garlic by any Other Name . . .

ERE IS A LIST of the garlic names (some marketing names, some arbitrary regional names, some quasi-scientific names) we've encountered:

Achatami	German White	Purple Stripe
Acropolis	Inchelium Red	Purple Tip
Artichoke	Italian	Redgrain
Asian Tempest	Italian Late	Red Revel
Brown Tempest	Italian Red	Red Rezan
Burgundy	Italian Purple	Red Toch
California Early	Japanese	Rocambole
California Late	Korean Red	Romanian Red
California White	La Panant Kari	Rose d'Albi
Carpathian	Leningrad	Rose d'Auvergne
Celaya Purple	Locati	Rose de Toulouse
Chesnok Red	Mahogany	Rose du Var
Chet's Italian	Metechi	Rosewood
Chilean	Mexican	Russian Redstreak
Creole	Mild French	Shatili
Creole Red	Nootka Rose	Silver Rose
Dukanskij	Oregon Blue	Silverskin
Elephant Garlic	Perle d'Auvergne	Skuri #2
French Messadrone	Persian Star	Spanish Roja
Georgian Crystal	Porcelain	Tipatilla
Georgian Fire	Purple Glazer	Xian
German Red	Purple Italian Easy Peel	Yugoslavian

THE BEST OF BOTH: GARLIC CHIVES

THESE TASTY, FLAT-LEAFED GREEN STALKS are often called Chinese chives because of their popularity in Chinese cooking. They have a pleasant garlic flavor as well as a delicate garlic fragrance. They are generally used as a tasty garnish. Garlic chives *(Allium tuberosum)* can grow to a height of more than a foot. The stalk is not tubular like that of its relative the ordinary chive (*A. schoenoprasum*). Some varieties have a thick, flat, gray-green leaf. Others are brighter green. Like the chive, it flowers handsomely, but the flowers are white, not the purple-pink of ordinary chives. Garlic chives are perennials; they can be raised from seed as well as propagated by division. Although they grow easily, they do not spread as quickly as chives.

fresh flavor. Others are more earthy, good for salsas and pestos. Some have a strange mineral quality when raw, yet when roasted are exceptionally pleasing. As with wine, the soil can have an influence on the flavor of garlic. Cloves from a single head, planted in two different places, can produce garlic heads that taste markedly different from each other. All of these nuances are interesting to the aficionado. But for the rest of us, there's no reason to fuss about a particular variety for any one dish.

Both hardnecks and softnecks can be roasted. It's just a little more difficult cutting across the top of the hardneck bulb as you prepare it for roasting. The very plump cloves of hardneck garlic may require a somewhat longer roasting time to become soft and creamy.

These are our favorite hardnecks:

Romanian Red has great flavor both raw and roasted. This garlic is rich and earthy, with strong herbal and mineral flavors. The cloves are plump and easy to peel. Even as the sprout develops in January and February, the rest of the flesh still tastes good.

German White also has a good shelf life and good flavor. The cloves are quite plump and easy to peel.

Chesnok Red is exquisite when very fresh, with a pink, silky skin that quickly darkens into a deep burgundy. This rather sharp Russian garlic is lush and sweet and has a rich caramel flavor when roasted. It, too, may have nice, plump cloves.

Here are our favorite designer softnecks:

Spanish Roja has a very easy-to-peel red skin. We love its bright garlic flavor when raw, so we like to use it in dishes that are not cooked. Garlic gurus Chester Aaron and Ron Engeland feel that this variety has *true* garlic flavor.

Creole Red looks like Spanish Roja, although the skin is often a darker red. Like its probably Spanish relative, it has a very fresh garlic flavor when raw. We find it a little more difficult to peel than the Roja. Both have smaller cloves than the other varieties.

Red Toch is ivory-skinned with deep burgundy streaks and blotches. From the Republic of Georgia, it's a very bright and earthy garlic. It is quite flavorful when roasted, although it lacks the full caramel flavor of the Chesnok Red.

THE CONTROVERSIAL ELEPHANT

WHILE THE LARGE BULB of elephant garlic does closely resemble garlic, its flavor is very mild and its texture is coarse and often mealy. Most scientists agree that elephant garlic does not belong to the garlic (*Allium sativum*) species at all, but is one of the leeks—*A. ampeloprasum*. In fact, many believe it to be the ancestor of today's leek.

The dispute over elephant garlic isn't confined to botanical circles. Most garlic enthusiasts dismiss it contemptuously—and we must confess we are among them. This is wimp garlic—contributing no real presence to a dish. But there are serious food writers who disagree, much to our astonishment.

Food writer Hugh Carpenter likes elephant garlic. He says it has sex appeal, a wonderful smell and plenty of flavor.

John Schumacher, chef-owner of Minnesota's New Prague Inn, likes elephant garlic, too. "It is milder, easier to peel," he says.

And another elephant garlic lover is Tod Kawachi, chef at Brix in Napa Valley. "It roasts up sweet and nutty," he says, "without the usual harsh 'rawness.' And it adds a fullness of flavor and roundness in the mouth." To each his own, we say.

GREEN GARLIC

GARLIC IS USUALLY PLANTED in the fall. Depending upon where you live, it begins to sprout sometime in early winter. Those young shoots are a little thicker than chives, with a tiny bulb at the bottom. Called green garlic, they're very delicious raw or cooked. When the leaves are young and tender, the taste is of garlic, to be sure, but the flavor is gentler and sweeter. Green garlic is easily purchased in late winter and early spring on the West Coast. But now that its reputation has spread across the country, some farmers are planting specifically for green garlic by spacing their cloves closer together (since you don't need to allow bulbing room). You can grow your own in windowsill pots for a taste of green garlic, but most recipes require a large quantity, too much for any windowsill. Green garlic is almost addictive; once you taste it, you'll be looking for it every year or growing it yourself.

ORGANICALLY GROWN GARLIC

Many farmers who grow hardneck garlic also farm organically. They offer something very different from the common and mass-produced garlic that fills the supermarkets, which has been sprayed with chemical fertilizers and fungicides. Does organically grown garlic taste better? It's hard to say, but we do know that most organic farmers place a great value on rich compost and healthy, natural fertilizers. And these materials influence the health of the soil, enriching the quality and flavor of what is grown in it.

BUYING FRESH GARLIC

Fresh garlic should feel very firm when pressed in your hand. Alas, garlic does not keep forever. Old garlic begins to sprout; that sprout has a rather bitter flavor, and in time the garlic will become soft and rot. Some people believe that eating the sprout causes indigestion.

TO STORE FRESH GARLIC

Except for a weekly supply in the kitchen, we keep our garlic in a cool, dark place in our basement. The refrigerator is too cold and too moist; refrigerated garlic loses its fresh flavor very quickly. Freezing garlic slowly destroys its taste, so we don't recommend it.

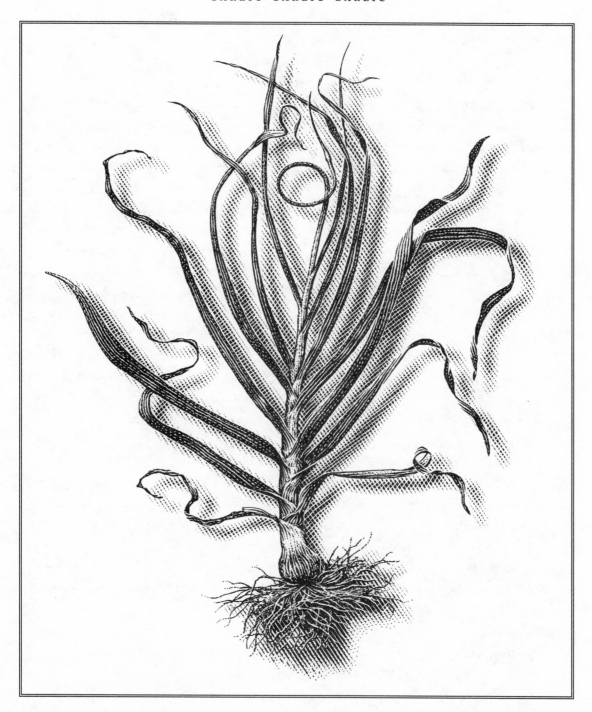

TASTE TEST

AAARRRGH!" CRIED THE WINEMAKER. "I can't go on!" Despite his sophisticated palate, he suddenly found himself unable to differentiate between one fiery clove of raw garlic and the next. No amount of crisp jicama sticks, ice-cold Perrier or water crackers could get his mouth, his tongue, his lips, his esophagus ready for the next potent insult—another chunk of one of a dozen varieties of *Allium sativum*. Still, he fared far better than most of the chefs, restaurateurs, food writers, caterers, wine merchants and winemakers who had come to evaluate and give us words to describe the differences among the various garlics.

We got the idea for such a tasting from the writer/garlic guru Chester Aaron, who put on a similar event at the restaurant Oliveto in Oakland with chef Paul Bertolli. Using Aaron's idea, we selected a dozen garlic varieties and invited 40 intrepid tasters to come on a Sunday evening. (It could have been even more complicated; we had at least 30 varieties in our kitchen but decided to restrict the tasting to 12. And heaven knows *that* was more than most could handle.)

At each setting we placed a whole head of garlic and some separate cloves so the tasters could see the differences. Then some whole roasted heads arrived with crackers. And finally, fresh raw slivers of the real thing. The guests had to taste it all as the price of the dinner they thought they had come to eat.

"It's just like a wine tasting," we lied. "So feel free to spit."

At Chester's California tasting, descriptions of the garlic included: muddy, piquant, caramel, artichoke-like, taste of the ground, garlic salt, dirty, starchy, not interesting, gritty and hot, like a chile, chemical.

A report on a New York taste test produced words like these: toasty, steely, soapy, dirty, pungent, too much acid rain, and aftertaste like ferocious walnuts.

Here are the varieties we tasted, as they are described in the Filaree Farm catalog, followed by some of the tasting notes of our guests.

None of the varieties emerged as the favorite. But at least four varietals got a 10, the highest number on our grading scale—Carpathian, Chesnok Red, Georgian Crystal and Red Toch. There were a few 9's. Most varieties were in the 4-to-8 range.

Variety	Roasted	Raw
Brown Tempest. Described in Filaree Farm catalog as a hardneck that has an initial fiery taste that mellows to a pleasing finish.	Nutty. Smooth. Sweet. Like baby food. Bland, an 8. Stayed strong in aftertaste.	Oniony and strong. Bites your tongue. Blows your head off. Fiery. Tinny aftertaste. Heat? What heat? It's for wimps.
California Early. An artichoke-variety softneck. Filaree says it is "mildly sweet with a controlled friendly taste."	Very nutty. Delicious. Sweet. Buttery. Creamy. Garlicky. A chemical taste. Not pleasant. Leathery. Soapy. Metallic. A 4.	Celeriaclike. Definite keeper. Surprisingly mild. One-dimensional. Too hot: I wouldn't use it. Hot as a fox, instantly. Maybe the fiercest burn of all.
Carpathian. A Rocambole hardneck from southeast Poland with "a nice overall tang, hot and spicy, strong and garlicky."	Bland. Strong and mushy. Rich. Sweet. Lemony. Nutty. Not enough flavor. Silky with slow heat and a bite at the back of the tongue.	Mild and crunchy. Mild, daikonlike. Like a radish. Like an apple. The best! A 10! OK: a 5. Pungent at the back of the palate. Strong but gentle. It made my nose run!
Chesnok Red. A Purple Stripe hardneck, an excellent baking variety with large cloves. Filaree says, "good aroma, good lingering flavor."	Buttery. Mild. Soapy. Skunky. Bland. Pasty. Bitter. Heavy. Musty. Holds up after roasting. Almost like candy. Excellent, complex.	The only 10. Mild, nutty, fresh. A slow build that burns the lips. Very strong and hot, from the front of the mouth to the back.

(continued)

Variety	Roasted	Raw
Creole Red. A Silverskin softneck. The Filaree catalog calls it the "winner of taste tests. Sweet."	Stronger. Very mild and bright. Very mild and creamy. Buttery, tart. Complex but balanced. It made the whole mouth warm. And the chin.	Sharp. No aftertaste. A 6. It burns my tongue. Tart. Bitter. Smoky. Peppery. Strong. Lingering. A slow build to an intense burn on the sides of the tongue.
Georgian Crystal. From the Republic of Georgia, a Porcelain hardneck. Filaree says, "Very mild and flavorful raw. Long storing."	Very mild, buttery, sweet. Sharp edge. Good flavor. Like a bad wine. Strong, chemical. Like potatoes. Flowery with a late-hitting heat.	Bitter. Hot right away. Too hot. Dirty finish. Taste is off. A 10. Super strong: bites the tip of the tongue, goes to the nose. Hot on roof of mouth, cheeks, tongue.
German White. A variety of German origin. A Rocambole hardneck.	Sweet. Buttery. Nutty. Creamy. Rich. Sweet. Too sweet, flavorless. Light, low heat.	Strong. Hot. Grainy. Spicy. Crunchy. Undistinguished, like elephant garlic. A terribly hot finish.
Metechi. Filaree lists it as a marbled Purple Stripe hardneck. "Raw taste, fiery but with a nice finish."	Pasty. Bland. Mild. Nutty. Buttery. Delicious. Bitter. Like caramel. Like bacon. Like jasmine. Like mashed potatoes. Oy veh! Delicious.	Mild to start and hot at finish. Pungent. Biting. Crunchy. Strong. Bitter. Sharp. Bright. Lively hot! Intense burn on the side of the tongue.

Variety	Roasted	Raw
Persian Star. From Uzbekistan, a hardneck. According to the Filaree catalog, "Very pleasant flavor—mild spicy zing."	Lightly nutty. Bland. Nice heat. Almost no heat. Sassy. Good acid. Like a water chestnut.	More tears! Mild, then hot. Crisp like a radish. Sharp. Sweet. Great spice flavors. Wow! Came on fast and hit the back of the mouth.
Red Toch. A softneck from Tochliavri in the Republic of Georgia. Filaree says, "raw taste described as perfect garlic flavor."	Mild like butter. Bitter, sweet. Spanish peanuts. Better raw. The richest, longest finish.	Very slight and subtle. An 8. The most balanced; my 10. Excellent flavor but not complex. A really slow build; some fire.
Romanian Red. A Porcelain variety hardneck imported to Canada from Romania. "Hot and pungent with a healthy, long-lasting bite."	Wonderful. Strong. Spicy. Hot. Warm. Mild. Sharp. Smooth. Buttery. Fragrant. Flinty flavor. Tingly heat.	Strong. Grainy. Biting aftertaste. Extremely hot. A wonderful 9.5. Brings a tear to the eye. At first not hot, but as it stands in your mouth, heat grows.
Spanish Roja. A popular Rocambole hardneck. Often described as having the flavor of "true garlic."	Mild. Definitely not hot. Bright, grows stronger. Another slow build, nice balance, not exciting or hot. Residual sweetness.	Hot!! Very biting, hot. Like a resin. Sharp and spicy. Stings! Hits you late and burns. A fast heat, not too intense, on the tip of the tongue.

A culinary life is simple when garlic is just garlic.
How amazing when varieties of garlic evoke such contradictory and passionate responses!

How to Prepare Garlic

GARLIC IN THE KITCHEN is many things: raw, cooked, roasted, powder, flakes and salt.

Fresh raw garlic is schizophrenic. A single clove of garlic dropped into the food processor and incorporated into a homemade mayonnaise becomes soft and subtle. That same single clove—cut in half and vigorously rubbed across the freshly toasted surface of good bread and drizzled with fine extra-virgin olive oil for *bruschetta*, page 113—becomes far more assertive. Finely minced and added to gazpacho, it takes on a vivid personality. Smashed and minced, it's hotter yet.

Roasted, it has a sweet caramel taste. A few cloves cooked in milk with potatoes are mild and a little sweet. Garlic cloves boiled for 20 minutes are soft and mild. A touch of garlic powder can be good in a rub for meat.

TO BREAK A HEAD INTO CLOVES

For a common softneck, put the head on the counter, root end up, and with the heel of your hand, press down firmly until the papery covering ruptures and the cloves fall out. To crack a hardneck, peel away the paper and then pull the cloves free.

TO PEEL A CLOVE

Cut off a bit of the stem end and peel the skin away. If this is very difficult to do, place the flat part of a chef's knife on the clove and press gently with the heel of your hand to release the skin. If you intend to chop or mince the clove, place the flat part of the knife on the clove and slam down hard with your fist, then press down on the knife with the heel of your hand. The peel should come away easily. There are devices on the market to help with the chore. (See page 35.)

TO PEEL A CLOVE

TO CHOP OR MINCE GARLIC

TO CHOP OR MINCE GARLIC

Minced into very fine bits, garlic yields a bright and lively flavor. If you smash the clove before you cut it (see above), the flavor will be a bit stronger.

With a sharp knife, depending on the size of dice you want, make several close-together vertical cuts into a peeled clove, but not through the root end. Then make some horizontal cuts, again not through the root end. Then make appropriate crosswise cuts until the garlic is diced as finely as you want it. Again make several horizontal and vertical cuts and then start cutting with a fine rocking motion of the knife. This is the technique used by experienced chefs. Some pieces will stick to the knife, so rub them off from time to time and scrape in the particles that have bounced away. Or chop the garlic with the salt in the recipe to avoid sticking and to increase flavor.

TO USE A PRESS

Garlic crushed and forced through a press will be very strong because so many more of the garlic's cells are broken, releasing the sulfurous chemicals. We press garlic when we want it to have a dramatic presence or when we dissolve it into a sauce. This is the best way to prepare garlic for garlic butter. Many cooks prefer to use a garlic press because they don't like

NO MACHINES, PLEASE

"I use garlic chopped or minced with a knife," says Marcella Hazan, "mashed with the flat side of a knife blade, or peeled and sliced into wafer-thin slices. I don't do anything to it that forces juice out of it, hence I don't press it or food-process it."

GARLIC MASTER

THE LATE, GREAT FOOD WRITER Bert Greene tells a fascinating story in his book *Greene on Greens*: "My grandmother . . . used garlic (like a fine perfumer I once observed selecting flower petals) with the meticulous concern for all other aromas in a creation. After bruising a kernel, she would rub it over the surface of a roasting chicken but never for a moment would she consider using more than that trace on the skin. I remember watching her rub a pan for a rib roast with garlic until it practically glistened; then she threw away the clove itself so that the seasoning would not overpower the beef's essential savor."

And while Greene's grandmother would insert little slivers of garlic into her leg of lamb, she would never, absolutely never, rub a salad bowl with it or use any garlic in a salad dressing. When asked why not, she answered, "Garlic in everything is just as bad as garlic in nothing."

Greene began to cook as a youngster. By the time he was 15, he had acquired a garlic press. Although his grandmother would never use one, preferring to chop her garlic by hand, Greene became quite attached to his handy gadget. An article in a 1974 issue of *House Beautiful*, however, gave him pause. Along with 13 other chefs, he was asked about his most cherished kitchen tools. Of course, Greene included his garlic press. Several paragraphs later, Craig Claiborne's list appeared—notably absent was a garlic press. "I wouldn't dare use a garlic press," he snapped, "because it transforms the flavor of garlic!"

With the passage of time, and experience, Bert Greene's own cooking techniques began to change. Finally he, too, substituted his fine carbon knife for his old garlic press. "And, indeed, I discovered that garlic minced with a knife does hold a more delicate bouquet and a subtler, less oily flavor than garlic mashed in a press."

And what technique did he employ when garlic ought to be *mashed*? He suggested chopping it very fine, first with vertical then with horizontal strokes, until the garlic has the texture of sea salt. Then, using the flat side of a knife blade, "whack it a few times."

chopping, but they should understand that pressed garlic is much stronger than chopped or minced.

Peel one large or two small cloves and put them into a garlic press; squeeze hard. The pressure crushes the garlic and forces the pulp through the tiny holes in the press. Use a knife blade to scrape the extruded garlic off the face of the press.

After the first pressing, you can scrape out what remains, mound it in the press and bear down again to yield a little more of the magic elixir. Then discard the juiceless peel left in the press.

CRUSHING GARLIC WITH SALT

Many Old World cooks, especially in Mediterranean countries, work their garlic to smoothness with a mortar and pestle, frequently adding some coarse salt to aid the process. It takes a little time, but you can keep crushing the garlic against the sides of the container until it becomes a completely smooth, creamy slurry. The chemistry is unclear, but the flavor is outstanding.

GRATING GARLIC

Grated garlic has about the same pizzazz as pressed garlic. Hold a large-tined fork stationary on the table with one hand, and with the other, rub a peeled clove back and forth against the tines until it is pulverized. Mediter-ranean culinary expert Paula Wolfert did this quickly and efficiently on our television program. She put the puree of garlic into a little olive oil and stirred it into a smooth paste, ready for cooking.

Small porcelain ginger graters with sharp, hard, glazed teeth can also do a very good job of pulverizing garlic.

SLICING GARLIC

Use a very sharp chef's knife for slicing garlic; the small mandoline-like slicer tears it too much.

PROCESSING GARLIC

For large quantities, it's possible to use a small food processor, but the garlic bits will be unevenly minced and very strongly flavored. For just a few cloves, it's hardly worth the bother of cleaning the machine.

Cooking Garlic

WHEN COOKING GARLIC on the stove, do so slowly over low heat in olive oil, vegetable oil or butter. Keep your eyes on it, because it will burn quickly; burned garlic is bitter and will ruin your dish. If you're cooking onions and garlic together as a sauce base, sauté the onions first, adding the garlic later to avoid burning or scorching it.

When cooking garlic, we often cover it for a

few minutes, just to braise it and release good, soft flavors. Italian cooks braise the garlic in a little water dipped from a pan of cooking greens. You can also just boil the cloves in water for 20 minutes to tame them.

Moist cooking makes garlic soft and mellow. Roasting makes it nutty and caramel-like.

DRY-ROASTING GARLIC

Unpeeled garlic cloves can be roasted in a dry skillet over medium heat as the Mexicans do. This method yields an excellent toasted flavor, one that is not as caramel-like as traditionally roasted garlic. Heat a cast-iron skillet over medium heat until hot. Cook garlic cloves, turning often, until soft to the touch and somewhat blackened in spots, about 15 minutes. Set aside until cool, then peel and mince.

Dry-roasting is good when you want the bits of toasted garlic to be recognizable, like little bursts of flavor, or when you do not want the very sweet taste.

OVEN-ROASTING GARLIC

Roasted garlic has a creamy texture and a splendid sweet flavor. We add a small bit of water to the garlic to stimulate the caramelization process.

Preheat the oven to 325°F. Slice off the top of a head of garlic. Gently remove outer papery skin from sides of head. Place head in a small ovenproof dish. Spoon 1 tablespoon of oil over top of garlic, then drizzle 1 teaspoon of water over it. Cover tightly with foil. Bake garlic for 1¼ hours. Uncover, baste with any remaining pan juices, and bake uncovered until golden, about 15 minutes more.

We store roasted garlic in the refrigerator, ready to use. It will keep for about 10 days.

USING ALL THOSE TINY CLOVES

We try to avoid buying garlic that has many tiny cloves; they're just too labor-intensive. Sometimes we press a number of them together,

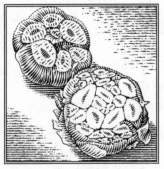

TO OVEN-ROAST GARLIC

hoping that the outer skin is not thin enough to come through the openings. These cloves are best, however, for adding some subtle garlic flavor to herb vinegars.

Preserving Fresh Garlic

Can you mince garlic ahead and refrigerate or freeze it? Minced garlic holds its fresh flavor for only a few hours. After that it becomes very bitter. Then, after a day in the refrigerator, minced garlic loses some heat and becomes dull.

We don't freeze garlic because extreme cold diminishes its unique flavor.

Can you store peeled garlic cloves in olive oil? Because of the possibility of botulism, this is not a good idea. However, if you soak the garlic in vinegar first for 12 hours, it is then safe.

What about the taste of prepared garlic in jars? These convenient consumer items are an excellent way for garlic farmers to add value to their produce. While the flavor of such products is somewhat less distinctive than that of garlic freshly peeled and/or minced, prepared garlic can be very handy for a busy cook—as long as it is then cooked. Left uncooked, it will sometimes have a slightly musty flavor.

Garlic powder, garlic flakes, garlic salt. If you have experienced Gilroy, California, at harvest time, you have smelled these products being made. Powder, flakes and salt are all dehydrated garlic, ground to particular textures. In making garlic salt, the finely ground dried garlic is mixed with table salt.

While garlic powder and garlic salt are fine in meat rubs, and all these products are useful in a pinch, none of them has the great flavor of fresh garlic. Keep in mind that part of the dehydration process subjects the garlic to extremely high heat, which can change some of its chemical components.

Garlic Equipment

Here are a few useful pieces of garlic handling equipment:

GARLIC PEELERS

E-Z-Rol Garlic Peeler (see page 36) from the Omessi Group, Northridge, CA 91326.

Chef'n, a garlic peeler from Progressive, has a small basket with flexible hooks surrounding an opening at the bottom. When the clove is pushed through, the hooks tear away the husk. Sometimes the hooks also cut into the clove.

Rubber mat. A small square sheet of rubber or plastic works on the same principle as the E-Z-Rol but without its foolproof efficiency.

ON A ROLL

SOMEONE TOLD ME that they want to put the E-Z-Rol garlic peeler in the Museum of Modern Art," said its inventor, retired architect Ben Omessi. "I asked why, and they said it was the least fussy and most useful kitchen tool they had seen. Less is more," he added, remembering the slogan of his famous mentor, architect Ludwig Mies van der Rohe. Omessi's simple flexible tube is the ultimate device for peeling a garlic clove. His little invention looks like an oversize piece of penne pasta or maybe a rubber cannoli. It's made of a silicone compound with just the right amount of stickiness to grab the papery garlic skin. Put a clove or two of garlic in it, roll it back and forth on a flat surface a couple of times, pressing down with the palm of your hand, and out come nude garlic cloves.

Omessi's previous claim to fame was that he designed those ubiquitous Playboy Clubs that featured voluptuous servers wearing the ears and tails of bunny rabbits. But his more significant contributions have been in the design of scores of hospitals and physical rehabilitation centers across the country.

Ben Omessi's garlic peeler inspiration came after a major change in his life. He developed heart trouble a few years ago and had a bypass operation. Afterward he felt too weak to stand at the counter to prepare his garlic for dinner. Eureka! Suddenly he got the idea for the plastic tube.

He could have retired at the age of 62 and spent the rest of his days by the pool. But he didn't. His hospital design work had made him sensitive to the needs of the ill and the

GARLIC PRESSES

There are garlic presses available from several different makers. All work the same way, some more easily than others. The peeled clove is put into a small receptacle with tiny holes in the bottom. It is then crushed and pressed through the holes with a plunger. Some presses have larger holes than others. We have not detected a difference between the taste of garlic pressed through one kind or another. But of course garlic pressed through large holes will have a more discernible texture. Deeper cylinders are best for hardneck cloves because they

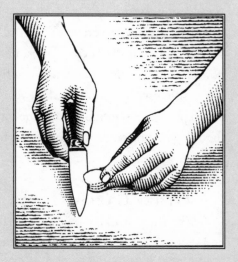 

physically challenged. "I concentrate on helping people with the ordinary activities of daily living," said the architect-inventor. After his official retirement he started designing devices to make things easier for those with special needs.

And how. Although the E-Z-Rol has never been advertised, Omessi is swamped with orders for the magical little garlic peeler. It's everywhere. Hundreds of thousands of them have been sold. The original is a sort of prosthetic beige. "But now we have them in red, green and cobalt blue," said Omessi.

"Julia Child has one," he said. "She came all the way up to our place to get it."

"What are you working on now?" we asked.

"An onion peeler!" he answered jubilantly. We can hardly wait.

better accommodate the larger cloves.

Many presses now have some type of plastic cleaning instrument with teeth, which can be removed from the handle and pressed into the outside of the press, loosening the pulp that remains in the holes. These gadgets are helpful for cleaning, but easy to lose.

Zyliss's Susi is made in Switzerland. This is a classic design made of cast aluminum. The cylinder is an inch and a quarter in diameter and one inch deep. It has 40 medium-size holes. The garlic is placed in the cylinder and the hinged plunger is positioned over it. When the handles are pressed together, the plunger stays parallel to the walls of the cylinder, ensuring even pressure on the whole area. Zyliss provides a plastic cleaning instrument that fits quite neatly into the upper handle. The Susi is handsomely machined. (Our much-used 1960 garlic press is also from Zyliss, but it has 139 tiny holes and requires a strong grip to crush the clove and force it through.)

Progressive International markets a very similar press made in Taiwan. The bottom handle of this press has gentle indentations that might make gripping it a little more comfortable. It also has 40 medium-size holes. It works like the Susi but is not quite as carefully machined, and the plastic cleaner is not as snugly housed in the handle.

The Good Grips Garlic Press, made by Oxo Division of General Housewares, is easy to use and efficient. The container for the cloves is U-shaped and larger than the cylinder on the Susi. There are 62 holes, which are somewhat larger than those on other presses. And it has heavy cushioned handles. A set of plastic teeth is bonded to the top of the plunger. After pressing, it is easy to swing the handle in the opposite direction until the teeth press into the holes to loosen the remaining garlic. This cast-steel press is the winner of the Tylenol/Arthritis Foundation Design Award.

Garlic press with screw top, from Progressive, is a cylindrical device with a perforated bottom. The bottom is unscrewed and the cylinder is filled with a number of cloves. Then a round plunger is screwed in from the top, pressing the garlic through. We found it a bit cumbersome to use.

Other Garlic Gadgets

Garlic slicer is like a miniature mandoline and slices a clove to the desired thinness by adjusting the cutting surface. Often it tears the clove rather than slicing it.

Fresh Fingers Odor Bar, from Progressive International, is an oval piece of stainless steel that removes garlic odors from your hands. Just rub hands with the bar under cold running water to remove garlic, onion and fish odors. An ionization process destroys lingering odors. From Progressive International.

Ceramic terra cotta garlic bakers made by a number of manufacturers, including Norpro, Canhome, Elkay, Himark and Via, are widely available in housewares stores and through major catalogs. While they are handy and attractive, a foil-covered ramekin will do just as well.

For Best Results

WE URGE CARING COOKS TO SEEK the very best ingredients available in their area.

♣ We try to cook seasonally and regionally, using the freshest organically grown local produce. If you need help finding organic growers in your region, check with the agricultural extension service or with chefs at fine restaurants, who often know local growers.

♣ We generally cook with fresh herbs since they impart full flavor without some of the bitterness associated with dried. We use kosher salt in our recipes, preferring its flavor to that of sea salt or ordinary table salt.

♣ We always try to use organic stone-ground flours, grains and beans.

♣ We prefer to grind pepper in a mill; that way, it's much fresher than the dusty preground kind.

♣ We usually cook with extra-virgin olive oil, using a relatively inexpensive fruity oil from the south of Italy sold in gallon containers. We use a lighter, more complexly flavored extra-virgin oil when it is not going to be subjected to high heat. When we call for a fragrant olive oil, we mean one with the aromas of fresh-cut grasses and herbs, signifying that the oil is especially fresh. When a vegetable oil is needed, we call for canola oil, which is polyunsaturated and has no discernible flavors.

♣ For Parmesan cheese, we always use genuine Parmigiano-Reggiano, from the region of Emilia-Romagna in Italy. Usually we grate it just before cooking.

♣ Our poultry is hormone-free, kosher-style processed, which means that it is dipped in cold rather than hot water before plucking. It not only tastes significantly fresher than ordinary poultry, it stays much moister during cooking. If you use kosher chicken, rinse it well because it is presalted, and do not salt it during cooking.

♣ Our meats are generally USDA-graded Prime unless otherwise indicated. We are equally particular about the freshness of fish and shellfish. Seek the very best purveyor.

🧄 All anchovies are not alike. If you have access to an Italian market, you can purchase salt-packed anchovies. When rinsed and filleted (an easy process), they taste significantly better than fillets in cans. They will keep for several weeks quite nicely.

🧄 We prefer the tangy flavor of low-fat (not no-fat) sour cream to that of the regular version. Occasionally, we call for evaporated milk (found on supermarket shelves with sweetened condensed milk) because of its particular flavor. You can use whole milk instead.

🧄 Two high-quality, modestly priced table wines are made by R. H. Phillips in Yolo Valley, California—Dunnigan Hills Sauvignon Blanc and Mistura (a Rhône-style red wine). We never cook with a wine we would not enjoy drinking.

🧄 Our recipes are generally quite flexible. Our full-flavored style gives the cook room to add a little more or a little less of most ingredients. Because we, like many passionate cooks, do not enjoy being tied to measurements, we try to allow latitude, especially when cooking with alliums.

SOME NOTES ON COOKING WITH ALLIUMS

🧄 When we call for diced onions, it means we want them to hold their shape in the finished dish. For "chopped onions," you can use a food processor, since the onions are intended to break down and cook into the sauce. With regard to scallions and green onions: We call them scallions when they have little or no bulb. We call them green onions when they have a large, fresh white bulb with no dried skin on it and a long, green quill attached.

🧄 We refer to sizes of onions as jumbo, large, medium and small. Jumbo is over 1 pound; large is ¾ to 1 pound. Medium is ½ to ¾ pound. Small is below ½ pound. A large, plump shallot will yield ⅓ to ½ cup when finely diced.

MEASURE FOR MEASURE

1 fresh plump clove yields 1½ rounded teaspoons of fresh minced garlic
⅛ teaspoon garlic powder equals 1 small clove
½ teaspoon garlic salt equals 1 clove

STARTERS

Spicy Mediterranean Olives with Garlic & Herbs 42

Brandade (a Creamy Cod Puree) 44

Roasted Garlic Pâté 47

Tapenade with Garlic & Sun-Dried Tomatoes 48

Anchovy & Kalamata Olive Tapenade with Garlic 49

Aegean Roasted Eggplant 50

Baba Ghanouj (Middle Eastern Eggplant with Sesame Paste & Toasted Pine Nuts) 51

Skordalia (Greek Garlic Sauce) 52

Caponata (a Simple Stew of Eggplant, Tomatoes & Garlic) 53

Gorgonzola Cheesecake with Garlic Salsa 54

Beer-Braised Shrimp with Creamy Mustard Dipping Sauce 56

Garlicky Marinated Mussels with Fresh Herbs 58

Artichokes with Minted Garlic Vinaigrette 60

Marinated Roasted Red Peppers with Garlic & Anchovies 62

Bagna Cauda (Warm Garlic Anchovy Dip with Vegetables) 63

Luscious Shrimp Toasts 64

Sautéed Oysters Piquante 65

Creole Crabmeat with Sherry, Green Onions & Garlic 66

Heavenly Crab Cakes 68

Garlicky Buffalo Wings with Blue Cheese Dip 70

Vegetarian Spring Rolls with Garlic Chives & Spicy Sauce 72

Silken Garlic Custards 74

Spicy Mediterranean Olives with Garlic & Herbs

THIS IRRESISTIBLE SNACK features a variety of imported olives, steeped in a garlic herb marinade. Olive trees grow all over the Mediterranean. Each region has favorite varieties, as well as preferred ways of curing them, dry or in brine. Happily, many of these olives are available in this country, often in Italian or Greek import stores. While we have a particular fondness for the lightly oiled, dry-cured olives from Morocco, we also love the Gaeta, Liguria and giant Cerignola of Italy. Other possibilities are the fabled French Nyons olives, as well as the Niçoise and Picholine, not to mention Greece's Kalamatas, Amfissas and Thasos (also dry-cured).

These olives keep for weeks in the refrigerator, but bring to room temperature before serving. If a garlic clove turns blue, discard it or save it for garlic aficionados (see note, opposite).

MAKES 5 TO 7 CUPS;
SERVES 10 TO 14

1 cup rich red wine vinegar,
plus more if needed

6 plump garlic cloves, peeled and
sliced in half lengthwise

4 small dried red chiles

2 teaspoons dried fennel seed

3 strips orange zest, about 1 x 3 inches

2 strips lemon zest, about 1 x 2 inches

2 teaspoons coarsely ground
black pepper

2 large (3-4 inches each)
branches fresh rosemary

1 cup extra-virgin olive oil,
plus more if needed

4 cups mixed imported olives,
thoroughly drained

In a nonreactive saucepan, combine vinegar, garlic, chiles, fennel, citrus zests and pepper. Cook over medium heat until mixture comes to a boil. Reduce heat and simmer for 3 minutes. Remove saucepan from heat, add rosemary and 1 cup olive oil and stir. Add olives. If more marinade is needed to cover olives, add equal amounts olive oil and vinegar. Stir to blend and cover saucepan. Let stand until absolutely room temperature.

Spoon mixture into a thoroughly clean large container, cover tightly, and let stand at room temperature for 24 hours, stirring from time to time. Remove any blue garlic cloves. Serve as a snack with apéritifs along with chunks of bread for mopping any excess oil.

Wine: Pol Roger Champagne NV Brut
(France: Champagne) or a good California sparkling wine

GARLIC BLUES

"This garlic is blue!"

Linda was astonished. She had made a mixture of good olives in oil and vinegar and had included a handful of whole garlic cloves. She was about to serve it, when she beheld a bizarre culinary development.

Some, but not all, of the garlic had turned a blue-jay blue.

So we put the question to Shirley Corriher, food scientist and author of *CookWise*.

"Sometimes vinegar makes garlic blue," she said. "A variation in the soil, or in the variety, causes certain proteins to be in the garlic, which then turn blue in an acidic environment. But it's safe to eat. It's just funny looking."

Brandade
(A CREAMY COD PUREE)

THE WORD *brandade* comes from the French verb *branler*, to crush or break. And *brandade* is a mixture of salt cod, olive oil and milk, traditionally crushed with a pestle until it makes a creamy puree. Looking rather like a bowl of mashed potatoes, ours makes a heavenly appetizer or a satisfying summer luncheon dish. With its origins in the South of France, it is found both with and without garlic, depending upon the region; near Marseilles, they use lots.

You can serve *brandade* at room temperature or brown it in a gratin dish and serve it hot. Linda likes hers with a little *harissa* (hot pepper sauce) on it, too. Serve it as a dip for raw vegetables or spread it on crusty bread or toasted croutons.

You need to start this recipe a day ahead.

MAKES ABOUT 2 CUPS

1 pound dried salt cod
5 plump garlic cloves, smashed
   and minced
½ cup warm milk or cream
½ cup warm extra-virgin olive oil,
   plus more if needed

Assorted crudités
Thin slices of toast, lightly
   brushed with garlic oil

The day before serving, place salt cod in a colander under the faucet in the sink. Trickle cold water over cod for 1 to 2 hours, moving pieces around (bottom to the top) occasionally. Transfer fish to a large bowl and cover with cold water. Keep refrigerated for 24 hours, changing water at least four times. Drain and rinse.

Place cod in a large sauté pan and cover with water. Bring to a boil, then simmer for 10 minutes. Drain fish and remove skin and bones. Break fish into pieces and place in a heavy bowl. Add garlic.

At the same time, gently heat milk and olive oil, each in a separate saucepan. Remove from heat.

Using a wooden spoon, or a wooden potato masher if you have one, vigorously pound fish and garlic together. (Or, if you are low on elbow grease, use a food processor.) Gradually add oil alternating with milk, continuing to beat vigorously, until both have been absorbed and mixture has the texture of creamy mashed potatoes.

If mixture seems too heavy, add olive oil, a tablespoon at a time, until the *brandade* is light and creamy.

Spoon *brandade* into a bowl or gratin dish. Serve at room temperature with crudités and garlic toasts. Or, if you prefer, brown in a gratin dish under a hot broiler. Tightly wrapped, this will keep at least 1 week in the refrigerator.

Wine: Compuget Viognier (France)
or a dry and fragrant white wine from the Rhône Valley

THE KINGDOM OF GARLIC

THE SCIENTIFIC NAME FOR GARLIC IS *Allium sativum*. It is the onion's cousin. And according to most botanists who study alliums, here is where it fits in the plant kingdom:

Division—Spermatophyta (from a Greek word meaning a seed-bearing plant)

Subdivision—Angiospermae (a Greek term for plants that grow their seed in a closed vessel)

Class—Monocotyledoneae (also from the Greek, meaning plants having only one leaf growing from a seed at germination—it fits, even though garlic makes no seeds)

Order—Liliales (from the Latin word for lily)

Family—Liliaceae (also from the Latin for lily)

Genus—*Allium* (from the Latin word for garlic)

Species—*sativum* (from the Latin word for cultivated)

Variety—*ophioscorodon* (hardneck) or *sativum* (softneck)

Cultivar—Rocambole, Silverskin, etc. (under these designations, more specific subcultivars such as Inchelium Red and California Early)

And how about the wild garlic we find in a field across the street from our house? The ethnobotanist Dr. Peter Gail says that it is *A. sativum,* genetically the same as the garlic we find in the supermarket. Other scientists disagree. They believe that *A. longicuspis* is the progenitor of contemporary garlic and that modern molecular biology confirms the connection. But if you bite into one of the tiny bulbs, you know it is garlic, whatever scientific name is used.

Roasted Garlic Pâté

WHEN SLOWLY ROASTED, all of garlic's sharp flavor rounds out into a very mellow, somewhat caramelized paste. Mixed with some pan juices, butter, white pepper and a touch of Tabasco, the garlic becomes a beguiling spread for crisp flatbread or toasted croutons.

SERVES 4 TO 6

4   large heads garlic
4   tablespoons extra-virgin olive oil
4   teaspoons water
3   tablespoons unsalted butter,
      room temperature
    Kosher salt (optional) and freshly
      ground white pepper
2-3   drops Tabasco sauce

Preheat oven to 325°F. Slice off tops of garlic heads. Gently remove papery outer skin from sides of heads. Place in a small ovenproof dish just large enough to hold them. Spoon 1 tablespoon oil over each head, then drizzle 1 teaspoon water over each. Cover tightly with foil. Bake garlic for 1¼ hours. Uncover, baste with any remaining pan juices, and bake uncovered until golden, about 15 minutes more.

Let garlic cool, then squeeze flesh from each clove into a shallow bowl. Add any remaining pan juices. Using a fork or potato masher, thoroughly mash garlic. Blend mixture with softened butter and season with salt, white pepper and Tabasco. Spoon into a small serving dish and wrap thoroughly. Store in refrigerator for up to 2 weeks. Bring to room temperature and serve with crusty bread or warm focaccia.

Wine: Mont-Marcal Brut Cava (Spain) or another dry
sparkling wine from Spain

Tapenade with Garlic & Sun-Dried Tomatoes

IN CAFÉS IN THE SOUTH OF FRANCE you will often find a crock of lusty olive paste on the table. It can be as simple as a combination of garlic, black Mediterranean olives and olive oil, or as complex as a lively mixture of anchovies, fresh oregano and sun-dried tomatoes as well. This makes a great spread for focaccia or a toothsome bread. Stored in a tightly covered container, tapenade will keep for weeks in the refrigerator. Just bring to room temperature before serving. If you have an herb garden, try including oregano flowers—they're especially delicious in this spread.

MAKES ABOUT 2 CUPS

- 2 packed cups pitted Niçoise or Kalamata olives
- 12 oil-packed or water-softened sun-dried tomatoes, drained
- 5 plump garlic cloves
- 2 teaspoons fresh oregano leaves, plus flowers if available
- 1 teaspoon freshly ground black pepper
- ¼ cup extra-virgin olive oil, plus up to 2 tablespoons more if needed

In the bowl of a food processor fitted with the metal blade, combine everything but oil. Pulse until pureed. Taste and add more tomato, if desired. With motor running, gradually add ¼ cup olive oil. Scrape and process again. Add more olive oil if needed to make a thick, spreadable paste. Scrape tapenade into a container, cover and store in the refrigerator. Bring to room temperature before serving.

Wine: Château Routas Rosé (France: Coteaux Varois) or another rosé from the South of France or California

Anchovy & Kalamata Olive Tapenade with Garlic

THIS UNUSUALLY ROBUST TAPENADE is a sturdy puree of kalamata olives, garlic and anchovies, with a generous taste of basil. Even if you think you don't like anchovies, try this— it's absolutely delicious, not at all fishy.

Try to purchase salt-packed anchovies, which can be found in Italian groceries in metropolitan areas around the country. Rinse them thoroughly, then carefully remove the bone. Pat them dry and pack into a container with a tight-fitting top. Cover with good extra-virgin olive oil and store in the refrigerator, bringing to room temperature as you need them. The excellent flavor of salt-packed anchovies is well worth the extra fuss.

MAKES 1¼ CUPS

1½ packed cups pitted Niçoise or Kalamata olives
1 2-ounce can oil-packed anchovies, drained, or 16 rinsed salt-packed anchovies, filleted
4 plump garlic cloves
6 large fresh basil leaves
1 teaspoon freshly ground black pepper
3 tablespoons extra-virgin olive oil

In the bowl of a food processor fitted with the metal blade, combine everything but olive oil. Pulse until pureed. With motor running, gradually add olive oil. Scrape sides and process again. Scrape tapenade into a container and store in refrigerator. It will keep for many weeks. Bring to room temperature before serving.

Wine: Billecart-Salmon Brut Rosé NV (France: Champagne) or a California brut (dry) rosé sparkling wine

Aegean Roasted Eggplant

THIS SMOKY, CREAMY PUREE of grill-roasted eggplant is sparked by a generous addition of fresh minced garlic and a judicious spritz of fresh lemon juice. Add some good-quality olive oil, and you have a snack enjoyed by millions throughout the eastern Mediterranean.

SERVES 6

3   eggplants, about 1 pound each,
     wrapped in foil
3   plump garlic cloves, smashed
     and minced
     Juice of 1 large lemon
3   tablespoons fragrant extra-virgin
     olive oil
     Kosher salt and freshly ground
     black pepper
1-2 tablespoons minced flat-leaf parsley

     Fresh pita bread for dipping

Soak for at least 15 minutes 1 cup of wood chips or 10 inches of wood for grilling. Drain. Preheat a gas or charcoal grill until it is hot.

Add wood to heated coals or briquettes, then place eggplants on grill rack and cover with lid or foil. Cook eggplants for 20 minutes, turn, and continue to cook until they feel very tender when gently pressed, 15 to 30 minutes more.

Remove cooked eggplants from grill and allow to cool. Remove foil, cut eggplants in half and scoop creamy flesh from skin into a bowl. Be sure to scrape caramelized flesh that adheres to skin. Mash thoroughly with a fork and stir in garlic, lemon juice, salt, pepper and parsley. Cover with plastic wrap and place in the refrigerator for at least 2 hours or up to 6.

Serve as a dip in an attractive bowl surrounded by wedges of pita bread.

Wine: Zardetto Prosecco di Conegliano Brut
(Italy: Veneto) or another light sparkling wine

Baba Ghanouj

(MIDDLE EASTERN EGGPLANT WITH SESAME PASTE & TOASTED PINE NUTS)

THIS ROASTED EGGPLANT APPETIZER is among the most famous of all Middle Eastern dishes. Our version adds mint and pine nuts to the classic. Whether enjoyed with a fork or used as a dip for pieces of pita bread, it is irresistible.

SERVES 8 TO 10

3   pounds eggplant
⅓   cup *tahini* (sesame paste), available in Middle Eastern and Greek markets
¼   cup water
4   plump garlic cloves, pressed
½   cup fresh lemon juice
¼   cup extra-virgin olive oil
2   teaspoons dried mint
1   teaspoon kosher salt
    Freshly ground black pepper
⅓   cup pine nuts

Pita bread for dipping

Roast eggplant, preferably over a grill or in a very hot oven, turning often, until it collapses and flesh feels very soft. The outside should be lightly charred. A 3-pound eggplant should take 45 to 55 minutes. Set aside to cool.

In a large bowl, thoroughly blend tahini and water together. Stir in garlic. Set aside.

Split eggplant and scrape flesh into the bowl of a food processor. Be sure to include any caramelized flesh you can scrape from skin. Pulse until mixture is finely chopped. Or chop by hand in a shallow wooden bowl.

Scrape eggplant into bowl with tahini mixture. Using a large fork, mix together with lemon juice, 2 tablespoons of the olive oil, mint, salt and pepper. Blend vigorously and set aside for at least 30 minutes at room temperature and up to 12 hours in the refrigerator.

Just before serving, bring *baba ghanouj* to room temperature. Spoon into a large shallow serving bowl.

Heat remaining 2 tablespoons olive oil in a small skillet over medium heat. Add pine nuts and stir until golden, 3 to 5 minutes. Pour nuts and oil over eggplant and serve surrounded by torn pieces of pita.

Wine: Bollinger Special Cuvée Brut NV
(France: Champagne) or another dry sparkling wine

Skordalia

(GREEK GARLIC SAUCE)

THIS THICK GREEK GARLIC SAUCE makes a marvelous dip to be served with vegetables as an accompaniment to fish or chicken. The potatoes can be mashed with a pestle in a shallow wooden bowl or with a potato masher. Avoid using a food processor or an electric mixer, which can make potatoes gluey.

SERVES 8 TO 12

2 large russet potatoes, peeled and cut into small (½-to-¾-inch) cubes

6 plump garlic cloves

½ teaspoon kosher salt

1 large egg yolk (optional, but makes a firmer dip)

¾ cup extra-virgin olive oil, plus more if needed

¼ cup fresh lemon juice

3 tablespoons white wine vinegar
Freshly ground white pepper

Pita bread, celery, carrot, bell pepper, and fennel sticks for dipping

Cover potatoes with water in a 3-quart saucepan and bring to a boil over high heat. Reduce heat to low and simmer until potatoes are tender, 15 to 20 minutes. Drain, rinse with cold water and process through a ricer or mash thoroughly.

Meanwhile, put garlic and salt in a large wooden bowl and pound with a pestle until thoroughly mashed. Gradually add potatoes and pound them with garlic. If mixture is still hot, let cool 15 minutes, then add egg yolk, if using, and vigorously mash or beat in with a wooden spoon. Alternating olive oil with lemon juice and vinegar, gradually add both to potato mixture, vigorously mashing or beating. Using a fork, add pepper, mixing briskly until very smooth. Mix in more olive oil, or even some water, a little at a time, if sauce is too thick to use as a dip.

Spoon into a container and store, covered, in refrigerator. It will keep for about 1 week. Bring to room temperature several hours before serving. Spoon into a bowl and serve with fresh vegetables and pita for dipping.

Wine: Jepson Vineyards Blanc de Blanc (California: Mendocino County) or another dry white sparkling wine

Caponata

(A SIMPLE STEW OF EGGPLANT, TOMATOES & GARLIC)

THIS DELICIOUS Sicilian eggplant dish often appears among a variety of small salads as part of the traditional Italian antipasto, or first course. While there are myriad variations on this flavorful eggplant stew, many without a trace of garlic, all versions have a sauce that is sweet and sour, or *agrodolce*. We, of course, prefer a *caponata* with garlic. We generally use eggplant varieties (such as long Japanese ones) that are not especially bitter, so salting before cooking is not necessary. This keeps very well for several weeks stored in a tightly covered container in the refrigerator.

SERVES 8 TO 10

½ cup plus 2 tablespoons extra-virgin olive oil

2½-3 pounds eggplant, peeled and cut into 1-inch cubes

3 plump garlic cloves, thinly sliced

1 sweet onion, cut into medium dice

1 cup thinly sliced celery

1½ cups tomato puree

3 tablespoons tomato paste

⅓ cup water

3 tablespoons sugar

½ cup rich red wine vinegar

3 tablespoons capers, rinsed and drained

¼ cup coarsely chopped green olives
Kosher salt and freshly ground
black pepper

Heat ½ cup olive oil in a large sauté pan over high heat. Add eggplant and cook, stirring often, until eggplant is somewhat browned and tender, about 10 minutes. Using a slotted spoon, transfer eggplant to a large bowl and reserve.

Adding remaining 2 tablespoons olive oil if needed, cook garlic and onion in same pan over medium heat until golden, about 10 minutes, stirring often. Add celery, tomato puree, tomato paste and water. Stir thoroughly. Simmer over medium heat until sauce has thickened, about 1 minute. Add eggplant, sugar, vinegar, capers and olives. Season generously with salt and pepper. Stir well, cover and simmer for 10 minutes over very low heat, or until eggplant is hot and liquids are bubbling. Remove from heat and let cool.

Store *caponata* tightly covered in the refrigerator. Serve at room temperature.

Wine: Regaleali Bianco or Rosato (Italy: Sicily)
or another very dry and fruity white or rosé wine

Gorgonzola Cheesecake with Garlic Salsa

SAVORY CHEESECAKES are always popular with our guests. This one gets the prize, especially when we use El Paso Chile Company's Cactus Paddle Salsa (available at specialty food markets everywhere; see Sources, page 414). We find the nontraditional blend of sweet and pungent Gorgonzola with spicy green salsa quite pleasing. The added garlic adds a mellow layer of flavor to the cheese. This recipe is inspired by one from Bayfield, Wisconsin's, Rittenhouse Inn, where owners/chefs Jerry and Mary Phillips continue to give new meaning to the word hospitality.

SERVES 10 TO 12

1 tablespoon unsalted butter, softened
1 cup plus 3 tablespoons grated Parmesan cheese
⅓ cup fine dry bread crumbs
12 ounces cream cheese, at room temperature
4 ounces imported Gorgonzola, at room temperature
1 cup sour cream
2 tablespoons unbleached flour
2 plump garlic cloves, smashed and minced
⅔ cup spicy salsa, preferably cactus paddle, drained of excess liquid
4 large eggs
Minced cilantro and more salsa for garnish

Preheat oven to 350°F. Select a large, deep baking dish or roasting pan to be used for a water bath in which cake is baked.

Evenly coat bottom and sides of a 9-inch springform pan with butter. Blend 3 tablespoons of the Parmesan with bread crumbs. Pour half of mixture into buttered pan and toss to coat evenly. Shake out excess. Carefully wrap bottom of pan in foil, leaving edges extending up so that no water can leak in.

In the bowl of an electric mixer, combine cream cheese, Gorgonzola and sour cream. Blend thoroughly, scraping sides several times. Add flour, the remaining 1 cup Parmesan, garlic and salsa. Scrape sides again.

With motor running on high, add eggs one at a time. Scrape sides thoroughly and beat again. Pour mixture into prepared pan.

Sprinkle evenly with remaining crumb mixture.

Place springform pan in baking dish. Slide oven rack partway out and set baking dish on rack. Pour boiling water into baking dish to go halfway up side of springform pan.

Bake 1¼ hours. Top of cake will be firm to the touch; don't worry if there are a few cracks in it. Remove water bath from oven and transfer cheesecake to oven rack. Cool for 1 hour in oven with door ajar.

Serve skinny slices of cheesecake warm or at room temperature. It can be wrapped in plastic wrap and chilled in the refrigerator overnight. Bring to room temperature before serving. Sprinkle with minced cilantro and serve extra salsa on the side.

Wine: Joseph Phelps Vineyards Vin du Mistral Grenache Rosé (California) or another rosé wine from California or the South of France

Beer-Braised Shrimp with Creamy Mustard Dipping Sauce

THESE SHRIMP MAKE a zesty appetizer for a casual summer supper, especially when served with our tangy mustard dipping sauce. In fact, the shrimp are even better when they can chill overnight in their garlic and herbed beer steaming liquid.

SERVES 6 TO 8

Shrimp

4   plump garlic cloves, smashed and minced
1   plump shallot, minced
½   teaspoon dry mustard
1   12-ounce bottle dark beer
1   teaspoon fresh thyme leaves (½ teaspoon dried)
1   bay leaf
¼   teaspoon Tabasco
½   teaspoon freshly ground black pepper
2   teaspoons kosher salt
1   tablespoon minced fresh chives
1   tablespoon minced fresh flat-leaf parsley
1½ pounds frozen peeled and deveined large shrimp (21-24 count)

Dipping Sauce

2   plump garlic cloves, pressed
2   tablespoons Colman's dry English mustard
2   tablespoons Dijon mustard
    Minced zest of 1 lemon
1½ cups low-fat sour cream
1   cup whole-milk yogurt
2   tablespoons Worcestershire sauce
    Freshly ground white pepper

To make shrimp: Have ready a bowl of ice water. Combine all ingredients in a large, heavy saucepan. Cover and bring to a boil over high heat. When you hear liquids bubble, reduce heat and simmer for 3 minutes. Uncover and check shrimp. If they are not all pink, stir, cover and cook 1 to 2 minutes more.

With a slotted spoon, quickly transfer shrimp to bowl of ice water and reserve cooking liquid. When shrimp are cool, drain. Let beer liquid cool. When it is cool, combine with shrimp in a large bowl. Cover with plastic wrap and chill for at least 4 hours and up to 1 day.

To make sauce: In a small bowl, blend together garlic, mustards and lemon zest. Whisk in remaining ingredients. Cover bowl and chill for at least 4 hours.

Serve shrimp on an attractive platter surrounding a bowl of dipping sauce.

Wine: Veuve Clicquot Vintage Brut Champagne
Gold Label (France: Champagne)
or another high-quality dry Champagne

Garlicky Marinated Mussels with Fresh Herbs

OUR GARLICKY MARINATED MUSSELS are, to quote our guests, "simply awesome." We always try to make more than we need so that we'll have leftovers to combine with tomato sauce and cooked pasta. Farmed mussels are the only way to go, since the cleaning is simple and there's no grit. This recipe has its roots in one given us by Pencove Mussels' Ian Jefferds, a pioneer mussel farmer in the state of Washington. But now we use the excellent Mediterranean mussels farmed by Washington's Taylor United, which ships them all over the country (see Sources, page 415). Remember, don't debeard mussels until just before you're ready to cook them.

SERVES 12

3   plump shallots, finely diced
3   plump garlic cloves, smashed
     and minced
2   teaspoons dried thyme
1   cup dry white wine
4   cups water
4   tablespoons (½ stick) unsalted butter
3   pounds farm-raised mussels,
     cleaned and debearded

Marinade

½   cup full-bodied red wine vinegar
3   plump garlic cloves, smashed
     and minced
1   cup extra-virgin olive oil
½   cup thinly sliced red onion
⅓   cup finely diced shallots
3   tablespoons minced fresh basil
     Kosher salt and freshly ground
       black pepper to taste
½   cup minced fresh flat-leaf parsley

Combine shallots, half of garlic, thyme, wine, water and butter in a large soup pot. Bring to a boil over high heat. Add mussels, cover tightly, reduce heat to medium-low and steam for 5 to 6 minutes, or until shells are open and mussel meats are opaque. Remove pot from heat. With a Chinese strainer or slotted spoon, transfer mussels from broth to a large bowl. Discard any mussels that did not open. Immediately place uncovered bowl in the refrigerator so mussels will cool quickly, about 1 hour.

Meanwhile, make marinade: Combine vinegar and garlic in a mixing bowl. Slowly whisk in olive oil to make a thick emulsion. Stir in onion, shallots, basil, salt and pepper. Pour marinade over thoroughly cooled mussels. Drain off marinade, then pour it over mussels again. Repeat this process several times to make certain all mussels are bathed in marinade.

Cover bowl and keep refrigerated, stirring from time to time, until mussels are to be served. Mussels should marinate at least 2 hours but not more than 2 days.

Just before serving, ladle marinade over mussels, sprinkle with parsley and gently toss. Serve with chunks of rustic bread and lots of napkins.

Wine: Cain Vineyards Sauvignon Blanc Monterey Musqué (California: Monterey) or a dry and fragrant Sauvignon Blanc from California or France

Artichokes with Minted Garlic Vinaigrette

ARTICHOKES AND GARLIC are a heaven-made match. Here we offer a minted fruity vinaigrette with enough garlic to lift the tasty thistle to soaring heights. If you pour it over the hot artichokes, the vinaigrette flavors are really well absorbed. Then serve the artichokes cold or at room temperature, spooning extra vinaigrette over the plated artichokes.

SERVES 4

Vinaigrette

10 mint leaves, bruised
    Juice of 1 lemon
3   tablespoons pear or white wine vinegar
1   tablespoon Dijon mustard
½   cup extra-virgin olive oil
3   tablespoons canola oil
2   plump garlic cloves, smashed and minced
1   plump shallot, minced
    Kosher salt and freshly ground black pepper
2   teaspoons minced fresh mint

4   large artichokes
    Juice of 1 lemon
1   large yellow onion, minced
2   unpeeled garlic cloves
1   lemon, thinly sliced
1   bay leaf
1   teaspoon kosher salt
2   teaspoons bruised black peppercorns
    Minced chives and mint for garnish

To make vinaigrette: A few hours before serving, combine mint leaves, lemon juice and vinegar in a small bowl and mix; let stand for 10 minutes, then discard mint. Thoroughly blend in mustard. Slowly whisk in olive oil, then canola oil, beating vigorously to make a thick emulsion. Add garlic, shallot, salt, pepper and minced mint. Set aside.

To prepare artichokes: Fill a large mixing bowl with cold water. Add lemon juice and reserve. Cut off and discard top third of each artichoke. With a sharp knife, remove stem, then break off and discard tough lower leaves. Finally, using sharp kitchen scissors, cut off upper half of all remaining leaves. Immediately plunge artichoke into lemon water. Repeat until all artichokes are prepared and soaking in lemon water.

Pour 1 quart cold water into the bottom of a heavy saucepan or deep sauté pan that is just large enough to hold the 4 artichokes. Add onion, garlic cloves, sliced lemon, bay leaf, salt and pepper. Remove artichokes from lemon water and place them in saucepan, stem side down.

Cover pan with a tight-fitting lid and place

over high heat until liquids begin to bubble. Reduce heat to low and simmer, adding more water if needed to keep a moist atmosphere. Cook until artichokes are very tender, 40 minutes or longer. To test for doneness, very gently tug a lower artichoke leaf; when it pops off easily, artichokes are done.

Using a slotted spoon or Chinese strainer, carefully remove artichokes from saucepan, gently tip them to drain any water and place in a shallow bowl just large enough to hold them.

Spoon vinaigrette evenly over hot artichokes. Serve at room temperature, spooning excess vinaigrette back over each serving. Sprinkle with minced chives and mint.

Wine: Artichokes tend to impart an unpleasant sweetness to any wine. If you must serve wine, it should be young and high in acid, such as a youthful Barbera from Piedmont. Or choose a handcrafted beer.

Marinated Roasted Red Peppers with Garlic & Anchovies

SERVE THIS SIMPLE DISH of roasted peppers as a perfect summer starter. What's unusual here is that the anchovies and garlic are baked together. The result is a very intense roasted pepper, with the anchovy melting into a rich accompaniment. Then the peppers marinate at room temperature overnight. (You can also refrigerate the finished dish for several days or up to 1 week, bringing it to room temperature about 3 hours before serving.) For optimum flavor, roast the peppers on a grill.

SERVES 6 TO 8

6   large red bell peppers
5   plump garlic cloves, smashed
       and minced
1   3-ounce tin of anchovies, drained
       and cut in half crosswise
2   tablespoons balsamic vinegar
½   cup extra-virgin olive oil
       Freshly ground black pepper
10   fresh basil leaves, julienned, plus
       more fresh basil for garnish

Preheat broiler until hot. Place peppers on a rack 4 inches from heat source and grill until blackened, 2 to 4 minutes. Turn and repeat until peppers are blackened on all sides. Or, better yet, blacken them on a grill.

Transfer roasted peppers to a paper bag and seal. When peppers cool, 45 minutes to 1 hour, remove from bag and peel away skin. Split peeled peppers and discard seeds and heavy membranes. Cut peppers lengthwise into 1½- to-2-inch-wide strips.

Preheat oven to 450°F.

Cover a very large rimmed cookie sheet or a large but shallow baking pan with foil. Arrange pepper strips in a single layer on prepared pan. Distribute garlic evenly over peppers. Place at least 1 anchovy piece on each pepper strip. Sprinkle evenly with vinegar, then drizzle with olive oil. Dust lavishly with pepper.

Bake peppers in hot oven for 10 minutes, or until anchovies begin to melt. Remove pan from oven and let cool. Transfer peppers to a serving bowl. Pour pan juices over them. Add julienned basil and stir very gently. Cover and let stand overnight at room temperature. Serve with a garnish of more fresh basil.

Wine: Lockwood Vineyard Sauvignon Blanc (California: Monterey County) or another Sauvignon Blanc from Monterey or Santa Barbara County

Bagna Cauda

(WARM GARLIC ANCHOVY DIP WITH VEGETABLES)

DIP SOME FRESH VEGETABLES into this warm garlicky sauce and you'll be hooked for life. The hot bath (*bagna cauda*) of butter, olive oil, anchovy and garlic is a traditional northern Italian dish. While the amounts vary from family to family, the basics remain the same. This particular recipe came from Italy to California with Helen Bonino, mother of our garlic farmer friend Lou. She learned how to make it from her mother. "It's so easy," Helen said. "Just remember a cup, a cup, a cup, a cup. And don't forget that the leftovers are fabulous on bruschetta." Helen cooks for multitudes, but even cut in half, this recipe is very generous.

SERVES 10 TO 20

½   cup unsalted butter
½   cup extra-virgin olive oil
½   cup chopped anchovy fillets
½   cup pressed garlic cloves
     (about 30 plump cloves)

Various crudités: Carrot and celery sticks, broccoli florets, trimmed green beans, pea pods, jicama slices, fennel slices, zucchini spears

In a small, heavy saucepan, melt butter over low heat. Add olive oil and anchovy fillets. Cook, stirring often, until anchovies have dissolved into the sauce, 1 to 3 minutes. Add garlic and stir until mixture is thoroughly blended, about 1 minute.

Pour mixture into a ceramic bowl and keep warm on a stand over a candle. Surround with fresh vegetables. If sauce gets too thick, thin with equal amounts of butter and olive oil.

Wine: Roederer Estate Brut Anderson
Valley L'Ermitage (California: Mendocino County)
or another dry sparkling wine

Luscious Shrimp Toasts

BITE INTO THESE CRISP TOASTS TO find a light and tasty shrimp mousse. Garlic, cilantro, bacon and ginger add to the pleasing flavors. Shrimp toasts can be prepared ahead and reheated on a cookie sheet in a very hot oven if need be, but they are best when served hot off the stove.

MAKES 20 TO 24 PIECES

1	tablespoon cornstarch
1	tablespoon rice wine
1	large egg white
½	pound raw shrimp, peeled and deveined
2	slices raw bacon, cut into small pieces
1	slice fresh gingerroot, 1½ inches thick
2	scallions, trimmed, white part with 1 inch of green
	3-inch piece celery rib
2	tablespoons fresh cilantro leaves
3	plump garlic cloves
2	teaspoons dark sesame oil
1	teaspoon dark soy sauce
5-6	slices good-quality white bread, each cut into 4 triangles
	Up to 2 cups peanut oil

Combine cornstarch and wine in a small bowl, stir well and set aside. Beat egg white until very frothy; set aside.

In the bowl of a food processor, combine shrimp and bacon. Puree until smooth. Add ginger, scallions, celery, cilantro and garlic. Pulse until vegetables are finely minced. Scrape mixture into a mixing bowl, blend in sesame oil and soy sauce, egg white, and cornstarch mixture. Using about 1 tablespoon paste each, spread shrimp paste evenly on bread triangles. Chill until ready to fry, up to 4 hours.

Just before serving, heat 2 cups of oil in a wok to 360°F, or until a piece of bread turns golden when tossed in. Carefully fry triangles, a few at a time, turning often, until they are golden on both sides, 30 seconds to 2 minutes. Drain on paper towels and serve immediately.

Wine: Domaine Albrecht Riesling (France: Alsace) or a dry-style Oregon white Riesling

Sautéed Oysters Piquante

THIS SPICY OYSTER DISH makes a great start to an evening of food from the grill. The simple citrus sauce contrasts with the peppery garlic butter in which the oysters are cooked. And there's a toasted crouton underneath to soak up all the delicious juices.

SERVES 8

2 tablespoons dry white wine
Juice of 1 lemon
Juice of 1 lime
2 teaspoons Worcestershire sauce

8 thick slices Italian bread croutons, crusts removed

4 tablespoons (½ stick) unsalted butter
2 tablespoons extra-virgin olive oil
1 plump shallot, minced
3 plump garlic cloves, smashed and minced
1 teaspoon freshly ground white pepper
½ teaspoon ground red pepper (cayenne)
1 teaspoon kosher salt
½ teaspoon Tabasco
1½ quarts shucked large oysters, including juices
¼ cup minced fresh parsley
¼ cup minced fresh chives

Lemon wedges

In a small bowl, combine white wine, lemon and lime juice and Worcestershire sauce. Blend well and set aside.

Lightly toast croutons and keep warm.

Combine butter and oil in a large skillet and place over medium heat until butter is melted. Add shallot and garlic, white and red pepper and salt. Stir over low heat until shallot wilts, about 3 minutes. Stir in Tabasco, then increase heat to high. Add oysters and their liquor; sauté, stirring constantly, until oysters begin to curl at edges, 3 to 4 minutes. Stir in reserved white-wine mixture. When liquids are bubbling vigorously, cook for 1 minute. Add parsley and adjust seasonings.

Place 1 crouton on each of 8 warmed plates. Divide oysters among plates, piled on top of croutons. Garnish with chives and lemon.

Wine: Domaine J.-A. Ferret Tête de Cru Le Clos Pouilly-Fuissé (France: Burgundy) or a Muscadet from France's Loire Valley

Creole Crabmeat with Sherry, Green Onions & Garlic

CRABMEAT IN A TASTY SAUCE served on toast points is a very old Louisiana-style appetizer. Garlic, tomato, green peppers and onions form the base for this pleasing dish, flavored with sherry and a bay leaf. When it's available, we use lemongrass instead of lemon zest—had it been available decades ago, any good Creole cook would have appreciated its special lemon flavor.

SERVES 6

3 tablespoons extra-virgin olive oil
1 dried chile pepper, crumbled
4 plump garlic cloves, smashed
   and minced
⅔ cup finely diced green onions,
   including tender parts of green
1 large celery rib, trimmed and
   finely diced
¼ cup finely diced green bell pepper
1 1-inch slice of lemongrass bulb,
   minced (or minced zest of 1 lemon)
1 cup finely diced peeled ripe tomatoes
1 tablespoon tomato paste
1 tablespoon unbleached flour
1 cup chicken stock

¼ cup dry amontillado sherry
1 bay leaf
   Kosher salt and freshly ground
   black pepper
1 pound lump crabmeat, carefully
   picked over to remove bits of shell
¼ cup minced fresh flat-leaf parsley
6 thin slices buttered fresh toast,
   crusts discarded
1 lemon, cut in half

Combine olive oil, chile pepper and garlic in a large skillet over medium heat. When hot, stir in green onions, celery, bell pepper and lemongrass. Cover and braise for 3 to 4 minutes, just to soften vegetables. Uncover and add tomatoes. Cook over high heat, stirring often, until tomatoes are hot, about 2 minutes. Add tomato paste and blend. Then blend in flour. Slowly stir in stock and sherry. Stir over high heat until mixture has thickened. Add bay leaf. Reduce heat to low and simmer for 15 minutes, stirring often, to cook flour. Season with salt and pepper. The sauce can be set aside at this time.

Just before serving, stir in crabmeat and heat until piping hot. Stir in parsley.

Place a slice of toast on each of 6 heated serving plates. Spoon crab mixture over toast. Add generous squeeze of lemon and serve.

Wine: Flora Springs Wine Company Sauvignon Blanc Napa Valley (California: Napa Valley) or another dry, rich Sauvignon Blanc from California

Heavenly Crab Cakes

E'VE NEVER MADE CRAB CAKES with mayonnaise, as most cooks do; instead we bind them with a simple white sauce and egg yolks. They're light but packed with a melange of flavors united by a good bit of garlic—which tastes roasted even though it is not. Serve these with fresh salsa or Creamy Mustard Dipping Sauce.

MAKES 10 CAKES

2   tablespoons butter
3   plump garlic cloves, smashed and minced
2   tablespoons minced shallot
½   teaspoon ground red pepper (cayenne)
2   teaspoons Colman's dry mustard
1   tablespoon unbleached flour
½   cup heavy cream
1   tablespoon minced fennel fronds or tarragon
1   tablespoon minced chives
    Minced zest from 1 lemon plus 1 tablespoon lemon juice
1   pound fresh lump crabmeat, carefully picked over to remove bits of shell
2   large egg yolks plus 1 large egg

¾   cup fine dry bread crumbs
¾   cup cornmeal
    Kosher salt and freshly ground black pepper
⅓   cup milk

¼   cup canola oil, plus more if needed
    Several bunches of watercress for garnish
    Fresh salsa or Creamy Mustard Dipping Sauce (page 56)

In a small skillet, melt butter over low heat. Add garlic and shallot; cover and cook until softened, about 2 minutes. Stir in cayenne and mustard. Sprinkle with flour and stir over low heat for 1 minute. Add cream and cook until mixture has thickened, stirring constantly, about 1 minute. Transfer mixture to a large mixing bowl.

Add fennel or tarragon, chives, lemon zest and juice and crabmeat. Blend gently but thoroughly. Then blend in egg yolks, ¼ cup each of the bread crumbs and cornmeal, salt and pepper. Cover bowl with plastic wrap and chill for 1 hour.

Gently form into 10 round cakes about 3 inches in diameter and 1 inch thick.

Combine whole egg and milk in a shallow soup plate. Combine remaining ½ cup each of bread crumbs and cornmeal in another. Very carefully, since these cakes are not sturdy, dip each first into egg mixture, then into crumbs. Chill coated crab cakes for 2 to 4 hours.

Heat oil in a large cast-iron skillet over medium-high heat. Sauté cakes until browned on bottom, 4 to 5 minutes. Turn and sauté on other side, about 5 minutes more.

Serve on heated plates, garnished generously with watercress. Offer salsa or dipping sauce.

Wine: Ferrari-Carano Chardonnay Alexander Valley (California: Sonoma County) or another Chardonnay from Sonoma County

Garlicky Buffalo Wings with Blue Cheese Dip

WE THINK THESE are the absolutely best wings in the world! Crisp, chile-hot chicken wings become addictive when dressed with lots of garlic. The original accompaniment of celery and a cheese dip is a genius idea—when your mouth is too fiery hot, munch on some celery and cooling dip. This particular recipe has evolved considerably from scorching taste memories of our first visit to the birthplace of wings, Buffalo's Anchor Bar. The Durkee's sauce should be readily available in supermarkets everywhere. El Paso Chile Company products can be found in specialty markets, or by mail (see Sources, page 414).

MAKES 40 PIECES;
SERVES 4 TO 10 AS AN
APPETIZER, OR 2 VERY HUNGRY
PEOPLE FOR SUPPER

Dip

½   cup crumbled blue cheese or Gorgonzola
⅓   cup plain yogurt
⅓   cup sour cream
1   plump garlic clove, minced
1   tablespoon red wine vinegar
2   teaspoons fresh lemon juice

½   teaspoon salt
½   teaspoon freshly ground white pepper

8   tablespoons (1 stick) butter
4   plump garlic cloves, pressed
20   chicken wings
½   cup Durkee's Red Hot sauce
¼   cup El Paso Chile Company's Hellfire Damnation sauce or another fiery hot sauce
1   tablespoon red wine vinegar

2-3   cups vegetable oil
    Kosher salt to taste
6-8   stalks of celery cut into thin sticks

To make dip: In a shallow mixing bowl, mash together cheese and yogurt. Whisk in sour cream. Then blend in remaining dip ingredients. Whisk vigorously. Scrape mixture into a serving bowl, cover tightly with plastic wrap, and chill at least 2 hours and up to 24.

To prepare wings: Melt butter over high heat in a small saucepan. Remove from heat and stir in garlic. Set aside.

Cut each wing into 3 joints; set tips aside for stock. Place remaining pieces in a large, shallow baking dish. Add chile sauces and vinegar to butter mixture; heat until very hot. Pour one-fourth of hot-sauce mixture over uncooked wings and toss well. Reserve remaining sauce. Let wings marinate for at least 30 minutes.

Preheat oven to 275°F.

Pour enough oil to allow for deep-frying into a wok or fryer. Heat until oil is hot enough to quickly brown a cube of bread (350°F). Add 10 to 12 chicken pieces and fry until golden brown on all sides, 4 to 6 minutes.

Transfer cooked wings to paper towels, then keep warm in preheated oven. Repeat until all wings are fried. Quickly reheat remaining sauce. Arrange chicken wings on a serving platter and pour sauce over them. Sprinkle with salt.

Serve with celery sticks and blue cheese dip on the side.

Wine: Georges Duboeuf Beaujolais-Villages (France: Beaujolais) or another medium-bodied, very fruity red wine

Vegetarian Spring Rolls with Garlic Chives & Spicy Sauce

OFTEN CALLED CHINESE chives, garlic chives have a thicker, broader leaf than regular chives. We love them and have many clumps of them around our gardens. Their pungent flavor enhances many dishes, especially these delicate, crunchy spring rolls. While Chinese chives are usually available in Asian markets, you can replace them with plain chives. Just add two more garlic cloves to the recipe. Made from just water and flour, spring roll wrappers are lighter and more delicate than egg roll wrappers. Despite the length of this recipe, these spring rolls actually take less than an hour to prepare.

MAKES 12

Filling

6 dried black mushrooms
6 plump garlic cloves, thinly julienned
½ cup minced scallions, whites only
2 tablespoons minced fresh gingerroot
1 dried chile pepper, crumbled
6 scallions, trimmed with 2 inches of green, finely julienned

½ cup finely chopped fresh snow pea pods
1½ packed cups finely shredded Napa cabbage
1 cup finely shredded carrots
4 ounces garlic chives (available in Chinese markets), cut into 2-inch lengths (½-⅔ cup)
1 tablespoon cornstarch
¼ cup chicken stock
2 tablespoons rice wine
3 tablespoons thin soy sauce
2 teaspoons dark sesame oil
3 tablespoons peanut oil
¼ cup minced fresh cilantro

Dipping Sauce

2 plump garlic cloves, smashed and minced
1 tablespoon minced fresh gingerroot
2 tablespoons soy sauce, preferably mushroom-flavored
3 tablespoons Chinese black vinegar
2 tablespoons rice wine
2 teaspoons Chinese chili sauce
2 teaspoons dark sesame oil
1 tablespoon minced fresh cilantro

1   tablespoon minced scallion

10   spring roll wrappers
1   large egg yolk, beaten
2-3   cups peanut oil

To make filling: Place dried mushrooms in a small bowl and cover with boiling water. Soak until mushrooms are softened, about 20 minutes. Drain mushrooms, discard stems and cut caps into matchsticks. Reserve.

Combine julienned garlic, minced scallions, ginger, and chile in a small dish.

In another dish, combine soaked mushrooms, julienned scallions, pea pods, cabbage, carrots and garlic chives. Finally, in a small bowl, mix cornstarch with chicken stock and rice wine until blended well, then mix in soy and sesame oil to make a sauce.

Heat peanut oil in a wok over high heat until hot. Add garlic mixture and stir over medium-high heat until very fragrant, about 15 seconds. Then add cabbage mixture, stirring over high heat for 1 minute, or until cabbage is wilted. Whisk sauce to make certain cornstarch is blended, then pour over cabbage. Vigorously stir over heat for 1 to 2 minutes, or until vegetables are softened and coated with sauce.

Turn contents of wok onto a large cold platter and let stand for ½ hour to cool. Stir in cilantro. (You can chill mixture for several hours at this point.)

To make dipping sauce: Blend all ingredients except cilantro and scallion. Let stand at room temperature for at least 1 hour or up to 2.

To finish spring rolls: Open wrappers and arrange on a large work surface with a point facing you. Place about 2 rounded tablespoons of filling in lower third of each wrapper, leaving enough space at bottom to fold over filling. Fold bottom up and tuck over and under filling; fold in each side. Dab some egg yolk in middle of remaining wrapper surface and roll into a tight tube. The dab of egg should help seal package. Repeat until all packages are made. (You can chill spring rolls for several hours at this point.)

To cook spring rolls: Preheat oven to warm (250°F). Pour peanut oil into wok or deep-fryer to a depth of 1½ inches and heat until hot enough to quickly brown a cube of bread (350°F). Deep-fry 3 spring rolls at a time, without crowding, until they are properly crisp and golden brown, 1 to 2 minutes (a bit longer if they have been chilled). Drain spring rolls well on paper towels and keep warm in oven until all are fried.

Add cilantro and scallions to dipping sauce and serve with spring rolls.

Wine: Hogue Fumé Blanc Dry Columbia Valley (Washington) or a rich Viognier from California

Silken Garlic Custards

THESE GARLIC CUSTARDS are as tender as a mother's heart. Sometimes we unmold them to accompany lamb. At other times we serve them in elegant ramekins as a first course, along with well-buttered asparagus. Our recipe is adapted from chef Jean Joho's in our very first book, *The Best of the Midwest* (Viking Studio Books, 1990). This transplanted Alsatian now displays his culinary skills at two celebrated Chicago restaurants: Everest and Brasserie Jo.

SERVES 6

10	plump garlic cloves, peeled
1½	tablespoons unsalted butter
1¼	cups milk
1	cup heavy cream
4	large eggs
4	fresh basil leaves, torn
	Kosher salt and freshly ground white pepper
	Fresh herbs for garnish

Preheat oven to 350°F. Have ready six 4-ounce ramekins.

In a small saucepan, combine garlic cloves with 1 cup water.

Bring to a boil and simmer for 1 minute. Drain and repeat process 3 more times. Pat dry.

Melt butter in a small skillet over medium-high heat. Add garlic cloves and stir until they begin to brown, 2 to 4 minutes. Remove garlic with a slotted spoon. Coat ramekins with browned butter and set aside.

Using a garlic press, squeeze garlic cloves into a blender or the bowl of a food processor. Add ½ cup of milk. Pulse until garlic is thoroughly pureed. Add remaining ¾ cup milk, cream, eggs, basil, salt and pepper. Mix thoroughly, then pour into prepared ramekins.

Place ramekins in a large baking pan. Slide oven rack partway out and set baking pan on rack. Pour in enough hot water to come halfway up sides of ramekins. Bake for about 45 minutes, or until custard is set. Remove pan from oven and set on a cooling rack, allowing ramekins to rest in water bath for 10 minutes.

Serve custards either in ramekins or unmolded with Amazing Creamed Corn and Roasted Garlic (page 381).

Wine: Domaine Marcel Deiss Pinot Blanc (France: Alsace) or another Alsatian Pinot Blanc

Soups

Chilled Cucumber Yogurt Soup with Garlic Dill Gremolata 78

Gazpacho 79

Buttermilk Carrot Soup with Herb Salsa, Cold or Hot 80

Chilled Fresh Tomato Soup with Roasted Garlic Cream 82

Tuscan Tomato & Garlic Bread Soup 84

Creamy Roasted Garlic Soup with Leeks & Potatoes 85

Garden Garlic Soup 86

Mexican-Style Soup of Roasted Tomatoes, Chiles & Garlic 88

Cream of Roasted Tomato Soup with Caramelized Garlic & Corn 90

Mouclade (a Creamy Mussel Stew with Garlic & Curry) 92

Simple Vegetable Chowder with Scallops 94

Creamy Lentil Soup 95

Winter Bean Soup with Lamb Shanks 96

Cabbage & Bean Soup au Pistou 97

Golden Curried Split Pea Soup with Smoked Ham, Apple & Fennel 100

Blue Cheese Soup with Roasted Garlic 101

Roasted Garlic Vegetable Chowder with Beer & Cheese 102

THE GREAT GARLIC MACHINE

IT WAS CRYING TIME. There we were, wearing hard hats and hair nets, with tears welling up in our eyes. We were in a building where a million pounds of sliced garlic was being dried on hot conveyors as long as a football field. The sulfurous essence of these powerful alliums was everywhere.

Pete Ramirez took sympathetic note of our tears. "I don't smell it," he said. "I never cry anymore."

Ramirez is the master of the drying operation at Gilroy Foods, which was founded in 1959 by some local garlic farmers who saw dehydration as a way to create new markets. When he started in 1961, the farmers dried the garlic in tunnels. But now Ramirez runs several computer-managed drying lines that hit thinly sliced garlic with a 260-degree blast for a few minutes, then move it along for 10 to 12 hours until it emerges from the line at 129 degrees—crisp, white, dry and ready for processing. As much as 150 million pounds of garlic is dehydrated here between the middle of July and the end of October, the garlic season.

Will Rogers once said that Gilroy, California, is the only place in the world where you can marinate a steak just by hanging it on a clothesline. The fact is, from the highway, you could find your way to the sprawling facilities of Gilroy Foods blindfolded, simply by following your nose. Want garlic on your lunch sandwich? Just unwrap it and hold it out in the air for a minute or two.

Long, open sheds hold hundreds of tons of fresh garlic, trucked in from all over California. The garlic is cured for four or five days to allow some of the moisture to evaporate so that the heads can be cracked easily and the cloves freed. Then the garlic is picked up by huge front-loaders and dumped into bins that feed conveyor belts. After the heads are broken down, the garlic is shaken to get rid of stones, sand, dirt and wood. Loose skin and leaves are blown away.

Just inside the main building is a big mural painted by some of the employees, depicting the flow of garlic from the fields to the dried product. There are 1,100 employees who keep the operation running 24 hours a day most of the year. (They dry other things too. Someone had painted a sign that read "You find it, we'll dry it.")

Once the cloves are washed and sliced, they're ready for the journey through the dryer and finally to the five-story mill, where, depending on what the market needs, the thin slices will be chopped, minced, ground, granulated or powdered.

We tasted some of the crisp dried slices, and they had lost none of their power. The sliced or chopped garlic is used when the processor wants recognizable pieces. The finer stuff provides the taste but no large particles. The biggest seller by far is granulated, which has the texture of sugar. Much of it is packaged by other processors for home use. Ground garlic, more like cornmeal, is also widely used. And there are three grades of powdered garlic. Most of it is packaged in drums that hold 300 pounds. One pound of garlic powder has the equivalent flavor of four or five pounds of raw garlic.

Most Americans never buy fresh garlic, even in this era of the garlic explosion. But almost everyone eats garlic whether they know it or not, because most big food processors (Campbell, Knorr, French's) use dried garlic in their products. Most Americans, it is safe to say, have eaten something from this plant.

As we were concluding our visit, we realized we were carrying more than a little of the facility's pervasive aroma out with us, on our clothes and in our hair. We asked Max Contin, the company's director of research and development, if he ever got used to the smell.

"Smell?" he said. "What smell?"

Chilled Cucumber Yogurt Soup with Garlic Dill Gremolata

THIS IS ONE OF OUR FAVORITE summer soups. It's thick and creamy, tangy and tasty. We especially enjoy the yin and yang of the various alliums. The real secret ingredient here is buttermilk, while a surprising touch comes from the lemon, dill and garlic gremolata sprinkled over the top.

SERVES 6

1   seedless cucumber, shredded and drained
⅔ cup finely chopped red onion
¼ cup finely chopped sweet onion
1   plump garlic clove, pressed
2   cups chicken stock
½ cup golden raisins
¼ cup finely chopped mixed fresh parsley, chives and dill
3   cups plain yogurt
½ cup buttermilk, or more as needed
Salt and freshly ground white pepper to taste

Gremolata
Zest of 1 lemon, minced
2   plump garlic cloves, smashed and minced
2   tablespoons minced fresh dill

Combine cucumber, onions, garlic and stock in a large mixing bowl. Stir in raisins. Let stand 15 minutes. Add herbs and yogurt. Stir until smooth. Add buttermilk, salt, and pepper; blend. Cover and chill until serving time, up to 5 hours.

To make gremolata: Blend together lemon zest, garlic and dill. Cover and chill until needed.

Just before serving, taste and adjust seasonings. If mixture is too thick, thin soup with more buttermilk. Ladle into shallow soup plates and sprinkle with gremolata.

Wine: Penfolds Sémillon Chardonnay South Australia Koonunga Hill (Australia: South Australia) or another Australian Sémillon/Chardonnay

Gazpacho

GARLIC AND TOMATOES make happy partners, especially in soups and sauces. And there are a great many tomato-and-garlic-based soups, each very different from the others. Gazpacho is a veritable salad and vinaigrette—cucumber and onions, garlic, vinegar and olive oil—in a soup bowl. In this recipe, the garlic, like everything else, is uncooked.

Tangy gazpacho is best made in late summer, when the tomatoes are right from the garden. Because our yard is filled with heirloom tomatoes, we mix them to get as complex a flavor as possible.

SERVES 6 TO 8

- 2 ½ pounds ripe tomatoes, peeled and seeded
- 3 plump garlic cloves, chopped
- 6 blanched almonds
- 1 English cucumber, peeled and diced
- ¾ cup finely diced sweet onion
- 3 cups rich chicken stock
- 2 teaspoons sugar (optional)
- 2 teaspoons kosher salt
- 6 drops Tabasco
- 1 teaspoon freshly ground white pepper
- ¼ cup extra-virgin olive oil
- 1 tablespoon sherry vinegar
- ¼ cup minced fresh cilantro

Combine tomatoes, garlic, almonds, half of the cucumber and ½ cup of the onion in the bowl of a food processor fitted with the metal blade. Pulse until mixture is finely pureed. Pour into a large bowl.

Whisk in chicken stock, sugar, salt, Tabasco and pepper. Blend well. Then vigorously whisk in olive oil, vinegar and half of the cilantro. Taste and adjust seasonings. Chill at least 4 hours.

Just before serving, adjust seasonings again. Ladle soup into serving bowls. Sprinkle with cilantro and remaining cucumber and onions.

Wine: Martinsancho Verdejo Rueda (Spain)
or a California Johannisberg Riesling

Buttermilk Carrot Soup with Herb Salsa, Cold or Hot

A SUBTLE SUGGESTION of garlic blends perfectly with curry and ginger in this refreshing carrot soup. If you serve it cold, buttermilk and yogurt give it the creamy tang that makes it a delicious summer dish. A simple mixture of garlic and herbs, blessed with a little lime juice, makes a great flavor contrast when stirred in at the last minute. Try to buy your carrots from a farm stand for optimum flavor. For a cold-weather variation, serve the soup hot, garnished with a watercress puree.

SERVES 8 TO 10

- 2 pounds young carrots, trimmed and well scrubbed
- 2 sprigs lemon thyme
- 1 tablespoon good-quality curry powder
- 1 rounded tablespoon minced fresh gingerroot
- 1 plump garlic clove
- 6 cups rich chicken stock
- 2 cups plain yogurt
- 1 cup buttermilk, plus more as needed
- ½ teaspoon kosher salt
- 1 teaspoon freshly ground white pepper

Herb Salsa

- ½ cup minced fresh herbs (cilantro, basil, thyme, verbena, parsley)
- 1 plump garlic clove, pressed
- 4 scallions, minced
- 1 tablespoon fresh lime juice
  Kosher salt and freshly ground white pepper to taste
- 2 tablespoons plain yogurt

Combine carrots, thyme and curry powder in a large, heavy saucepan. Add ginger, garlic and stock. Bring to a boil over high heat. Cover, reduce heat to low and simmer briskly until carrots are falling apart, 40 to 50 minutes.

Remove pot from heat and cool for 1 hour. Remove thyme and discard. Spoon solids and half of liquid into bowl of a food processor and puree. Add yogurt and process until smooth.

Pour carrot mixture and remaining stock mixture into a large mixing bowl. Add 1 cup of the buttermilk, salt and pepper. Whisk until well blended. Taste and adjust seasonings. Chill for at least 5 hours or up to 24. Bring soup to room temperature before serving.

Shortly before serving, make salsa: Blend together herbs, garlic, scallions and lemon juice. Season with salt and pepper. Blend in yogurt.

Stir soup; add more buttermilk if too thick. Ladle soup into shallow soup plates. Garnish with a dollop of salsa in center of bowl and stir into soup ever so slightly.

Wine: Columbia Crest Sémillon Columbia Valley
(Washington: Columbia Valley)
or a Pacific Northwest white Riesling

Chilled Fresh Tomato Soup with Roasted Garlic Cream

THE SECRET TO THIS COLD LIGHT SOUP is the superb flavor you get from cooking sweet onions and garlic with fresh-from-the-garden tomatoes. A swirl of roasted garlic cream provides a refreshing counterpoint. You can easily freeze the soup without its garlic cream and have the pleasure of garden-fresh flavors in the middle of winter. We always use a variety of tomatoes for this, including plenty of yellow plum tomatoes. The evaporated milk and the light sour cream give the cream a tangy taste.

SERVES 8 TO 10

¼ cup olive oil

½ cup finely diced shallots

4 plump garlic cloves, smashed and minced

6 pounds various vine-ripened tomatoes, stemmed and coarsely chopped

1 bouquet garni
   Kosher salt and freshly ground white pepper

Roasted Garlic Cream

1 cup light sour cream

2 tablespoons evaporated milk, plus more if desired

1 large head garlic, roasted (page 34)

¼ cup minced fresh chives, preferably garlic chives
   Freshly ground white pepper

Heat olive oil over low heat in a heavy-bottomed 3-quart pot. Add shallots and minced garlic. Cover and cook over very low heat until onions become transparent, 5 to 8 minutes. Stir in tomatoes, bouquet garni, salt and pepper. Cook, covered, until tomatoes are very soft, 40 to 50 minutes. Let cool for 15 minutes. Discard bouquet garni.

Puree tomato mixture in a food mill, discarding skin and seeds. Transfer puree to a large, heavy saucepan and cook over high heat until bubbling. Reduce heat and simmer briskly for 15 minutes to reduce soup slightly and thicken a bit. Remove from heat.

When soup is cool, transfer to a large bowl,

cover with plastic wrap and refrigerate until cold, at least 2 hours or up to 24.

Just before serving, make garlic cream: Blend together sour cream, evaporated milk and mashed roasted garlic in the bowl of a small food processor. If cream is very thick, thin with more evaporated milk. Cream should be a little thicker than pancake batter.

To serve, ladle soup into shallow soup plates and garnish with a dollop of garlic cream. Swirl slightly with a fork. Sprinkle with chives and freshly ground white pepper.

Wine: Adelsheim Pinot Gris Willamette Valley (Oregon: Willamette Valley) or an Alsatian Pinot Gris from France

Henry IV of France worried about his sex appeal and his capacity to perform. His prescription for both concerns was to eat a lot of garlic before bedding the *femme de la nuit*.

Tuscan Tomato & Garlic Bread Soup

ASIMPLE AND TASTY WAY to use stale bread, this old Tuscan soup is best made with right-off-the-vine tomatoes. The other ingredients are basic—water, garlic, bread and basil. Some Italian cooks add sliced onions and celery to the pot, others do not. While most old recipes do not call for peeling the tomatoes, Fred prefers to peel his; Linda feels that the skins add important flavor. Whatever you do, this recipe will become a summer favorite.

SERVES 8 TO 10

¼	cup extra-virgin olive oil
4	plump garlic cloves, smashed and minced
6	basil leaves, slivered, plus additional for garnish
5	large vine-ripened tomatoes, coarsely chopped
8	cups hot water
½	pound stale bread, cut into 1½-inch cubes, lightly toasted, preferably from a rustic country loaf
	Kosher salt and freshly ground black pepper

In a large, heavy saucepan, combine olive oil and garlic. Cook over low heat until garlic has softened, 3 to 4 minutes. Add basil, tomatoes and water. Increase heat and bring to a boil. Add bread cubes, reduce heat and simmer for 1 hour. Season with salt and pepper.

Ladle into soup bowls and garnish with more basil.

Wine: Dievole Chianti Classico (Italy: Tuscany) or another Tuscan Chianti Classico

Creamy Roasted Garlic Soup with Leeks & Potatoes

HERE'S A CREAMY SOUP without a drop of cream or milk. We use Yukon gold potatoes, which give any soup a pleasing texture. But the real flavor treat comes from the roasted garlic. The final touch: sautéed thinly sliced garlic for a crunchy, toasty garnish.

SERVES 8 TO 10

½ cup olive oil

5 plump heads garlic, roasted (page 34), plus 3 plump garlic cloves, thinly sliced

4 cups well-washed, thinly sliced leeks, including tender green

3 pounds large Yukon gold potatoes, peeled and cut into 1-inch cubes

½ teaspoon dried thyme

10 cups vegetable stock
Kosher salt and freshly ground white pepper to taste

1 tablespoon minced chives

Heat olive oil in a small saucepan or skillet over medium heat. Add sliced garlic and sauté just until crisp and golden brown, 2 to 4 minutes. Do not let garlic get too dark or it will be bitter. Using a slotted spoon, transfer garlic to paper towels to drain. Reserve.

Combine hot olive oil and leeks in a large, heavy soup pot. Cover tightly and cook over very low heat until leeks are quite wilted, 15 to 20 minutes, stirring from time to time. Add potatoes, thyme and stock. Cover and cook over medium heat until liquid is bubbling, about 5 minutes. Reduce heat to low and simmer until potatoes are very tender, 30 to 40 minutes.

Remove soup from heat. Pour 2 cups of potato liquid into a measuring cup and reserve.

Working in batches, puree soup and roasted garlic together. Return puree to pot, season with salt and pepper, and stir over medium-high heat until bubbling. If soup is too thick, thin with as much reserved stock as necessary to give the soup a pleasing thickness. If it's too thin, simmer briskly for 5 to 10 minutes to thicken. Adjust seasonings, adding more salt and pepper to taste.

Ladle into heated soup plates and sprinkle with crisped sliced garlic and chives.

Wine: Zenato Tocai (Italy: Veneto) or another Italian Tocai

Garden Garlic Soup

SPINACH, CARROTS, ONIONS and garlic are cooked and pureed to make the base of a light and refreshing soup. Once pureed, it's pleasingly creamy, but you can also add a cup of heavy cream for extra richness. This recipe comes from Russ Vernon, owner of the West Point Market in Akron, Ohio.

SERVES 8

8 cups vegetable or chicken stock
1 pound spinach, washed, drained
   and stemmed
4 cups grated carrots
4 tablespoons (½ stick) unsalted butter
2 cups chopped white onions
16 plump garlic cloves, smashed
   and minced (or 8-10 spring
   green garlics)
⅓ cup unbleached flour
1 cup heavy cream (optional)
¼ teaspoon grated nutmeg
5 drops Tabasco
   Kosher salt and freshly ground
   white pepper
   Minced fresh chives for garnish

Bring stock to a boil in a large, heavy saucepan. Add spinach and carrots and cook over medium heat for 10 minutes, or until carrots are tender.

Meanwhile, melt butter in a large sauté pan. Add onions and garlic; cook over low heat until onions are tender but not browned, about 5 minutes. Sprinkle flour evenly over and cook, stirring often, for 3 to 5 minutes.

Combine spinach and onion mixtures in a food processor, in batches if necessary, and puree until smooth. Return to saucepan and bring to a boil; reduce heat to low and simmer for 5 minutes. Add cream (if using), nutmeg, Tabasco, salt and pepper. Simmer briskly for 5 minutes more.

Ladle into heated soup plates and garnish with chives.

Wine: Bonny Doon Vineyard Il Pescatore (California) or another full-bodied white wine with fruit flavors

SOME SIMPLE OLD-WORLD GARLIC SOUPS

GARLIC SOUP PROVENÇAL (BOILED WATER SOUP)

AUGUST ESCOFFIER'S CELEBRATED BOOK *Ma Cuisine*, first published in 1934, gives a garlic soup recipe that is exquisitely simple and absolutely delicious.

Boil together 8¾ cups of water, 1 cup olive oil, 1 teaspoon salt, some pepper, 8 garlic cloves, and some bay leaf, thyme, sage and parsley. The soup is done when the garlic is soft. Strain the broth into a soup bowl over a toasted crouton, with or without a poached egg on top. Sprinkle with parsley and serve.

Sopa de Ajo

Another version of garlic soup is made in Spain. The garlic cloves are crushed, then tossed into hot oil along with the croutons. When the bread and garlic turn golden, the water and seasonings are added. After the broth simmers for a while, the eggs are added, one at a time, to poach. Add a sprinkle of parsley once the soup is in the bowls and you have an awesome dish.

Mexican-Style Soup of Roasted Tomatoes, Chiles & Garlic

THIS INTENSELY FLAVORED SOUP incorporates three different ways of roasting vegetables: on the grill, in the oven, and on top of the stove. Pasilla chile powder provides some smoky berry overtones. This recipe was inspired by a soup we enthusiastically devoured at the celebrated Chicago restaurant Topolo-bampo, owned by Rick and Deann Bayless. The traditional Mexican technique of dry-roasting unpeeled garlic cloves on the stovetop contributes a lot to this soup.

SERVES 4 TO 6

4 large fresh poblano chiles
3 pounds mixed ripe tomatoes, preferably including plums, halved
3 tablespoons olive oil
7 plump garlic cloves, unpeeled
1 large sweet onion, minced
1 teaspoon ground cumin
1 teaspoon pasilla chile powder or 1 dried pasilla chile, toasted and cooked with the stock (see Sources, page 414)
2 cups chicken or vegetable stock Kosher salt and freshly ground white pepper
2 tablespoons fresh lime juice, plus more to taste
3 tablespoons fresh cilantro Finely diced fresh avocado and sour cream for garnish

To roast and peel chile peppers: Preheat grill or broiler. Roast peppers close to heat, turning often, until totally charred on outside, 10 to 15 minutes. Or set directly on flames of a gas burner, watching closely and turning often, until peppers are blistered. Transfer them to a paper bag and fold shut. Let peppers stand until cool, then carefully remove skins. Seed, dice coarsely and set aside.

To prepare tomatoes: Preheat oven to 450°. Place cut side up on a large foil-lined shallow-sided cookie sheet. Drizzle with 2 tablespoons of the olive oil. Place pan on a rack and roast tomatoes until tops are partially browned and somewhat crinkled, 40 to 50 minutes. (If necessary, brown lightly under broiler, being careful not to let juices that have collected around tomatoes dry up). When done, immediately remove pan from oven and set aside.

To roast garlic: While tomatoes are roasting, place garlic cloves on a griddle or small cast-iron skillet and roast on top of stove, turning often, until dark brown-black on exterior, about 15 minutes. Transfer to a plate and squeeze flesh from skin when cool. Reserve.

To finish soup: Heat the remaining 1 tablespoon of oil over low heat in a large nonreactive saucepan. Add onion, cumin and chile powder (if using whole chile, add with tomatoes). Cover and sauté until onion has softened, about 5 minutes. Add stock and bring to a boil. Cover and keep warm until tomatoes are ready.

To onion/stock mixture add diced roasted peppers, garlic, and tomatoes, along with any juices and browned bits accumulated on pan. Season with salt and white pepper. Cover and cook over low heat until onion is very soft and tomatoes fall apart, 25 to 30 minutes. Discard dried whole chile if using.

Pass mixture through a food mill into a clean pot, or puree in a food processor and pass through a strainer. Add lime juice and heat soup until hot. Taste and adjust salt and pepper; add more lime juice for additional tang.

Ladle soup into heated soup plates. Sprinkle with cilantro.

Garnish with diced avocado and a dollop of sour cream.

Wine: Beringer Vineyards White Zinfandel (California) or a French Tavel Rosé from the southern Rhône Valley

Cream of Roasted Tomato Soup with Caramelized Garlic & Corn

ROASTING TOMATOES brings out all their natural sugars and intensifies their flavor, giving this thick soup a comforting character. The generous topping of caramelized garlic and corn offers a grand counterpoint. This is a soup to make on the first chilly day at summer's end when you still have access to those delicious vine-ripened tomatoes. It just won't taste the same with out-of-season pseudo-tomatoes.

SERVES 4 TO 6

10 large vine-ripened tomatoes,
      cut in half
 3 tablespoons olive oil
 1 small dried red chile, crumbled
 1 medium yellow onion, finely diced
 1 large fresh basil leaf, finely torn (¼
      teaspoon dried), plus 4-6
      leaves for garnish
 2 cups milk
      Kosher salt and freshly ground
        white pepper
 3 tablespoons unsalted butter
 2 plump garlic cloves, slivered
 ¾ cup corn kernels, fresh or
        defrosted frozen

 ½ teaspoon sugar
 ½ cup low-fat sour cream
 1 tablespoon minced fresh chives

Place broiler rack about 3 inches from source of heat. Preheat oven to 450°F. Line a low-sided cookie sheet with foil.

Arrange tomato halves cut side up and close together on prepared pan and drizzle with 1 tablespoon of the olive oil. Roast until tops are crinkled, about 50 minutes. Turn oven to broil. Place tomatoes under broiler until tops begin to glaze, about 8 minutes. Be careful not to let juices that have collected around tomatoes dry up.

While tomatoes are roasting, heat remaining 2 tablespoons oil over low heat in a medium-sized nonreactive saucepan. Add crumbled chile, onion and basil. Cover and sauté, stirring occasionally, until onions are translucent and tender, 6 to 8 minutes. Set aside until tomatoes are ready.

Spoon tomatoes and juices into pot with onion, scraping in any browned bits on the foil. Cover and cook over low heat until tomatoes fall apart, 25 to 30 minutes.

Pass tomato mixture through a food mill into a clean pot or puree in a food processor and pass through a strainer. (You should have close to 4 cups of puree.) Stir in milk, salt and white pepper. Bring mixture, uncovered, to a vigorous simmer over medium heat, and cook for 8 to 10 minutes.

Meanwhile, melt butter in a small sauté pan. Stir in garlic and corn. Cook over medium heat, stirring often, until butter and garlic slivers have browned lightly, about 5 minutes. Sprinkle with sugar and cook until sugar has melted, 2 to 3 minutes more. (You can prepare 1 hour ahead and reheat just before serving.)

To finish soup, whisk together ½ cup of hot soup with sour cream. Whisk this mixture into soup pot and season with salt and pepper. Reduce heat to low and cook just until soup begins to simmer. Ladle into heated soup plates and use a slotted spoon to distribute garlic/corn mixture equally. Sprinkle with chives. Place a basil leaf in center of each plate and serve.

Wine: Cooper Mountain Pinot Gris Willamette Valley (Oregon: Willamette Valley) or a Pinot Grigio from Italy

Mouclade

(A CREAMY MUSSEL STEW WITH GARLIC & CURRY)

A TRADITIONAL FRENCH STEW of mussels and cream, *mouclade* is usually enlivened by a pinch of curry powder and thickened with egg yolks. This version of a soup we first tasted in Brussels is generous with both curry powder and garlic. It's a special indulgence, to be sure, but one that is wonderfully satisfying. Remember not to debeard the mussels too soon before cooking or they will die and spoil.

SERVES 4

¾ cup heavy cream

¼ cup light sour cream

3 large egg yolks

3 tablespoons unsalted butter

1½ teaspoons good-quality curry powder, preferably Madras-style

⅛ teaspoon ground red pepper (cayenne)

2 plump shallots, minced

3 plump garlic cloves, smashed and minced

2 cups very dry white wine
   Juice of 1 lemon

⅛ teaspoon saffron

4 pounds mussels, scrubbed and debearded

Kosher salt and freshly ground black pepper

3 tablespoons minced fresh flat-leaf parsley

2 tablespoons minced fresh chives

Whisk together heavy cream and sour cream in a medium-sized mixing bowl. Add yolks, one at a time, whisking until thoroughly blended. Set aside.

In a large saucepan, melt butter over medium heat. Add curry powder and cayenne; stir for 1 minute. Add shallots and garlic; cook just until shallots become translucent, 3 to 4 minutes. Stir in ¼ cup of the wine, lemon juice and saffron. Stir until saffron is dissolved. Set aside.

In a 6-quart pot, combine mussels and remaining 1¾ cups wine. Cover and cook over high heat, shaking from time to time, until mussels open, 5 to 6 minutes.

Discarding any that haven't opened, use a Chinese strainer or slotted spoon to quickly transfer mussels from broth to a large heated serving bowl. Cover with foil to keep warm.

Working quickly, pour mussel cooking liquid through several layers of cheesecloth into saucepan with seasoned shallots and garlic.

Bring to a boil over medium heat. When mixture is very hot, temper egg yolk and cream mixture by adding some of the hot liquid a bit at a time, whisking well. When yolk mixture is warmed, add all of it to saucepan, reduce heat to low and stir constantly for 5 minutes to thicken. Do not allow soup to get too hot or it will curdle. Mixture should be creamy but not thick.

Add salt and pepper. Taste and adjust seasonings.

Divide mussels among large, heated soup plates. Ladle soup over mussels. Sprinkle with parsley and chives.

Wine: Calera Wine Co. Viognier
(California: Mt. Harlan) or another rich and
aromatic Viognier from France's Condrieu region

Simple Vegetable Chowder with Scallops

PEOPLE OFTEN THINK chowder is by definition milk-based, but actually the name is derived from the *chaudière*, or cauldron, that French fishermen used for making fish soups. This is a light, tomato and garlic-piqued vegetable chowder, studded with corn, scallions and bell peppers. There's not even a hint of dairy here, but you'll find a special surprise in the bottom of each soup plate—silky slices of tender sea scallops. A generous sprinkling of fresh cilantro gives it a very fresh finish. This is a favorite company first course at our house, often followed by rack of lamb.

SERVES 6 TO 8

2 tablespoons vegetable oil

1 dried red chile, crumbled

2 plump garlic cloves, slivered

½ cup finely diced plump green onions or scallions

½ cup finely diced red bell pepper

2 large, very ripe tomatoes, peeled, seeded and finely diced

1 cup fresh corn kernels

½ cup dry white wine

2 teaspoons soy sauce

6 cups fish stock or clam juice

Kosher salt and freshly ground black pepper

1 pound sea scallops, cut into ¼-inch slices

2 tablespoons finely chopped fresh cilantro for garnish

Heat vegetable oil in a large, heavy saucepan over medium heat. Add chile and garlic. Stir for 1 minute, just to release flavors. Add green onions or scallions, pepper and tomatoes. Cover, reduce heat to low, and cook for 10 minutes, or until onions are translucent and peppers are tender. Be sure to stir from time to time. Add corn, wine, soy sauce and fish stock or clam juice. Cover, increase heat to medium and cook until mixture begins to bubble, about 5 minutes. Reduce heat and simmer briskly for 5 minutes. Season to taste with salt and pepper.

Remove pot from heat. Stir in sliced scallops, cover and let stand 3 minutes. Ladle hot chowder into heated soup plates. Sprinkle generously with cilantro and serve immediately.

Wine: Chalk Hill Sauvignon Blanc
(California: Sonoma County) or an Australian
Sémillon Chardonnay

Creamy Lentil Soup

SLOW COOKING with a base of browned onions and garlic gives an earthy richness to this hearty lentil soup, and pureeing makes it creamy. If you wish, you can use the fat from a few slices of bacon to replace the olive oil. Save the crisp bacon for a crumbled garnish. Another garnish alternative is a small dollop of sour cream.

SERVES 8 TO 10

- 3 tablespoons olive oil
- 1 jumbo Spanish onion, finely chopped
- 4 plump garlic cloves, smashed and minced
- 2 large carrots, finely chopped
- ½ teaspoon dried thyme
- 1 bay leaf
- 2 cups (about 1 pound) green or brown lentils, preferably French, picked over and rinsed
- 8 cups vegetable or chicken stock, plus more if needed
  Kosher salt and freshly ground white pepper
- ⅓ cup dry sherry
- 2-3 tablespoons minced fresh chives

Heat oil in a heavy 4- or 5-quart saucepan over medium heat. Add onion, increase heat and cook, stirring often, until golden, 8 to 12 minutes. Be careful not to burn. Stir in garlic and carrots. Cook until garlic has softened, 2 to 4 minutes. Add thyme, bay leaf, lentils and stock. Cover and cook over high heat until liquid is bubbling. Reduce heat and simmer briskly until lentils begin to fall apart, 1 to 1¼ hours.

Discard bay leaf. Working in batches, puree soup in a food processor or food mill. Transfer puree to a clean saucepan. Season with salt and pepper. Stir in sherry and heat until simmering. While this should be a very thick soup, you may wish to thin it a little with some reserved stock.

Ladle into heated soup plates and garnish with fresh chives.

Wine: Michele Chiarlo Barbera d'Asti (Italy: Piedmont) or another Barbera from Piedmont

Winter Bean Soup with Lamb Shanks

LAMB AND GARLIC have a splendid affinity for each other, especially in this hearty bean soup. The original recipe came to us more than a decade ago from chef Richard Perry, one of the best chefs in the Midwest. Over the years we have settled on this particular adaptation as one of our favorite winter treats, especially when we have dried cannellini beans from Wisconsin's Kingsfield Gardens (see Sources, page 412).

SERVES 6 TO 8

2 tablespoons olive oil
2 lamb shanks (about 1 pound each)
1 cup finely diced yellow onion
6 plump garlic cloves, smashed
  and minced
1 pound dried cannellini beans, or
  other white beans, picked over
  and rinsed
2 large carrots, coarsely chopped
1½ cups peeled and diced tomatoes,
  or 1½ cups canned crushed tomatoes
1 bay leaf
¼ cup minced fresh flat-leaf parsley
1 teaspoon fresh thyme
  (½ teaspoon dried)

2 whole allspice
1 teaspoon freshly ground black pepper
1 tablespoon kosher salt
10 cups water, plus more if needed
1½ cups tomato juice (optional)

Heat oil in a heavy soup pot over high heat and brown lamb shanks on all sides, about 5 minutes. Add onion and garlic. Stir until wilted, about 2 minutes. Add dried beans, carrots, tomatoes, seasonings, water, and tomato juice (if using).

Bring to a boil. Reduce heat and simmer for 1 hour, covered. After 1 hour, place lid just slightly ajar and continue to simmer until beans and shanks are very tender, 1½ to 2 hours more. Remove bay leaf and allspice.

Carefully transfer lamb shanks to a carving board. Remove meat from bone and cut into bite-size pieces. Return meat to soup.

Just before serving, heat soup until hot. If soup is too thick, thin it with more water, tomato juice, or a combination.

Wine: Bruno Giacosa Barbera d'Asti (Italy: Piedmont)
or another Barbera from Piedmont

Cabbage & Bean Soup au Pistou

PISTOU IS A GARLICKY BUT NUTLESS Provençal version of Italy's pesto, commonly served as a substantial garnish for a rich French vegetable and vermicelli soup. This refreshingly light bean soup includes some quickly cooked shredded cabbage. The *pistou*, made with basil, Parmesan, garlic and olive oil, is generously dolloped into the center, to be swirled about by the lucky diner. Serve this soup with a very crusty bread.

SERVES 8 TO 10

1	pound dried Great Northern beans, picked over and rinsed
½	cup grated Parmesan cheese
½	cup packed fresh basil leaves
3	plump garlic cloves, peeled
¼	cup extra-virgin olive oil
¼	cup olive oil
2	cups coarsely chopped yellow onion
3	plump garlic cloves, smashed and minced
10	cups rich chicken stock, heated
4	large carrots, scraped, cut into 1-inch pieces
	Kosher salt and freshly ground white pepper
6	cups shredded Savoy cabbage

Place beans in a large saucepan. Add enough water to rise 2 inches above them. Bring to a boil over high heat. Reduce heat, cover and simmer over very low heat until beans are somewhat tender, 1¼ to 1½ hours.

Meanwhile, make *pistou*: In the bowl of a food processor, combine Parmesan, basil and garlic cloves. Pulse to chop finely. With motor running, slowly add all of the extra-virgin olive oil to make a smooth paste. Transfer *pistou* to a bowl. If holding more than 1 hour, cover and refrigerate.

While beans are cooking, heat ¼ cup olive oil over low heat in a heavy-bottomed soup pot. Add onion and minced garlic. Cook over low heat, stirring often, until quite wilted, 6 to 8 minutes. Add chicken stock, carrots, salt and pepper. Keep warm until beans are ready.

Drain beans and add to stock mixture. Cover and bring to a boil over high heat. Reduce heat to low and simmer for 20 minutes, or until beans are tender. Stir in cabbage and cover and cook for 10 minutes more, or until carrots and cabbage are done.

Ladle into heated soup plates. Garnish lavishly with *pistou*.

Wine: Château Compuget Blanc (France: Languedoc) or a white Burgundy from the Mâcon region of France

PLINY—GARLIC'S ANCIENT CHAMPION

ALIO MAGNA VIS," WROTE PLINY THE ELDER 2,000 YEARS AGO. "Garlic has powerful properties." In chapter 23 of the twentieth book of his *Natural History*, citing historical and contemporary authorities, this keen observer of the world around him makes the case for garlic's strength.

♣ It repels serpents and scorpions by its smell, but if one of them should happen to sting or bite you, garlic will heal the wound. The bites of dogs and shrew-mice, bruises and blisters, scalp lesions, sprains and ruptures—all yield to garlic therapy.

♣ Accidentally ingest a little aconite or henbane? Work fast, and garlic will save you.

♣ Take garlic for asthma, catarrh, coughs, dropsy, earache, epilepsy, erysipelas, freckly eruptions of the skin, hoarseness, iliac passion, infections, jaundice, leprous sores, lichen, pains in the temples, phrenitis, phthiriasis, quinsy, scrofula, scurf, suppuration of the chest (however severe), tenesmus, toothache and tumors.

♣ Should you be seized by a quartan ague, a little garlic in dry wine with "an obolus of silphium" will take care of it.

♣ Tapeworms and other intestinal parasites are blasted away by garlic.

♣ If you are tired, garlic helps you sleep. If there is a madman in the family, get relief by giving him raw garlic. If you are pale, it will give your skin a ruddier color. If you are planning a move, it will protect you from the changes of water and of residence.

♣ If you'd care to pound a little garlic with fresh coriander and take it with some wine, those sex problems will be a thing of the past; passion will be restored.

♣ Farmers take note: if garlic is added to their feed, chickens will be protected from pip, and beasts of burden will pass urine without pain if the farmer will just treat their parts with a garlic paste.

♣ On the other hand, it won't do much for diarrhea, chronic fluxes or graying hair. Here, according to Pliny, you must look to leeks; garlic can't cure everything. Still, there is no other plant in Pliny's classic work that can do as much for you as garlic.

♣ What are those mysterious afflictions and poisons Pliny mentions, for which garlic is the antidote?

> aconite—wolfsbane, a poisonous plant
> catarrh—inflammation of any mucous membrane
> dropsy—fluid retention or bloat
> erysipelas—a type of streptococcus infection
> henbane—a poisonous plant of the nightshade family
> iliac passion—probably a term for intestinal distress
> jaundice—dysfunction of the liver
> lichen—skin eruption
> obolus of silphium—a small measure of a medicinal plant
> phrenitis—probably inflammation of the brain
> phthiriasis—lice
> pip—a disease of fowl
> quartan—malaria
> quinsy—tonsillitis
> scrofula—tuberculosis of the lymph glands
> scurf—dry skin
> suppuration—an abscess
> tenesmus—constipation and perhaps an inability to urinate freely

—Adapted from the 1951 W.H.S. Jones translation of Pliny's Natural History.

Golden Curried Split Pea Soup with Smoked Ham, Apple & Fennel

THIS COLORFUL SOUP of yellow split peas includes a smoked ham hock for an earthy touch. An apple adds a delicate sweetness, balanced by a splash of lemon juice.

SERVES 6

2 tablespoons olive oil
1 dried chile, crumbled
2 teaspoons ground fennel
2 plump shallots, minced
4 plump garlic cloves, smashed and minced
2 large carrots, trimmed, scrubbed and finely chopped
½ cup finely chopped peeled celery root (or equal parts chopped celery and chopped parsnip)
   Kosher salt to taste
1 tablespoon Madras-style curry powder
½ teaspoon ground red pepper (cayenne)
½ teaspoon freshly ground black pepper, plus more if desired
1 pound green split peas
1 large tart apple, peeled, cored and finely diced
9 cups hot water, plus more

as needed
1 smoked ham hock (or a bone from a smoked ham)
1 bay leaf
1 lemon, cut into 6 pieces

Heat olive oil in a large, heavy soup pot over medium heat. Add chile and stir for 1 minute. Then add fennel, shallots, garlic, carrots and celery root. Cover, reduce heat and cook for 5 minutes, or until vegetables begin to soften. Stir in salt, curry powder, cayenne and black pepper. Add peas, apple, water, ham hock and bay leaf.

Cover pot and bring to a boil over high heat. Reduce heat to low and cook until peas have fallen apart, 2½ to 3 hours. Remove ham hock and slice meat into small pieces. Return meat to pot. Add more water if soup is too thick. Taste and adjust seasonings.

Ladle into heated soup bowls. Squeeze lemon juice into each and serve.

Wine: Harpersfield Vineyards Gewürztraminer (Ohio: Lake Erie) or an Alsatian Gewürztraminer from France

Blue Cheese Soup with Roasted Garlic

THICK AND SILKY, sweet and fruity, rich and creamy, this is a remarkable, complexly flavored soup indeed. Our friend John Ash knows more about garlic than almost anyone else we know. This soup was inspired by a recipe from this celebrated chef's beautiful book *From the Earth to the Table* (Dutton, 1995).

SERVES 6 TO 8

- 2 tablespoons unsalted butter
- 3 plump garlic cloves, smashed and minced
- ¾ cup minced leeks, white part only
- 1 cup finely diced parsnips
- 2 cups peeled and finely diced tart apples
- ¼ cup applejack or Calvados
- 3 cups chicken stock
- 2 cups (9 ounces) crumbled blue cheese, such as Gorgonzola, Blue Castello, or Maytag Blue
- 2 cups light cream
  Kosher salt and freshly ground white pepper
- 3 tablespoons pureed roasted garlic (page 34)
  Minced fresh tarragon or fennel fronds for garnish

In a large, heavy saucepan, melt butter over low heat. Add minced garlic and leeks; cover and cook until translucent but not brown, about 5 minutes. Remove from heat and let sit 5 minutes, covered.

Stir in parsnips, apples, applejack, and stock. Bring to a boil, cover and simmer until parsnips are tender, about 20 minutes. Add cheese and stir until it melts. Transfer mixture to a food processor and pulse until solids are pureed. Return mixture to saucepan. Stir in cream; if mixture is too thick, thin with more stock.

Season with salt and pepper and set pan over medium heat. When soup is hot, ladle into heated soup plates, swirl in a teaspoon of garlic puree and sprinkle with fennel.

Wine: Patz and Hall Napa Valley Chardonnay (California: Napa Valley) or a very rich and complex Chardonnay from Burgundy

Roasted Garlic Vegetable Chowder with Beer & Cheese

A CREAMY, THICK, CHEESY chowder, this is an ideal vegetable soup for cold weather. Its special sweetness comes from dry-roasting the garlic. Make sure the beer is *not* cold; let it stand uncapped for several hours before cooking to reduce the foam.

SERVES 8

12	plump garlic cloves, unpeeled
3	tablespoons olive oil
1	dried red chile, crumbled
1	cup thinly sliced leeks
2	large carrots, scrubbed and sliced into thin disks
2	cups broccoli florets
1	cup corn kernels
1	teaspoon dried thyme (2 teaspoons fresh)
¼	cup unbleached flour
5	cups hot milk
1	cup dark beer
3	cups shredded sharp Cheddar cheese Kosher salt and freshly ground white pepper
2	teaspoons Worcestershire sauce Minced fresh dill, chives or parsley for garnish

One hour prior to cooking, prepare garlic: Place cloves in a single layer on a cast-iron skillet or griddle over medium-high heat. Roast cloves, turning often, until brown spots appear on skins and flesh is somewhat soft when lightly pressed, about 10 to 15 minutes. When garlic has cooled, carefully remove skins. Mince flesh and set aside.

Heat oil and chile in a large nonreactive saucepan. Add leeks and carrots; cover tightly and braise over very low heat for 10 minutes, or until carrots begin to soften. Add minced garlic, broccoli, corn kernels and thyme. Stir well, cover, and cook over very low heat for 5 minutes. Sprinkle evenly with flour, stir, and cook for 2 minutes more, stirring constantly. Slowly add hot milk, stirring gently until milk is hot and mixture has thickened. Stir in beer.

Cook over low heat until carrots and broccoli are tender, 10 to 15 minutes. Add cheese and stir until it melts. Season with salt, pepper, and Worcestershire sauce. Serve in heated bowls and sprinkle with fresh herbs.

Wine: Di Majo Norante Aglianico (Italy: Molise) or another fruity, spicy red wine from Italy, such as a Chianti Classico

BREADS

SERIOUS GARLIC

NO ONE IN THE WORLD grows more garlic than Don Christopher—at last count, 60 million pounds a year. When we arrived at Christopher Ranch, it looked as if it were snowing. A billion white flakes were swirling around in the California breeze, the by-product of the compressed-air peeling of tons of cloves of garlic.

The 5,000-acre ranch has been in the Christopher family for 40 years. At first they grew sugar beets and prunes. Then they turned to garlic and the rest is agricultural history. Christopher grows California Early and California Late, which he harvests throughout the summer and into the fall. At Blythe, he grows 400 acres of a hardneck Chinese strain that he can harvest in May. He contracts with other farmers for what he can't grow himself. And there are big refrigerated, low-oxygen storage facilities that can hold the garlic for several weeks without appreciable loss of quality.

When Christopher really got serious about garlic, most Gilroy growers were still sending their crop to the dehydrators. Even today most Americans get their garlic dried, in processed foods. In an effort to find new markets and encourage consumers to discover the beauty of the real thing, the growers started the Fresh Garlic Association in 1978 and the Gilroy Garlic Festival in 1979.

Inside the processing buildings of Christopher Ranch, big bins of bulbs are poured onto the conveyor system, inspected, cleaned, sized and boxed. In another area, heads of garlic are being cracked by machine to free the cloves. They are peeled with blasts of air (the source of the snowstorm) and packaged in jars for the restaurant and supermarket trade. There's even a cannery that turns out fresh sauces and pickled garlic.

Serious business, to be sure. But Christopher is clearly enjoying himself. We asked him why garlic has become so popular.

"We've made garlic fun," he said. "You've got garlic festivals everywhere. And all of those health considerations. It's always in the news. Those garlic pills—no odor. People can use garlic instead of salt. It makes your food better. Garlic is terrifically versatile."

Ham & Garlic Butter Biscuits

THIS RECIPE has a serendipitous origin. One day Fred forgot that he was to cook on his *Morning Exchange* program, so he had to quickly create a recipe from ingredients in the refrigerator. Inspired by some aged Virginia ham from the S. Wallace Edwards Company, he came up with these marvelous biscuits. They are thin and crisp, owing to the amount of shortening, and they are really delicious—especially when generously spread with really good butter. They've become a family favorite.

MAKES 2 TO 3 DOZEN

2½   cups unbleached flour
2   teaspoons baking soda
2   teaspoons baking powder
¼   teaspoon kosher salt
1   teaspoon freshly ground pepper
6   tablespoons unsalted butter,
    cut into small pieces
2   plump garlic cloves, peeled
5   long chives, cut into large pieces
1¼   cups buttermilk
½   cup finely chopped Virginia
    smoked ham

Preheat oven to 450°F. Place rack in upper third of oven.

In the bowl of a food processor fitted with the metal blade, combine dry ingredients. Add butter, garlic and chives. Pulse until mixture has the texture of coarse cornmeal. Add buttermilk and ham. Process just until mixture forms a ball.

Roll dough on a lightly floured board to a thickness of ½ inch. Cut out rounds with a 1½-inch biscuit cutter. (Reroll scraps once.) Place rounds on an ungreased baking sheet and bake for 10 minutes, or until golden.

Serve hot, preferably split with a sharp knife and lightly buttered.

Three-Peppers Under-Cover Corn Bread

OUR EARLY SETTLERS and covered-wagon pioneers made corn bread by placing a cast-iron Dutch oven directly in the fire and covering the lid with hot coals, a technique that results in a tender, full-flavored bread because of the steamy atmosphere. Here we add a variety of hot and sweet peppers lightly sautéed in garlic butter to make an even more flavorful bread. It makes a marvelous stuffing (see page 274).

You will notice that we preheat our Dutch oven. We want the pot hot enough to start cooking the batter immediately. A last-second oil spraying will keep the bottom from sticking if the Dutch oven is not well seasoned. Be sure to use a pot that is cast iron, cast aluminum, or cast iron clad in enamel.

MAKES ONE 10-INCH BREAD

6   tablespoons unsalted butter
3   plump garlic cloves, smashed
    and minced
½   medium-sized red bell pepper,
    seeded and finely diced
1   Anaheim or poblano chile pepper,
    seeded and finely diced
1   small fresh hot chile, seeded
    and minced
2   cups stone-ground cornmeal
1¼   cups unbleached flour
3½   teaspoons baking powder
2   tablespoons sugar
1   teaspoon kosher salt
½   teaspoon baking soda
2   cups buttermilk
3   large eggs, beaten
¼   cup vegetable oil

Preheat oven to 400°F.

Lightly but thoroughly coat a 5½-quart cast-iron Dutch oven or a 9-inch lidded cast-iron skillet with vegetable oil spray. As soon as you have assembled your ingredients and are ready to mix the batter, place the prepared pan in the oven to preheat.

In a medium-sized skillet, melt butter over medium heat. Add garlic and peppers. Reduce heat to low, cover and cook until peppers are somewhat softened, 3 to 5 minutes. Shake pan several times. Remove from heat.

Combine dry ingredients and sift into a mixing bowl. In another mixing bowl, combine buttermilk, eggs, vegetable oil and garlic-pepper mixture, using an electric mixer. With motor running on low, add buttermilk mixture to dry ingredients and mix well. Scrape sides of bowl once and mix again briefly.

Let batter rest for 15 minutes. Carefully transfer heated baking pan to a heatproof surface. Blend batter well, remove cover from baking pan, and pour batter into pan. Cover and bake 30 minutes in oven without opening lid. Test by inserting a toothpick into middle of corn bread. When toothpick comes out dry, corn bread is done.

Transfer baking pan to a rack. Uncover and let stand for 15 minutes. Place another rack over top and carefully turn pan upside down so corn bread slips out. Cool slightly before serving.

Spiral Loaf with Caramelized Onions & Garlic

THIS GETS OUR VOTE as one of the all-time best garlic breads. A yeasty, tender white bread is filled with a heady mixture of caramelized onions and garlic. Add some rosemary and oregano and you have a terrific filling for this deceptively simple bread—flavors permeate every crumb. You'll find that the center of the baked loaf will separate a bit from the top; that's just the nature of a spiral loaf.

MAKES ONE 10-x-5-INCH LOAF

- 1 tablespoon active dry yeast
- ¼ cup lukewarm water
- 1 tablespoon sugar
- 1½ cups warm milk
- ¼ cup vegetable oil
- 4½-5 cups unbleached flour
- 1 tablespoon plus 1 teaspoon kosher salt

Filling

- ¼ cup olive oil
- 1 teaspoon dried rosemary
- 1 teaspoon dried oregano
- 1 jumbo Spanish onion, finely chopped
- 6 plump garlic cloves, smashed and minced
- 1 tablespoon melted butter

In a small bowl, mix together yeast, water, and sugar. Let mixture stand until creamy, 5 to 10 minutes.

In the bowl of an electric mixer fitted with a paddle (if mixing by hand, use a wooden spoon), combine milk, vegetable oil and yeast mixture. Slowly add 4 cups of the flour, then 1 tablespoon salt.

Remove paddle, change to dough hook and knead until dough is smooth and elastic, adding flour as needed to make a soft, just slightly tacky dough. Transfer dough to a large, lightly oiled bowl. (We use a very large wooden salad bowl.) Cover with plastic wrap and let rise in a warm place until doubled in size, about 1 to 1½ hours.

While bread is rising, prepare filling: Heat olive oil over medium heat in a medium-sized, heavy skillet. Add rosemary and oregano and stir for 30 seconds to release flavors. Add onion and garlic. Cover tightly, reduce heat to low and cook, stirring often, until onion is golden, 20 to

30 minutes. Stir in remaining 1 teaspoon salt and let cool.

Oil a 10-x-5-inch bread pan. Punch dough down and turn out on a lightly floured board. Roll or pat into a rectangle 9 inches wide and 18 inches long. Spread onion-garlic mixture evenly over surface of dough, leaving a ½-inch clear edge all around. Tightly roll dough up from short side, jelly-roll fashion. Pat ends so it is 9 inches across. Place roll in bread pan, seam side down. Loosely cover with plastic and let rise in a warm place until top is 1½ inches above pan, 45 to 60 minutes. Meanwhile, preheat oven to 375°F.

Bake in preheated oven for 45 minutes. Gently remove bread from pan and place directly on oven rack. Continue to bake 10 to 15 minutes more, or until loaf is golden brown and bottom sounds hollow when rapped (an instant-read thermometer inserted into center should read 210°F).

Immediately brush top of bread with butter to give it a nice sheen. Let cool on a rack for at least 30 minutes before eating. Serve warm or at room temperature.

Salt-Rising Garlic Bread with Potato-Cornmeal Starter

THIS UNUSUAL GARLIC BREAD has a crisp crust and a very full-flavored crumb. The distinctive flavor comes from garlic blended with the unusual potato and cornmeal starter, which is modeled on the old-fashioned salt-rising bread Fred's stepgrandmother made. It's called "salt-rising" because the starter was made in a bowl kept toasty warm by placing it in the box of salt kept on the wood-burning stove.

Today, when we need a very warm place in our kitchen, we put the mixing bowl inside a shallow wooden bowl near the pilot light of our gas range. That's where the starter begins its life, and that's also where the bowl rests while the dough rises. This starter is quite versatile. Just refresh it every few weeks. If yours is very bubbly, you can use two cups of it and omit the commercial yeast.

Begin the starter three days before you bake the first loaf.

MAKES 1 LARGE ROUND BREAD, PLUS A LONG-LIVED STARTER

Starter

1	large russet potato, peeled
½	teaspoon salt
½	teaspoon sugar
1	teaspoon baking soda
½	teaspoon ground ginger
2	cups boiling water
¼	cup cornmeal
1½	cups warm water
2¾	cups unbleached flour

Bread

1¼	cups warm water
2	teaspoons active dry yeast
2	tablespoons olive oil
6	plump garlic cloves, pressed
3½	cups unbleached flour, plus more if needed
1	tablespoon kosher salt
1	cup plus 1 tablespoon finely ground cornmeal or semolina

12-14 ice cubes

To make starter the first time: Three days ahead, slice potato into a 2-quart mixing bowl. Add salt, sugar, baking soda and ginger. Pour

WHEN WORKING WITH STARTER

AFTER REMOVING UP TO 1½ cups of starter to make bread, whisk in ⅔ cup flour and ⅔ cup warm water. Let stand in a warm place covered with plastic wrap for 24 hours. Then cover and refrigerate until 24 hours before you intend to use it.

At that time, refresh starter by stirring in ⅓ cup flour and ⅓ cup warm water. Let stand in a warm place for 24 hours. It is ready to use.

boiling water over mixture and stir. Sprinkle cornmeal and 1 cup of the flour over mixture and stir. Place bowl, uncovered, in a very warm place until it forms a very thick, frothy and yeasty-smelling sponge, 24 to 30 hours. Stir mixture well. Remove potato slices to a small bowl, scraping froth back into sponge. Add ½ cup warm water to potatoes and swish them around in it. Then pour that water back into sponge. Discard potatoes. Whisk sponge with water, then whisk in ½ cup of the flour.

Return uncovered bowl to a very warm place until surface is well covered with bubbles, 4 to 6 hours. Stir in ½ cup water and ½ cup of the flour, to make a pancakelike batter. Cover with plastic wrap and let stand at room temperature overnight.

Whisk in remaining ¾ cup of flour and ½ cup water. Cover and let stand at room temperature for 24 more hours or until surface is very bubbly. Starter should be ready to use.

To make bread: In a small bowl, combine ¼ cup of the warm water with yeast. Set aside in a warm place until mixture begins to foam, 5 to 10 minutes.

In a warmed mixing bowl, combine yeast mixture with 1½ cups starter and remaining 1 cup warm water. Stir in olive oil, garlic, 1 cup of the flour and salt. Beat thoroughly, then add 1 cup of the cornmeal. Mix well.

Gradually mix in enough of the flour to make a shaggy mass. Lightly flour a clean work surface. Scrape dough from bowl. With heavily floured hands and a pastry scraper, begin to knead, slowly adding flour as needed. Knead until dough is elastic and rather smooth, although still soft and somewhat tacky, 15 to 20 minutes.

Oil a large, preferably wooden, bowl. Place dough in bowl and turn to lightly coat with oil. Cover with plastic wrap and let rise in a warm place until it has doubled, 2 to 3 hours.

Prepare your shaping bowl: A round, shallow wooden salad bowl, 10 inches in diameter and 3 inches deep in the middle, lined with a tea towel, works perfectly. Sprinkle cloth generously with flour.

When dough has doubled, punch down. Turn onto a lightly floured work surface and knead for 5 minutes. Shape into a firm round and place, top side down, in shaping bowl. Take a large plastic bag and stand it like a dome over bread and bowl. Let dough rise in a very warm place until large and rounded, 1 to 1½ hours.

About 45 minutes before you want to bake, place unglazed tiles or a baking stone on an oven rack in upper third of oven. Place a broiling pan on rack below. Preheat oven and tiles to 450°F.

To bake bread: Carefully but quickly, slide oven rack with tiles partly out of oven and sprinkle tiles with cornmeal. Turn bread upside down onto tiles. Using a razor blade, make three or four long parallel slashes across top of bread, first in one direction, then in the other (to make diamonds).

Push oven rack back into oven and quickly toss ice cubes into pan below. Bake for 50 minutes, or until bread is a rich golden brown (an instant-read thermometer inserted into center of bread should read 210°F).

Let bread cool on a rack.

BRUSCHETTA

ITALY GIVES US one of the greatest-tasting bread snacks in the world—*bruschetta*. Cut a thick slice of country bread. Toast it thoroughly, preferably over an open fire. Cut a plump clove of garlic in half and rub it vigorously across the surface. Then drizzle the toast generously with the best extra-virgin olive oil you can find. Spectacular!

Variation: Follow the garlic rub with a good rub of half a garden-fresh tomato, then drizzle with oil. Or, as they do in Piedmont, place both fillets of a cleaned, salt-packed anchovy over the garlic-rubbed bread and then drizzle with oil.

WHEN IN BARCELONA—*Pa Amb Tomàquet*

Catalans rub garlic on both sides of their toasted bread and then rub both sides with half a right-from-the-vine tomato before drizzling each side with olive oil and dusting with salt.

OLD-FASHIONED AMERICAN GARLIC BREAD

Soften 8 tablespoons of unsalted butter. Mix with several pressed garlic cloves. If you like, add some minced fresh basil. Split a loaf of Italian bread in half lengthwise. Spread most of the garlic butter over bottom piece. Replace the top and dot with remaining garlic butter. Wrap well in foil and bake at 400°F for about 20 minutes, or until bread is slightly toasted and butter has melted into it. Cut in thick wedges. For a real treat, send those wedges to the grill to crisp.

Sourdough Bread with Garlic, Basil, Sun-Dried Tomatoes & Cheese

THE FIRST TIME we made this bread, Fred couldn't stop eating it. The crumb is coarse and studded with bits of tomato and garlic. Besides the tang from the potato-cornmeal sourdough starter, this bread gets oodles of other flavors from the rye flour and fontina cheese. And you'll love the pumpkin color from the sun-dried tomatoes!

MAKES 1 LOAF

2 teaspoons active dry yeast
  Pinch sugar
¾ cup warm water
  Up to 6 cups unbleached flour
1 cup stone-ground rye flour
1 tablespoon kosher salt
1 cup Potato-Cornmeal Starter (page 110) or other sourdough starter
½ cup drained oil-packed sun-dried tomatoes, chopped
5 plump garlic cloves, smashed and minced
⅓ cup coarsely chopped fresh basil
1 cup grated fontina cheese
1 tablespoon cornmeal

Combine yeast, sugar and ¼ cup of the water in a small bowl. Mix thoroughly and set aside until foamy, 5 to 10 minutes.

In the bowl of an electric mixer, combine 3 cups of the flour, rye flour and salt (if mixing by hand, use a wooden spoon). Stir in yeast mixture, starter and remaining ½ cup water. Add tomatoes, garlic, basil, cheese and 1 cup flour. Blend thoroughly. Blend in 1 more cup flour.

Turn dough out onto a well-floured board and knead, gradually adding as much flour as needed to make a dough that is elastic, moderately smooth and just slightly tacky to the touch.

Oil a large, preferably wooden, bowl. Place dough in bowl and turn to coat lightly with oil. Cover with plastic wrap and let rise in a warm place until it has doubled in volume, 1½ to 2 hours.

Prepare your shaping bowl: You can use a round, shallow wooden salad bowl, 10 inches in diameter and 3 inches deep in the middle, lined with a tea towel. Sprinkle towel generously with flour.

When dough has doubled, punch down and turn out onto a lightly floured work surface. Knead for 5 minutes. Form into a round and place in shaping bowl, smooth side down. Cover with a large inverted plastic bag. Let rise in a warm place until dough has doubled in volume, about 1 hour.

About 45 minutes before you plan to bake, put a rack in top third of oven and line it with unglazed tiles or a baking stone. Preheat oven and tiles to 450°F.

To bake bread: Sprinkle a pizza peel or cookie sheet with cornmeal. Very gently, keeping rounded top facing up, tip bread onto it. Carefully slide oven rack with tiles partly out of oven. Slip bread from peel onto tiles. Using a sharp razor, slash an X across top of loaf.

Slide rack back into oven. Reduce oven temperature to 425°F and bake bread for 50 minutes, or until it is a rich, golden brown (an instant-read thermometer inserted into its center should read 210°F).

Remove bread from oven and cool on a rack.

MANGO MARTINI

WE'VE TASTED GARLIC-STUFFED OLIVES BEFORE, but none as delicious as those three gracing each martini at Chicago's trendy restaurant Mango. Bartender Carolyn Canfield makes them herself. The plump cloves are roasted. "You need to watch your garlic," she advises. "You want the cloves to be soft, but not mushy." Chill the roasted garlic, then carefully lift each clove individually from the head.

"You have to have large, green pitted olives," she said. "Not the ones stuffed with pimentos, which aren't salty enough." Save the brine they come in.

Carefully insert one roasted clove into the opening of each large pitted olive. After you've done it a few times you'll get the hang of it. Pack the olives gently into a container and cover them with the reserved brine. "Vodka lovers should cover them with Ketel One," she suggested. Stored in the refrigerator, they will keep for at least a week (not that you'll be able to leave them alone that long).

The garlic-loving bartender had a final martini-olive-stuffing suggestion for us: "Blend softened Gorgonzola cheese with chopped roasted garlic and a little port wine."

THE GARLIC MARKETS OF SOUTHWEST FRANCE

THE ROBUST CUISINE OF SOUTHWESTERN FRANCE is rich in garlic as well as fat. From *cassoulet* to *confit*, garlic is an essential flavoring. (Perhaps the French give too much credit for long life to red wine and not enough to garlic!) Lautrec is the beautiful pink garlic growing near Albi that we used to buy every August. We brought special large plastic bags with us in those years. If we were going to be traveling a lot after we made our purchases, we triple-bagged the garlic braids at night, so that their wonderful "fragrance" would not permeate the car. During the day we traveled with them *un*bagged, so the air could flow around them. For our trip back to Cleveland, they were tightly wrapped once more. We brought enough home to last almost through the winter. It was wonderful. And now it's illegal.

To try the rich and vivid garlics of the region for yourself, check out these towns, which have special garlic markets and events:

CADOURS (NEAR TOULOUSE)

The garlic market is the last weekend of August; it lasts for two days. The garlic here is violet in color because of certain elements in the soil in this region. If you want to see a castle made of garlic braids, this is the place! There are special competitions for decorations made with braided garlic.

For information, call Cadours Town Hall: 5-61-85-60 01.

Lautrec (near Albi)

This town gives its name to the pink garlic we enjoyed for so many years. The garlic market is held here every Friday below the medieval market. A special market on the first Friday of August features all kinds of competitions and celebrations. For dinner there is the tasting of the *sabounade*, a special dish made with beans and garlic.

For information, call Lautrec Tourist Office: 5-63-75-31-40.

Beaumont de Lomagne (near Montauban)

You will find both white and violet garlic in this town. The garlic market is held each Tuesday and Saturday morning from June to December. A special celebration, complete with garlic exhibitions, is held on the second weekend of September.

For information, call Beaumont de Lomagne Tourist Office: 5-63-02-42-32.

Saint Clar (Tarn-et-Garonne)

The garlic market here takes place every Thursday, beginning with the second Thursday in July. There is a special garlic fair on the second Thursday in August—with entertainment and a garlic lunch cooked by the local farmers. If you go on the fourth Thursday of August, you can see a special garlic cooking competition.

Toulouse

In Toulouse, the noble city of *cassoulet*, there are garlic markets at the Place du Salin on both August 24 and October 15. You will find three kinds of garlic: white, which lasts until Christmas; violet garlic from Gascony, which lasts until April; and "the wonderful pink garlic of Lautrec, which the connoisseurs fight for in the early morning!" Here you will also find garlic braided with lemon verbena and shallots.

Country Bread
with Red Wine, Olives & Garlic

I F TAPENADE IS GOOD on top of the bread, it has to be even better mixed into it! The basics of that zesty Mediterranean olive spread are cured black olives, olive oil and garlic. We add red wine and Mediterranean herbs to deepen the flavors. The robust stone-ground whole wheat flour not only contributes to the great taste but gives added texture to this terrific loaf. Here, as in some of our other bread recipes, we toss a dozen ice cubes into a shallow pan placed on a lower oven rack to create the steam needed for a rich crust.

MAKES 1 LARGE ROUND LOAF

1	tablespoon active dry yeast
1	teaspoon sugar
1½	cups warm water
¼	cup extra-virgin olive oil
⅓	cup dry red wine
½	cup stone-ground whole wheat flour (red wheat if possible)
4	plump garlic cloves, smashed and minced
1	cup pitted Kalamata olives
2	teaspoons kosher salt
2	teaspoons herbes de Provençe, or mixture of dried rosemary, thyme, basil and savory
4½	cups unbleached flour, plus more if needed
1	tablespoon cornmeal
12-14	ice cubes

In a small, warm bowl, combine yeast, sugar and ¼ cup of the water. Blend thoroughly, then put in a warm place until foamy, about 7 to 10 minutes.

In the bowl of an electric mixer (or, if mixing by hand, in a large bowl with a wooden spoon), combine oil, wine, whole wheat flour, garlic, olives, salt and herbs. Blend in remaining 1¼ cups water and yeast mixture. Gradually mix in flour, adding enough to create a slightly tacky dough. Knead for 10 minutes with a dough hook or about 20 minutes by hand. Form into a firm ball.

Oil a large, preferably wooden, bowl. Place dough in bowl and turn to lightly coat with oil. Cover with plastic wrap and let rise in a warm place until doubled, about 2 hours.

Prepare your shaping bowl: You can use a round, shallow wooden salad bowl, 10 inches in diameter and 3 inches deep in the middle, lined with a tea towel. Sprinkle towel generously with flour.

About 45 minutes before baking, place a large shallow pan on the lower rack of your oven. Place upper rack in top third and line it with unglazed tiles or a pizza stone. Preheat oven to 450°F.

When dough has doubled, punch down and turn out onto a lightly floured work surface. Knead for 5 minutes. Form into a nice round and place in the lightly floured shaping bowl. Cover with a large inverted plastic bag. Let rise in a warm place until bread has doubled in volume, about 1 hour.

To bake bread: Sprinkle a pizza peel or a rimless cookie sheet with cornmeal. Very gently, keeping rounded top facing up, tip bread onto it. Carefully but quickly, slide oven rack with tiles partly out of oven. Slip bread from peel onto tiles. Slash an X across top with a razor. Immediately slide rack back into oven and dump ice cubes into hot pan below.

Bake for 30 minutes. Reduce heat to 425°F and continue to bake for 10 more minutes, or until top is a rich butterscotch color and an instant-read thermometer inserted into center reads 210°F.

Remove bread from oven and cool on a rack.

Anchovy, Garlic & Olive Bread

EVERYONE LOVES THIS COARSE BREAD, with its crisp exterior and textured, chewy crumb, inspired by a remarkable anchovy and olive bread served by Paul Mincelli in his eponymous Paris restaurant. The anchovies, olives and garlic bake into little bits of warm flavor that folks love but cannot quite identify. The French make it with a sponge called a *poolish;* the Italians call theirs *biga.* The important thing to keep in mind is that a wet dough will yield the textured crumb with uneven holes that we associate with a peasant bread. Although this dough is a bit messy to handle, it is worth the effort.

Start this bread the day before you plan to bake it.

MAKES 1 LARGE ROUND BREAD

Sponge
- 1 scant tablespoon active dry yeast
- 1¼ cups warm water
- 1 cup unbleached flour
- ½ cup whole wheat flour

Dough
- 1½ teaspoons active dry yeast
- 2 cups warm water
- 1 tablespoon honey

- 4½ cups unbleached flour, plus more if needed
- 2 teaspoons kosher salt
- 1 cup whole wheat flour
- 3 plump garlic cloves, smashed and minced
- ⅔ cup pitted Niçoise olives
- 1 2-ounce can anchovy fillets, drained and chopped
- 1 teaspoon olive oil
- 1 tablespoon cornmeal

- 12-14 ice cubes

To make sponge: The night before you plan to bake, in a medium bowl, proof yeast by thoroughly blending it with ¼ cup of the water. Let stand in a warm place until mixture begins to foam, 6 to 10 minutes. Mix in remaining cup of water, then gradually stir in flours, beating well with a wooden spoon. Cover bowl with plastic wrap and let stand overnight in refrigerator. Let stand at room temperature for 1 hour before mixing.

To make dough: Place yeast in a small bowl with ¼ cup of the water and honey. When foamy, combine with sponge and remaining 1¾ cups water in the bowl of an electric mixer and blend (if mixing by hand, use a wooden spoon). Gradually beat in 3 cups of the flour, salt, whole wheat flour, garlic, olives and anchovies.

Using some of remaining 1½ cups flour, generously flour a clean work surface. Turn dough onto prepared surface and begin to knead, gradually adding remaining flour. After 15 minutes, dough should be elastic, smooth, but still slightly tacky. Add more flour only if dough is very sticky.

Oil a large, preferably wooden, bowl. Place dough in bowl and turn to coat lightly with oil. Cover with plastic wrap and let rise in a warm place until it has more than doubled, about 1¼ hours.

Prepare your shaping bowl: You can use a round, shallow wooden salad bowl, 10 inches in diameter and 3 inches deep in the middle, lined with a tea towel. Sprinkle towel generously with flour.

When dough is ready, punch down, then turn out onto a lightly floured work surface. Knead for 2 to 3 minutes, then shape into a tight, smooth round. Place top side down in shaping bowl. Cover with a large inverted plastic bag and let rise in a warm place for 1 hour, or until dough has risen slightly above bowl.

To bake bread: Half an hour before bread is fully risen, place a large shallow pan on the lower rack of your oven. Place upper rack in top third and line it with unglazed tiles or a pizza stone. Preheat oven to 450°F.

When bread is ready to bake, quickly but carefully slide oven rack with tiles partly out of oven and sprinkle tiles with cornmeal. Invert shaping bowl and gently tip bread upside down onto tiles so that bottom becomes top. With a sharp blade, cut three slashes about 1½ inches apart, then three slices across to make diamonds. Slide rack back into oven and add ice cubes to baking pan.

Bake for 35 minutes. Reduce temperature to 425°F and bake for 15 minutes more, or until bread is a rich brown and an instant-read thermometer inserted into center reads 210°F.

Let bread cool on a rack.

Garlic Walnut Bread with Rosemary

WALNUTS AND GARLIC bring out the best in each other, especially in the company of piney rosemary. Here they're combined in a tender-crumbed loaf to make a great bread for cheese or sandwiches. Adding some walnut oil enriches its flavor. Hats off to Odessa Piper, owner/chef of Madison, Wisconsin's, acclaimed restaurant L'Étoile, who taught us how to make walnut bread.

MAKES 1 LOAF

1 cup warm milk

1 tablespoon active dry yeast

2 teaspoons sugar

½ cup rye flour

2½ cups unbleached flour, plus more if needed

2 teaspoons kosher salt

¼ teaspoon freshly ground white pepper

1 tablespoon minced fresh rosemary (2 teaspoons dried)

3 plump garlic cloves, smashed and minced

¼ cup walnut oil

½ cup walnuts, coarsely chopped

Combine ½ cup of the milk, yeast and sugar in a small bowl. Blend well and let stand until foamy, 5 to 10 minutes.

Combine rye flour, 2 cups of the flour, salt, pepper, rosemary and garlic in the bowl of an electric mixer (if mixing by hand, use a wooden spoon). In a medium-sized bowl, blend together remaining ½ cup milk, walnut oil and yeast mixture.

With mixer running on low, add milk mixture to flour mixture. Then add nuts. Blend well, adding more flour if dough is very wet and sticky. Knead dough for 7 to 10 minutes with a dough hook or 12 to 15 minutes by hand on a lightly floured board until smooth and elastic. Form dough into a smooth round.

Lightly oil a large mixing bowl. (We prefer a large wooden salad bowl.) Turn dough over in bowl, coating it with oil. Cover bowl with plastic wrap and let rise in a warm place until doubled in volume, 2 to 3 hours.

Lightly knead dough to eliminate any bubbles. Shape into a round and place on an oiled pizza pan. Cover loosely with a kitchen towel and let rise in a warm place for 1 hour, or until nearly doubled in volume. About 45 minutes before baking, preheat oven to 375°F.

Bake for 45 to 55 minutes, or until loaf is golden brown (an instant-read thermometer inserted into center should reach 210°F).

Transfer bread to a cooling rack.

As Good as Ten Mothers

PRODUCERS OF VAMPIRE MOVIES usually manage to have enough garlic on their sets to make everyone in Gilroy happy. But in those films you never see anyone eating it; the garlic is there as though it were aspirin for a headache.

From time to time in other movies, we see garlic being consumed. In *Goodfellas*, for example, Paul Sorvino and Ray Liotta, a couple of Mafia guys in the pen, are shown chopping garlic with a razor blade in an effort to upgrade the quality of prison grub.

But we know of only one film in which garlic is the star: Les Blank's documentary *Garlic Is as Good as Ten Mothers*. A San Francisco garlic lover, Blank turned his attention to garlic at about the time that Alice Waters was making Americans rethink dinner through her work at Chez Panisse in Berkeley. She loved garlic and used tons of it in her restaurant. Les Blank came to watch her cook and got into the garlic subculture that was starting to make its way into the mainstream.

"Garlic is the spice of life, the spice of life, the spice of life," sings the young soprano at the opening of the Gilroy Garlic Festival, the first scene in Blank's film.

Blank found barbecue kings, chefs, musicians, writers, children and assorted odd characters whose lives had been influenced by garlic. One Spanish gypsy came to California out of a life butchering the by-product of the bullfighting craft. And at one point, as he puts together a garlicky sausage, he sings out this advice:

"If you want to be happy in your life,
You had better tell your wife,
To throw five nice heads of garlic in the pot."

And Blank directly confronts something that anyone raised in the country knows about. He shows some sows chowing down on huge quantities of garlic. Then, a little later, we see a dozen piglets dining at their mother's teats.

"Oink, oink, oink," they say greedily and in unison. "More garlic milk."

Focaccia with Garlic, Leeks & Rosemary

THIS POPULAR ITALIAN FLATBREAD can be made with many toppings. We thoroughly enjoy this bread topped with pungent garlic, mellow leeks and fragrant rosemary and with pepper and rosemary kneaded right into the dough. Our dough is soft and silky, easy to handle. We've made focaccia for years, but our results improved after reading Carol Field's marvelous book *The Italian Baker* (Harper & Row, 1985). That's where we learned about "dimpling" the shaped dough in the final rising. The dimples catch the oil from the topping, making a much better bread.

SERVES 4 TO 6

Focaccia

1 tablespoon active dry yeast
1 cup warm water
3 cups unbleached flour,
    plus more as needed
1½ teaspoons kosher salt
1 rounded teaspoon freshly ground
    black pepper
1 tablespoon minced fresh rosemary
3 tablespoons olive oil

Topping

¼ cup plus 2 tablespoons extra-virgin
    olive oil
4 cups thinly sliced leeks, trimmed
    to include tender greens
¼ cup thinly sliced garlic cloves
1 rounded tablespoon minced
    fresh rosemary

12-14 ice cubes

To make focaccia: Dissolve yeast in ¼ cup of the warm water and let stand until foamy. In the bowl of an electric mixer fitted with a paddle, combine 3 cups flour, salt, pepper and rosemary. Add yeast mixture, remaining ¾ cup water and olive oil. Mix on low speed until thoroughly blended. Once dough is mixed, change to dough hook and knead for about 5 minutes, gradually adding flour to make a smooth dough. (Or mix yeast and flour with a wooden spoon, then turn dough out on a floured surface and knead until smooth, gradually adding only enough flour to keep dough from sticking.) When dough is smooth and shiny, place in a large, well-oiled bowl and turn to coat lightly with oil. Cover with plastic wrap and let rise in a warm place.

It should double in bulk in about 1 hour.

Meanwhile, make topping: Heat ¼ cup of the olive oil in a heavy saucepan over medium heat. Add leeks, garlic and rosemary. Stir, cover tightly, reduce heat to low and cook until leeks are tender, about 15 minutes. Reserve.

Lightly coat a 14-inch pizza pan with 1 tablespoon olive oil. After dough has doubled, turn it out on a lightly floured surface and roll or pat it into a 12-inch circle. Lift it onto prepared pan, then gently stretch dough to cover pan. It should be about ½ inch thick. Using the tips of your fingers, vigorously press "dimples" all over surface of stretched dough. Cover lightly with a towel and let rest for 20 minutes. Drizzle evenly with remaining 1 tablespoon olive oil. Distribute cooked garlic-leek mixture evenly over surface. Lightly cover with towel again and let focaccia rise for 1 hour.

Place a shallow baking pan on a lower oven rack. If using a baking stone, place it on upper rack. Preheat oven to 450°F. Slide focaccia from pan to hot stone and toss ice cubes into hot baking pan. Reduce heat to 425°F. Bake focaccia for 20 to 25 minutes, or until top and edges are golden.

Transfer focaccia to a cake rack for a few minutes. Cut into wedges and serve while quite warm.

If serving as a starter:
Wine: Badia a Coltibuono Chianti Classico
(Italy: Tuscany) or a medium-bodied Zinfandel
from California

Focaccia with Roasted Garlic, Oregano & Kalamata Olives

THIS FOCACCIA is redolent of fresh oregano, pungent olives and sweet and smoky garlic. It's a simple topping to prepare, but wonderfully complex to taste. Serve this in summer as an appetizer along with a clutch of simple salads, a melange of olives and—to make a real hit—the roasted garlic pâté on page 47.

You can prepare this dough somewhat ahead of baking. Follow instructions right up till dough finishes its first rising. Punch dough down, cover loosely with plastic and refrigerate until 1½ hours before baking. Let stand in a warm place and it will rise perfectly for you. To make an even better crust, stretch focaccia onto a flat-sided cookie sheet or pizza peel that has been sprinkled with cornmeal, then slide it directly onto hot tile (this is a little tricky) and bake.

SERVES 4 TO 6

Focaccia

1 tablespoon active dry yeast

1 cup lukewarm water

3 cups unbleached flour,
  plus more as needed

1 teaspoon kosher salt

1 teaspoon freshly ground black pepper

2 tablespoons fresh oregano

3 tablespoons olive oil

Topping

3 large heads garlic, roasted,
  with any pan juices, page 34

1½ teaspoons kosher salt

1 teaspoon freshly ground black pepper

3 tablespoons extra-virgin olive oil

2 tablespoons minced fresh oregano,
  preferably Greek

3 tablespoons extra-virgin olive oil

1 cup pitted Kalamata olives,
  coarsely chopped

12-14 ice cubes

To make focaccia: Dissolve yeast in ¼ cup of the warm water and let stand until mixture is creamy. In the bowl of an electric mixer fitted with a paddle, combine 3 cups flour, salt and pepper. Add yeast mixture, remaining ¾ cup water and olive oil, then run motor on low until mixture is well blended. Once dough is mixed, change to dough hook and knead for 5 to 7 minutes, until smooth. Or turn dough out on a floured surface and knead by hand until smooth, gradually adding 1 tablespoon of the oregano and adding only enough flour to keep dough from sticking. When dough is smooth and shiny, place it in a large, well-oiled bowl, cover with plastic wrap and let rise in a warm place. It should double in bulk in 1 to 1½ hours.

Lightly coat a 14-inch pizza pan with olive oil. After dough has doubled in volume, turn it out onto a lightly floured surface and pat or roll it into a 12-inch circle. Lift onto prepared pan, then gently stretch dough to cover. It should be about ½ inch thick. Using the tips of your fingers, vigorously press "dimples" all over surface of stretched dough. Cover lightly with a towel and let rest for 20 minutes.

Meanwhile, make topping: Squeeze roasted garlic flesh into a shallow mixing bowl. Add pan juices, 1 tablespoon of the oregano and 1 tablespoon of the olive oil. Mash together until mixture is spreadable.

After focaccia rests for 20 minutes, drizzle evenly with remaining 2 tablespoons olive oil. Spread evenly with roasted garlic mixture, then scatter olives over surface. Sprinkle with remaining 1 tablespoon oregano. Lightly cover with towel again and let focaccia rise for 1 hour.

Place a shallow baking pan on a lower oven rack. If using a baking stone, place it on upper rack. Preheat oven to 450°F. Slide focaccia onto hot stone and toss ice cubes into hot baking pan. Reduce heat to 425 degrees and bake focaccia for 20 to 25 minutes, or until top and edges are golden.

Transfer focaccia to a cake rack for a few minutes. Cut into wedges and serve while quite warm.

If serving as a starter:
Wine: Renato Ratti Dolcetto d'Alba (Italy: Piedmont)
or a light California Pinot Noir

MORE FOR THE MONEY

Louie and Judy Bonino own 350 acres in San Martin, California. They plant 40 acres in garlic—the usual Californias and a little Roja, a pretty Spanish red. Their employees are masters of the braid, wreath and *ristra*. The 12 heads in a braid or 24 in a wreath bring in a lot more money than one or two dozen in a brown paper bag, and vastly more than if sold in bulk for dehydrating.

So just before the harvest, the foreman walks the fields, noting plants that would be handsome enough for braiding. They are gathered first and allowed to dry. Then, when the harvest is done, the Boninos start the process of creating 10,000 braids.

In a large, barnlike salesroom, hundreds of braids of garlic hang from the wall, wonderfully crafted and tied with elaborate corsages at the top. Several women sit at tables making more, trying to stay ahead of the demand. Thousands are sold through the mail.

Louie Bonino's family has been on this farm since 1917. His grandfather, who had come to California from the mines in Illinois, started out with grapes. But Prohibition drove him to prunes, then row crops. Louie and Judy have been working the farm for 30 years, continuing the tradition. Garlic was something they'd always grown for their own kitchen, but as the nation got hooked, so did they, and they got into big-time growing. Now their two sons, both recent college graduates, work with them, learning the vagaries of growing garlic.

We asked Louie if he thought garlic was growing in popularity because of its medicinal properties. "I won't make health claims," he said, "but it couldn't hurt." Very long lives in the Bonino family.

As we were leaving, Louie asked if we had eaten at the Stinking Rose Restaurant in San Francisco. "You know that 36-foot garlic braid? We made it."

SALADS

Tomato Salad with Red Onions, Herbs & French Dressing   130

Minted Cucumber Yogurt with Garlic & Dill   132

Tapawingo's Greens with Rosemary Honey Garlic Vinaigrette   133

Greek Salad with Feta & Garlicky Yogurt Dressing   135

Wilted Spinach Salad with Garlic & Bacon   136

Endive & Prosciutto Salad with Garlic & Walnuts   137

Buttermilk Slaw with Garlic   138

Two-Cabbage Slaw with Peppers & Herbs   139

Shredded Carrots & Fennel with Spicy Garlic Vinaigrette   140

Lentil Salad with Minted Garlic & Lime Vinaigrette   141

Green Beans with Basil Garlic Vinaigrette & Hazelnuts   144

Tomato Salad with Red Onions, Herbs & French Dressing

WE'RE COOKS AND WRITERS, not farmers. But even we are able to grow luscious heirloom tomatoes for late-summer enjoyment. We mix a variety of them for this salad, tossing them with red onions, fresh basil and a garlicky French dressing. What makes this dressing French? We never did find out. Perhaps it's the paprika, which lends a robust flavor and a rosy color to a very tasty oil and vinegar dressing. The optional horseradish adds a pleasing freshness to the flavors. If you have horseradish in your garden, scatter some minced leaves over the tomatoes.

This recipe makes about 1½ cups of dressing. Stored in a tightly closed container in the refrigerator, it will keep for several weeks. If you strain out the garlic and onion before storing, it won't get bitter.

SERVES 6 TO 8

French Dressing

¼ cup fresh lemon juice

¼ cup tarragon vinegar

2 teaspoons Colman's dry mustard

1 tablespoon hot Hungarian paprika

2 teaspoons kosher salt

1 teaspoon sugar

1 teaspoon freshly ground white pepper

2 teaspoons grated horseradish (optional)

2 plump garlic cloves, pressed

¼ cup grated sweet onion

½ cup extra-virgin olive oil

¼ cup canola oil

Salad

6 large vine-ripened tomatoes, mixed varieties

½ cup coarsely chopped red onion
   Kosher salt and freshly ground black pepper

6 large leaves fresh basil, julienned

1 tablespoon capers, drained (optional)

To make dressing: In a medium-sized mixing bowl, blend together lemon juice, vinegar, mustard and paprika. Whisk in salt, sugar, pepper, horseradish (if using), garlic and grated onion. Very slowly whisk in olive oil, then canola oil. Pour into a container with a tight cover and refrigerate for at least 4 hours and up to 2 weeks. Let stand at room temperature for 30 minutes before using.

To make salad: In a salad bowl, gently mix tomatoes and onions together. Add ½ cup French dressing and blend. Season with salt and pepper, adding more dressing if you like. Sprinkle with basil and capers (if using) just before serving.

> "What garlic is to salad,
> insanity is to art."
> —Anonymous

Minted Cucumber Yogurt
with Garlic & Dill

A SALAD OF CUCUMBER, garlic and yo-gurt appears on many Eastern Mediter-ranean tables in various guises. Our recipe is inspired by a salad we enjoyed one hot afternoon in Istanbul. Not only did it include both mint and dill, but it also had a bit of heat to it—cayenne, we decided. Use regular cucum-bers and lightly seed them with your fingers (some seeds are fine). And remember that the better the yogurt and the garlic, the better this delicious dish will be. Serve as one of a number of small cold dishes for an appetizer buffet or as a salad accompanying grilled lamb.

SERVES 6 TO 8

2 medium-sized cucumbers, peeled, lightly seeded, finely diced and drained for 30 minutes

2 cups plain yogurt, preferably whole-milk

4 plump garlic cloves, smashed and minced

2 tablespoons minced fresh dill

¼ cup minced fresh mint or 1 tablespoon dried

¼ teaspoon ground red pepper (cayenne) Kosher salt and freshly ground black pepper

Combine all ingredients in a medium-sized bowl. Blend thoroughly. Cover with plastic wrap and refrigerate for at least 2, and up to 6, hours. Serve in a colorful bowl.

Tapawingo's Greens with Rosemary Honey Garlic Vinaigrette

ALTHOUGH THERE ARE FIVE CLOVES of garlic in this salad, it's amazingly subtle. Pete Peterson, owner/chef of the celebrated Tapawingo, in Ellsworth, Michigan, lightly browns most of the garlic in olive oil for both a toasty garnish and a tasty oil. A spicy blend of greens is best—arugula, mâche, mizuna, frisée, dandelion, radicchio and Belgian endive.

Try this dressing as a marinade for swordfish or chicken breasts on the grill. Pete's recipe calls for a garnish of red bell peppers and jicama, but you can use other vegetables as well. In fact, the night we first enjoyed this at Tapawingo, it was garnished with haricots verts (fine string beans) and pencil-thin blanched asparagus.

SERVES 8

½ cup olive oil
3 plump garlic cloves, thinly sliced, plus 2 plump garlic cloves, smashed and minced
⅓ cup white wine
3 tablespoons good-quality honey
2 tablespoons soy sauce
2 teaspoons grated fresh gingerroot
1 teaspoon minced fresh rosemary
½ teaspoon freshly ground white pepper
½ teaspoon kosher salt
¼ cup fresh lemon juice

1 pound mixed spicy greens (see description), washed, dried and trimmed
1 roasted bell pepper (page 62), cut into ¼-inch-wide strips
1 cup julienned jicama

Heat olive oil in a small skillet over medium heat. Add sliced garlic and sauté until crisp and golden brown, 2 to 4 minutes. Lift out garlic with a slotted spoon and drain on paper towels; set aside. Let oil cool.

In a large bowl, combine cooled oil with wine, honey, soy, ginger, minced garlic, rosemary, pepper and salt. Whisk to blend. Slowly drizzle in lemon juice, whisking constantly.

Pour desired amount of vinaigrette over greens and toss lightly to coat. Transfer greens to platter or large salad bowl. Add red pepper and jicama to vinaigrette remaining in bowl and toss. Sprinkle over greens. Taste and add more salt and pepper, if desired. Top with crumbled reserved sautéed garlic and serve.

THE STINKING ROSE

WE WONDERED WHAT A MARTINI WOULD BE LIKE at The Stinking Rose restaurant. Big surprise: it was garnished with an olive stuffed with garlic and, for good measure, a big clove of pickled garlic as well. The Stinking Rose is on Columbus Avenue in San Francisco's North Beach neighborhood. The place is big and busy, sort of like a Houlihan's with attitude. It sprawls through several rooms, each with a different kind of funky look. Design is creative, with lots of painted murals on the walls, including animated cloves of garlic carrying on all the activities of human life except sex, of course, since garlic is asexual. Colors are bright. The world's longest braid of garlic stretches for about 36 feet through the rooms of the restaurant. Three hundred people at one time can partake of foods in which "the stinking rose" is the featured player. In fact, garlic is unavoidable; don't go there unless you are ready for the nutritive, curative and culinary power of garlic. And, yes, it will even be in your dessert.

We started with a plate of well-cooked cloves of garlic in oil with anchovies and bread, followed by a garlic and potato soup and a plate of heavily garlicked mussels and clams. There was more to come: a pork chop, very thick, with pickled garlic cloves scattered about, and a serving of garlicked mashed potatoes. Big scampi on a bed of pasta and some bouillabaisse, all charged with garlic. And for dessert, a stunning garlic ice cream.

At The Stinking Rose prices are low. And, strangely, there is no pervasive garlic presence. Restaurateurs Dante Serafini and Jerry Dal Bozzo knew the territory, since they'd been successful in another nearby restaurant called Calzone. They used so much garlic there, to the approval of their customers, that the idea hit—a garlic restaurant. So in the early '90s they started the enterprise. As far as anyone knows, it was the first, and it is enormously successful. They have since opened another Stinking Rose in Los Angeles. And now others are setting up garlic restaurants all around, including Johnnie's Garlic in Santa Rosa, The Garlic Café in Las Vegas, Garlic and Shots in London's Soho and Kynsilaukka Ravintola in Helsinki, which serves garlic beer with dinner.

On the way out, we bought a copy of the restaurant's pride and joy, *The Stinking Cookbook*. On the cover it says, "We season our garlic with food."

Greek Salad with Feta & Garlicky Yogurt Dressing

THE BASICS OF GREEK SALAD are similar throughout the Middle East and along the Mediterranean from Turkey through Greece. Some cooks top it with a preserved-lemon-based dressing; others prefer olive oil. We like this yogurt dressing, especially with organic whole-milk yogurt. The dressing keeps well for several days in the refrigerator.

SERVES 8 TO 10

1½ cups plain yogurt, preferably organic

⅓ cup fresh lemon juice

4 plump garlic cloves, pressed

½ teaspoon kosher salt

½ teaspoon freshly ground white pepper

1 teaspoon dried oregano

1 teaspoon dried mint

1 large head Boston lettuce, trimmed and coarsely shredded

1 large head romaine lettuce, trimmed and coarsely shredded

2 packed cups coarsely chopped escarole

1 medium-sized English cucumber, unpeeled and thinly sliced

1 medium-sized red onion, thinly sliced

3 large, very ripe tomatoes, cut into wedges

1 green bell pepper, thinly sliced into rings

10 ounces good-quality feta cheese, cut into ¾-inch cubes

1 2-ounce tin anchovies, drained

20-30 imported black olives, such as Kalamata

2 tablespoons extra-virgin olive oil

In a medium-sized mixing bowl, blend together yogurt and lemon juice. Add garlic, salt, white pepper, oregano and mint. Blend thoroughly and set aside.

On a large, somewhat concave platter, arrange lettuces in an attractive layer. Scatter escarole over lettuce, then arrange cucumber slices on escarole. Next scatter onion rings, then tomatoes and green pepper. Scatter feta, anchovies and olives over platter. Drizzle with olive oil.

Spoon dressing evenly over platter. Sprinkle with salt and pepper. We serve this salad without tossing.

Wilted Spinach Salad with Garlic & Bacon

THIS TANGY AND SMOKY salad dressing is poured right from the hot skillet over the spinach to wilt it. Hot bacon dressings have always been popular in this country, especially served with spinach. For added flavor, we include garlic and onion.

SERVES 4

1¼ pounds raw spinach, trimmed of stems, washed and spun dry

4 thick slices bacon, preferably lightly cured and heavily smoked, cut into matchsticks

Up to ⅓ cup extra-virgin olive oil

1 small dried chile

½ large sweet onion, thinly sliced

2 plump garlic cloves, smashed and minced

½ teaspoon celery seed

2 teaspoons Dijon mustard

Juice of ½ lemon

¼ cup cider vinegar

Kosher salt and freshly ground black pepper

Tear spinach into bite-sized pieces and place in a large bowl. Sauté bacon in a heavy skillet over medium heat until crisp, then remove with a slotted spoon and drain on paper towels. Pour bacon fat into a measuring cup. Add enough olive oil to bring total measure to ½ cup, then return oil mixture to skillet. Place over medium heat until hot; add chile, onion and garlic. Stir over low heat until onion slices are wilted, 2 to 4 minutes. Stir in celery seed; remove and discard chile. Add mustard to skillet and whisk until blended. Slowly whisk in lemon juice and vinegar. Return crisped bacon to skillet.

When bacon and dressing are hot, pour over spinach. Season salad liberally with salt and pepper. Toss thoroughly and serve.

Endive & Prosciutto Salad with Garlic & Walnuts

IN ITALIAN COOKING, walnuts and garlic are often combined to make a pungent topping for pasta, as well as a pleasing counterpoint in an antipasto salad. This sharply flavored salad has its roots in such dishes. The pleasantly bitter freshness of Belgian endive is complemented by toasted walnuts, fresh garlic and salty prosciutto.

SERVES 6

¼   cup extra-virgin olive oil
3   plump garlic cloves, minced
1   cup walnut pieces
8   medium-sized Belgian endives
2   ounces thinly sliced imported
     prosciutto, julienned
1   teaspoon Dijon mustard
1   tablespoon fresh lemon juice
1   tablespoon white wine vinegar,
     preferably with garlic chives
     Kosher salt and freshly ground
     white pepper

Preheat oven to 400°F.

Combine olive oil and garlic in a small saucepan. Heat very slowly over low heat just until oil is hot but not simmering, 2 to 3 minutes. Remove from heat and set aside to cool.

Scatter walnuts on cookie sheet and bake until golden, 10 to 15 minutes. Reserve.

Trim and discard coarse end of endives. Cut each endive into rings about ¼ inch thick. Transfer to a salad bowl.

Add prosciutto to endives. With a slotted spoon, transfer garlic to salad bowl.

In a small bowl, whisk together mustard, lemon juice and vinegar. Slowly whisk in olive-oil mixture to make an emulsion.

Pour dressing over salad and toss. Blend in toasted nuts, salt and white pepper. Serve immediately.

Buttermilk Slaw with Garlic

THIS TANGY, CREAMY SLAW provides a remarkably cooling contrast to anything served with a hot and spicy barbecue sauce. Garlic, tarragon and cider vinegar give it the zip; sour cream and buttermilk add soothing elegance. Cabbage slaw with mayonnaise was never this good!

SERVES 8 TO 10

3 plump garlic cloves

2 tablespoons fresh tarragon leaves

¼ cup hot water

3 tablespoons sugar

⅓ cup cider vinegar

2 teaspoons kosher salt

1 teaspoon freshly ground white pepper

1 cup sour cream

1 cup buttermilk

1 large cabbage (2½-3 pounds), cored and finely shredded

1 bunch scallions, trimmed and finely shredded

Mince garlic and tarragon together; set aside. In a large mixing bowl, stir together hot water and sugar. Whisk in vinegar, salt, pepper, sour cream and buttermilk until smooth, then stir in garlic and tarragon. Add cabbage and scallions and toss to coat evenly with dressing. Cover bowl with plastic wrap and refrigerate, stirring occasionally. Slaw should stand for at least 4 hours and up to 8.

Just before serving, taste and adjust seasonings, adding more salt, pepper or vinegar if desired.

Two-Cabbage Slaw with Peppers & Herbs

THIS COLORFUL CABBAGE SALAD is tossed with a garlic-enriched vinaigrette spiked with grated horseradish, sweet onion and mellow poppy seeds. It's great for outdoor barbecues on sizzling summer days when you're reluctant to serve a mayonnaise-based dressing because of the heat.

SERVES 10

3 plump garlic cloves, smashed
   and minced
2 tablespoons grated sweet onion
1 tablespoon grated white horseradish
2 teaspoons kosher salt
1 teaspoon freshly ground white pepper
1 teaspoon dry mustard
¼ cup fruit vinegar or garlic chive
   vinegar
1 tablespoon honey
½ cup extra-virgin olive oil
1 tablespoon poppy seeds

1 pound Savoy cabbage, finely shredded
1 pound red cabbage, finely shredded
2 bell peppers, preferably red and
   yellow, seeded and julienned
1 medium-sized red onion, thinly sliced
⅓ cup minced fresh herbs: tarragon,
   basil, lovage, borage, thyme,
   lemon verbena, lemon balm

In a medium-sized bowl, blend together garlic, onion, horseradish, salt, pepper and mustard. Whisk in vinegar, then honey. Slowly whisk in olive oil to make a thick emulsion. Stir in poppy seeds. Set dressing aside.

In a large bowl, toss together cabbages, peppers, onion and herbs. Add dressing and blend thoroughly. Taste for seasoning, adding more salt and pepper if needed. Cover with plastic wrap and chill for at least 4 hours and up to 6.

Serve cold.

Shredded Carrots & Fennel with Spicy Garlic Vinaigrette

THE COMBINATION of carrots and fennel makes a salad that is both colorful and savory. Tossed with this vinaigrette, it is especially bold. The dressing gets judicious additions of horseradish and lime. Add some golden raisins for a sweet contrast. Our versatile dressing is good for a grilled chicken dinner salad as well as for a simple chopped salad of iceberg lettuce, red onions, tomatoes and blue cheese.

SERVES 6 TO 8

3   tablespoons rich red wine vinegar
2   tablespoons fresh lime juice
1   teaspoon grated white horseradish, fresh or preserved
1   teaspoon sugar
1   teaspoon Colman's dry mustard
1   teaspoon kosher salt
½   teaspoon ground ginger
¼   teaspoon ground cardamom
2   pinches ground red pepper (cayenne)
½   teaspoon freshly ground white pepper

2   plump garlic cloves, pressed
1   plump shallot, minced
½   cup extra-virgin olive oil
1   large fennel bulb, trimmed, cut in half, cored, cut very thinly crosswise
7   medium-sized carrots, scrubbed and coarsely grated
½   cup golden raisins (optional)

In a small mixing bowl, combine vinegar and lime juice. Blend in horseradish, sugar, mustard, salt, ginger, cardamom, cayenne and white pepper. Then blend in garlic and shallot. Very slowly whisk in olive oil and beat until dressing emulsifies. Set aside or pour into a container and chill until needed. Dressing can be stored for at least a week; shake or whisk vigorously just before using.

Up to 4 hours before serving, prepare salad. Combine fennel, carrots and optional raisins in a serving bowl. Add half of dressing and blend thoroughly. Toss with remaining dressing. Cover and chill until serving.

Lentil Salad with Minted Garlic & Lime Vinaigrette

LENTILS MAKE an outstanding salad, especially in summer. We are particularly fond of serving them with this vinaigrette brightened with garlic, lime juice and mint. This pleasing salad is a fine accompaniment to highly seasoned dishes like the Out-of-India Grilled Butterflied Leg of Lamb with Spicy Mint Sauce (see page 326) and Skewered Lamb with Chiles, Cumin and Garlic (page 330).

SERVES 4 TO 6

1¼ cups lentils, preferably French
    Le Puy brand, sorted and rinsed
4 cups water
1 whole clove
1 small yellow onion, peeled
¼ cup fresh lime juice
1 tablespoon red wine vinegar
1 teaspoon Dijon mustard
⅓ cup extra-virgin olive oil
2 plump garlic cloves, smashed
    and minced
1 bulb lemongrass, minced
    (or zest of 1 lemon, minced)

1 teaspoon dried mint
⅓ cup finely diced red onion
⅓ cup finely diced celery
    Kosher salt and freshly ground
    black pepper
½ cup ¼-inch-diced feta, preferably
    imported (optional)

Put lentils and water in a large saucepan. Stick onion with clove and add to lentils. Bring to a boil over high heat, then reduce heat to low. Cover and simmer briskly until lentils are tender, 20 to 30 minutes. Remove and discard onion. Drain lentils and rinse with cold water until cool.

In a large bowl, blend together lime juice, vinegar and mustard. Slowly whisk in olive oil to make a thick emulsion. Add garlic, lemongrass, mint, onion and celery. Blend together and season with salt and pepper. Blend in lentils. Cover with plastic wrap and chill for at least 2 hours and up to 6. Gently blend in feta just before serving.

KYNSILAUKKA RAVINTOLA

GET US TO KYNSILAUKKA RAVINTOLA! We put that on our list the instant we started this project. We had heard a lot about it, but going there just didn't seem possible. Unexpectedly, other business led us to Helsinki, and on a dark winter Sunday evening, there it was, intimate, inviting, welcoming, comfortable, fragrant. Kynsilaukka Ravintola means garlic restaurant. In just ten years it has become perhaps the most famous dining spot in all of Finland.

While not a natural part of Finnish cuisine, garlic (*kynsilaukka* or *valkosipuli*, another word for it) grew in popularity as Helsinki became a cosmopolitan restaurant city. Pizza was everywhere, and Chinese and Thai restaurants were thriving. What single ingredient was common to these exotic cuisines? Garlic. The Finns met it and fell in love with it. Now, when you stroll through Helsinki's fabled covered markets, you see garlic everywhere— mostly marinated raw whole garlic cloves in bulk. Some are hot and spicy. Others are mild, lavishly seasoned with herbs like basil or oregano. And others are cured like pickles, with mustard seed, dill and onions. One stand even offered freshly made sauerkraut richly studded with coarsely chopped garlic.

Early in 1987, Jan-Erik Berg, Hannu Lautamäki and M.Tapio Metsola laid the plan for a big Helsinki restaurant with broad appeal, open 365 days of the year, affordable to every-one (where folks went "on their own money" as the Finns would say). And they decided to focus on one particular seasoning—garlic.

Garlic was not grown in quantity in Finland, but was easily available, already peeled, from Spain. Late that year Kynsilaukka Ravintolo opened for business. It is, as the team planned, a warm and attractive restaurant with terrific service, offering hearty and famil-iar Finnish dishes that feature garlic in appealing ways.

While sipping a garlic beer, you might have fresh salmon served with a garlic marinade, or a hearty lamb stew enriched by caramelized garlic in the silky sauce and garnished with a dollop of garlic rosemary cream. Garlic adds a pleasing touch to marinated beets, as well as to a delicate gratin of whitefish and a creamy shellfish stew. Chopped raw garlic and peanuts make a heady topping for fried potatoes. And chopped garlic and parsley are served as a table condiment, lest some dish require a garlic boost. All of this, of course, is perfectly finished by some garlic schnapps—garlic-marinated vodka, frozen and served in a well-chilled glass.

The restaurant's success can be measured by the volume of garlic used—9 kilos, or close to 20 pounds, every day. They keep track of it in the kitchen. When we were there they had just passed the 33,000-kilo mark—more than 36 tons in the first ten years. And the folks just keep on coming.

Green Beans with
Basil Garlic Vinaigrette & Hazelnuts

AFTER A QUICK BLANCHING in hot water and chilling, the beans are tossed with crunchy red onions and a vinaigrette. The addition of fresh basil is perfect in summer with beans fresh from the garden.

You can prepare both the beans and the vinaigrette ahead, but toss together no more than one hour before serving to avoid discoloring the beans. To make this even more delicious, toss with hazelnuts or pecans, toasted in a 350°F oven.

SERVES 4 TO 6

1½ pounds green beans, preferably young and thin, trimmed
2   plump garlic cloves, pressed
½   teaspoon Dijon mustard
3   tablespoons garlic-chive, fruit or white wine vinegar
⅓   cup extra-virgin olive oil
½   large red onion, thinly sliced
    Kosher salt and freshly ground white pepper
10 leaves fresh basil, julienned
½   cup coarsely chopped toasted hazelnuts or pecans (optional)

Have ready a large bowl of ice water. Fill a large saucepan with salted water and bring to a boil over medium-high heat. Add beans and blanch for 45 seconds. Quickly drain beans and refresh in ice water. When beans are cold, pour into a colander and drain again while you prepare dressing.

Combine garlic and mustard in a large bowl; blend thoroughly. Whisk in vinegar, then slowly whisk in olive oil. Pat beans dry, then add to dressing with onion, salt and pepper. Toss together until beans are evenly coated with dressing. Add basil and blend again. Let stand for up to 1 hour.

Toss with nuts (if using) just before serving.

SAUCES & RELISHES

FILAREE

WATERSHINE PICKED UP A HEAD OF HARDNECK GARLIC, its stiff woody stem and dried leaves still attached. Carefully she rubbed off the garden dirt clinging to it. Then she peeled away the bulb's papery covering to reveal eight brilliant red cloves, symmetrical, alive.

"It's called Chesnok," she said. "It's a wonderful variety from the Republic of Georgia. I love it. It's the best roasting garlic there is."

We had come to Filaree, the ultimate garlic farm, 10 acres outside the town of Okanogan in north central Washington. Filaree is where Ron Engeland, Watershine's former husband, learned the garlic business and wrote one of the great books on the subject, *Growing Great Garlic*, thus becoming a garlic guru.

There was no sign or street number on a mailbox to tell us we had arrived, only a picture of a garlic clove incised into a board nailed to the shed. The place looked like a typical little farm—small buildings here and there, cars and pickups standing around, pieces of farm machinery, and a small old house that serves as the office.

We were greeted by Tom Cloud, whose T-shirt featured a coyote baying at a garlic moon. Watershine, now Maya Watershine Woods, appeared from the office with paychecks for the farm's workers. We walked with them to the barn, where half a dozen people were cleaning, topping, sizing and packing the garlic heads by hand, one by one.

"It's a Third World kind of an operation," she said, handing the workers their pay. The garlic, about 20,000 pounds of it, had been curing in the sheds for a couple of weeks, carefully tagged with red ribbons.

Much of it is sold by mail order as seed for amateur growers across the country, and the rest goes to fanciers of gourmet garlic, people who are not satisfied with ordinary California Early. The farm grows more than 400 varieties or strains, and the record-keeping is meticulous.

In addition to the original 10 acres, Watershine leases another 5 across the road. Garlic is tough on the soil, so after a plot has been harvested, it's sown with buckwheat and vegetables for three years before being used for garlic again.

In the middle of the orchard, among apples of various kinds, peaches, apricots, and even a big olive tree, there is an open patch used to test new strains of garlic. Also among the trees are occasional huts or tents where the part-time summer workers stay. One of the workers is a chef who loves the farm so much that he always quits his winter job to come back to help with the summer's chores.

We carefully wrapped up our prize, the peeled head of Georgian garlic, and took off, wondering how such a small operation is able to survive. And we marveled at the influence this little farm has had on thousands of growers of garlic across the country.

That night, in the Willamette Valley, after a long drive, we sat at the table of Jack and Heidi Czarnecki, who have closed their great mushroom restaurant in Reading, Pennsylvania, and moved west to start anew near the wild mushrooms and pinot noirs of Oregon. We sliced the cloves of Chesnok and ate them raw, savoring the pungency.

Jack lifted his glass. "To the people who have grown this wonderful food and made this remarkable wine." And we said, "To Watershine, and the men and women of Filaree Farm."

And everybody drank to them all.

Minted Sauce of Garlic & Cilantro

A PUREE OF FRESH CILANTRO, mint and garlic is bound together with olive oil and a white wine, fruit or chive vinegar. This cold sauce makes a pungently pleasing accompaniment for such varied dishes as lamb—chops, rack or grilled leg—grilled bluefish or mackerel. It can be held for up to a week in the refrigerator; just bring it to room temperature before serving.

MAKES 1 CUP

1 packed cup fresh mint leaves
1 packed cup fresh cilantro leaves
4 plump garlic cloves
2 tablespoons white wine, chive or fruit vinegar
3 tablespoons extra-virgin olive oil
  Kosher salt and freshly ground white pepper

In a food processor, combine mint, cilantro and garlic. Pulse until finely chopped. Add vinegar and pulse until mixture is well blended. Scraping sides down several times, gradually add olive oil, then salt and pepper. Pulse to make a thick puree. Scrape into a dish, cover tightly with plastic wrap, and let stand for several hours before serving.

A Simple Summer Pesto

Garlic, fresh basil, pine nuts, Parmesan cheese and olive oil—these simple ingredients are combined into a heavenly paste that melts luxuriously over hot pasta. In recent years, pesto has appeared in a variety of guises, but this one is fairly straightforward. Our personal touches include some butter and fresh flat-leaf parsley for depth of flavor. You can make this pesto in large quantities, freeze it in ice cube trays, and pop it out as you need it all winter long. If you have an herb garden, experiment. Often we'll add some lemon basil or even cinnamon basil. We use ⅓ to ½ cup of pesto for ½ pound of pasta.

MAKES 2 CUPS

3 packed cups fresh basil leaves
1 cup fresh flat-leaf parsley leaves, stems discarded
4 plump garlic cloves
1 cup coarsely grated Parmesan cheese
4 tablespoons (½ stick) unsalted butter, softened
1 rounded teaspoon freshly ground black pepper
1 teaspoon kosher salt
½ cup pine nuts
⅔ cup extra-virgin olive oil

In the bowl of a food processor, combine basil, parsley, garlic, Parmesan cheese, butter, pepper and salt. Pulse until finely chopped, 25 to 30 pulses. Add pine nuts and pulse to chop, about 10 pulses. With motor running, slowly add oil. Scrape sides and blend briefly. Mixture should be thick and creamy.

Spoon into a clean container and refrigerate or freeze.

Walnut & Opal Basil Pesto with Mint

OUR YARD IS A VISUAL SMORGASBORD of basils, many of them planted right in among the flowers. Especially beautiful are the large burgundy-colored leaves of opal basil. We find that opal basil has a somewhat earthier flavor than the green types, and it blends beautifully with slightly bitter walnuts and pungent garlic. Here we add some mint, sun-dried tomatoes and olives for further richness of flavor. It's also fun to add some cinnamon basil as well. This unusual pesto is stunning with goat cheese or poultry. Try inserting it under the skin of a butterflied chicken to roast in a hot oven (page 261). This pesto also makes a fine base for a pizza with chicken, as well as a great sauce for a simple dish of pasta.

MAKES 1½ CUPS

1½	packed cups fresh opal basil leaves
½	packed cup fresh mint leaves (orange, pineapple or spearmint)
½	cup grated Parmesan cheese
3	plump garlic cloves
4	large oil-packed sun-dried tomatoes (⅛ cup)
¼	cup pitted Kalamata olives
	Zest of 1 lemon
4	tablespoons (½ stick) unsalted butter, softened
½	teaspoon kosher salt
½	teaspoon freshly ground white pepper
½	cup walnut pieces
⅓	cup extra-virgin olive oil

In the bowl of a food processor, combine basil, mint, cheese, garlic, tomatoes, olives, lemon zest, butter, salt and pepper. Pulse until mixture is finely chopped, about 20 pulses. Add nuts and pulse until chopped, about 10 pulses. With motor running, add olive oil in a slow but steady stream. Scrape sides of bowl and pulse to blend.

Spoon pesto into a clean container. Cover tightly and store in the refrigerator. This pesto can also be frozen. We divide it into ½-cup portions, wrapping each thoroughly in several layers of plastic wrap.

Chimichurri

(A SOUTH AMERICAN PESTO)

THIS SPICY AND TANGY SAUCE OF GARLIC, herbs, plums and figs is outstanding as an accompaniment to grilled chicken and fish. But it also makes a most unusual dip for summer vegetables, as well as a surprising addition to a platter of sliced pineapple and melons. This comes from Linda's Memphis cousin Susan Cavitch, a woman of many talents. Susan has a large family and a vast garden (including an awesome fig tree), and she is a well-respected herbalist. In a letter accompanying her recipes, she suggested a number of infusions of garlic and vinegar with herbs. One of white wine vinegar, garlic, rosemary, lavender and rose petals is our favorite and would be terrific in this sauce.

MAKES 3 CUPS

1   cup coarsely chopped fresh figs
1   cup coarsely chopped fresh plums
2   bay leaves
1   teaspoon whole black peppercorns
8   plump garlic cloves
1½   cups tightly packed fresh flat-leaf parsley
3   tablespoons fresh oregano
2   tablespoons fresh thyme leaves
2   teaspoons fresh rosemary needles
½   teaspoon crushed dried red chile
2   tablespoons vinegar, preferably garlic vinegar
½   cup extra-virgin olive oil
½   teaspoon kosher salt

Using a small vegetable steamer insert (or another type of steamer), gently steam figs and plums until they are just tender and not too soft, about 4 minutes. Drain and set aside.

Combine bay leaves and peppercorns in a spice grinder and grind thoroughly.

Put bay leaf mixture into the bowl of a food processor, along with garlic, parsley, herbs, crushed chile, plums and figs. Pulse until ingredients are finely ground and blended, scraping sides of bowl several times. With motor running, drizzle in garlic vinegar, then olive oil, processing only until ingredients are well blended.

Scrape sauce into a clean container and cover tightly. Chill until needed, bringing to room temperature 1 hour before serving.

GARLIC BREATH, GARLIC HANDS

SOME PEOPLE CAN EAT A TON OF GARLIC and you would never know it. Others can just look at a clove and exude its essence for a whole day. For those worried about garlic breath, we got tips from people who work with it all the time.

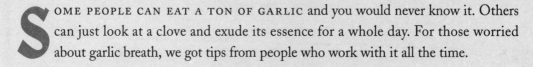

- "Chew a coffee bean." —Bob Bowersox, chef/host of QVC; also Gray Kunz, chef of Lespinasse in New York City

- "Roasting makes it milder."—Jimmy Schmidt, chef of the Rattlesnake Club in Detroit

- "When in Rome, do as the Romans do. At my house, you eat garlic or you go hungry."—Vid Lutz, executive chef of Johnny's in Cleveland

- "Drink some wine!"—Kim and Ciro Pasciuto, proprietors of Seattle's La Panzanella

- "Whiskey and toothpaste."—David Burke, chef of Park Avenue Café in New York City

- "This is a problem only when garlic is used improperly, browned too long or used raw in excessive quantities."—Marcella Hazan, doyenne of Italian cooking

- "Remove the potent green center of the garlic."—Patricia Quintana, Mexican food expert

- "Altoids."—Cindy Pawlcyn, Bay Area restaurateur

As for garlic on the hands:

- "Lemon juice and coffee grounds."—Lydie Marshall, culinary educator and writer

- "A special olive oil soap. Sometimes lemon. But why do I want to get rid of the garlic smell?"—Carol Field, Italian cooking authority

Lemon Pepper Aioli

THIS LUSTY GARLIC MAYONNAISE HAS its roots in Provence and is similar to *rouille,* the roasted pepper and saffron mayonnaise served with bouillabaisse. (In Spain they call it *allioli.*) While it is traditionally made with a mortar and pestle, *aioli* can also be prepared in a food processor, as it is here. We use bread for thickening, but you could just as easily use a heaping tablespoon of plain mashed potato instead. *Aioli* served in a white-wine-based fish soup turns the soup into *bourride.* But *aioli* is equally delicious with grilled or poached chicken, poached salmon or grilled bluefish. Be sure to try it on a baked potato!

MAKES ABOUT 1½ CUPS

- 1 1-inch-thick slice French bread, crust removed
  Zest of 1 lemon
- 3 tablespoons fresh lemon juice

6-8 plump garlic cloves
1 teaspoon kosher salt
2 large egg yolks
¾ cup canola oil
¾ cup very fruity extra-virgin olive oil, plus more as needed
1½ teaspoons freshly ground black pepper

Soak bread, lemon zest and juice in the bowl of a food processor for 2 to 3 minutes. Add garlic cloves and salt. Pulse until mixture is combined. Add egg yolks and pulse again to blend. With motor running, very slowly add oils, scraping sides of bowl several times. Mixture should be thick and creamy. If too thick, slowly add more olive oil. Add pepper and pulse to blend.

Scrape *aioli* into an attractive serving bowl. Cover tightly and store in the refrigerator until 20 minutes before serving.

Great Rémoulade

WITH ITS ROOTS in Louisiana cookery, American rémoulade sauce is mayonnaise-based and packed with all kinds of extra goodies like garlic, scallions, anchovies and horseradish, to give it exceptional richness and zip. Linda's version has been evolving for almost 40 years. At our house, guests often prefer to eat the sauce alone with a fork rather than with the shrimp, crab, grilled chicken or fish that it accompanies. For best flavor, prepare this sauce at least one day ahead of serving. You can keep rémoulade sauce for at least a week in a clean container, tightly covered in the refrigerator.

MAKES ABOUT 1 QUART

1 tablespoon Colman's dry mustard

¼ cup grated white horseradish, fresh or preserved

¼ cup chili sauce, preferably Bennett's

1 tablespoon Worcestershire sauce

1¼ teaspoons Tabasco

3 cups homemade mayonnaise, or Hellmann's or Best Foods

4 plump garlic cloves, smashed and minced

6 scallions, trimmed with 1 inch of green, minced

3 hard-boiled eggs, finely chopped

12 anchovy fillets (preferably rinsed salt-packed or drained oil-packed), finely chopped

¼ cup minced fresh chives

¼ cup minced fresh flat-leaf parsley

2 tablespoons minced fresh tarragon

2 rounded tablespoons capers, rinsed and drained

Zest of 2 lemons, minced

In a large mixing bowl, blend together dry mustard, horseradish and chili sauce. Blend in remaining ingredients one at a time. Spoon into a clean container. Cover tightly and store in refrigerator until needed.

Spoon into an attractive serving bowl and surround with cooked seafood, chicken or fish.

A Special Marinara Sauce

THIS IS A SIMPLE SAUCE OF GARLIC, onions and tomatoes. What makes it so special is the combination of really good olive oil and butter. Linda has been enjoying Frances Santosuosso's marinara sauce since the mid 1970s, when she first visited the Santosuossos' tavern, Johnny's Bar. Fran and her husband, Eugene, have long since retired; their sons have turned the bar into one of Cleveland's most popular upscale restaurants. This marinara sauce is always available, even when it's not listed on the menu. Whether served over a simple bowl of spaghetti or ladled on some heavenly veal meatballs, it is always exceptional. This marinara freezes well.

MAKES 2 QUARTS

⅓ cup extra-virgin olive oil, preferably very fruity

6 tablespoons unsalted butter

6 plump garlic cloves, smashed and minced

1 large yellow onion, minced

1 large carrot, scraped and shredded

2 28-ounce cans Italian plum tomatoes, crushed, with their juice

2 teaspoons dried basil

½ teaspoon dried oregano

1 teaspoon crushed dried red chiles

⅛ teaspoon ground red pepper (cayenne) Kosher salt and freshly ground black pepper

½ teaspoon baking soda

In a large, heavy nonreactive saucepan, heat olive oil and butter over medium heat. Add garlic, onions and carrots, and sauté, stirring often, until carrots are soft, 4 to 6 minutes. Add tomatoes, basil, oregano, chiles and cayenne. Bring sauce to a boil and simmer for 20 minutes. Add salt, pepper and baking soda. Blend thoroughly and serve.

When served with pasta:
Wine: Rex Hill Pinot Noir Willamette Valley
(Oregon: Willamette Valley) or a Chianti Classico
from Italy

Barbecue Sauce with Roasted Tomatoes, Horseradish & Bourbon

THIS THICK, SMOOTH SAUCE has pleasing smoky overtones from the roasted tomatoes. Vinegar, horseradish and bourbon blend with garlic and onions to add a marvelous depth of flavor. This is not an especially sweet sauce. We've come to prefer it above all others for ribs.

MAKES 6 TO 7 CUPS

5½	pounds ripe plum tomatoes, cut in half lengthwise
6	tablespoons olive oil
3	plump garlic cloves, smashed and minced
1	fresh hot chile, minced
1	large sweet onion, minced
2	teaspoons ground cumin
½	teaspoon ground red pepper (cayenne)
1	teaspoon freshly ground white pepper
1	teaspoon ground oregano
1	teaspoon Colman's dry mustard
¼	cup dark unsulfured molasses
¼	cup rich red wine vinegar
½	cup bourbon whiskey
½	cup grated white horseradish, fresh or preserved
	Kosher salt

Place tomatoes, cut side up, on two large, foil-lined cookie sheets. Either roast in two batches or in two ovens simultaneously.

Place oven rack about 3 inches below broiler. Preheat oven (or broiler) to 450°F.

Drizzle tomatoes with 2 tablespoons of the olive oil. Roast until tops are partially browned and somewhat crinkled, about 50 minutes. Turn oven up to broil. Keep tomatoes under broiler until tops begin to glaze and crinkle more, 5 to 8 minutes. Be careful not to let juices that have collected around tomatoes dry up. When done, immediately remove pan from oven and set aside. Repeat for second batch.

While tomatoes are roasting, heat remaining 2 tablespoons olive oil over low heat in a medium-sized nonreactive saucepan. Add garlic, chile and onions. Cover and cook until onions have softened, about 5 minutes. Uncover and add cumin, cayenne, white pepper, oregano and mustard. Increase heat to medium and stir mixture for 2 minutes to release flavors. Add molasses and vinegar. Stir over medium heat until liquids begin to bubble. Stir in bourbon, then horseradish. Remove from heat.

Spoon roasted tomatoes and juices into pot with onion, scraping in any browned bits that have accumulated on foil. Add salt to taste. Cover and cook over low heat until onions are very soft and tomatoes fall apart, 25 to 30 minutes.

Pass mixture through a food mill into a clean pot, or puree in a food processor and pass through a strainer. Taste and adjust seasonings, adding salt and more white pepper if desired. Reheat just before serving with barbecued ribs.

> **"Garlic is not only a flavor,
> it is the secret of happiness."**
> —Chef Antoine Bouterin, New York

Fresh Caramelized Tomato Sauce

ROASTING THE TOMATOES brings out all of their natural sugars and intensifies their flavor. This delicious sauce makes a satisfying addition to any pasta dish, especially one that is baked.

SERVES 4 TO 6

- 10 large, vine-ripened tomatoes, cut in half
- 3 tablespoons olive oil
- 1 dried chile, crumbled
- 3 plump garlic cloves, smashed and minced
- 1 large white onion, finely chopped
  Kosher salt and freshly ground black pepper
- ½ cup chopped fresh basil (optional)

Place oven rack about 3 inches below broiler. Preheat oven or broiler to 450°F. Line a cookie sheet with foil.

Arrange tomato halves cut side up and close together on prepared pan, then drizzle with 1 tablespoon of the olive oil. Roast until tops are crinkled, about 50 minutes. Turn oven up to broil. Keep tomatoes under broiler until tops begin to glaze, about 8 minutes. Be careful not to allow juices that have collected around tomatoes to dry up—add a little water if necessary.

While tomatoes are roasting, heat remaining 2 tablespoons of olive oil over low heat in a medium-sized nonreactive saucepan. Add crumbled chile, garlic and onions. Cover and cook until onions have softened, about 5 minutes. Remove from heat.

Spoon tomatoes and juices into pot with onion mixture, scraping in any browned bits that have accumulated on foil. Cover and cook over low heat until tomatoes fall apart, 25 to 30 minutes.

Pass tomato mixture through a food mill into a clean pot, or puree in a food processor and pass through a strainer. (You should have close to 4 cups of puree.) Bring mixture, uncovered, to a vigorous simmer over medium heat, 4 to 6 minutes. Taste and adjust seasonings, adding salt and pepper if needed. Stir basil (if using) into sauce and serve.

Blueberry Ketchup

THIS ZESTY DARK FRUIT KETCHUP gets a pleasing tang from a generous measure of fresh ginger. It's great with smoked poultry or ham, as well as slathered on a thick grilled burger with a slice of raw onion.

MAKES ABOUT 4 CUPS

2	tablespoons olive oil
1	dried red chile, crumbled
5	plump garlic cloves, thinly sliced
1½	tablespoons minced fresh gingerroot
1	large yellow onion, finely diced
3	medium-sized tomatoes, peeled, seeded and chopped
12	ripe plums, preferably prune plums, cut in half and pitted
2	pints fresh blueberries
	Zest of 1 lemon, minced
1	tablespoon fresh lemon juice
1	tablespoon rich red wine vinegar
1	cup firmly packed dark brown sugar
1	teaspoon ground cardamom
1	teaspoon ground coriander
1¼	teaspoons ground cinnamon
¼	teaspoon ground cloves
1	teaspoon kosher salt
1	teaspoon freshly ground white pepper

In a heavy-bottomed nonreactive saucepan, heat olive oil and chile. Add garlic and ginger; cook over low heat until fragrant, 1 to 2 minutes. Add onion, cover and cook until transparent, 4 to 6 minutes. Stir in remaining ingredients. Increase heat to high, cover and cook until liquids begin to bubble. Reduce heat and simmer for 30 minutes.

Remove from heat and let cool for 15 minutes. Puree mixture in a food processor, transfer to saucepan. Place over high heat, cover and cook until mixture begins to boil. Place lid slightly ajar. Reduce heat to medium-low and simmer briskly for 30 minutes, stirring often. Sauce will be very thick. When it has cooled, spoon into 1-cup containers and store in freezer. When ready to use ketchup, defrost and store in refrigerator.

Terzalua

CALABRIAN GREEN TOMATOES, GARLIC & FENNEL

THIS VERY OLD, TRADITIONAL RECIPE is for patient, passionate lovers of green tomatoes. It takes little effort, but it does require time. The process needs a little more than 3 weeks to complete.

Our friend Lou Turi, a retired law director of Willoughby, Ohio, has been carefully recording his late father's recipes to hand down to subsequent generations. Papa Turi was born and raised in Fossato ser Alta, a small village in the mountains of Calabria.

You will need a 4-quart crock for this, along with a wooden lid that is at least 1 inch thick and cut to just fit inside the crock. We wrap our lid in foil to keep mold at bay. Serve with grilled chicken or with any dish you'd normally accompany with pickles.

MAKES ABOUT 2 QUARTS

Up to 1 cup kosher salt

6 pounds green tomatoes, stems removed, cut into ¼-inch-thick slices

2 heads hardneck garlic or 1 large head softneck garlic, smashed and minced

¼ cup fennel seed, preferably from the garden

1 cup extra-virgin olive oil

Have ready a 4-quart crock with a 1-inch-thick wooden weight cut to just fit inside of crock.

Measure ½ cup kosher salt. Layer tomatoes in crock, sprinkling every second layer with 1 tablespoon of salt. Repeat until crock is filled to top. Sprinkle with 1 tablespoon salt. Wrap wooden top in foil and place directly over tomatoes. Refrigerate.

During the first week, drain every 2 days, adding 1 tablespoon salt to top each time.

For at least 2 more weeks, or up to 3 weeks, drain off any liquid and add salt 2 times each week. (If tomatoes on top get a little moldy, discard those tomatoes and wipe mold from crock and wooden top.)

After 3 to 4 weeks, fill crock with water, then drain. Repeat several times. Transfer tomatoes to a colander and rinse thoroughly several times more. Return to crock and cover with wooden top. Keep for 2 days in refrigerator.

Drain tomatoes once more, then transfer to a large mixing bowl. Add garlic, fennel seed and olive oil. Toss thoroughly and serve.

Leftover *terzalua* will keep, refrigerated in a covered container, for several weeks.

Lovely Pickled Green Tomatoes

THESE CRISP, garlicky pickled tomatoes pack a little heat. We especially enjoy the touch of fennel that serves as a pleasing licorice contrast to the spicy pepper. While all the books say that it is not necessary to process high-acid pickles—which these are—you certainly may if you wish. They will, however, lose some of their pleasing crunch.

MAKES 5 QUARTS

1¼	cups kosher salt, plus more if needed
3	quarts water
1	quart cider vinegar
4½	pounds green tomatoes, preferably plum tomatoes, wiped clean
5	fresh red chile peppers
15	plump garlic cloves
5	heads fresh fennel seeds (or 5 teaspoons dried seeds)
5	heads fresh dill
20	stalks fresh dill weed

Have ready 5 freshly sterilized wide-mouth quart canning jars, still in their hot water, and 5 jar tops, prepared according to package directions.

In a large nonreactive saucepan, combine salt and water. Mix until salt is dissolved; let brine rest for 10 minutes. If a raw egg in the shell does not float in brine, add salt, a few tablespoons at a time, until it does float. Remove egg. Add vinegar and bring brine to a boil. Simmer briskly for 2 minutes.

Using special canning tongs, carefully drain sterilized jars. Divide tomatoes among them, leaving about 1 inch of headroom. Then pack 1 chile, 3 garlic cloves, 1 fennel head, 1 dill head and 2 stalks dill weed into each jar.

Ladle brine into jars to just above neck. Cover jars with sterile rings and lids. Let stand on a towel in a cool place for 24 hours. Tighten lids and store.

If you prefer, process jars in a water bath for 15 minutes.

Rose-Scented Fig Preserves with Garlic & Ginger

THE SWEETNESS OF THE FIGS and sugar is brightened by lime juice and ginger. In this particular dish, the garlic assumes a warm character, even though it is not roasted. And the rose-scented geraniums, available at any nursery, add a note of the exotic. Not only do we spread this on warm biscuits and toast, but we also use it as a sauce, tossing it with grilled Thai sausage from our friend Mr. Brisket (see Sources, page 415). This is one of Susan Cavitch's marvelous recipes.

MAKES 8 HALF-PINT JARS

2 quarts fresh figs, chopped
    into ½-inch chunks
5½ cups sugar
¼ cup fresh lime juice
¾ cup water
2 tablespoons minced crystallized ginger
10 plump garlic cloves, thinly sliced
    and julienned
¾ cup minced rose-scented
    geranium leaves
8 nicely formed rose-scented
    geranium leaves

In a nonreactive container with a tight-fitting lid, combine figs, sugar, lime juice, water, ginger and garlic. Refrigerate overnight or up to 24 hours, stirring periodically.

Transfer mixture to a heavy-bottomed saucepan and add minced geranium leaves. Over medium-low heat, bring to a boil. Gently simmer, skimming off surface foam and stirring every 10 to 15 minutes, until mixture thickens, 1 to 2 hours.

When thickened, allow preserves to rest for 5 minutes. Pour into sterilized jars. Using a sterilized utensil, gently ease a geranium leaf into each jar.

Seal jars according to manufacturer's directions. Process preserves for 15 minutes in a water bath.

Summer Fruit Marmalade with Roasted Garlic & Basil

THIS MARMALADE IS a great morning spread, and it is excellent served with grilled duck or veal tenderloin. The recipe is from herbalist Susan Cavitch.

MAKES 6 HALF-PINT JARS

1   large grapefruit
1   large orange
1   medium lime
1   medium lemon
9   cups water
3   peaches, peeled and chopped
    into ½-inch pieces
3   nectarines, peeled and
    chopped into ½-inch pieces
    Flesh of 1 large head roasted garlic
1   cup Grand Marnier or
    Triple Sec liqueur
8   cups sugar
1   tablespoon finely chopped
    fresh lemon verbena
2   tablespoons finely chopped fresh basil
¼   teaspoon vanilla extract

Peel thin strips of skin, avoiding white pith, from grapefruit, orange, lime and lemon. Slice each into uniform slivers and set aside. Gently break citrus pulp by hand into ½-inch pieces. Combine with peaches and nectarines and set aside.

In a small saucepan, bring 2 cups water to a boil. Add citrus peel and boil for 5 minutes. Pour peel into a strainer and hold under running cold water until peels cool completely, 1 to 2 minutes. Repeat these steps, using 2 cups more of fresh water. After second boiling, place peel in a large, heavy-bottomed nonreactive saucepan along with the fruits, garlic, remaining 5 cups water and Grand Marnier. Cover and refrigerate overnight or up to 18 hours.

Place saucepan over medium-high heat and bring to a boil. Cook uncovered for 35 minutes. Reduce heat to medium, add sugar, lemon verbena and basil. Stir and bring to a boil, stirring often. Increase heat to medium-high and cook until marmalade reaches the jell point (220°F) or to desired consistency, 30 to 35 minutes. Stir frequently and gently.

Remove marmalade from heat and let rest 5 minutes. Skim off any foam that forms, then blend in vanilla extract. Pour marmalade into sterilized jars and seal according to manufacturer's directions. Process in a water bath for 10 minutes.

GARLIC GODFATHER

JOSEPH GUBSER, JR., was the only man we met in Gilroy who wore a coat and tie. We said we had read about him in a *Smithsonian* article on garlic. He was amazed to have been included in the piece even though, as we reminded him, in Gilroy he's famous as the Garlic Godfather.

He's much too modest to be comfortable with that. Gubser has a different idea about who ought to be called the Garlic Godfather. When we mentioned the landmark book on alliums *Onions and Their Allies,* by Henry Jones and Louis Mann, Gubser jumped up.

"For three days," said Gubser, "Dr. Louis Mann sat on that couch, puffing on his pipe and talking about raising garlic. He may have known more about it than anyone. *He's* the Garlic Godfather."

Gubser's father started farming in Gilroy in 1922 and grew garlic (and other crops) for 47 years. "My job, when I was 12 or 13, was to dump the unsold garlic in the creek. In 1942, I started to grow, and I'm now in my 55th year."

The farmer became an entrepreneur during World War II. Soldiers and sailors overseas needed onions and garlic to make the army food taste better. The only way they could have either was through dehydration.

"The folks at Basic in Vacaville were dehydrating pioneers and they needed product," Gubser told us. "That season the farmers here had surplus garlic, so why not? Basic would pay me 2¾ cents per pound and I could buy it for ¾ of a cent per pound." The transaction earned him enough money to start his business. And the farmers got some money for the garlic they were going to throw out.

Today Gubser may well be the world's leading authority on the business of garlic. One year he was in 38 different countries on garlic matters—consulting, investing, buying, selling. After more than half a century in the garlic business, he swears he's not tired. "Every day I come to work is like a vacation day," he said. His grandson, Jake Levine, is majoring in business and learning about garlic.

"He's very smart," said his grandfather. "He'll be good here." But you get the feeling that the Garlic Godfather is in no hurry to retire.

Light Meals

Turkish Poached Eggs with Spicy Garlic Yogurt   169

Dilly Salmon Cakes with Garlic Tartar Sauce   170

Goat Cheese Soufflé with Sauce of Fresh Peas & Tarragon   172

Spanakopita (Spinach Pie)   174

Artichoke Pie in Cream Cheese Pastry   176

Gert's Cream Cheese Pastry   178

Chèvre & Tomato Tart with Roasted Garlic   179

Tapenade Tart with Fontina & Escarole   180

Savory Bread Pudding with Sun-Dried Tomatoes & Pesto   183

A Simple Spicy Quiche with Dry-Roasted Garlic & Broccoli   184

Coosa Mih' Shee (Stuffed Squash in Tomato Sauce with Garlic & Mint)   186

Couscous Salad with Grilled Chicken & Roasted Garlic Vinaigrette   188

Açorda (Portuguese Dry Soup)   190

The First Four Books of Garlic

THESE ARE THE FOUR BEST BOOKS WE'VE COME ACROSS in our study of the stinking rose. They are the Matthew, Mark, Luke and John in the gospel of garlic. In each case, garlic was just the starting point, the subject that stimulated these authors to write. All of these books can be found in libraries.

Garlic Is Life by CHESTER AARON

Chester Aaron is a farmer. But he is also a novelist, professor and teacher of creative writing. Retired from academia, he now works his little farm, tending his garlic and developing close relationships with the people who buy some of the 55 varieties that he grows. Around his house are 40 small raised beds, undergirded by mesh screens to keep out garlic-loving gophers. He lives alone with Sadie, the gopher-loving cat who more than earns her keep.

In his book he has drawn together the history of his Georgian Jewish family, who fled the pogroms early in the century and came to western Pennsylvania for a life of hard work. That background helps give structure and meaning to his academic career, his friendships, his writing, and, in his later life, his work as a shepherd and farmer.

Aaron is a complex and fascinating man who has found some of the basic answers of life in the quiet of cultivation. Garlic and his work with it became for him a metaphor for creativity, love and friendship, but also for difficulty, disappointment and loss, and, as his title says, for life itself. When the day's toil in the garden is over, the light is always on in his study, where he writes something more about garlic and life.

A Garlic Testament by STANLEY CRAWFORD

Another academic, Crawford is a University of Chicago intellectual who escaped the rat race and found fulfillment as a marginal farmer on some marginal land in an economically depressed part of a dry southwestern state. His book is a rare look at the power of the attachment one can have to a little patch of farm and the things that can grow on it.

But Crawford doesn't let his contemplation of philosophical matters hide the hard work demanded of him and his wife in running a small organic farm. He describes what they do with elegance, but you know it's no picnic. He became one of those farmers who know how to do everything, from fixing the transmission on the old tractor to calculating how many of his garlic heads he could afford to hold back for planting and still have enough money left to buy some clothes and pay the propane bill.

By the end of the book, as he contemplates again the harsh economics of what he does, you are almost afraid that he won't want to continue this hardscrabble life or, worse, not be able to continue if he wants to. The book is a celebration of the beauty of the processes that one way or another sustain us all.

Growing Great Garlic by RON L. ENGELAND

Filaree Farm in the Okanogan region of north central Washington was the setting where Ron Engeland, his wife, Watershine, and the people who worked with them developed the best book yet on understanding where garlic came from, why it is so good and, most important, how to grow it.

Although he's left Filaree for a different life, Engeland has given the rights to the book to the farm. Those who buy the book will travel through seasons on the farm and learn about the work it takes to make things grow. They will learn how and when to plant, when to harvest, how to cure, and how to get the crop to market. But more than that, readers of *Growing Great Garlic* will come to understand the passion for growing, and how it can connect us to the soil.

It is the best book yet on how to grow garlic.

The Book of Garlic by LLOYD J. HARRIS

What a bizarre book, we thought. The cover grabs you at once. Designed by the brilliant Seymour Chwast, it shows a vampire, a chef, a doctor and a magician, one in each corner of the cover contemplating a single head of garlic. The subtitle is *The Incredible Story of Allium Sativum as Magic Bulb, Potent Medicine, Unrivaled Culinary Herb, and Stinking Rose of Mirth*. Lloyd Harris was certainly way ahead of the curve in recognizing the possibilities of garlic in the modern world.

Harris has searched all of literature for funny and clever anecdotes about garlic and has made his own substantial contributions to the lore. Everything of importance written about garlic before the book's 1975 publication is noted here. Clearly Harris was a man driven by passion; no herb in human history has been saluted with such knowledge, interest and concern as garlic is in this funny, creative, entertaining book.

Harris is elusive. We asked a number of people around San Francisco how to reach him. No one could tell us. We will have to be content with seeing him in the documentary *Garlic Is as Good as Ten Mothers*, in which he wears a white garlic-head hat and declaims on garlic's curative powers and its wonderful taste.

Turkish Poached Eggs with Spicy Garlic Yogurt

We HAVE FOUND MANY exotic garlic dishes in the Eastern Mediterranean. If you're a fan of poached eggs, as we are, you will adore this recipe, adapted from one in Inci Kurt's *Turkish Cookery*. In combination, the hot eggs, cool yogurt, garlic and cayenne all work together to make a scrumptious breakfast—especially in summer. We like to place the eggs on a toasted crouton to sop up the juices and serve in heated soup plates.

SERVES 2

1   cup plain yogurt, preferably
       whole milk
2   plump garlic cloves, smashed
       and minced
2   teaspoons minced fresh mint
       (1 teaspoon dried)
1½   tablespoons unsalted butter
⅛   teaspoon ground red pepper
       (cayenne)
4   large eggs
2   tablespoons cider vinegar or
       other fruit vinegar
       Kosher salt and freshly ground
       white pepper
2   ¾-inch-thick slices toast,
       crusts removed

In a medium-sized mixing bowl, blend together yogurt, garlic and mint. Set aside.

In a small saucepan or in a microwave, melt butter and cayenne together. Keep hot.

Break eggs into separate small dishes or saucers and place beside stovetop.

Fill a large sauté pan with water. Add vinegar and some salt. Bring to a softly rolling boil. Have heated serving plates nearby. Carefully tilt eggs, one at a time, into the bubbling water. Using a slotted spoon, quickly flip whites around the yolk, trying to keep each egg in an oval shape. Cook for 2 to 3 minutes, depending upon preference.

While eggs are cooking, quickly place toast in bottom of two soup plates. Place two eggs on each plate. Spoon yogurt mixture around and over eggs. Pour some cayenne butter over each. Season with salt and white pepper.

For a festive brunch:
Wine: Pommery Brut Champagne "Apanage"
(France: Champagne) or another dry Champagne
from France

Dilly Salmon Cakes with Garlic Tartar Sauce

THESE DELICIOUS SALMON CAKES are crisp on the outside and feather light inside. Frying under cover allows us to use a minimum of oil and creates superb, delicate cakes. Serve them for brunch with scrambled eggs and mushrooms or, better yet, topped with a perfectly poached egg. Our special tartar sauce has plenty of zip for either combination. You can make the sauce a day ahead. The salmon cake recipe multiplies quite nicely. Fry the cakes in batches of four, keeping the finished ones warm on a cookie sheet in a heated oven.

SERVES 2 TO 4

Garlic Tartar Sauce

- 1 teaspoon Colman's dry mustard
- 1 teaspoon grated horseradish, fresh or preserved
- ¾ cup mayonnaise, preferably homemade or Hellmann's or Best Foods
- 1 plump shallot, minced
- 2 plump garlic cloves, pressed
- 1 tablespoon sweet pickle relish
- 1 tablespoon minced fresh dill
- 1 teaspoon hot Hungarian paprika

Kosher salt and freshly ground white pepper

Salmon Cakes

- 1 large russet potato, baked and chilled
- 4 ounces (½ packed cup) poached salmon
- ½ cup coarsely chopped sweet onion
- 1 tablespoon chopped fresh dill, plus fresh dill for garnish
- 2 plump garlic cloves, smashed and minced
- 1 large egg yolk
- 2 tablespoons unsalted butter, melted Kosher salt and freshly ground white pepper
- ⅓ cup fine dry bread crumbs
- 3 tablespoons canola oil

To make tartar sauce: In a medium-sized mixing bowl, blend together mustard and horseradish. Blend in remaining sauce ingredients. Scrape into a serving bowl. Cover tightly with plastic wrap and refrigerate until needed.

To make salmon cakes: Remove potato skin and slice potato. In the bowl of a food processor fitted with the metal blade, combine potato, salmon, onion and dill. Pulse until mixture is very coarse. Turn into a large mixing bowl and blend thoroughly with garlic, egg yolk, butter and generous amounts of salt and pepper. Divide mixture into four portions and pat into four cakes about 2½ inches in diameter and ¾ inch high. Pour bread crumbs onto a plate, then coat fish cakes evenly on all sides.

Heat oil in a large cast-iron or stamped-steel skillet over high heat. Place fish cakes in skillet, cover and reduce heat to medium. Fry for 3 minutes, or until golden on the bottom. Turn, cover, and fry until other side is golden brown, 3 to 4 minutes. Serve on heated plates garnished with fresh dill. Pass tartar sauce separately.

Wine: Colle Salato Verdicchio (Italy: Marches)
or another Verdicchio

Goat Cheese Soufflé with Sauce of Fresh Peas & Tarragon

GARLIC AND TARRAGON flavor this goat cheese soufflé, and a simple fresh pea sauce makes a festive addition. Serve this as a luncheon dish or a casual supper. A soup or salad is all you need to complete the meal.

SERVES 6

Soufflé

6 tablespoons (¾ stick) unsalted butter
¼ cup finely grated Parmesan or Asiago cheese
1⅔ cups milk
4 plump garlic cloves, pressed
5 tablespoons unbleached flour
6 large egg yolks, beaten
6 ounces fresh goat cheese (chèvre), crumbled
2 teaspoons minced fresh tarragon (1 teaspoon dried)
Kosher salt
½ teaspoon freshly ground white pepper
¼ teaspoon freshly grated nutmeg
Pinch of ground red pepper (cayenne)
7 large egg whites

Sauce

1 tablespoon unsalted butter
1 plump garlic clove, pressed
3 scallions, trimmed with 1 inch tender green, minced
½ cup finely chopped butter (Boston) lettuce
1 cup fresh peas
1 cup chicken stock
1 teaspoon minced fresh tarragon (½ teaspoon dried)
Kosher salt and freshly ground white pepper
2 tablespoons heavy cream

To make soufflé: Prepare a 2-quart soufflé dish. Butter well with 1 tablespoon of the butter; dust evenly with half of the grated cheese. Generously butter a foil "collar" and tie it around soufflé dish so that it extends 3 inches above rim.

Place an oven rack in middle of oven and preheat oven to 400°F.

Scald milk and set aside. Melt remaining 5 tablespoons butter in a heavy saucepan over medium-low heat. Stir in garlic, then whisk in flour, blending well. Slowly whisk in scalded milk to make a very thick béchamel sauce. Reduce heat and cook, stirring constantly, for 2 minutes to cook flour. Remove sauce from heat.

Slowly whisk a little hot sauce into beaten egg yolks until yolks are thoroughly heated. Stir eggs back into pan of béchamel sauce. Add crumbled goat cheese, tarragon, ½ teaspoon salt, white pepper, nutmeg and cayenne. Stir over very low heat until cheese has melted. Reserve.

Beat egg whites with a pinch of salt just until they hold stiff peaks. Stir one-quarter of egg whites into cheese mixture to lighten it, then gently fold in remaining egg whites. Spoon into prepared soufflé dish and sprinkle with reserved grated cheese.

Bake soufflé for 35 minutes, or until nicely browned and firmly set. It should be slightly creamy in center. While soufflé is baking, prepare sauce.

To make sauce: Melt butter in a small saucepan over low heat. Add garlic and scallions. Cover and cook until scallions wilt, about 1 minute. Add lettuce, peas and stock. Cover, increase heat and simmer slowly until peas are very tender, 6 to 10 minutes. Puree mixture in a food processor. Season with tarragon, salt and white pepper.

Transfer mixture back to saucepan. Stir in cream and heat, but don't allow to boil. Serve immediately, accompanied by sauce.

Wine: Didier Dagueneau Clos des Chailloux Pouilly-Fumé (France: Loire Valley) or another rich and complex Pouilly-Fumé

Spanakopita
(SPINACH PIE)

THIS IS A SOMEWHAT NEW LOOK at the very traditional Greek spinach pie made with crispy thin layers of pastry. In a salute to our friends who love dandelion greens, we include them in our filling. (Use escarole instead, if you prefer.) If you like Gorgonzola, use it in equal measure instead of the cottage cheese. Serve this splendid dish as a meatless meal, a first course or even as a side vegetable dish to accompany chicken or fish from the grill. We would never freeze this, but we reheat it with great success.

SERVES 10 TO 15

3   tablespoons olive oil
1   cup finely chopped yellow onions
6   plump garlic cloves, smashed
     and minced
1   pound dandelion greens, rinsed
     and coarsely chopped
1   pound spinach, stemmed, rinsed
     and coarsely chopped
½   cup minced fresh flat-leaf parsley
¼   cup minced fresh tarragon
¼   cup minced fresh mint
¼   teaspoon freshly grated nutmeg
6   large eggs, beaten

½   pound feta cheese, preferably
     imported, crumbled
½   pound 4-percent cottage cheese
     or crumbled Gorgonzola cheese
     Up to 1¼ cups fine dry bread crumbs
     Kosher salt and freshly ground
     white pepper
3   sticks (¾ pound) unsalted butter,
     melted
1   pound phyllo sheets, defrosted in
     refrigerator if frozen

Heat olive oil in a large sauté pan over medium heat. Add onions and garlic. Cook, stirring often, until mixture is lightly browned, 5 to 7 minutes. Add dandelion greens and spinach to onion mixture. Cover and cook, stirring from time to time, until greens are thoroughly wilted and tender, about 10 minutes. Transfer mixture to a large bowl and cool.

Add parsley, tarragon, mint, nutmeg, eggs, cheeses, ¼ cup of the bread crumbs, salt and white pepper. Mix vigorously and set aside.

Preheat oven to 350°F.

Generously butter an 18-x-12-inch baking dish. Open phyllo package and place it next to your work area. Cover with a damp tea towel.

Have melted butter handy in a small bowl and a pastry brush.

If possible, enlist another pair of hands for assembly. Working very quickly, place a sheet of phyllo in pan, brush with butter and sprinkle with 1 scant tablespoon crumbs. Repeat until you have 10 layers. Spoon spinach mixture evenly into pan, covering entire surface of pastry. Sprinkle top with 1 tablespoon crumbs. Cover spinach mixture with 8 to 10 more sheets of pastry, buttering and sprinkling with crumbs as you continue. Sprinkle top layer with crumbs, then cover evenly with remaining melted butter.

Using a very sharp knife, lightly score top pastry layers into squares. Bake for 1 hour, or until top is crisp and golden.

Transfer pan to a rack. Using sharp knife, complete cutting spanakopita into squares. Let cool for at least 15 minutes before serving.

Wine: Vietti Dolcetto "Lazzarito" (Italy: Piedmont) or another Dolcetto from Italy

Artichoke Pie in Cream Cheese Pastry

LINDA HAS BEEN MAKING this unusual dish in one form or another for more than 35 years. We love the blend of artichokes, mushrooms and alliums in a cheesy custard. Bits of sun-dried tomatoes provide a counterpoint. Whether served as the main dish for a meatless meal or as the accompaniment to roasted chicken, fish or beef, this is a great treat. We like to use white onion in this dish; its bright flavor works well with the artichokes.

SERVES 8 TO 10

Juice of 1 lemon
5 medium artichokes
3 tablespoons olive oil
1¼ cups shredded carrot
¾ cup minced white onion
½ cup chicken stock
4 tablespoons (½ stick) unsalted butter
3 ounces shiitake mushrooms, stemmed and sliced
6 ounces cremini mushrooms, sliced
4 plump garlic cloves, smashed and minced
4 sun-dried tomatoes, packed in oil, minced
2 teaspoons minced fresh basil
2 teaspoons minced fresh thyme
¼ cup minced fresh flat-leaf parsley
1 cup whole-milk ricotta cheese
5 large eggs
¾ cup grated Parmesan cheese
Kosher salt and freshly ground white pepper to taste
1 recipe Gert's Cream Cheese Pastry (page 178)

Fill a large mixing bowl with water and add lemon juice. Trim artichokes by removing all outer leaves, leaving only pale inner leaves. Cut off top 2 inches of each artichoke and trim dark green part off bottom. Slice bulb in half vertically and trim out fuzzy choke with a sharp knife and a spoon. Slice each artichoke half into very thin vertical slices and put into lemon water. Drain and rinse sliced artichokes just before using.

Heat olive oil in a large skillet. Sauté carrot and onion until golden. Add drained artichokes and stock. Cover and simmer slowly until artichokes are very tender, 20 to 30 minutes. Add more stock if needed. Set aside uncovered.

Meanwhile, melt 3 tablespoons of the butter in another large skillet. Add mushrooms, garlic and sun-dried tomatoes. Cover and cook over low heat until mushrooms are tender, 10 to 15 minutes. Uncover and stir over medium heat until moisture has evaporated. Stir in herbs and set aside uncovered.

Combine ricotta, eggs, and grated cheese in a large mixing bowl. Mix thoroughly. Carefully add contents of the two skillets, season with salt and white pepper and blend.

Preheat oven to 450°F.

Roll half of cream cheese pastry between two floured sheets of wax paper to make a 12-inch circle. Carefully fit pastry into a 10-inch, preferably Pyrex, pie plate. Spoon filling evenly into prepared plate. Roll out top crust in same fashion and make decorative slits in center, then fit top crust over pie. Trim excess dough to hang 1 inch over edge of plate. Seal and crimp to make a decorative edge.

Melt remaining 1 tablespoon of butter and brush top of pie. Bake for 30 minutes, or until top is nicely browned. Let rest for 10 minutes on a cooling rack before serving.

Wine: Louis Jadot Beaujolais-Villages (France: Beaujolais region of Burgundy) or a fresh, young, very fruity red wine

Gert's Cream Cheese Pastry

WHEN LINDA WAS FIRST MARRIED, her mother taught her how to make a hot chopped-liver-filled nibble, using this pastry. We've lined small tarts and large pies with it. Over the years it has seen a wide variety of savory fillings, but none quite as remarkable as the artichoke pie. One other change from earlier years is that we now make the delicate pastry in a food processor.

MAKES TWO 10-INCH CRUSTS

- 2 sticks (½ pound) unsalted butter, softened, cut into pieces
- ½ pound cream cheese, softened, cut into pieces
- 2 cups unbleached flour
- ¼ teaspoon kosher salt

In the bowl of a food processor, combine all ingredients. Pulse 10 times, then let motor run just until a ball begins to form. Scrape mixture from bowl. Pat pastry into a large round. Cut in half and form into two disks about 1 inch thick. Wrap thoroughly in wax paper and chill at least 1 hour before rolling out.

Chèvre & Tomato Tart with Roasted Garlic

HERE'S SOMETHING out of the ordinary to serve with grilled chicken or on its own: a savory pie with a luscious filling of goat cheese, roasted garlic and vine-ripened tomatoes and a topping of crispy fresh bread crumbs. If the pie is served hot, the cheese will be a bit runny; when cooled, it firms up.

SERVES 8 TO 10

5   large, firm but ripe tomatoes,
       cut into ½-inch-thick slices
1   large egg yolk beaten with
       1 teaspoon water
1   partially baked 10-inch pie shell
       (page 180)
6   ounces soft fresh goat cheese (chèvre)
       Flesh of 1 large head roasted garlic
       (page 34)
¼   cup heavy cream
3   tablespoons sour cream,
       plus more if needed
1   tablespoon minced fresh parsley
1   tablespoon fresh thyme or
       1 teaspoon dried
½   teaspoon salt
1   teaspoon freshly ground black pepper
3   tablespoons extra-virgin olive oil
2   cups fresh, soft bread crumbs
⅔   cup minced shallots

Place tomato slices on cooling racks and let drain while preparing pie.

Preheat oven to 400°F.

Lightly brush egg wash on bottom and sides of pie shell to seal. Let stand while preparing filling.

In the bowl of an electric mixer, combine goat cheese, garlic, heavy cream, sour cream, parsley, thyme, salt and pepper and beat until light and creamy. If mixture appears too dry to spread easily, add more sour cream, 1 tablespoon at a time. Mixture should have consistency of sour cream. Set aside.

Heat olive oil in a small saucepan. Add crumbs and shallots. Toss well to coat and cook over medium heat for 2 minutes, tossing often. Remove from heat and set aside. Season with salt and pepper.

Spoon goat-cheese mixture into pie shell and spread to distribute evenly. Layer tomatoes evenly over filling. Cover top evenly with bread-crumb mixture.

Bake for 20 to 25 minutes, or until crumbs and pastry are browned. Remove from oven and cool on a rack for 30 minutes before serving.

Wine: Charles Joguet Chinon Rosé (France: Loire Valley)
or dry Rosé from California

Tapenade Tart with Fontina & Escarole

GARLIC AND KALAMATA OLIVES, the basic ingredients of most tapenades, along with a dollop of sun-dried tomatoes, give this cheesy quiche its dramatic flavors. We add escarole for flavor and color. The pastry shell is wonderfully flaky. We learned the technique for it from Lydie Marshall during one of her Thanksgiving visits with us.

SERVES 8 TO 10

Pastry Shell

1⅓ cups unbleached flour
¼ teaspoon kosher salt
8 tablespoons (1 stick) cold unsalted butter, cut into ½-inch pieces
3 tablespoons ice water

Filling

1 tablespoon olive oil
3 plump garlic cloves, pressed
2 tablespoons minced oil-packed sun-dried tomatoes
5 large eggs, beaten
1 cup heavy cream
⅓ cup milk, preferably whole
1 teaspoon kosher salt
¼ teaspoon freshly ground black pepper
Generous pinch freshly grated nutmeg

2 cups coarsely chopped escarole, blanched and drained, pressed dry
1¼ cups grated fontina cheese
⅓ cup finely chopped Kalamata olives

To make pastry shell: Combine flour and salt in the bowl of a food processor. Add butter bits and pulse 15 to 20 times, until mixture has the texture of cornmeal. Sprinkle evenly with ice water. Pulse 15 more times; mixture will be crumbly and not at all gathered. Dump mixture in a mound on a lightly floured work surface. Using the heel of your hand, quickly push small amounts of dough away from you across the work surface until all of it has been worked. With the help of a pastry scraper, gather blended dough together. If it seems to need more blending, repeat process one more time. Then form dough into a disk about 4 inches in diameter, wrap with wax paper, and chill for 20 minutes.

Generously flour work surface and rolling pin. Roll pastry into a 13-to-14-inch circle and carefully fit into an 11-inch tart pan with a removable bottom. Trim edges to 1 inch above top of rim and fold half toward inside, leaving a firm half-inch rim above edge of pan. Prick bottom and sides of pastry with a fork and chill shell for 40 minutes.

While shell is chilling, preheat oven to 400°F.

Line shell with foil and fill with pie weights or rice so that sides will not slip down. Bake for 15 minutes, remove weights and foil, and bake another 10 minutes. Take shell from oven and cool on a wire rack until time to fill.

Place baking rack in middle of oven. Lower oven heat to 350°F.

To make filling: Heat olive oil in a small skillet over medium heat. Add garlic and sun-dried tomatoes. Stir over low heat for 1 to 2 minutes, just to lose raw flavor of garlic. Set mixture aside to cool.

In a large mixing bowl, thoroughly beat eggs together with cream and milk. Blend in salt, pepper and nutmeg. Add cooled garlic mixture to egg mixture. Add escarole, 1 cup cheese and olives. Blend thoroughly. Pour into prepared shell. Sprinkle evenly with remaining ¼ cup cheese.

Bake until custard has set and top is golden, 30 to 40 minutes.

Let cool on a rack for at least 20 minutes before serving.

Wine: Weingut Familie Zull Schrattenthaler Ödfeld Grüner Veltliner (Austria) or an Italian Pinot Grigio

THE BARD'S GARLIC

GOOD NEWS!" came the word on the telephone. Mervyn Sopher, peripatetic polylingual polymath and retired physician, had just returned from Stratford, Ontario, where Shakespeareans gather every summer. "There is only one garlic mention in all of Shakespeare, and it is in *Hamlet*," he said. "I just got the authoritative word." He sent us to Act Two, where the prince is lecturing the traveling players.

We started to read, and eventually came to this: "I remember, one said there were no sallets in the lines to make the matter savoury, nor no matter in the phrase that might indict the author of affectation." "Sallets" is a word that had a number of Elizabethan meanings. It could be the headpiece of a suit of armor or a protective visor or even a salad. But there was still another, more obscure meaning—a spicy herb. Our guess is that someone, trying to make the lines more understandable, changed "sallets" to garlic, which, heaven knows, is some spicy herb. On the other hand, Shakespeare knew garlic, and the word was available. Why didn't he use it, if that was what he meant?

We got to wondering. Could it be that the bard, who knew everything and wrote so much, never mentioned garlic? This led us to the major Shakespearean concordances, which list every word he ever used, and where. The people in Stratford got it wrong. There is no garlic in *Hamlet*. But garlic is mentioned in five of the other plays.

♠ In *Measure for Measure* (iii 2-195), the following: "Though she smelt brown bread and garlic."

♠ "Eat no onions nor garlic, for we are to utter sweet breath." That one is from *A Midsummer-Night's Dream* (iv 2-43).

♠ From *The Winter's Tale*, "Mopsa must be your mistress: Marry, garlic, to mend her kissing with" (iv 4-162).

♠ "I had rather live with cheese and garlic in a windmill"—*King Henry IV* (iii 1-162).

♠ From *Coriolanus* (iv 6-98), "You that stood so much upon the voice of occupation and the breath of garlic-eaters."

Clearly Shakespeare shared with most of his countrymen a disdain for garlic. Actually, we don't think living with cheese and garlic in a windmill would be so bad.

Savory Bread Pudding with Sun-Dried Tomatoes & Pesto

WE FIRST LEARNED about savory bread puddings from the folks at D'Amico Cucina in Minneapolis. This recipe combines the special flavor of sun-dried tomatoes with the garlic-and-basil pungency of pesto in a tender bread pudding. It makes a great supper on its own or a fine accompaniment to grilled fish or chicken.

SERVES 6 TO 8

- 6 packed cups 1-inch cubes Italian bread
- 3 tablespoons unsalted butter, melted
- 1 cup heavy cream
- 3 cups milk, plus more if needed
- 5 large eggs
- ⅓ cup Simple Summer Pesto (page 149) or another pesto sauce
- 8 oil-packed sun-dried tomato halves, drained and minced
  Salt and freshly ground black pepper to taste
- 2 tablespoons grated Parmesan cheese

Place bread cubes in a large bowl. Add melted butter and toss well to coat. In another bowl, blend together cream, milk, eggs and pesto. Pour over bread cubes and blend well. Let bread mixture stand 1 hour at room temperature. Mixture should be very creamy; if it seems dry, slowly add more milk. Stir in sun-dried tomatoes, salt and pepper.

Lightly butter a 3-quart shallow casserole. Pour bread mixture into it and smooth top. Sprinkle evenly with cheese. Let stand 1 more hour at room temperature.

Preheat oven to 400°F. Bake pudding 50 minutes, or until top is golden brown and pudding is firm to the touch. Remove from oven and let stand in a warm place for 10 minutes before serving.

Wine: Martini & Prati St. Elmo's Blend
(California: Sonoma County) or a light and fruity
red wine from Italy

A Simple Spicy Quiche
with Dry-Roasted Garlic & Broccoli

BROCCOLI, CHEESE AND EGGS combine to make a tender crustless quiche that's great for either brunch or supper. The garlic's special sweetness is imparted by dry-roasting it Mexican style. A good-quality curry powder and mace add some exotic notes to this very flavorful and flexible dish. You can vary the cheeses according to your personal taste. Should you wish, you can omit the spices and use some fresh herbs instead. And finally, if you wish, you can mix this the night before, bring it to room temperature and bake it right before serving.

SERVES 6 TO 8

- 6 plump garlic cloves, unpeeled
- 2 cups medium-size-diced broccoli
- 1 tablespoon butter, softened
- 2 tablespoons fine dry bread crumbs
- 9 large eggs, beaten
- 2 cups (4-percent fat) cottage cheese
- ½ pound (2 cups) grated Jarlsberg cheese
- ½ pound (2 cups) grated Jack cheese, flavored if possible
- ¼ cup unbleached flour
- 1 teaspoon baking powder
- 1 teaspoon Madras curry powder
- 1 teaspoon kosher salt
- ½ teaspoon freshly ground white pepper
- ½ teaspoon ground mace
- ½ cup finely diced red bell pepper
- ⅓ cup finely diced shallots
  Sour cream (optional)

Place a small cast-iron skillet over medium heat until hot. Dry-roast garlic cloves, turning often, until soft to the touch and somewhat blackened in spots, about 15 minutes. Set aside until cool, then peel and mince. Reserve.

While garlic is roasting, prepare broccoli: Fill a small saucepan with salted water and bring to a boil over high heat. Add broccoli and cook for 1 minute. Drain and refresh with cold water. Drain again and set aside in a small bowl.

Preheat oven to 375°F. Butter a shallow 3-quart gratin or baking dish. Coat with crumbs; invert dish to discard excess crumbs.

In a large mixing bowl, combine eggs, cottage cheese and grated cheeses. Blend vigorously. Add flour, baking powder, curry powder, salt, white pepper and mace; blend thoroughly. Add reserved garlic, broccoli, bell pepper and shallots. Blend gently but thoroughly. Pour into prepared baking dish and smooth top.

Bake for 45 minutes, or until golden brown and firm to the touch. Cut quiche into generous portions and serve immediately. Garnish if desired with sour cream.

Wine: Henriot Brut "Souveraine" (Champagne: France) or Martinsancho Verdejo from Spain

Aristophanes believed that garlic could be useful in sports. He urged competitive athletes to stoke up on the big G before going to the stadium. Today, some runners believe chewing a piece of garlic in a race will keep others from overtaking them.

Coosa Mih' Shee
(STUFFED SQUASH IN TOMATO SAUCE WITH GARLIC & MINT)

OUR FRIENDS HELEN AND WEDAD Shaheen prepare many Syrian recipes taught them by their mother and grandmother nearly 60 years ago. One of our favorites is this—small squash with a tender stuffing of lamb and rice. The mint-laced and garlic-piqued tomato sauce is light. This is a good side dish for dinner or main dish for lunch. The Shaheens use a nifty pale green summer squash called *coosa* for this dish—look for it at farmers' markets. You can use any small green summer squash that is about 1¼ inches in diameter at the neck with a plumper bottom. A *coosa* corer, available in most Middle Eastern markets, looks like a long, sharp marrow spoon.

Note: If you wish, prepare squash pulp for another vegetable dish: Squeeze out excess moisture, then sauté pulp in some butter with a small chopped onion, a dash of allspice and a chopped fresh tomato. Simmer, covered, for 10 minutes. Season with salt, pepper and some mint.

SERVES 12 AS A SIDE DISH OR 6 AS A MAIN DISH

14 coosa or zucchini squash, 5-6 inches long

½ cup long-grain rice, rinsed in cold water

¾ pound coarsely ground lamb or beef

4 tablespoons (½ stick) unsalted butter, softened

1 tablespoon minced fresh flat-leaf parsley

½ cup canned tomato sauce
Kosher salt and freshly ground pepper

1 cup tomato puree or canned crushed tomatoes

3 plump garlic cloves, smashed and minced

2 cups water

1 teaspoon dried mint

Remove stem ends of squash. Using a slender paring knife and a long thin spoon, gently hollow out squash from stem end, leaving a shell about ⅛ inch thick. You have 2 extra squash. Reserve pulp (see Note). Rinse squash in cold salted water, then drain thoroughly.

In a large bowl, blend together rice, lamb or

beef, butter, parsley, tomato sauce, salt and pepper. Stuff squash about four-fifths full, leaving some room for rice to swell. Place squash in a very large, heavy-bottomed pan. Pour tomato puree evenly over squash. Sprinkle with garlic. Then pour water evenly over them. Finally, sprinkle with mint and more pepper.

Cover and cook over high heat until liquids bubble, 3 to 4 minutes. Reduce heat to low and simmer until tender, 30 to 35 minutes.

Wine: Château Trignon Côtes-du-Rhône Village, Sablet (France: Rhône) or Thomas Mitchell Shiraz (Australia) or a lighter-styled Australian Shiraz

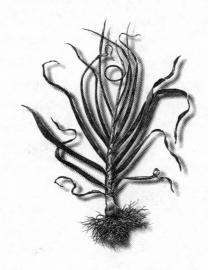

Couscous Salad with Grilled Chicken & Roasted Garlic Vinaigrette

COUSCOUS, THAT MIDDLE EASTERN grainlike pasta, lends itself to all kinds of summer supper salads. We like to combine it with either grilled chicken breast or some grilled shrimp. And if you have a summer herb garden, add a variety of herbs along with a mixture of diced fresh vegetables.

This recipe calls for pureeing the roasted garlic with the vinegar. Some roasted garlic is very creamy, while other varieties soften but aren't as easy to smash. It's easiest to combine garlic flesh and vinegar in a mini-food processor and puree. But you can also use a mortar and pestle.

SERVES 4

1 cup chicken stock
2 tablespoons unsalted butter
1 cup uncooked couscous
1 cup frozen peas, defrosted
½ large red onion, in medium dice
1 sweet red, yellow, or orange bell pepper, in medium dice
2 chicken breasts, split, boned, skinned, and grilled
Flesh of 1 large head roasted garlic
⅓ cup fruit vinegar, such as cherry, raspberry, peach or cider
Juice of 1 lime
¼ teaspoon ground ginger
½ cup extra-virgin olive oil
Kosher salt and freshly ground white pepper
2 cups mixed salad greens, cleaned and dried
1 tablespoon minced fresh chives
1 tablespoon minced fresh mint
1 teaspoon minced fresh tarragon
½ cup toasted pecans, chopped coarsely
Edible flowers for garnish, such as nasturtiums, calendula, borage

In a heavy 2-quart pot bring chicken stock to a boil. Add butter and couscous. Stir well, cover, and remove from heat. Let stand for 15 minutes, then fluff with a fork. Set aside until cold.

In a large bowl, combine couscous with peas, onion and pepper; toss to blend. Slice chicken into ½-inch strips and add to couscous mixture.

Puree roasted garlic with vinegar (see headnote). Transfer mixture to a small bowl and whisk together with lime juice and ginger. Slowly add oil, whisking constantly to form a thick emulsion. Add salt and white pepper. Remove 2 tablespoons of dressing and reserve. Add remaining dressing to couscous mixture and blend gently.

Just before serving, toss lettuces and herbs with remaining vinaigrette and divide among dinner plates.

Serve couscous on bed of lettuces. Sprinkle with pecans and garnish with edible flowers.

Wine: Franz Prager Grüner Veltliner Smaragd

(Austria: Wachau) or another crisp,

but very concentrated, white wine

Açorda

(PORTUGUESE DRY SOUP)

ÇORDA IS USUALLY MADE with stale bread, stock, lots of garlic and cilantro. Sometimes a poached egg is served on top. Our *açorda* is inspired by two different versions at one of Lisbon's most popular restaurants, Pap' Açorda. Like those two recipes, this is a very moist "pudding." Serve it with spicy sautéed shrimp, a grilled chicken or simply prepared fish. Or stir in Somewhat Portuguese Shrimp Piri Piri (page 244).

SERVES 4 TO 6

6-7 cups ¾-inch sourdough bread cubes

4 cups chicken stock

1 bay leaf

1 small branch rosemary or
   ¼ teaspoon dried

2 large eggs

2 tablespoons vinegar

⅓ cup extra-virgin olive oil

3 plump garlic cloves, smashed
   and minced

2 crushed dried chiles

½ cup minced fresh cilantro

Kosher salt and freshly ground
   white pepper
Juice of half a lemon

Toss bread cubes onto a cookie sheet; let stand at room temperature for 1 to 2 hours to dry out.

Pour stock into a small saucepan. Add bay leaf and rosemary. Bring to a boil, reduce heat and simmer for 15 minutes.

Meanwhile, break eggs into little dishes and reserve. Fill a shallow 2-quart saucepan with 2 inches of water. Add vinegar and bring to a boil. Keep warm, bringing back to a boil before cooking eggs.

Heat a large serving bowl.

Combine oil, garlic and chiles in a large skillet. Heat over high heat. Add bread cubes and stir until they begin to brown, 3 to 4 minutes. Place in serving bowl. Pour 3 cups of the hot stock through a strainer over cubes and toss well. Keep warm.

Slip eggs into simmering water. With a slotted spoon, spoon whites over yolks to make a neat package. Cook until firm, about 2½ to 4 minutes. Transfer eggs with a slotted spoon onto softened bread. Add salt and white pepper and stir in lemon juice.

Using 2 large spoons, break eggs into bread mixture. Keep cutting and tossing until mixture becomes puddinglike. If mixture appears too dry, add more stock. Stir in fresh cilantro and serve.

Wine: R. H. Phillips Toasted Head Chardonnay (California: Yolo Valley) or a white Burgundy from the Mâcon region of France

BIG AND BIGGER

GARLIC HEADS VARY GREATLY IN SIZE, but size seems to have no effect on taste. Some heads are almost as small as a large marble, while others are nearly as big as a baseball. No grower, however, will admit to having small garlic. Even when heads are diminutive, packers never use the word "small." California growers have come up with a standard set of designations that is well accepted. Here's how Christopher Ranch, the world's largest garlic grower, does it, with the company's marketing label:

Designation	Heads per pound	Label	Diameter in inches
Super Colossal	5½	Festival	2¾
Colossal	6½	Festival	2⅝
Super Jumbo	7½	Gilroy	2⅜
Extra Jumbo	8½	Christopher	2¼
Jumbo	10½	Chef's Choice	2⅛–2¼
Giant	12½	California 1	⅞–2

Tiny garlics are called:

Large Tube	14–15½	California	1¾
Medium Tube	17–18½	California	1½
Small Tube	19–24	California	1–1¼

PASTA & PIZZA

Spaghetti al Aglio e Olio (Spaghetti with Garlic and Oil)   196

Spaghetti with Hazelnut Pesto   197

Orecchiette (Little Ears) with Fresh Tomatoes, Arugula & Garlic   198

Spaghettini with Garlic, Lemon & Anchovies   199

Conchigliette (Little Shells) with a Sauce of Caramelized Tomatoes,
Roasted Peppers, Garlic & Basil   200

Spaghetti Carbonara   202

Pasta with Winter Squash, Shallots, Garlic & Mascarpone   206

Lemon Linguine with Green Tomatoes & Sage   207

Linguine with Red Clam Sauce   208

Baked Fusilli with Savoy Cabbage, Endive & Dandelion Greens   210

Macaroni & Cheese with Tomato Topping   211

Thai-Style Noodles with Garlic Peanut Sauce   212

Pizza with Caramelized Onions & Garlic   213

Fontina Pizza with Roasted Garlic, Mashed Potatoes & Clams   214

Pizza with Eggplant, Garden Tomatoes & Garlic   216

Red, White & Green Pizza   217

Dough for Thin Pizza   218

RECIPE FOR A FESTIVAL

THE PYRO-CHEFS ARE THE STARS of the world's most famous food festival, always appearing in the national magazines and on television. For the three days of the annual celebration of garlic in Gilroy, they stand behind high-fire burners and cook calamari with garlic. "Fire in the hole!" they shout. And then in go the ingredients and up goes the huge, structure-threatening flame.

The pyro-chefs are all volunteers—in real life, golf pros, firefighters, financial planners, car dealers, farmers. Some of them have been at it since the first Gilroy Garlic Festival in 1979. And they will proudly show you the scars on their arms from hot oil, hot pans and hot fire.

Val Filice, a veteran chef who understands the dynamics of big events, is the long-time manager of "Gourmet Alley," where the chefs work and where crowds line up for food the moment the gates open. He gave us the recipe for successfully feeding 100,000 festival guests over three days:

> 18,000 lbs. top sirloin (for the pepper and garlic steak sandwiches)
> 7,000 lbs. calamari (for the fiery show)
> 4,200 lbs. scampi (also fiery)
> 8,000 loaves fresh French bread (for garlic toast and sandwiches)
> 4,500 lbs. mushrooms (stuffed with you know what)
> 6,000 lbs. pasta (con pesto)
> 4,000 lbs. chopped garlic
> 185 gallons olive oil
> An endless supply of dry vermouth (for the scampi)
> White jug wine (for the calamari)

And this is just for Gourmet Alley, the main fund-raising activity of the festival, not including what private food booths sell or give to the festival goers. (For example, 40,000 garlic ice cream cones are given out free at the Gilroy Foods booth.)

When the festival started, organizers hoped to make people more aware of the joys of garlic and also call attention to their town, by then the garlic capital of the world. And they figured they could raise some money for good causes at the same time. They planned for

5,000 visitors that first year and got 15,000. By 1987, attendance reached 156,000—far more people than they were equipped to handle. So they cut back and began to plan for more orderly growth, adding acres to the grounds and setting up a shuttle system from the parking lots. The growth of the festival has mirrored the growth of garlic use in the United States, both having expanded exponentially.

NEARLY 5,000 VOLUNTEERS work 48,000 hours to put on the festival (this in a city of just 34,000 people). We don't know of a comparable enterprise. This is way beyond any county fair. The entire community gets swept up in the hard work of planning and making it happen. Depending on hours worked, each volunteer gets a share of the profits for the charity he or she designates. So far, the festival has raised well over $5 million for 152 organizations.

Competition for the 100 private booths is intense and standards are high. Entrepreneurs who want to rent one of the booths must compete. A committee grades the entrants on past performance, the quality and taste of their product, the presentation, customer satisfaction rating and participation in the effort to raise money for charity.

In 1997, 123,000 guests came, just about the number the organizers wanted, and festival receipts were up nearly a quarter of a million dollars.

The festival queen and her court accompanied young women from their garlic sister cities, Takko Machi in Japan and Monticelli in Italy. New was a kissing contest, designed to show that garlic can be romantic. There were arts, crafts and music as well as garlic books, garlic paraphernalia, garlic garments. (One T-shirt proclaimed, "It's chic to reek.") Of course there was a cooking competition, with big prizes for the best new garlic recipes, not to mention a topping contest and a braiding contest. And in the hot California sun, there was relief in the "rain rooms," where you can stand for a moment or two in a cooling mist. And if someone should swoon from the hot sun, emergency medical technicians on their mountain bikes were only seconds away.

Near the main gate, Gerry Foisy, dressed as the world's largest head of garlic, posed endlessly with festival goers for 10,000 photographers, earning money for his favorite charity. And not far away Herbie and the Clovettes tirelessly diverted and entertained the children, who couldn't quite understand their parents' infatuation with fiery garlic and calamari.

Spaghetti al Aglio e Olio

SPAGHETTI WITH GARLIC AND OIL

FOR ITALIANS, this dish is the ultimate comfort food; variations depend upon region and personal taste. The better the ingredients, the better the final dish. Use good extra-virgin olive oil. The following method ensures that the oil is not overheated, which would ruin its character. "The fixins" for this dish are always in our cupboard and refrigerator. It's incredibly easy and very, very good.

SERVES 4

2   tablespoons unsalted butter

6   tablespoons extra-virgin olive oil

1   small dried chile, crumbled

1   pound spaghetti

6   plump garlic cloves, smashed
    and minced
    Kosher salt and freshly ground
    black pepper

½   cup freshly grated Parmesan cheese

½   cup minced fresh flat-leaf parsley

Fill a 6-quart soup pot with salted water and bring to a boil.

Combine butter, oil and chile in a small saucepan or skillet and set aside.

Cook spaghetti according to package directions. As soon as it begins to boil, melt butter in oil over medium heat. When butter has melted, stir in garlic and immediately remove from heat.

About 2 minutes before spaghetti will reach *al dente* stage (according to package directions), return skillet to very low heat. When butter begins to foam, stir garlic and count to 15. Remove from heat.

When spaghetti is done, drain well and return to pot. Add garlic and oil mixture and toss well. Stir in salt, pepper and cheese, toss with parsley, and divide among heated soup plates.

Wine: Terre del Principe Vernaccia di San Gimignano "San Biagio" (Italy: Tuscany) or another crisp, aromatic white wine from Italy

Spaghetti with Hazelnut Pesto

WHEN SHE HEARD we were working on this book, Lynne Rosetto Kasper, author of *The Splendid Table* (Morrow, 1992), told us about a pesto she encountered nearly two decades ago. Her description of a sauce made of hazelnuts, pine nuts, garlic and basil sent us rushing into the kitchen. This toasty, creamy dish is the stuff of our own food memories now. It will keep for up to a week in the refrigerator in a carefully sealed container.

SERVES 4 TO 6

1   packed cup fresh basil leaves

½   cup fresh flat-leaf parsley leaves, stems discarded

4   plump garlic cloves

½   cup grated Parmesan cheese

¼   cup grated Romano cheese

2   tablespoons unsalted butter, softened

½   rounded teaspoon finely ground black pepper

½   teaspoon kosher salt

1   cup peeled hazelnuts, toasted

⅓   cup pine nuts, toasted

¾   cup extra-virgin olive oil

1   pound spaghetti

More grated cheese for garnish

In the bowl of a food processor, combine basil, parsley, garlic, cheeses, butter, pepper and salt. Pulse until finely chopped, 25 to 30 pulses. Add nuts and pulse until finely chopped. With motor running, slowly add oil. Scrape sides and blend briefly. Mixture should be thick and somewhat creamy.

Cook spaghetti *al dente* according to package instructions. Reserve ⅔ cup cooking water, then drain pasta thoroughly. In a large heated bowl, combine pasta and pesto. Toss thoroughly, slowly adding reserved cooking liquid, until sauce is very creamy.

Divide among heated soup plates and garnish with cheese.

Wine: Honig Cellars Sauvignon Blanc
(California: Napa Valley) or another rich
Sauvignon Blanc from California

Orecchiette (Little Ears) with Fresh Tomatoes, Arugula & Garlic

THIS IS A DISH that celebrates summer and early fall, when all is fresh in the garden and greenmarket. The big-flavored pressed garlic and peppery arugula combine to add pungent notes to right-from-the-vine tomatoes (if at all possible, use several varieties). The cuplike orecchiette catch the soupy sauce, but this garlicky dish is most pleasurably served in a soup bowl with a spoon. Should you wish to make a winter version, substitute two cups of chopped canned tomatoes and one tablespoon of tomato paste for the fresh tomatoes and watercress for the arugula.

SERVES 4

3 tablespoons olive oil, preferably extra-virgin
4 plump garlic cloves, pressed
1 dried chile, crumbled
4 large vine-ripened tomatoes, coarsely chopped (about 5 cups)
1½ cups coarsely chopped arugula
Kosher salt and freshly ground black pepper
¾ pound orecchiette

Fill a large soup pot with salted water and bring to a boil.

Meanwhile, heat olive oil in a large sauté pan over medium heat. Add garlic and chile; stir until aromas are released, about 1 minute. Add tomatoes and stir together. Cover and cook over low heat, shaking pan occasionally, for 10 minutes, or until tomatoes are softened and juices are released. Remove pan from heat.

Quickly cook orecchiette according to package directions until *al dente*. Reserve 2 tablespoons of cooking water and drain.

When pasta is nearly done, bring sauce to a vigorous simmer.

Add drained pasta, arugula and reserved water to sauce. Stir over medium heat until arugula is wilted, about 1 minute.

Season with salt and pepper and divide among heated dishes.

Wine: Renato Ratti Dolcetto d'Alba (Italy: Piedmont)
or another Italian Dolcetto

Spaghettini with Garlic, Lemon & Anchovies

THIS DISH COMBINES THREE of our favorite flavors—dried chiles, lemons and anchovies—with the wonderful pasta basics of garlic and olive oil. Even if you think you don't like anchovies, try this dish; they cook into an amazingly subtle sauce, brightened by the lemons and tossed with a sprinkling of fresh basil.

SERVES 4

Minced zest and juice of 1 large lemon
6 tablespoons extra-virgin olive oil
2 small dried chiles, crumbled
1 2-ounce tin anchovies, drained and minced (or 7 salt-packed anchovies, rinsed and filleted)
3 tablespoons unsalted butter
1 pound spaghettini
6 plump garlic cloves, smashed and minced
Kosher salt and freshly ground black pepper
⅔ cup freshly grated Parmesan cheese
⅓ cup finely julienned fresh basil (lemon basil if available)

Fill a 6-quart soup pot with salted water and bring to a boil.

Combine lemon zest, lemon juice, oil, chiles and anchovies in a small saucepan or skillet. Cook over medium heat until hot. Add butter and stir until butter melts and anchovies have dissolved into the sauce, 3 to 5 minutes. Set aside.

Cook spaghettini in boiling water according to package directions. About 2 minutes before pasta has reached *al dente* stage, return sauce to very low heat. When hot, stir in garlic and count to 15. Remove skillet from heat.

Drain pasta and return to pot. Add sauce and toss well. Blend in salt, pepper and most of cheese. Then toss with basil.

Divide among heated soup plates. Sprinkle with remaining cheese.

Wine: Tiefenbrunner Pinot Grigio (Italy: Alto Adige) or a rich and fragrant Pinot Grigio from Italy's Friuli region

Conchigliette (Little Shells) with a Sauce of Caramelized Tomatoes, Roasted Peppers, Garlic & Basil

GILROY GARLIC FARMER LOU BONINO was roasting Anaheim peppers in a fiery tumbler the day we came to visit. "We add them to our tomato sauce," he told us. "That's how you get a really rich, smoky flavor." Here we've gone one step further by roasting the tomatoes, too. Serve this thick basil-and-garlic-rich sauce with any pasta that has indentations to catch the sauce.

SERVES 4

4	large Anaheim or mild poblano chiles
3	tablespoons olive oil
2 ¾-3	pounds ripe plum tomatoes, cut in half lengthwise
3	plump garlic cloves, minced
1	large sweet onion, minced
	Kosher salt and freshly ground black pepper
1	pound conchigliette
1	cup freshly torn basil
	Grated Parmesan cheese (optional)

Preheat grill or broiler. Roast peppers, turning often, until totally charred on outside. Transfer to a paper bag and fold shut. Let peppers stand until cool, then carefully remove skin. Seed, coarsely dice and set aside.

While peppers are roasting, prepare tomatoes. Place them cut side up on a large foil-lined cookie sheet. Drizzle with 2 tablespoons olive oil. Place pan in oven and roast at 450°F until tomato tops are partially browned and somewhat crinkled, about 50 minutes. (If necessary, brown lightly under broiler, being careful not to let juices that have collected around tomatoes dry up.) When done, immediately remove pan from oven and set aside.

While tomatoes are roasting, heat remaining tablespoon of oil over low heat in a large nonreactive saucepan. Add garlic and onions. Cover and cook until onions have softened, about 5 minutes. Remove from heat and reserve.

Spoon diced roasted peppers as well as tomatoes and juices into pot with onions, scraping in any browned bits accumulated on pan. Add salt and pepper to taste. Cover and cook over low heat until onions are very soft and tomatoes fall apart, 25 to 30 minutes.

Pass mixture through a food mill into a clean pot, or puree in a food processor and pass through a strainer. Taste and adjust salt and pepper. Keep warm.

Fill a soup pot with salted water and bring to a boil. Cook pasta according to package direc-tions until *al dente*. Reserve ¼ cup cooking water, then drain pasta thoroughly.

Add pasta, basil and reserved liquid to sauce. Toss thoroughly and serve in heated soup plates. If you wish, garnish lightly with cheese.

Wine: Rabbit Ridge Zinfandel
(California: Sonoma County) or another Zinfandel
from California

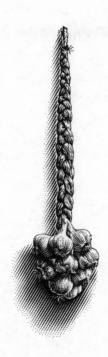

Spaghetti Carbonara

CARBONARA is an old-fashioned Italian pasta sauce of garlic, crisp bacon, raw eggs and cheese. The eggs "cook" when combined with the hot pasta and hot bacon sauce. Some cooks use lots of black pepper and no garlic. All Italian cooks use pancetta, a cured, unsmoked bacon; however, you may also use a lightly cured, heavily smoked Virginia bacon. There are many theories about carbonara's origins. Italian cooking authority Marcella Hazan suggests that it goes back only to World War II, when GIs brought their rations of bacon and eggs to Italian cooks. Others say the name comes from the very generous use of black pepper. Fred has always thought it was a favorite food of coal miners. Linda, who believes that a dried chile "lifts" the flavor of most food, uses one in this and then discards it. Fred believes that discarding the browned garlic is heresy. He minces it, adding it back to the pasta along with the parsley. If you are concerned about using raw eggs, this recipe is not for you.

**SERVES 2 FOR DINNER,
4 AS A FIRST COURSE**

4 ounces pancetta or bacon,
　cut into ¼-inch cubes

2 tablespoons olive oil

3 plump garlic cloves, smashed

1 dried red chile (optional)

⅓ cup dry white wine

4 large egg yolks

2 teaspoons freshly ground black
　pepper, plus more if you wish

½ cup grated Parmesan cheese

½ cup grated Romano cheese
　Kosher salt

½ pound spaghetti

⅓ cup minced fresh flat-leaf parsley

Combine pancetta or bacon, olive oil, garlic and chile, if using, in a very small saucepan. Cook over low heat, stirring occasionally, until bacon is crisp, 10 to 12 minutes. Remove and discard chile; set browned garlic aside if you want to use it in the final dish. Add wine to pan and simmer 5 minutes to reduce alcohol flavor. Set aside.

In a large mixing bowl, combine egg yolks, pepper, ¼ cup of the Parmesan cheese and the Romano cheese. Beat together vigorously.

Fill a large soup pot with water. Bring to a vigorous boil, add 1 teaspoon salt, then pasta. Cook until pasta is *al dente*, 8 to 10 minutes. While pasta cooks, heat bacon sauce until hot. Drain pasta well, but do not rinse.

Transfer pasta to bowl with egg mixture and toss thoroughly.

Pour hot bacon sauce over pasta and toss again to coat evenly. Add parsley, remaining ¼ cup Parmesan and (if desired) minced browned garlic and toss again.

Divide pasta among heated soup plates and serve.

Wine: Riccardo Falchine Chianti Colli Sensi "Titolato Colombaia" (Italy: Tuscany) or a Barbera from Italy

THE MYSTERIOUS WOLFSBANE STRATEGY

WE HAD TO SEE IT AGAIN. On a project like this one, no research opportunity can be missed, so we went to the video store to rent the 1931 film *Dracula*, with Bela Lugosi. Instead of garlic heads and flowers woven into a wreath and placed on Lucy's pillow and others draped above her door, Dr. Van Helsing uses wolfsbane to protect her. As the sweet Lucy dreams, the nurse, not knowing of the strategy, unlatches the door, moves the wolfsbane away and leaves the room, opening the way for the hungry (and thirsty) count to work his will on her.

Wolfsbane is a potent poison, and it is well known that it can keep werewolves at bay. But there is no evidence that it can repel a greedy vampire. Was the substitution of wolfsbane for garlic a business decision? Can it be that the director and the screen writer were fearful of offending the garlic-hating movie-going public of the early 1930s? Or were they themselves allium wimps? We'll never know why, since the creators of this film classic, like Dracula himself, have long since started taking their dirt naps.

Roman Polanski, on the other hand, got it right. In his 1967 film *The Fearless Vampire Killers*, garlic is everywhere. It is first mentioned in one of the earliest scenes. And at the inn where the vampire hunter and his apprentice are staying, there is more garlic than at Gilroy, clear evidence that the locals are on a vampire alert. The only problem is that there is no garlic in the bathroom, and Sara, the innkeeper's daughter, is joined by His Excellency in a sudsy tub, where he partakes of her blood.

Polanski, playing the assistant, munches frequently on whole raw garlic heads to protect himself while at work, and at the end of the film, although he has not killed any vampires, he himself has not been bitten. (Polanski has recently produced a stage musical based on his film, and, yes, garlic is big in it.)

The most brilliant of the Dracula films is *Bram Stoker's Dracula*, produced in 1992 by Francis Ford Coppola. Guided by Dracula expert Leonard Wolf, Coppola crafted a sweeping and breathtaking movie. On the other hand, he gives short shrift to garlic. It is never mentioned, although at one point we see one hefty braid in a fleeting shot. Hardly enough to win approval of the California garlic establishment.

Chronicling the legend in 1995, Mel Brooks brought out *Dracula: Dead and Loving It*, with Leslie Nielsen as the vampire. Brooks was true to the story and stuck with garlic. Lucy is back, but not for long. Her four-poster bed and all the windows and doors in her room are festooned with long braids of Super Colossal California Early, more than enough, one would think, to take care of any interloper. But Renfield, Dracula's beetle-and-bug-eating assistant, creeps in and removes just enough cloves from one window to allow the thirsty count passage, and suddenly Lucy is in the netherworld, awaiting the bloodiest staking of a heart in movie history.

Clearly, garlic can work. But it has to be directly in the path of the monster if he is to be held at bay.

Pasta with Winter Squash, Shallots, Garlic & Mascarpone

IF PUMPKIN OR SQUASH-FILLED RAVIOLI are delicious, it stands to reason that nuggets of winter squash, slowly braised with garlic and shallots for added complexity, are an outstanding topping for pasta, especially with the luxurious addition of mascarpone and freshly grated Parmesan cheese.

SERVES 4

2-2½ pounds winter squash
     (acorn or butternut)
⅓ cup olive oil
1 dried chile, crumbled
½ cup finely diced shallots
3 plump garlic cloves, minced
    Kosher salt and freshly ground
     white pepper
    Freshly grated nutmeg
1 pound pasta such as orecchiette
    or fusilli
1 tablespoon minced fresh tarragon
    or fennel weed
⅔ cup mascarpone
½ cup freshly grated Parmesan cheese

Cut squash in half and then in quarters. Remove seeds and carefully peel or cut away skin. Cut flesh into ¼-inch-thick slices, then cut coarsely into medium-sized pieces. Set aside.

Heat olive oil over high heat in a large sauté pan or skillet. Add chile and stir for 30 seconds. Reduce heat to medium-low and stir in shallots, garlic and squash. Season with salt, white pepper and several generous gratings of nutmeg. Cover tightly and cook, stirring occasionally, until squash is tender, 15 to 25 minutes. (If squash cooks quickly, set it aside, uncovered. Then reheat it over high heat while pasta drains.)

While squash is cooking, cook pasta according to package directions. Drain thoroughly.

Add tarragon or fennel, mascarpone and half of the Parmesan to pasta. Stir gently but thoroughly to melt mascarpone. Stir in squash mixture.

Divide among 4 heated soup plates. Garnish with remaining Parmesan and serve.

Wine: Maculan Breganze di Breganze (Italy: Veneto)
or a Tocai from Italy's Friuli region

Lemon Linguine with Green Tomatoes & Sage

OHIO'S EARLY FALL generally leaves us with a multitude of green tomatoes. Besides frying, pickling, preserving and turning them into jam, we also serve green tomatoes as a piquant and tangy, slightly peppery pasta topping, perfect for lemon linguine or even plain linguine.

SERVES 4

¼ cup extra-virgin olive oil

1 dried red chile pepper, crumbled

3 plump garlic cloves, smashed
   and minced

   Minced zest of 1 lemon

6 cups coarsely chopped green tomatoes

1 teaspoon minced fresh sage

1 pound lemon linguine
   (available in specialty markets) or
   ordinary linguine

   Kosher salt and freshly ground
   black pepper

3 tablespoons grated Parmesan cheese

Heat oil, chile pepper and garlic in a large sauté pan over medium heat. When garlic is softened, stir in lemon zest, tomatoes and sage. Cook, stirring often, until tomatoes are tender, about 15 minutes.

Meanwhile, bring a large pot of salted water to a rolling boil.

Cook linguine according to package directions to *al dente* stage. Drain well.

Add cooked linguine to cooked sauce and stir together over medium heat for 2 minutes. Season generously with salt and pepper.

Divide among heated plates and sprinkle with cheese.

Wine: Domaine Marcell Deiss Pinot Blanc
(France: Alsace) or an Italian Pinot Bianco
from the Trentino region

Linguine with Red Clam Sauce

THIS RICH AND GARLICKY tomato sauce perfumed with fresh clam stock and studded with meltingly tender clams is one of our very best dishes. We begin the meal with prosciutto, melon and lime juice. Then we add a crisp salad and some good bread, and as Fred always says, "We are in Yum City."

SERVES 4

⅓ cup olive oil
2 plump garlic cloves, smashed
1 cup dry white vermouth
3 dozen cherrystone clams, scrubbed and soaked for 1 hour (or 3 cups good-quality fresh chopped clams with liquor)
1 sprig fresh thyme, or pinch of dried
1 large sweet onion, finely diced
2 dried chiles, crumbled
5 plump garlic cloves, pressed
1 28-ounce can crushed tomatoes with their juice
1 3-ounce can tomato paste
1 teaspoon fresh thyme leaves
2 teaspoons minced fresh oregano
Kosher salt and freshly ground black pepper

1 pound linguine
¼ cup minced fresh flat-leaf parsley
15 fresh basil leaves, julienned
Grated Parmesan cheese for garnish

Combine 1 tablespoon olive oil, smashed garlic and vermouth in a large soup pot over medium heat. When bubbling, add clams and thyme. Cover and cook over medium-low heat until shells open, 8 to 12 minutes. Remove pan from heat. Take clams from shells, making sure that clam juices spill into pot. Strain pot liquid through a coffee filter or cheesecloth to eliminate any sand. Set aside. Coarsely chop clams and reserve.

In a large, heavy saucepan, heat remaining olive oil over medium heat. Add onion and chiles. Cover and reduce heat to low. Cook until onions have wilted, about 4 minutes. Stir in garlic, cover and cook until softened, about 2 minutes.

Add crushed tomatoes, tomato paste, 2 cups reserved clam juices, thyme and oregano. Increase heat to high and cook until mixture begins to boil. Lower heat and simmer, with cover somewhat ajar, for 30 minutes. If sauce seems too thick, stir in remaining clam juices. Season with salt and pepper.

Shortly before serving, fill a large pot with salted water and bring to a rolling boil. Add linguine and cook according to package directions.

Reheat sauce. When bubbling, add clams and parsley. Drain pasta, reserving 2 tablespoons of cooking water. Add drained pasta to sauce and toss thoroughly.

Divide among heated serving plates and sprinkle with fresh basil and cheese.

Wine: Regaleali Rosso del Conte (Italy: Sicily)
or another light and fruity red wine from Italy

""Dragon-breath therapy"
calls for eating six raw cloves of garlic
a day to protect against colds.

Baked Fusilli with Savoy Cabbage, Endive & Dandelion Greens

GARLIC AND BITTER GREENS make a dazzling marriage, especially when combined with the mellow sweetness of cabbage. This unusual baked pasta is one of our favorites, especially in springtime when we are able to get baby dandelion greens. If they are unavailable, use the larger cultivated ones or a large head of radicchio. And if you have some, include a handful of wild garlics.

SERVES 4 TO 6

½   cup olive oil
1   dried red chile pepper, crumbled
4   garlic cloves, minced
    Minced zest of 1 lemon
1   large red onion, thinly sliced
4   cups shredded Savoy cabbage
2   Belgian endives, trimmed and
    finely shredded crosswise
2   cups baby dandelion greens or
    1 head radicchio, trimmed
    and finely shredded
    Kosher salt
1   pound fusilli
2   tablespoons unsalted butter
    Freshly ground black pepper

¾   cup freshly grated Parmesan cheese,
    plus more for topping
¼   cup julienned fresh basil

Preheat oven to 450°F. Using 1 tablespoon oil, thoroughly grease a 3-quart ovenproof casserole.

Combine remaining oil and chile pepper in a large sauté pan and cook over medium heat until hot. Add garlic, lemon zest, onions, cabbage, endives and dandelion greens. Blend well, cover and cook over low heat until cabbage is tender, about 25 minutes, stirring occasionally.

While cabbage is cooking, fill a large pot with water, add salt, and bring to a boil over high heat. Cook fusilli at a very slow boil for 5 minutes less than directed on package. Reserve ½ cup liquid, draining the rest. Toss fusilli with cooked cabbage mixture, reserved pasta liquid, butter, salt and pepper to taste, ½ cup cheese and basil. Spoon into prepared casserole. Sprinkle evenly with remaining cheese. Bake in preheated oven for 10 minutes, or until top is golden brown.

Serve in heated soup plates and garnish with more cheese.

Wine: Anselmi Soave (Italy: Soave) or another good Soave

Macaroni & Cheese with Tomato Topping

THIS IS A WONDERFULLY hearty dish. If you make it ahead, combine sauce with macaroni just before baking.

SERVES 8

- 1 pound elbow macaroni
- ½ cup fine dry bread crumbs
- ½ cup finely grated Parmesan cheese
- 3 tablespoons minced fresh flat-leaf parsley
- 6 tablespoons unsalted butter, melted
- 1 medium onion, minced
- 3 plump garlic cloves, pressed
- 1 fresh red chile, seeded and minced
- 3 tablespoons unbleached flour
- 3 cups whole milk, heated
- 3 cups grated sharp yellow Cheddar
- 1 cup low-fat (not no-fat) sour cream
- 1 teaspoon kosher salt
- 1 teaspoon freshly ground white pepper
- 1 tablespoon minced fresh chives
- 2 teaspoons fresh thyme or 1 teaspoon dried
- 2 large ripe tomatoes, cut into ¼-inch slices

Preheat oven to 375°F. Generously butter a 3-quart casserole.

Cook macaroni for 2 minutes less than directed on package, or until *al dente*. Drain and set aside.

Combine bread crumbs, Parmesan and 2 tablespoons parsley in a small bowl and set aside.

In a small nonstick skillet, melt 2 tablespoons of the butter over medium heat. Add onion, garlic and chile. Cover tightly, reduce heat to low and cook until vegetables are softened, 3 to 5 minutes. Using a slotted spoon, transfer solids to a small bowl. Stir any remaining butter into bread-crumb mixture.

In a large, heavy saucepan, melt remaining 4 tablespoons butter over medium heat. Whisk in flour, then gradually whisk in milk and bring just to bubbling point. Reduce heat to simmer, stirring for a few minutes, until thickened. Stir in Cheddar, sour cream, salt and white pepper. Add onion mixture, remaining 1 tablespoon of parsley, chives and thyme. Add salt and macaroni; blend well.

Pour into casserole. Distribute sliced tomatoes over top. Sprinkle bread-crumb mixture evenly over tomatoes.

Bake until top is browned and sauce is hot and bubbly, 30 to 40 minutes. Serve hot.

Wine: Elk Cove Pinot Gris (Oregon: Willamette Valley) or rich Marsanne from California

Thai-Style Noodles with Garlic Peanut Sauce

WE HAVE NO IDEA whether our creamy, tangy peanut sauce is authentic. All we know is that the sourness of tamarind and the warm flavor of peanut butter blend well with fresh garlic and the heat of chile paste. Sesame oil and soy sauce speak of Asia, while lime juice and coconut milk enhance the flavor contrasts. Toss the sauce with tasty buckwheat noodles and you have a silky but crunchy room-temperature noodle salad. Should you wish to serve this as a main dish for supper, add cooked shrimp or strips of grilled chicken breast.

SERVES 6 TO 8

- 1 pound buckwheat noodles
- 1 tablespoon tamarind paste (available in most Indian and Asian markets)
- ½ cup boiling water
- ½ cup chunky peanut butter
- 3 plump garlic cloves, smashed and minced
- 1 tablespoon Chinese chili paste
- ½ cup unsweetened coconut milk (available in many supermarkets and all Asian markets)
- 3 tablespoons minced fresh gingerroot
- 1 tablespoon minced fresh lemongrass
  Juice of 3 limes
- ¼ cup dark soy sauce
- 2 tablespoons dark sesame oil
- 1 cup bean sprouts (optional)
- ⅓ cup minced fresh cilantro

Cook noodles according to package directions. When done, drain thoroughly and refresh with cold water. Set aside.

In a large bowl, combine tamarind paste and boiling water. Stir until paste is dissolved. Add peanut butter and stir vigorously until mixture is smooth. Stir in garlic and chili paste. Blend in coconut milk, ginger, lemongrass, lime juice, soy sauce and sesame oil.

Add noodles and bean sprouts, if using, to peanut sauce. Blend gently but thoroughly. Just before serving, stir in cilantro. Serve at room temperature.

Wine: Zind-Humbrecht Riesling (France: Alsace)
or R. H. Phillips Dunnigan Hills Viognier EXP
or another good Alsatian Riesling

Pizza with Caramelized Onions & Garlic

WHEN COOKED UNDER COVER very slowly, onions and garlic caramelize into a luscious mixture that is almost jammy. Rosemary adds a delicate piney flavor, prosciutto some smoky notes. Creamy fontina cheese melts into a sublime topping for this lustrous pizza.

MAKES ONE 12-TO-14-INCH PIZZA

- 6 tablespoons butter
- 1 jumbo sweet onion, coarsely diced
- 3 plump garlic cloves, smashed and minced
- 1 teaspoon minced fresh rosemary or ½ teaspoon dried
- 2-3 tablespoons cornmeal
  Dough for 1 pizza (page 218)
- 1 tablespoon olive oil
  Freshly ground black pepper
- 3 ounces thinly sliced prosciutto, cut into medium-wide strips
- ½ cup grated Italian fontina cheese

Melt butter in a heavy-bottomed skillet over low heat. Stir in onions and garlic. Cover and cook over very low heat, shaking pan from time to time, until onions begin to caramelize, 45 to 60 minutes. Stir, uncovered, until onions are darkly caramelized, 5 to 10 minutes. Using a slotted spoon, transfer onion mixture to a bowl. Stir in rosemary and reserve.

Place a baking stone or pizza tile, if using, on the lowest oven rack. Preheat oven to 500°F. Sprinkle a peel or pizza pan with cornmeal.

On a lightly floured surface, pat and roll out dough into a large round. Begin stretching dough over closed fists to make a thin 14-inch round. Place round on prepared pan or peel. Using your fingertips, dimple entire surface of dough. Then brush with olive oil.

Distribute onion mixture evenly over pizza. Sprinkle lavishly with pepper. Then scatter prosciutto over surface. Sprinkle with grated cheese.

Place pan in oven or transfer pizza from peel to baking stone. Bake pizza until bottom of crust is nicely browned, 12 to 15 minutes. Serve at once.

Wine: Dessilani Barbera (Italy: Piedmont)
or another Barbera from Italy

Fontina Pizza with Roasted Garlic, Mashed Potatoes & Clams

IN THIS SIMPLE PIZZA, roasted garlic and mashed potatoes blend together into a glorious topping. The briny, tender clams and fontina cheese make a winning combination.

If you have thin-skinned potatoes, just scrub them; don't bother peeling. And if you can capture the clams' juices, blend those into the potatoes, too. For the best results when making pizza, treat yourself to a large, rectangular tile and the flat wooden shovel called a peel. There is nothing better than the very crisp pizza you get when you bake it on the tile. You'll make your breads that way, too.

MAKES ONE 12-TO-14-INCH PIZZA

1 pound Yukon gold potatoes, peeled and cut into ¾-inch cubes
2 tablespoons unsalted butter
1 tablespoon minced fresh chives
2 teaspoons minced fresh thyme leaves
Salt and freshly ground white pepper to taste
2 tablespoons cornmeal
Dough for 1 pizza (page 218)
1 tablespoon olive oil
1 plump head of garlic, roasted (page 34) and mashed
2 dozen small fresh clams, shelled
⅔ cup shredded Italian fontina cheese

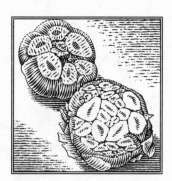

Cover potatoes with salted water in a large saucepan. Bring to a boil over high heat. Cover, reduce heat and simmer until potatoes are tender, about 20 minutes. Reserve ½ cup of potato water, then drain potatoes well and return them to saucepan. Over very low heat, mash potatoes and butter with a masher. Then beat in enough reserved cooking liquid to make a fairly creamy mixture. Remove from heat, blend in chives, thyme, salt and pepper to taste. Set aside.

Place a baking stone or tile, if using, on the lowest oven rack. Preheat oven to 500°F. Evenly sprinkle a peel or pizza pan with cornmeal.

On a lightly floured surface, pat or roll out dough into a large round. Begin stretching dough over closed fists to make a thin 14-inch round. Place round on prepared pan or peel. Using your fingertips, dimple entire surface of dough. Then brush with olive oil.

First spread garlic, then potato mixture over surface. Distribute clams over mashed potatoes. Sprinkle evenly with fontina.

Place pan in oven, or carefully transfer pizza from peel to hot tile. Bake until bottom of crust is nicely browned, 12 to 15 minutes. Serve at once.

Wine: Lockwood Vineyard Chardonnay
(California: Monterey County)
or another Chardonnay from Monterey County

Pizza with Eggplant, Garden Tomatoes & Garlic

EGGPLANT, TOMATOES, GARLIC and basil blend beautifully as a topping for this pizza. It is at its best in late summer when the tomatoes are at their peak of flavor.

MAKES ONE 12-TO-14 INCH PIZZA

2   small Japanese eggplants, about
    6 inches long and 2 inches in
    diameter (or 4 very small, short
    regular eggplants)
    Up to ¼ cup olive oil
2-3 tablespoons cornmeal
    Dough for 1 pizza (page 218)
3   medium-sized ripe garden-fresh
    tomatoes, cut into ⅓-inch-thick
    slices, then cut in half crosswise
3   plump garlic cloves, thinly sliced
6   fresh basil leaves, julienned
    Kosher salt and freshly ground
    black pepper
⅓   cup grated Parmesan cheese

Carefully cut a very thin slice off each side of each eggplant. Then cut eggplants lengthwise into thin (⅓-inch-thick) slices. Preheat a gas grill or broiler, with a rack 3 inches from ele-ment. Lightly brush eggplant slices with olive oil. Grill or broil slices until golden brown on each side, 2 to 4 minutes a side. Reserve.

Place a baking stone or pizza tile, if using, on lowest oven rack. Preheat oven to 500°F. Sprinkle a peel or pizza pan with cornmeal.

On a lightly floured surface, pat and roll out dough into a large round. Begin stretching dough over closed fists to make a thin 14-inch round. Place round on prepared pan or peel. Using your fingertips, dimple entire surface of dough. Then brush with 1 tablespoon olive oil.

Distribute eggplant evenly over pizza. Then distribute tomatoes evenly over eggplant. Scatter with garlic slivers, then with basil. Sprinkle with salt and pepper. Drizzle with 1 tablespoon olive oil. Sprinkle evenly with cheese.

Place pan in oven, or carefully transfer pizza from peel to baking stone. Bake pizza until bottom of crust is nicely browned, 12 to 15 minutes. Serve at once.

Wine: Ravenswood Zinfandel Sonoma County (California: Sonoma County) or a Dolcetto from Italy's Piedmont

Red, White & Green Pizza

THIS PIZZA TASTES as good as it looks. The three cheeses and the garlic work especially well together, sparked by the peppery quality of the arugula. You can also use nasturtium leaves; if neither is available, use escarole or julienned green bell pepper instead.

MAKES ONE 14-INCH PIZZA

Dough for 1 pizza (page 218)
2   tablespoons cornmeal
2   tablespoons olive oil, plus more
      for drizzling
1½   cups grated Italian fontina cheese
⅔   cup crumbled Roquefort, Maytag
      Blue or Gorgonzola cheese
4   plump garlic cloves, smashed and
      minced
¼   cup drained sun-dried tomatoes,
      cut into thin strips
½   cup thinly sliced red onions
12-14   arugula leaves
6   fresh basil leaves, julienned
½   cup coarsely grated Parmesan cheese

Place a baking stone or pizza tile, if using, on lowest oven rack. Preheat oven to 500°F. Sprinkle a peel or pizza pan with cornmeal.

On a lightly floured surface, pat or roll out dough into a large round. Begin stretching dough over closed fists to make a thin 14-inch round. Place round on prepared pan or peel.

Brush dough with 1 tablespoon olive oil. Sprinkle evenly with half of the fontina and Roquefort cheeses. Then sprinkle with garlic. Distribute tomatoes over cheeses, then onions, arugula and basil. Sprinkle evenly with remaining cheeses.

Place baking pan in oven or carefully transfer pizza from peel to baking stone. Bake until bottom of crust is nicely browned, 12 to 15 minutes. Serve at once.

Wine: Howell Mountain Vineyards "Old Vines" Zinfandel
(California: Napa Valley) or another rich Zinfandel

Dough for Thin Pizza

ADDING HONEY and a small amount of whole wheat flour makes this a very tasty dough and one that handles quite easily. It will keep in the refrigerator for several days before using; just bring it to room temperature before stretching. If you like your pizza very crisp on the bottom, bake it directly on a pizza stone or bread tile.

MAKES TWO 14-INCH PIZZAS

¾ cup warm water, plus more if needed
1 tablespoon wildflower honey
1 tablespoon active dry
   (not instant) yeast
¼ cup milk
2 tablespoons olive oil
2¾ cups unbleached flour
¼ cup whole wheat flour
1 teaspoon kosher salt

To proof yeast, blend ¼ cup warm water, honey and yeast in a small bowl and let rest in a warm place until mixture is foamy, 5 to 10 minutes.

In a glass measure, combine remaining ½ cup water, milk and oil. Combine flours and salt in the bowl of a food processor. With motor running, pour in yeast mixture, then water mixture. Process just until dough leaves side of bowl and forms a ball. If dough seems too dry, add more water, 2 tablespoons at a time. Process briefly again. Dough should be nice and elastic.

Lightly flour a board and knead dough for a few minutes. Turn dough into a lightly oiled bowl, cover with plastic wrap, and let rise in a warm place until doubled, about an hour.

To bake, follow directions in individual pizza recipes, pages 213-16.

FISH & SHELLFISH

Beer-Battered Walleye with Garlic   224

Pan-Fried Trout with Garlic Pecan Lemon Butter   225

Bourride with Lemon Pepper Aioli   226

Red Snapper with Bay Leaves, Cumin & Garlic   228

Lime & Cilantro Marinated Swordfish with a Fruited Salsa   230

Braised Swordfish in Raïto (a Garlic, Onion & Tomato Ragout)   232

Braised Alaskan King Salmon with Simple Garlic Ratatouille   234

Baked Mackerel with Olives, Onions & Garlic   235

Grilled Tuna Steaks with Green Olive & Garlic Pesto   236

Cape Cod Bluefish with Garlic, Onions & Exotic Spices   238

Calamari in Brazilian Tomato Garlic Broth   239

Oyster Po'Boy with Spicy Lemon Garlic Mayonnaise   240

Chinese-Style Fried Soft-Shell Crabs with Garlic Chile Confetti   242

Somewhat Portuguese Shrimp Piri Piri   244

Steamed Clams with Garlic & White Wine   245

Shrimp & Sausage Stew with Corn   246

Amazing Mussels with Saffron, Garlic & Sun-Dried Tomatoes   248

Mussels Marinara   249

Baked Lobsters with Clam Chowdered-Garlic Potato Hash Stuffing   250

Celebration Paella   252

DRIVING MR. GARLIC

GIVE US GARLIC," we told the state of Ohio. But it was already taken. Wendy Lindemuth had gotten there 10 years ahead of us. And so had Bob Zimmerman, a garlic farmer, who wore "Garlic 1" on his car. We had to settle for "Garlic 2." We wondered about other states, and after endless negotiations with motor vehicle bureaucracies, we learned that 22 of the 50 had issued garlic plates. Twelve of those who drive with Mr. Garlic were willing to talk about it.

Wendy Lindemuth confesses to having been garlic crazy for most of her life. When she and her husband, Bruce, went to Europe on a four-year business assignment, they traveled widely, exploring regional cuisines and taking good note of how creatively garlic was used.

She brought what she learned to her own Ohio kitchen and has been converting garlic-resisting family and friends into true lovers of "this awesome food of the gods."

In 1987 she bought her garlic license plate. She will soon give the vehicle to their daughter Ashley, but with mixed emotions. Ashley not only wants the car, she wants the license plate!

When John Romeo of Pittsburg, California, was in high school, they called him "Johnny Garlic." He regularly ate raw garlic in class, a practice that got him his nickname and frequently got him banished to the principal's office for offenses against the environment.

He and his wife, Anne, have collected a ton of garlic memorabilia. And to this day he wears a solid gold head of garlic on a chain around his neck. He recently turned down an offer, by a man from Gilroy, of $1,000 for his garlic license plate.

Margaret Leitch, cofounder of the Washington, D.C., Garlic Festival, got the Maryland garlic plate in 1994. "There is something about garlic that brings passion, love and life to people," she said. It was the abuse garlic suffered in restaurant kitchens that made her a such a passionate defender of it.

That passion cost her dearly. She was an executive in a computer software company, but her boss hated garlic; he told Margaret she could eat garlic only on weekends. That was unacceptable. So after nearly 10 years, she resigned. (Her former boss has seen the light and is now taking garlic pills.)

Harold E. Johnson, at 75, no longer drives. But he sent us a photograph taken in his driveway. It shows him sitting in a wheelchair looking at the license plate on his perfect 1985 Oldsmobile. Standing nearby, admiring the car, is his 21-year-old grandson.

The license plate has been a familiar sight in his town of East Walpole, Massachusetts, for 16 years. Now Johnson has decided to pass along his well-loved car to his grandson, together with the quixotic license plate, as a kind of reminder to enjoy life.

"I love garlic," said Jean Garlick, of Lansing, Michigan. "And as a nurse, I have always been interested in its medicinal use. Besides, I love the human Garlick, too—my husband." So when she got her first brand-new car in 1989, he got a garlic license plate for her, and she has had it ever since—a celebration of both culinary and family love.

(continued)

Mary Stevens wrote from Montana that when her late husband, Garland, was young, an older brother-in-law called him "Garlic." The nickname endured, and when the CB radio craze hit in the '70s, Garlic became his handle. He then decided to make it official; he ordered a garlic plate for his car and used it for the rest of his life.

For years Jeffrey Freehoff moved around Concord, New Hampshire, with "Chef" on his license plate. But when he became a restaurant manager, he relinquished the old plate and applied for one that would celebrate what he had always regarded as the one indispensable ingredient in the kitchen.

Joan Gussow, an emeritus professor of nutrition and an avid organic gardener, grows most of her own food, including garlic.

Her first choice for a vanity plate several years ago was "Compost." But the word seemed confusing: is it "a noun, a verb or a command?" So she asked the state of New York for "Broccoli," and her late husband asked for "Onions." Onions was taken, so he settled for "Garlic." Later they gave "Broccoli" to their son but kept their automotive salute to the stinking rose.

"I used to have license plate PAX 007," said Bibby Moore. "Pax for peace and 007 for you know who. I was an undercover agent for peace. But around age 45, I decided that I was too serious. So I got something on my tag that I believe in. I believe in garlic."

Salty and Gisela Green live on the Honey Grove Farm in Alsea, Oregon. Since 1989, their truck has carried the banner for Oregon garlic. That was when Salty retired from a sales career and became a full-time farmer. Soon thereafter he began growing garlic for a local restaurateur. When word got out, demand grew, and the Greens found themselves in the garlic business. Now when Salty drives up to make a delivery, there is no question about what he is bringing: it's right there on his license plate.

Joanne and Johnny Esau are garlic lovers. Both are famous in Vermont—Johnny for giving pickled garlic to his high-achieving fifth grade students, and Joanne for her high-profile Vermont Garlic Company, specializing in all kinds of garlic products. One day she wondered if anyone had bought Vermont's garlic license plate. No one had. And to her surprise and delight, her new plate bore the name of her fledgling company: Vermont Garlic.

A garlic license plate in the middle of Chicago?

No way it could belong to a farmer. Maybe just a garlic fanatic. We heard from Jim and Sandee Hempleman, who said it was as simple as that.

"We love garlic!" they told us. "We've had the plate since 1980. That was even before garlic was cool."

Beer-Battered Walleye with Garlic

ROUND THE GREAT LAKES, walleye is king. Broiled, fried or baked, this meaty freshwater fish is simply delicious. Our favorite version, however, is fried in a garlicky beer batter. We've found that the dark beer rounds out the garlic's flavor, making an especially tasty coating that enhances the delicate sweetness of the fish. You can accompany it with Lemon Pepper Aioli (page 153) or Spicy Lemon Garlic Mayonnaise (page 240) or even a sweet-and-sour sauce. And you must serve walleye with crispy potatoes. If you cannot find walleye, try this recipe with thick fillets of pike or perch.

SERVES 4

1	cup plus 2 tablespoons unbleached flour
	Kosher salt
1	teaspoon freshly ground white pepper
4	plump garlic cloves, pressed
1	cup dark beer, plus more if needed
2-2½	pounds boneless, skinless walleye or pike or perch fillets, cut in half crosswise
	Up to 1 cup canola oil

In a large mixing bowl, blend together flour, 1 teaspoon salt and white pepper. Add garlic and 1 cup beer, whisking well until smooth. Let stand at room temperature for 30 minutes.

Stir batter. It should be somewhat thicker than pancake batter in order to thoroughly coat fish. If it is too thick, slowly thin with a bit more beer.

Preheat oven to 250°F for warming.

Pour oil ¼ inch deep into a large, cast-iron skillet and place over medium-high heat until hot. Dip fish fillets into batter, making certain they are well coated. Place in hot fat without crowding and cook until golden brown on one side, about 4 minutes. Turn and fry on other side until golden. Transfer cooked fish to paper towels to drain. Keep fried fillets warm in oven while you fry the rest of fish.

Sprinkle with salt and serve.

Wine: Calera Wine Co. Chardonnay "Central Coast" (California: Central Coast) or another Chardonnay from California's Central Coast region

Pan-Fried Trout
with Garlic Pecan Lemon Butter

THESE PAN-FRIED TROUT, lightly coated with nuts, are just delicious, especially with our special topping. There's enough garlic in this pecan-and-lemon-butter sauce to give it a kick. Pecans and baked sweet potatoes seem made for each other, so we usually serve them with this dish.

SERVES 4

1   teaspoon kosher salt

1   teaspoon freshly ground white pepper

2   tablespoons finely ground pecans

2   tablespoons fine dry bread crumbs

¼   cup milk

4   dressed trout, 8-10 ounces each

3   tablespoons canola oil

4   tablespoons (½ stick) unsalted butter

½   cup pecan pieces

3   plump garlic cloves, smashed
      and minced

¼   teaspoon ground red pepper (cayenne)

1   tablespoon fresh lemon juice

1   tablespoon minced fresh chives

1   tablespoon minced fresh
      flat-leaf parsley
    Lemon slices for garnish

In a shallow soup plate, blend together salt, white pepper, ground pecans and bread crumbs. Pour milk into another soup plate. Dip fish in milk, then roll in crumb mixture to coat evenly. Place fish on a cake rack until ready to cook, letting stand up to ½ hour.

Heat oil and 1 tablespoon butter in a large, heavy skillet over medium-high heat. Add fish, reduce heat to medium and cook until golden, about 4 minutes. Turn and cook on other side until golden and fish feels firm to the touch, 4 to 5 minutes more. Transfer fish to heated serving plates.

Drain off fat. Place remaining 3 tablespoons butter in skillet and melt over medium-high heat. Add pecans and garlic. Cook, stirring constantly, until pecans are nicely browned. Add cayenne and stir for 30 seconds. Remove skillet from heat and stir in lemon juice, chives and parsley.

Pour sauce over each fish, making certain that nuts are evenly divided among them. Garnish with lemon slices and serve.

Wine: Patz & Hall Chardonnay "Russian River Valley"

(California: Sonoma County)

or a rich white Burgundy from France

Bourride with Lemon Pepper Aioli

BOURRIDE IS A HEAVENLY FISH STEW with roots in Provence. It's a tomato-less version of bouillabaisse, thickened with *aioli* to give a very special flavor and texture. We've kept this process simple; some old recipes call for first thickening the stock with egg yolks, then adding the *aioli* as well. Bourride is often made with monkfish or mullet. We prefer red snapper or cod, or you could use several varieties of fish and shellfish, as well as boiled new potatoes. A crunchy salad is all you need to complete your meal.

SERVES 4 TO 6

¼ cup olive oil
1 small dried chile, crumbled
4 garlic cloves, chopped
2 cups coarsely chopped yellow onions
2 large carrots, coarsely chopped
1 medium-sized fennel bulb, coarsely chopped
9 cups rich fish stock
½ cup dry white wine
    Strip of orange peel, 1 x 3 inches
¼ teaspoon saffron
    Kosher salt and freshly ground black pepper

3 pounds red snapper fillets, cut into six 8-ounce portions
    Lemon Pepper Aioli (page 153)
8-12 slices French bread, toasted (croutons)
    Minced fresh chives, preferably garlic chives

Heat olive oil in a large, heavy soup pot over medium heat. Add chile, garlic, onions, carrots and fennel. Cover and reduce heat. Cook, stirring occasionally, until onions soften, about 5 minutes. Add fish stock, wine, orange peel and saffron. Increase heat until liquids bubble. Cover and simmer for 1 hour. Strain soup into a 2-quart glass measure, pressing solids to extract flavor. There should be 7 cups soup; if there is more, simmer briskly to reduce. Stir in salt and pepper.

Just before serving, bring soup to a brisk simmer. Add fish, reduce heat and simmer slowly until fish is done, about 8 minutes per inch of thickness. To check for doneness, gently insert the tines of a fork into thick part of fish to check appearance of flesh. It should be almost opaque.

While fish is cooking, liberally coat 6 croutons with *aioli*. Place a crouton in each of 6 heated soup plates. Spoon ½ cup remaining *aioli* into a small mixing bowl.

Carefully transfer a portion of fish to top each crouton. Gradually add 1 cup soup to ½ cup of *aioli*, whisking vigorously to blend. Then add mixture to pot of fish soup and blend together. Ladle soup into soup plates with fish. Sprinkle with chives.

Serve with extra croutons and remaining *aioli* on the side.

Wine: André Brunel Domaine Becassone
White Côtes-du-Rhône (France: Rhône Valley)
or a Viognier from California

Red Snapper
with Bay Leaves, Cumin & Garlic

WHILE THERE ARE MANY IMITATORS, there is only one real American red snapper. Its fillets are thick and meaty, with a very firm flesh when cooked. The tomato-based sauce with green olives is most delicious and unusual. Our cooking time is based on fish that's about 1¼ inches thick at its center. Reduce the time accordingly for thinner fillets. You can substitute halibut for snapper. If you have preserved lemons, they would make a superb garnish for this dish.

SERVES 4 TO 6

4 tablespoons olive oil
1 small dry chile, crumbled
5 plump garlic cloves, smashed
   and minced
¾ cup minced shallots
2 bay leaves
1 teaspoon ground cumin
1 generous pinch ground allspice
½ cup dry white wine
2 cups canned crushed tomatoes
¾ cup peeled, seeded and finely
   diced ripe tomatoes
¼ cup chopped green olives,
   preferably imported

1 tablespoon fresh lime juice
   Kosher salt and freshly ground
   white pepper
2½-3 pounds American red snapper fillets
   or black sea bass or striped bass,
   cut into 4-6 portions
½ cup unbleached flour

Preheat oven to 450°F.

In a medium-sized saucepan, heat 2 tablespoons olive oil with chile. Add garlic, shallots and bay leaves. Cover and cook over low heat until shallots are softened, 3 to 4 minutes. Stir in cumin and allspice. Add wine, increase heat to medium-high and simmer uncovered until liquid is reduced by half. Add crushed tomatoes, diced tomatoes, olives, lime juice, salt and white pepper. Bring to a simmer, cover, reduce heat and cook for 15 minutes. Remove bay leaves and reserve.

Season fish fillets with salt and pepper. Dredge in flour to coat lightly.

Heat remaining 2 tablespoons oil over high heat in a large, heavy skillet just big enough to hold fish in a single layer. Lightly brown fillets on both sides, about 4 minutes total. Carefully transfer fish to a warm plate.

Wipe out skillet. Return fish to pan and place skin side down in a single layer.

Pour reserved sauce over fish. Cover tightly with a lid or heavy foil. Place in oven and braise for 9 minutes. Uncover and gently insert the tines of a fork into thick part of fish to check appearance of flesh, which should be firm and almost opaque.

Transfer portions to heated plates. Cover generously with sauce.

Wine: Saintsbury Chardonnay Carneros (California: Napa Valley) or an Australian Chardonnay

Lime & Cilantro Marinated Swordfish with a Fruited Salsa

LIME JUICE AND CILANTRO brighten this dish; they're incorporated into both the fruity marinade and the accompanying fruit-based salsa. This is a sensational summer fish dish.

SERVES 6

Marinade

2 plump garlic cloves, smashed and minced
1 teaspoon Dijon mustard
¼ cup fruit vinegar (peach, cherry, pear, raspberry)
1 tablespoon fresh lime juice
⅔ cup extra-virgin olive oil
2 tablespoons minced fresh cilantro
4 scallions, trimmed with tender green and minced
   Freshly ground white pepper
3½-4 pounds swordfish or grouper steaks, cut 1½ inches thick
   Kosher salt to taste

Salsa

½ cup finely diced fresh pears
½ cup finely diced fresh peaches or mango
¼ cup finely diced cucumber
¼ cup finely diced red onion
2 plump garlic cloves, smashed and minced
1 tablespoon finely diced pickled jalapeño pepper
2 tablespoons fruit vinegar
1 tablespoon fresh lime juice
1 tablespoon walnut oil
2 teaspoons honey
3 tablespoons minced fresh cilantro
   Kosher salt and freshly ground white pepper

To marinate fish: In a small bowl, thoroughly blend garlic, mustard, vinegar, lime juice, olive oil, cilantro, scallions and white pepper. Arrange fish in a single layer in a nonreactive shallow dish. Pour marinade over fish; turn to coat well on both sides. Let stand, turning several times, for 1 hour at room temperature or up to 3 hours in the refrigerator.

To prepare salsa: In another bowl, combine all ingredients. Blend well and refrigerate until needed.

To grill fish: Shortly before serving, thoroughly clean the surface of a gas or charcoal grill with a metal brush, then coat surface evenly with a vegetable spray. Heat grill until hot.

Remove fish from marinade and salt generously. Place on grill and cover. Turn after 5 minutes. Turn and grill 5 minutes on second side, or until done. To check for doneness, uncover and gently insert tines of a fork into thick part of fish. Flesh should be almost opaque, but with some rareness along bottom of the flakes.

When fish is cooked, transfer to heated serving dishes. Spoon fruit salsa over each piece. Sprinkle generously with additional white pepper.

Wine: Sanford Sauvignon Blanc Central Coast
(California: Santa Barbara County)
or a Sauvignon Blanc from New Zealand

Braised Swordfish in Raïto

(A GARLIC, ONION & TOMATO RAGOUT)

LINDA FIRST READ ABOUT RAÏTO, an unusual Provençal sauce, in the late Elizabeth David's celebrated work *A Book of Mediterranean Food*, published in 1950. David wrote lovingly about a "ragoût made of onions, tomatoes, garlic, pounded walnuts, thyme, rosemary, fennel, parsley, bay leaves, red wine, capers, and black olives, all simmered in olive oil." Served in Provençe on Christmas Eve, it was a sauce in which either dried salt cod or eels were cooked. We think it also makes a marvelous sauce for swordfish.

SERVES 6

⅓ cup olive oil

2 cups finely diced yellow onion

6 plump garlic cloves, smashed and minced

6 large vine-ripened tomatoes, peeled and finely diced

2 cups dry red wine, plus more if needed

⅓ cup ground walnuts

2 bay leaves

⅓ cup finely chopped pitted Niçoise olives

1 teaspoon ground fennel seeds

1 teaspoon fresh thyme leaves or ½ teaspoon dried

1 teaspoon minced fresh rosemary or ½ teaspoon dried

2 tablespoons capers, drained Kosher salt and freshly ground black pepper

3 pounds swordfish or halibut steaks cut 1 inch thick

¼ cup minced fresh flat-leaf parsley

Heat olive oil in a large, heavy skillet over low heat. Add onion and garlic. Cook, stirring often, until softened, 4 to 6 minutes. Add tomatoes and 1 cup wine. Increase heat and cook until mixture begins to bubble. Stir in walnuts, bay leaves, olives and fennel. If using dried herbs, add them as well. Cover, reduce heat to low and cook for 20 minutes.

Add ½ cup wine and stir vigorously, thoroughly scraping bottom of pan (nuts tend to stick). Cover and cook for 10 minutes more, or until tomatoes are absorbed into sauce. If using fresh herbs, stir in along with capers. Season generously with salt and pepper. This sauce can be prepared several hours ahead; hold at room temperature in skillet.

Preheat oven to 450°F. Stir remaining ½ cup wine into sauce and bring to a boil. Simmer for 2 to 3 minutes to reduce alcohol. Remove bay leaves. Arrange fish on top of sauce. Season fish with salt and pepper. Spoon some sauce over top as well.

Cover pan loosely with a sheet of foil and braise fish for 14 minutes, or until done. To check for doneness: when top of fish is firm and just opaque, cut into center of a fillet; fish should be opaque but very moist.

Carefully transfer fish to heated serving plates. If sauce seems too dry, add more wine and simmer for a few minutes. Stir parsley into sauce and spoon generously over fish.

Wine: Mommessin Morgon Beaujolais (France: Burgundy) or another fruity Beaujolais

Braised Alaskan King Salmon with Simple Garlic Ratatouille

ONE OF THE MOST FLAVORFUL salmons in the world is Alaskan King. Even better is the silky White, or Ivory, King, often available in late July and early August. Here we braise it with a simple, aromatic mixture of diced tomatoes, celery, garlic and onions—the basic ingredients for ratatouille. Minced green olives add a special note. This recipe was inspired by one generously shared with us by Ives Roubaud, executive chef of Chicago's celebrated Shaw's Crab House.

SERVES 4

2 plump garlic cloves, smashed and minced

4 imported green olives, rinsed, pitted and minced

¼ cup finely diced eggplant

¾ cup finely diced tomatoes

⅓ cup finely diced white onions

⅓ cup finely diced celery

2 tablespoons olive oil

4 8-ounce 1-inch-thick, fillets Alaskan king salmon, pin bones removed

⅓ cup dry white wine

¾ cup fish stock or bottled clam juice

Kosher salt and freshly ground white pepper

Preheat oven to 400°F.

In a small bowl, blend together garlic, olives, eggplant, tomatoes, onions and celery. Set aside.

Heat olive oil over medium-high heat in a heavy ovenproof skillet. Add salmon, skin side down, and sauté for 5 minutes. Remove skillet from heat. Pour wine over fillets. Cover evenly with vegetable mixture, allowing some to fall into pan juices. Braise fish in oven, uncovered, for 3 minutes. Add fish stock or clam juice, baste thoroughly and cook for an additional 3 minutes, or until fish is done to your preference. To check for doneness, gently insert tines of a fork into thick part of fish. Flesh should be almost opaque, but with some rareness along bottom of flakes.

Transfer fish to heated serving plates. Divide ratatouille among them. Season generously with salt and pepper.

Wine: Au Bon Climat Pinot Noir Santa Barbara County "La Bauge au Dessus," Bien Nacido Vineyard (California: Santa Barbara County) or a rich Pinot Noir from Oregon

Baked Mackerel
with Olives, Onions & Garlic

W'RE NOT SURE we've ever met a fish we didn't like. From delicate gray sole to oily fish like mackerel and bluefish, we enjoy them all, especially the rich ones. We've learned, however, that these luxurious fish are best when the seasonings have their own big personalities. In this recipe, a topping of green olives, garlic and onions with lemon and oregano is the perfect foil for the mackerel. A side of fried potatoes, a salad and a glass of wine are all you need to complete this simple meal.

SERVES 4

1   lemon
    Up to 2 tablespoons extra-virgin
     olive oil
⅔   cup finely chopped pimento-stuffed
     green olives
3   plump garlic cloves, smashed
     and minced
⅔   cup finely chopped yellow onion
¼   rounded teaspoon dried oregano
4   small (¾-1 pound each)
     mackerel, butterflied
    Kosher salt and freshly ground
     white pepper

Preheat oven to 475°F.

Remove zest from lemon and mince. Slice lemon in half and reserve. Lightly oil a shallow baking sheet.

In a small bowl, combine lemon zest, olives, garlic, onions and oregano. Arrange fish, skin side down, on baking sheet. Sprinkle with salt and white pepper. Spread olive mixture over tops of fish. Drizzle with a little oil.

Bake in preheated oven for 8 to 10 minutes, or until fish is done. To check for doneness, uncover and gently insert tines of a fork into thick part of fish. Flesh should be almost opaque.

Transfer fish to heated serving plates. Squeeze fresh lemon juice over each, then sprinkle generously with white pepper.

Wine: Michele Redde Sancerre Les Tuilières
(France: Loire) or a fruity, but crisp and flinty,
California Sauvignon Blanc

Grilled Tuna Steaks with Green Olive & Garlic Pesto

A SIMPLE MARINADE adds flavor and moisture to this grilled tuna. But what really makes the dish is the unusual pesto topping of green olives, garlic and basil—a fresh, zesty counterpoint to the tuna's wonderful richness. You might also enjoy serving this pesto with mackerel or bluefish.

SERVES 4

- 3 tablespoons rich red wine vinegar
- 2 teaspoons Dijon mustard
- ⅓ cup extra-virgin olive oil
- 2 plump garlic cloves, smashed and minced
- 1 small yellow onion, minced
  Freshly ground black pepper
- 4 tuna steaks, preferably yellowfin, 1 inch thick

Green Olive and Garlic Pesto

- ¾ cup coarsely chopped, pitted imported green olives
- 3 plump garlic cloves
- ¼ cup loosely packed fresh flat-leaf parsley
- ¼ cup loosely packed torn fresh basil leaves
  Zest of 1 lemon
- 2½ teaspoons fresh lemon juice
- 2 tablespoons extra-virgin olive oil
- ½ teaspoon kosher salt, plus more as needed
- ¼ teaspoon freshly ground black pepper, plus more as needed

In a small mixing bowl, blend together vinegar and mustard. Slowly whisk in olive oil to make a thick emulsion. Blend in garlic, onion and black pepper.

Place fish fillets in a glass or ceramic dish just large enough to hold them. Thoroughly coat fish with marinade and let stand for 1 hour, turning from time to time.

Meanwhile, make pesto: In the bowl of a food processor, combine olives, garlic, parsley, basil and lemon zest. Pulse until mixture is pureed. Add lemon juice. With motor running, slowly add olive oil, blending until mixture makes a thick puree. Blend in salt and pepper. Scrape pesto into a small dish and reserve.

Shortly before serving, thoroughly clean the surface of a gas or charcoal grill with a metal brush, then coat surface evenly with a vegetable spray. Heat grill until hot.

Remove fish from marinade and season with salt and pepper. Place on grill. Cook for 3 minutes, turn and grill for 3 minutes more. To check for doneness, carefully insert a knife into center and check color. We like our tuna rare in center.

Transfer fish to heated serving plates. Spread some pesto over top of each and serve.

Wine: Siduri Pinot Noir Sonoma Coast "Hirsch Vineyard"
(California: Sonoma County) or another
rich and complex California Pinot Noir

Cape Cod Bluefish
with Garlic, Onions & Exotic Spices

BLUEFISH IS A FULL-FLAVORED summer treat. Those from waters off Cape Cod—Cape blues as they are known—are considered by aficionados to be the very best. We often rub them with some mayonnaise, then treat them to serious, zesty seasonings, here a cumin-laced spice blend.

SERVES 4 TO 6

Olive oil
2 teaspoons kosher salt
½ teaspoon ground cumin
½ teaspoon ground cardamom
½ teaspoon ground coriander
½ teaspoon ground ginger
½ teaspoon dried oregano
½ teaspoon freshly ground white pepper
¼ teaspoon ground allspice
2 large bluefish fillets, each about 1¼ pounds
3 plump garlic cloves, pressed
½ large sweet or white onion, finely diced
⅔ cup Hellmann's or Best Foods mayonnaise
1 lemon, cut in half

Lightly coat a large, shallow baking dish with olive oil.

In a small bowl, blend together salt, cumin, cardamom, coriander, ginger, oregano, pepper and allspice.

Arrange bluefish fillets, skin side down, in the prepared dish. Divide seasonings between fillets, sprinkling evenly. Lightly rub surface to coat thoroughly. Let stand for 30 minutes, or up to 1 hour.

Preheat oven to 400°F.

In a small bowl, blend together garlic, onions and mayonnaise. Divide between fillets, spreading evenly.

Bake in preheated oven for 18 to 22 minutes, or until fish flakes easily when tested with a fork. If fillets are smaller than 1 pound, test after 16 minutes.

Squeeze lemon juice over fillets, divide into portions and serve on heated plates.

Wine: Peter Michael Winery L'Après-Midi Sauvignon Blanc (California: Napa Valley) or another complex Sauvignon Blanc

Calamari in Brazilian Tomato Garlic Broth

THIS HIGHLY SPICED tomato sauce with a suggestion of coconut milk makes a perfect background for calamari. We like to serve the soupy calamari ladled over a toasted crouton of garlic bread, or even focaccia, with more croutons on the side. A version of the dish was originally served to us by Sergio Abramov, a talented Cleveland chef who came here from Brazil as a youth. We like our calamari quite spicy, but you can control the heat by using less Tabasco.

SERVES 6

¼ cup olive oil
3 pounds cleaned squid, body sacs cut into ½-inch rings, juices drained but reserved
8 plump garlic cloves, smashed and minced
2½ cups finely diced yellow onions
2 small hot chiles, seeded and minced
1 tablespoon minced fresh gingerroot
2 teaspoons ground fennel seed
1 teaspoon ground red pepper (cayenne)
1 3-ounce can tomato paste
5 cups tomato puree
¾ cup unsweetened coconut milk
2 tablespoons fresh lemon juice
1 tablespoon fresh lime juice

Up to 2 teaspoons Tabasco
Kosher salt and freshly ground black pepper
12 thick toasted garlic croutons
¼ cup minced fresh flat-leaf parsley
2 tablespoons minced fresh cilantro

Heat olive oil over high heat in a large non-reactive sauté pan. Add squid and sauté, stirring often, until rings become more opaque and tentacles firm up, 3 to 5 minutes. Add garlic, onions, chiles, ginger, fennel and cayenne. Stir until onions are softened, about 3 minutes. Stir in tomato paste, then tomato puree, coconut milk, lemon and lime juices, ½ teaspoon Tabasco, salt and pepper. When liquids bubble briskly, reduce heat and simmer until squid rings are fork-tender, about 25 minutes. If sauce is too thick, thin with reserved squid juices. Taste and adjust seasonings by adding more salt, pepper and Tabasco if desired.

Place 1 crouton in each soup bowl. Ladle in squid and sauce. Sprinkle generously with parsley and cilantro. Serve with more garlic croutons for mopping.

Wine: Allegrini Valpolicella (Italy: Veneto)
or another very fruity Valpolicella

Oyster Po'Boy
with Spicy Lemon Garlic Mayonnaise

NOTHING IS MORE DELICIOUS than fried oysters, garlic butter and mayonnaise nestled in toasted bread ready for sauce-sopping. The food of Louisiana is some of the most inspirational we've encountered. Anything Louisianians do with oysters may be addictive, but this is one of our favorites.

SERVES 2 TO 4

Spicy Lemon Garlic Mayonnaise

⅔ cup mayonnaise, preferably homemade or Hellmann's or Best Foods

2 plump garlic cloves, smashed and minced

3 scallions, trimmed with 1 inch green and minced
Minced zest of 1 lemon

1 tablespoon fresh lemon juice

1 teaspoon Tabasco
Freshly ground white pepper to taste

1 loaf crusty Italian bread

6 tablespoons unsalted butter

2 garlic cloves, smashed and minced

1-3 teaspoons Tabasco

24 large shucked oysters with their liquor

⅔ cup buttermilk

¼ teaspoon freshly grated nutmeg

2 large eggs, beaten

¼ teaspoon ground red pepper (cayenne)

¼ teaspoon freshly ground black pepper

1 cup finely ground cornmeal

⅓ cup corn flour (available in health food stores, or use durum wheat flour)
Kosher salt

2-3 cups canola oil
Juice of 1 lemon

2 tablespoons minced fresh flat-leaf parsley

To make mayonnaise: Combine all ingredients in a small bowl and blend vigorously. Scrape into a serving bowl, cover and refrigerate until needed.

To prepare bread shell: Preheat oven to 425°F.

Using a serrated knife, cut a large oval out of top of loaf and scoop out soft center, leaving at least 1 inch of bread on all sides. Combine butter, garlic and 1 teaspoon Tabasco in a small saucepan; simmer briskly over medium heat until garlic is softened. Generously brush inside of shell with butter mixture, reserving remaining butter. Place shell on baking sheet to brown in oven, about 15 minutes. Set aside when golden brown, keeping warm.

Drain oyster liquor into a bowl. Combine with buttermilk, 1 teaspoon Tabasco, nutmeg and eggs. In another bowl, combine cayenne, black pepper, cornmeal, corn flour and salt.

Heat 2 cups oil in a wok. When oil reaches 365°F (hot enough to quickly brown a cube of bread), quickly dip each oyster first into buttermilk batter, then into cornmeal mixture. Drop oysters into hot oil. Repeat with remaining oysters, but do not crowd them. Fry until nicely brown on both sides, 4 to 5 minutes. Drain on a paper towel and keep warm. Repeat until all are cooked.

Pile oysters into prepared bread shell. Quickly add lemon juice to reserved butter. Taste and add more Tabasco if desired. Heat butter sauce and pour over oysters. Sprinkle with parsley.

Serve wedges of Po'Boy with spicy garlic mayonnaise on the side.

Wine: Rabbit Ridge Sauvignon Blanc Russian
River Valley (California: Sonoma County)
or a good Muscadet from France

Chinese-Style Fried Soft-Shell Crabs with Garlic Chile Confetti

ONE OF OUR FAVORITE food places in the whole world is San Francisco's Yank Sing, where the *dim sum* are spectacular. When we are very lucky, during fresh soft-shell crab season, we enjoy exquisitely battered and crisply fried soft-shell crabs served under a lavish blanket of garlic and chiles. This is our version.

SERVES 2

1 cup unbleached flour
2 teaspoons baking powder
1 teaspoon salt
1 cup ice-cold sparkling water
1 large red bell pepper, finely diced
⅔ cup finely diced scallions
6 plump garlic cloves, smashed
   and minced
2 small fresh chiles, preferably
   serrano, minced
3 tablespoons minced fresh cilantro
2 tablespoons minced fresh chives,
   preferably garlic chives

2 tablespoons soy sauce
1 tablespoon Chinese black
   vinegar or a rich red wine vinegar
1 tablespoon fresh lime juice
2 teaspoons dark sesame oil
2-3 cups peanut oil
4 large soft-shell crabs, cleaned
   and dried
2 lime wedges

In a large mixing bowl, sift together flour, baking powder and salt. Add water and mix vigorously. Set aside while you prepare sauce.

In another bowl, blend together bell pepper, scallions, garlic, chiles, cilantro, chives, soy sauce, vinegar, lime juice and sesame oil. Reserve.

Preheat oven to 250°F. Line a baking sheet with paper towels or brown paper.

Pour oil into wok to about 1½ inches. Heat to 365°F on a deep-fat thermometer. Working quickly, dip crabs in batter and drain excess.

Drop crabs one at a time into hot oil and cook until golden on both sides, about 2 minutes a side. Drain on paper towels, then keep warm on prepared baking sheet in oven. Adding oil if needed and reheating, repeat until all crabs are fried.

Serve on heated plates and cover with garlic chile confetti.

Garnish with lime wedges.

Wine: Honig Cellars Sauvignon Blanc "Reserve"
Napa Valley (California: Napa Valley)
or another rich and complex Sauvignon Blanc

In Gary, Indiana, it is against the law to eat garlic and then go to the movies. That city carries on a Grecian tradition that made it a high crime to enter the temple of Cybele after eating garlic. (You would think that if anyone would be tolerant of garlic it would be the goddess of nature.)

Somewhat Portuguese Shrimp Piri Piri

In Portugal, chile peppers, olive oil and vinegar are combined to make the very hot *piri piri* sauce. In this simple preparation, an olive oil, garlic and hot pepper marinade is cooked into a zippy sauce for the shrimp. The last-minute addition of vinegar gives just the right piquancy to this brightly flavored dish. Bold cooks should add lots of hot pepper sauce.

SERVES 4 TO 6

2 pounds shrimp, shelled and deveined
3 garlic cloves, finely minced
3 dried chiles, crushed
¼ cup extra-virgin olive oil
2 tablespoons rich red wine vinegar
   Hot pepper sauce to taste
   Kosher salt and freshly ground
     white pepper
1 lemon, cut in half

If shrimp have been frozen, pat dry. Place shrimp in a nonreactive bowl and add garlic, chiles and olive oil. Toss well and let stand at room temperature for 1 hour or in refrigerator for 2, stirring frequently.

Just before serving, drain oil into a large skillet. Heat until hot. Add shrimp and seasonings. Toss over high heat until shrimp are firm and pink, 3 to 5 minutes. Stir in vinegar, hot sauce, salt and pepper. Squeeze fresh lemon juice over shrimp and serve.

Wine: Calhandriz Vinho de Mesa White (Portugal)
or an Oregon Pinot Gris

In a medium-sized cast-iron skillet, heat 5 tablespoons oil. Whisk in flour and cook over medium heat, whisking constantly, until roux is very dark brown, 4 to 6 minutes. Gradually add roux to hot stock, stirring after each addition. Simmer briskly, stirring frequently, until sauce thickens, 6 to 12 minutes.

Wipe skillet clean with paper towel. Pour in remaining 2 tablespoons oil and place over medium heat. Add garlic-onion mixture and stir until onions are somewhat softened, 2 to 4 minutes. Spoon vegetables over sausage in sauté pan.

Pour thickened sauce over sausage and vegetables. Heat over medium heat until sauce begins to bubble. Reduce heat, partially cover and simmer slowly, stirring occasionally, for 10 minutes. Skim off obvious surface fat. (Stew can be prepared up to this point and reheated just before finishing at serving time.)

When stew is simmering briskly, stir in shrimp and corn. Cover and cook until shrimp are just firm and opaque, about 6 minutes. If stew becomes too thick, thin with more stock. Add Tabasco if you wish, and adjust salt and pepper. Remove bay leaf.

Serve in shallow soup plates with rice; garnish with chives and parsley.

Wine: Berberana "Dragon" Tempranillo (Spain)
or another medium-bodied, fruity wine from Spain

Amazing Mussels with Saffron, Garlic & Sun-Dried Tomatoes

JUST INHALE AND ENJOY when the bowl comes to your place at the table. This simple dish is redolent with the heady aromas of tomatoes, garlic, briny mussels and saffron. It was served to us by Cory Schreiber, owner/chef of Wildwood, a smashing restaurant in Portland, Oregon. At Wildwood, the dish is roasted in the wood-burning brick oven. But it can also be prepared on top of the stove or on an outdoor grill with wood chips added to the coals.

SERVES 4

½ cup white wine vinegar
1 pinch saffron
½ cup extra-virgin olive oil
1 cup vegetable oil
Kosher salt and freshly ground black pepper
4 pounds mussels, scrubbed and debearded just before cooking
½ cup drained oil-packed sun-dried tomatoes, thinly julienned, or 1 cup julienned tomato flesh
2 plump shallots, thinly sliced
1 tablespoon minced garlic
1 lemon, cut in half

½ cup fresh flat-leaf parsley
Thick slices sourdough bread, toasted and rubbed with garlic

Combine vinegar and saffron in a small saucepan and heat until hot. Stir briskly for 30 seconds, then set aside. When cool, whisk in oils; season with salt and pepper.

Place mussels in a large, heavy, wide soup pot. Add vinegar-oil mixture, tomatoes, shallots and garlic. Cover pot with a tight-fitting lid and place on high heat. Bring to a boil and cook until all mussels open and meats are opaque, 6 to 8 minutes. Do not overcook.

Distribute mussels among 4 large heated soup plates. Taste broth, adding as much fresh lemon juice as you prefer. Add parsley and ladle soup over mussels. Serve with toasted croutons.

Wine: Didier Dagueneau Pouilly Fumé Au Sang (France: Loire Valley) or a very good Pinot Blanc from Alsace

Mussels Marinara

GARLIC, ONIONS AND TOMATOES form the base of a great many marvelous Italian dishes. In this recipe, we combine them to make a robust sauce for meaty mussels. The briny juices provide a perfect counterpoint to our basic sauce. We often ladle the mussels and sauce into a soup plate and serve as is, with lots of grilled bread for mopping the sauce. Or you can serve the mussels tossed with linguine.

SERVES 4 TO 6

¼ cup olive oil

2 dried red chiles, crumbled

5 plump garlic cloves, smashed and minced

1 large yellow onion, finely diced

5 cups canned crushed Italian plum tomatoes

¼ cup dry vermouth

¼ teaspoon dried oregano

1 tablespoon chopped fresh basil plus ¼ cup minced fresh basil Kosher salt and freshly ground black pepper

3 pounds mussels, scrubbed and debearded just before cooking

2 pounds dried linguine or bucatini (optional)

¼ cup minced fresh flat-leaf parsley

Heat olive oil over high heat in a large non-reactive sauté pan. Add crumbled chiles, garlic and onions. Stir briskly until onions are softened, about 3 minutes. Stir in tomatoes, vermouth, oregano, 1 tablespoon basil, salt and pepper. Cover tightly and cook until liquids begin to bubble. Reduce heat to very low and simmer for 20 minutes. Add mussels to sauce and cover. Increase heat to high and cook until liquids bubble, 2 to 4 minutes. Reduce heat to low and cook until shells are fully open and mussels are firm and opaque, about 6 minutes.

Ladle mussels and sauce into heated soup plates. Sprinkle generously with ¼ cup fresh basil and parsley.

If serving with pasta: While sauce is cooking, fill a soup pot with generously salted water and bring to a rolling boil. Cook linguine until tender but still firm to the bite, about 10 minutes. Drain well. If pan is large enough, add cooked pasta to marinara and stir well over low heat for 1 to 2 minutes. Toss with herbs and serve.

Wine: Fattoria Montellori Chianti Moro (Italy: Tuscany) or a California Sangiovese

Baked Lobsters with Clam-Chowdered Garlic Potato Hash Stuffing

ONE CHILLY LATE FALL EVENING we experienced nirvana at New York chef David Burke's Park Avenue Café—half a five-pound lobster stuffed with New England clam chowder potato hash. Our version of this exceptional recipe may take a little preparation time, but it's not difficult and can be prepared several hours ahead. Trust us, it's worth the effort; it could be the best shellfish dish we have ever made. A tasty blend of garlic-and-shallot-flavored hash-brown potatoes studded with clams and moistened with cream makes a lusty stuffing.

SERVES 8

4   large russet potatoes
2   thick slices bacon, preferably
        heavily smoked
8   tablespoons (1 stick) unsalted butter
1   small dried red chile, crumbled
6   plump garlic cloves, smashed
        and minced
2   plump shallots, finely diced
½   cup finely diced red bell pepper
½   cup finely diced celery
¼   cup minced fresh flat-leaf parsley
¼   cup minced fresh chives

1   teaspoon freshly ground black pepper
1   teaspoon minced fresh thyme
1   teaspoon minced fresh tarragon
8   2-pound lobsters
3   cups chopped clams or 3 dozen clams,
        shucked and chopped, with liquor
        Kosher salt
⅔   cup heavy cream, or more as needed
        Juice of 1 lemon
2   pinches ground red pepper (cayenne)
        Lemon wedges
        Melted butter with lemon for dipping

Preheat oven to 375°F. Bake potatoes until they are almost tender. Let cool, then remove skin. Coarsely chop potatoes and set aside.

Fry bacon in a large cast-iron skillet over medium heat until crisp. Transfer strips to paper toweling. Add 4 tablespoons butter to skillet with bacon fat and melt.

Add chile and garlic to skillet. Stir until hot, then add shallots. Reduce heat and stir until shallots begin to soften, 2 to 3 minutes. Stir in potatoes. Increase heat and cook, gently tossing with a spatula, until potatoes begin to brown, 4 to 5 minutes. Add bell peppers and celery. Cook until peppers begin to soften, 3 to 4 minutes, stirring occasionally. Stir in parsley, chives, pepper, thyme and tarragon. Blend and remove from heat.

Transfer potato hash to a large mixing bowl. Crumble bacon and add to hash.

To split lobsters, place shell side down on work surface. Insert a sharp knife into abdomen and cut through shell toward tail. Pry halves apart with your hands. If you prefer, you can boil them for 5 minutes to kill them before splitting.

Arrange lobsters split side up on baking sheets. Discard stomachs and intestines. Scrape runny tomalley and coral roe, if any, into bowl with potato hash.

Add chopped clams and clam liquor to potato hash. Season generously with salt, adding more pepper if desired. Stir in ⅔ cup cream and gently blend stuffing. If it seems too dry, slowly add more cream.

Divide stuffing among lobsters, lightly mounding it in each cavity. Melt remaining 4 tablespoons butter in a small saucepan. Stir in lemon juice and cayenne. Pour some over stuffing in each lobster. (You can refrigerate lobsters for several hours now. Just bring them to room temperature 30 minutes before baking.)

Bake lobsters for 20 to 25 minutes, or until they are red and stuffing is lightly browned.

Place lobsters on serving plates and serve with lemon wedges and melted butter.

Wine: Patz & Hall "Hyde Vineyard" Carneros Chardonnay (California: Carneros & Napa) or a lush white Burgundy from France

Celebration Paella

THIS EXTRAORDINARY CASSEROLE of rice, shellfish, chicken and sausage is guaranteed to garner raves. It was the first dish Linda ever prepared for Fred. Its complex flavors are particularly enhanced by generous additions of garlic and saffron. The recipe is long, but it's not difficult to make, and most of the preparation can be done early in the day. We prepare this in a 14-inch paella pan. Any 14-inch casserole that's at least 2 inches deep will work. We like to serve paella on its own, followed by a large salad of bitter greens.

SERVES 8 TO 10

1½   pounds chorizo or smoked garlic sausage

3   pounds chicken breasts and thighs, each cut in half
    Up to ½ cup olive oil
    Salt and freshly ground black pepper to taste

¾   pound smoked ham, cut into ¾-inch cubes

½   cup finely diced yellow onion

¼   cup minced scallions, including 1 inch green

8   plump garlic cloves, smashed and minced

1   red bell pepper, deveined, seeded and julienned

½   green bell pepper, deveined, seeded and julienned

1½   cups peeled, seeded and chopped fresh tomatoes

8   cups rich fish stock

½   teaspoon saffron

¼   teaspoon ground red pepper (cayenne)
    Kosher salt and freshly ground black pepper

4   cups long-grain jasmine rice

1   pound large raw shrimp, peeled and deveined

1   pound sea scallops

20   littleneck clams, scrubbed

10-20   mussels, scrubbed and debearded

1   2-pound lobster, stomach and intestines discarded, cut into pieces

¾   cup fresh or frozen peas (do not thaw)

2   lemons, cut in wedges

2   hard-cooked eggs, chopped

Lightly prick sausages in many places. Fill a saucepan with water, add sausage and bring to a boil over high heat. Lower heat and simmer briskly for 5 minutes to release fat. Drain and pat dry. Slice into ¼-inch-thick slices and set aside.

Meanwhile, heat 3 tablespoons oil in a large skillet over medium heat. Working in batches and adding oil as needed, brown chicken pieces until golden on both sides, about 10 minutes. Sprinkle browned chicken lightly with salt and pepper and reserve.

Add sausage to skillet and brown on both sides. Transfer with a slotted spoon to a plate and set aside.

Drain oil from skillet and wipe it. Add 3 tablespoons more oil and heat until hot. Add ham cubes and cook until lightly browned, 2 to 4 minutes. Add onions, scallions, garlic and bell peppers. Stir over medium-high heat until onions soften, about 3 minutes. Add tomatoes. Stir and cook over medium heat until liquids in pan evaporate. Set mixture aside until 1 hour before serving.

Remove racks from oven and preheat to 400°F.

In a large saucepan, combine stock, saffron, cayenne and ½ teaspoon each salt and pepper. Bring to a boil, blend thoroughly and keep warm.

Combine rice and garlic-onion mixture in bottom of paella pan; mix well. Pour boiling stock over mixture and place pan on high heat. Stir constantly until mixture begins to boil.

Quickly scatter chicken, sausage and shellfish over pan. Sprinkle evenly with peas. Set pan on floor of oven and bake for 25 to 30 minutes, or until liquids are absorbed. Rice should be somewhat *al dente*.

Remove paella from oven and wrap pan with a large bath towel. Let rest for 8 minutes so rice finishes steaming.

Scatter lemon wedges about and sprinkle with chopped egg.

Wine: Kistler Vineyards Sonoma Valley "Durell Vineyard" Chardonnay (California: Sonoma County) or another lush and concentrated Chardonnay

ANCIENT GARLIC

OUR WORD "GARLIC" COMES FROM THE OLD ENGLISH: *gar*, meaning spear, and *leac*, meaning leek—a leek with spear-shaped leaves. But long before the English cultivated it and gave it that name, it had been grown and used for thousands of years in scores of places under any number of names.

Where did garlic come from? Almost certainly from south-central Asia. The nomadic peoples who traveled the barren areas of Asia probably learned very early to use those tasty and pungent plants that came up through the melting snow in spring. And surely they found that those plants, allowed to mature and then to cure or dry a little, were hardy and tough, resisted decay and were appealingly portable. These characteristics allowed garlic to be distributed widely, along what some have called "the garlic crescent," across Asia and west to the Mediterranean.

Botanists believe that garlic may have been among the earliest plants to be cultivated. Perhaps 10,000 years ago, someone first put a few cloves into the soil near a dwelling and found that they could have easier access to the useful plant the next season. And those early growers surely discovered that garlic kept other foods from spoiling quite so quickly.

Archaeologists have documented the presence of garlic in the earliest civilizations. Early writings from countries all around the Mediterranean and the Middle East tell of the uses of garlic. Garlic was also carried east, to China and southeast Asia. Lisa Manniche in her *Ancient Egyptian Herbal* says that garlic was used as a food in Egypt in the earliest times, though there was relatively little written about its medicinal properties. Clay models of garlic heads were crafted in Egypt over 5,000 years ago. Like onions, garlic heads were placed in tombs, including Tutankhamen's (six heads, to be precise).

When the Jews went into exile, they missed five foods—three of which were alliums. The Book of Numbers in the Bible tells us that along with cucumbers and melons, the Jews pined for onions, leeks and garlic. We doubt that the garlic-loving Egyptians and Jews were thinking medicine; they were thinking dinner. They loved garlic for the same reasons we do, and that is what drove its domestication into every corner of the world.

POULTRY

Chicken with Forty Cloves of Garlic   257

Crisp Roast Chicken with Garlic, Lemon & Herbs   258

Chicken Braised with Many Cloves of Garlic & Root Vegetables   260

Butterflied Lemon Chicken with Walnut & Opal Basil Pesto   261

Pollo alla Diavolo (Deviled Chicken)   262

Amazing Curried Chicken with Eggplant and Lime   264

Kung Pao Chicken   267

Hazelnut-Crusted Chicken Breasts with Garlic Lemon Mustard   268

Chinese Five-Spice Chicken   270

Sweet & Spicy Butterflied Hens   272

Piquant Roasted Capon with Corn Bread Stuffing   274

Sicilian Roast Turkey with a Surprising Stuffing   276

Grilled Marinated Duck Breasts with Peppered Pineapple Sauce   280

Sauerkraut-Stuffed Duck with Candied Garlic & Apples   282

SEX & THE SINGLE GARLIC

HOW REMARKABLE THAT GARLIC, the potent and lusty allium, a vegetable that writers as early in history as Pliny considered to be an aphrodisiac, should turn out to be a sexless plant. No sex for garlic. Its reproduction is managed not by seed and pollen, or egg and sperm, but by planting the plump cloves, which contain the blueprint for the new plant. Some scientists believe garlic may have had the power in the past to make flowers and seeds, but that it was lost through what they call "inbreeding depression."

Since cultivated garlic cannot produce seed, it is not possible for botanists to develop new cultivars. (Some strains produce spathes, but they contain tiny replicas of the cloves, not seed.) How, then, can we explain the different varieties that grow across the world? In their classic *Onions and Their Allies*, Henry Alfred Jones and Louis Mann say that in the world of garlic there are great differences in "plant size, yield, content of solids, time of maturity, ease of bolting, storability, and the number, size, shape and colour of the cloves." And they probably should have included "taste." But these differences "must have arisen as vegetative mutations during the long period of garlic cultivation." Those plants that were carried throughout the Mediterranean changed over the years as a result of their new environments.

In 1963, when their book was published, Jones and Mann were not thinking about making true seeds. But in more recent times other researchers have. A mega California operation that produces 50 million pounds of garlic a year has to buy (or save) perhaps 5 million pounds of "seed cloves" for the next crop. If garlic could grow true seed, garlic farming will be a lot easier. Instead of requiring a giant warehouse for seed cloves, growers could store enough seed to produce 50 million pounds of garlic in one small room.

At the University of Wisconsin, Philipp Simon and Margaret Pooler have stimulated seed production in a few plants, but the time when garlic growers will plant true seed instead of cloves is still years in the future.

Chicken with Forty Cloves of Garlic

NO BOOK ABOUT GARLIC would be complete without this legendary Provençal dish. There are many versions. James Beard's calls for chicken legs and thighs, others use the whole chicken. We're partial to this very simple one—a whole chicken roasted inside a tightly covered Dutch oven on a bed of onions and celery, perfumed by herbs and garlic cloves. When roasted, the chicken is exquisitely flavorful, the garlic cloves buttery tender. Serve this with freshly toasted bread croutons, squeezing the garlic right from its skin onto the toast. We prefer kosher chicken because it is exceptionally juicy.

SERVES 4

- 2 cups coarsely chopped yellow onions
- 2 large celery stalks, coarsely chopped
  Kosher salt and freshly ground
  black pepper
- 1 3½-to-4-pound frying chicken,
  preferably kosher
- 40 plump garlic cloves, unpeeled
- 3 tablespoons extra-virgin olive oil
- ¼ cup dry white wine
- ⅓ cup mixed fresh herbs, such as tarragon, thyme, lemon verbena, lovage, chervil, flat-leaf parsley, rosemary, lavender

Preheat oven to 375°F.

Combine onions and celery in a 5½-quart Dutch oven, preferably cast-iron. Rub salt and pepper inside chicken and place bird over onion mixture. Scatter garlic cloves around chicken. Pour olive oil, then white wine, over chicken and garlic. Season generously with more salt and pepper. Place 2 tablespoons herbs inside chicken. Scatter remaining herbs over chicken and garlic cloves. Cover pot tightly, first with heavy foil, then with the lid.

Roast chicken for 1½ hours. Chicken should be fork-tender; it will not be browned.

Carve chicken into quarters. Serve with garlic cloves and pan juices.

Wine: Domaine Ogier Couvé Syrah
(France: Rhône Valley) or a rich,
earthy Côtes-du-Rhône from France

Crisp Roast Chicken with Garlic, Lemon & Herbs

ALEMONY, CRISP SKIN is just the beginning. Wait until you taste the flesh of this delicious bird after it absorbs all the marvelous fragrant flavors of its herb-and-roasted-garlic "stuffing." It's accompanied by a lemon-punctuated garlic pan sauce. The best roasted chicken we ever ate was served at L'Ami Louis in Paris years ago. That's when we learned to roast chicken in a cast-iron skillet at a very high temperature, which is the secret of this great chicken.

SERVES 4

1 head garlic, cut in half crosswise

3 tablespoons olive oil

2 teaspoons water

1 3½-to-4-pound frying chicken
Kosher salt and freshly ground black pepper

2 lemons, cut in halves

2 large branches fresh rosemary (1 tablespoon dried)

1 large branch fresh lemon verbena or lemon balm, if available

4-5 branches other fresh herbs, such as thyme, pineapple sage, basil

½ cup rich chicken stock

1 tablespoon minced fresh flat-leaf parsley
More fresh herbs for garnish

At least 1 hour before you roast chicken, preheat oven to 325°F. Place garlic on a large square of foil and drizzle with 1 tablespoon oil. Then drizzle each half with 1 teaspoon water. Seal packet closed and roast for 45 minutes. Remove packet from oven and open. Garlic will still be firm. Let cool somewhat.

Meanwhile, increase oven temperature to 475°F.

Pour any oil from garlic packet into a 10-to-12-inch cast-iron skillet. Add more if needed to thoroughly oil skillet.

Rub cavity of chicken with salt and pepper. Place 1 lemon half in cavity, along with garlic halves. Then pack in herbs. Transfer chicken to skillet, breast side up.

Rub chicken with remaining 2 tablespoons olive oil. Squeeze juice of second lemon half over it. Rub surface with salt and pepper.

Roast, basting once with third lemon half, for 60 minutes, or until skin is very dark and thigh is exceptionally tender when pierced with a fork; juices should run clear.

Transfer chicken to a carving board. Using a heavy potholder, transfer skillet to stove. Over high heat, whisk in chicken stock and juice of remaining lemon half, scraping up any browned bits that stick to skillet. Boil rapidly to thicken sauce, 2 to 3 minutes. Skim off obvious surface fat and season to taste with salt and pepper. Keep warm.

Remove garlic and herbs from cavity of chicken. Squeeze garlic from skin and mash; add to sauce, whisking well to blend. Cut chicken into quarters. Blend any accumulated juices into gravy and heat thoroughly.

Transfer chicken quarters to heated serving plates. Sprinkle with parsley. Garnish lavishly with fresh herbs and serve with pan sauce.

Wine: Raymond Vineyard and Cellar Chardonnay "Private Reserve" (California: Napa Valley) or another rich California Chardonnay

THE SOURCE OF THE STING

GARLIC, LIKE ITS COUSIN ALLIUMS, burns the eyes and the tongue because it is alliaceous; it contains powerful sulfur compounds. Alliin is principal among them. You are not likely to ever experience it directly, because the instant it is exposed to the outside world by a bite or a cut or a crush, an enzymatic reaction takes place, and the alliin yields alliinase and allicin. It is allicin that is famous for its powerful aroma, tears (although they may be tears of joy) and pain. That is what hurts your tongue and your gut.

Chicken Braised with Many Cloves of Garlic & Root Vegetables

THIS IS ONE OF THE MOST POPULAR of our recipes. After browning the chicken, we braise it on a bed of onions, turnips, potatoes and carrots, seasoned with herbs and lots of garlic. The caramelized vegetables add a succulent sweetness to the pan juices. The garlic cloves make a creamy spread for accompanying bread.

SERVES 4 TO 6

2   tablespoons unsalted butter

2   tablespoons extra-virgin olive oil

3   whole chicken breasts, with bone
     and skin, split and patted dry

6   small turnips, scrubbed and cut in half

6   small white onions, peeled

6   small red, white or yellow potatoes,
     scrubbed and cut in half

3   carrots, scrubbed and cut into
     2-inch lengths

2   large heads plump garlic, cloves
     separated and left unpeeled

1   rounded tablespoon dried herbes de
     Provence or ⅓ cup mixed minced
     fresh parsley, sage, rosemary, thyme
     plus fresh herbs for garnish

Kosher salt and freshly ground
black pepper

Lightly toasted sturdy bread for accompaniment

In a 12-inch sauté pan or large Dutch oven, heat butter and olive oil over medium-high heat. Brown chicken on both sides, about 10 minutes. Transfer to a platter. Add turnips, onions, potatoes and carrots and sauté, stirring, over medium-high heat for several minutes to brown lightly. Remove from heat.

Arrange chicken, skin side up, over vegetables. Scatter garlic cloves over all. Sprinkle with herbs, salt and pepper. (Chicken can be prepared to this point several hours ahead and refrigerated. Bring to room temperature before cooking.)

Cover skillet tightly, place over very low heat, and cook for 50 minutes, occasionally giving pan a good shake while holding lid tightly with one hand. Dish is done when chicken and onions are fork-tender.

To serve, distribute among heated serving plates. Spoon some pan juices over chicken and garnish with fresh herbs.

Wine: Martin Ray Chardonnay "Mariage" (California) or an Alsatian Pinot Gris

Butterflied Lemon Chicken with Walnut & Opal Basil Pesto

THIS BUTTERFLIED BIRD is cooked over a sprinkling of garlic, while a luscious layer of walnut and opal basil pesto is spread directly on its flesh, beneath the skin. The crisped chicken is redolent of exotic seasonings and mellow garlic. This particular pesto fills the entire chicken with fragrant flavors, but regular pesto will work here too. Carve this butterflied chicken right in front of your guests.

SERVES 4

2   tablespoons olive oil

2   plump garlic cloves, smashed
     and minced

1   3½-to-4-pound frying chicken, split
     down back, backbone removed
     Kosher salt and freshly ground
     white pepper

⅔   cup Walnut & Opal Basil Pesto
     (page 150) or another pesto sauce

3   lemon halves

Lightly oil a shallow baking pan. Sprinkle minced garlic over surface where butterflied chicken will be placed.

Place chicken skin side down on work surface. Season generously with salt and pepper. Turn over. Carefully loosen skin with your fingers. Generously spread pesto under skin, all the way down thighs. Rub surface of skin with remaining olive oil; season with more salt and pepper. Spritz evenly with juice of one lemon half. Let stand at room temperature for 30 minutes.

Meanwhile, preheat oven to 500°F. Roast chicken for 15 minutes. Baste with juice of second lemon half. Reduce temperature to 375°F and roast 25 minutes longer. To test, gently insert point of a knife into thigh; when juices run golden yellow, chicken is done.

Cut chicken into quarters. Baste with juice of third lemon half and serve.

Wine: Oakville Ranch Vineyards Chardonnay
Napa Valley "ORV" (California: Napa Valley) or another
rich and concentrated Chardonnay from California

Pollo alla Diavolo
(DEVILED CHICKEN)

THE TECHNIQUE OF COOKING something pressed under a heavy weight is a very old one, and the preparation can be done on top of a stove or on a grill. Here we butterfly a chicken and marinate it with oil, red chile, garlic and rosemary. We cook it in a cast-iron skillet, weighted with a somewhat smaller one filled with bricks. Then we splash the finished chicken with some fresh lemon juice and parsley. The marinade and sauce become the base of the Italian *diavolo* sauce. The first time we tasted such a deviled chicken was about a decade ago at Omero, a restaurant in the hills outside of Florence, Italy. The bird was prepared over a wood fire and flattened under a huge, heavy weight called a *mattone*. It was sublime; this is as close as we can get.

SERVES 2 TO 4

Marinade

⅓ cup olive oil

2 plump garlic cloves, pressed

3 tablespoons fresh rosemary
(1 rounded tablespoon dried)

1 dried chile, crumbled

1 tablespoon coarsely ground
black pepper, plus more to taste

1 3½-to-4-pound frying chicken,
split down back, backbone removed

1 lemon, cut in half
Kosher salt

⅓ cup chopped fresh flat-leaf parsley

To make marinade: In a small bowl, whisk together olive oil, garlic, rosemary, chile and pepper.

Place chicken, skin side down, on large work surface. With a heavy implement such as a meat pounder, smash chicken flat. Cut small slashes in thighs and wings so that they flatten too. Put flattened chicken in a nonreactive dish large enough to hold it. Coat thoroughly with oil mixture and marinate for 1 hour at room temperature, or for 8 hours in refrigerator. Bring to room temperature before cooking.

If cooking on top of stove: Place chicken, skin side down, in a 12-inch cast-iron skillet, add marinade and place over high heat until skillet is hot. Reduce heat to low and cover flattened chicken with another skillet weighted with 6 to 8 pounds of heavy objects (we use bricks). Cook for 30 minutes, then turn chicken, replace weighted skillet on it, and cook for 20 minutes more. Chicken is done when thigh is pierced with a sharp knife and juices run golden.

If cooking on grill: Spray grill with vegetable oil spray and preheat. Remove chicken from marinade, place skin side down on grill, cover with a large skillet holding 6 to 8 pounds of weight. Baste chicken with marinade and turn every 10 minutes for 35 to 40 minutes. Chicken is done when thigh is pierced with a fork and juices run golden.

Place cooked chicken on a heated platter, skin side up. Baste with lemon juice and sprinkle with salt, pepper and parsley. Serve on heated plates.

Wine: Taurino Salice Salentino Riserva (Italy: Puglia)
or a Valpolicella from Italy

Amazing Curried Chicken with Eggplant and Lime

A MULTIPLICITY OF SPICES AND HERBS gives an exotic flavor to this curried chicken. It is simmered in a rich, thick garlic-and-onion gravy incorporating pureed roasted eggplant and tomatoes. Since this curry reheats quite nicely, you can make it a day ahead; just add a bit more water when you reheat it. Serve it with buttery rice or even saffron rice.

SERVES 8

2¼   pounds eggplant

Seasonings

2¼   teaspoons kosher salt
1¼   teaspoons freshly ground black pepper
1¼   teaspoons freshly ground white pepper
1   teaspoon ground red pepper (cayenne), or more to taste
1   teaspoon ground cardamom
1   teaspoon dry mustard
1   teaspoon turmeric
½   teaspoon ground coriander
½   teaspoon ground ginger
¼   teaspoon ground cloves
¼   teaspoon ground fenugreek
2   small dried chiles, crumbled
1   bay leaf

2   3½-to-4-pound frying chickens, cut into 6 pieces each, wing tips and backbones removed
⅔   cup unbleached flour
      Up to ⅔ cup vegetable oil
2   cups coarsely chopped yellow onions
4-5   plump garlic cloves, pressed
2   rounded tablespoons minced fresh gingerroot
2   cups water
2   cups crushed tomatoes
1   large russet potato, grated
8   scallions, trimmed with 1 inch green and finely chopped
⅓   cup minced fresh cilantro
2-4   large limes, quartered

To prepare eggplant: Preheat gas grill on high heat or broiler. Wrap eggplant in heavy foil and roast, turning several times, until very soft when pressed, 25 to 40 minutes, depending on size. Or cook wrapped eggplant under broiler, turning several times until very soft. When eggplant is somewhat cool, split it and scoop flesh and juices into the bowl of a food processor. Pulse until pureed and reserve.

Meanwhile, prepare seasonings: Combine salt, ground peppers, spices, dried chiles and bay leaf in a small bowl and set aside.

Rinse chicken pieces and pat dry. Place flour in a heavy plastic bag or doubled paper bag. Add chicken pieces, a few at a time, and shake to coat evenly. Place coated chicken on a cake rack.

Pour ¼ cup oil into a large cast-iron skillet; heat over high heat until smoking. Add chicken pieces, but do not crowd; reduce heat to medium and cook until golden brown, 3 to 5 minutes; turn and brown other side. Repeat this process, adding oil if needed, until all pieces are browned. Transfer browned chicken to a heavy 5½-quart Dutch oven. Wipe skillet clean with a paper towel.

Heat ¼ cup oil in skillet over medium heat. Add onions and cook, stirring often, until golden, 8 to 10 minutes. Add garlic and ginger and stir for 30 seconds. Add seasoning mixture and cook, stirring constantly, for 1 minute more.

Add water and stir until all seasonings are thoroughly blended. Add tomatoes, pureed eggplant and grated potato. Cook over medium heat until bubbling. Taste sauce; add more cayenne if sauce is too mild.

Pour sauce over chicken, then sprinkle with scallions. Cover tightly. Cook over medium heat until liquids bubble; reduce heat to low. Simmer for 1 hour, or until chicken is very tender when pierced with a fork. If sauce is too thick, gradually add more water.

Sprinkle with cilantro. Serve on heated plates with buttered rice; spritz lavishly with lime juice.

Wine: Thomas Mitchell Marsanne (Australia)
or another Marsanne from Australia

HORACE SHAW'S TORNADO JUICE

I CAN TALK SHALLOTS WITH YOU," said Jim Robison, the Walla Walla farmer. "But if you want to talk garlic, call Horace Shaw." And John Swenson, the Illinois lawyer turned allium scientist and shallot grower, gave us the same advice. "Horace Shaw is the best garlic grower ever," he told us.

On his farm in Weston, Oregon, Shaw has grown as many as 400 different garlic cultivars over the years. Now retired, he grows only a little for his own kitchen. The earliest garlic he remembers is some his family brought to Nebraska from China in 1934. He has never been far from garlic since.

In the pure garlic establishment, it is sometimes thought heretical to talk about elephant garlic, or drying garlic or even pickling garlic. But Horace Shaw waxed rhapsodic about all three.

"Some say it's not garlic, but I don't care," he told us. "I like elephant garlic." He finds it milder than regular garlic. And he likes it even after it has been dried in a processing plant and made into a powder. "No bitterness when you put it on your toast," he said. And he loves pickled garlic, too.

Horace is convinced that garlic has great health benefits, and he gave us his recipe for Tornado Juice. "Start with equal parts of ginger, garlic, cayenne peppers, onion and horseradish. Chop them all together and put in a quart jar until it is three-quarters full. Pour on cider vinegar until it is full. Let it stand two weeks. Strain through nylon hose or cheesecloth. Put one tablespoon in a cup of tea and drink. It's really good for you."

We're thinking about it.

Kung Pao Chicken

GARLIC, GINGER AND CHILES may be our favorite "holy" triumvirate. Add Asian flavorings and you have a splendid version of this popular Chinese chicken dish.

SERVES 4

- 2 whole chicken breasts, boned, skinned and split, cut into 1-inch pieces
- 3 tablespoons cornstarch
- 3 tablespoons rice wine
- ¼ cup soy sauce
- 1 tablespoon Chinese black vinegar or red wine vinegar
- 2 teaspoons dark sesame oil
  Up to 1½ cups peanut oil
- ¾ cup roasted peanuts
- 1 medium red bell pepper, cut into ½-inch pieces
- 5 small dried chiles
- 3 plump garlic cloves, smashed and minced
- 1 ½-inch-thick slice fresh gingerroot, peeled and minced
- ¼ cup minced scallions, including tender green
- ¼ cup minced fresh cilantro

Place diced chicken in a medium-sized mixing bowl. Sprinkle with 2 tablespoons cornstarch and toss to coat evenly. Then sprinkle with 1 tablespoon rice wine and blend again. Let stand 5 minutes.

In a small dish, blend together remaining 1 tablespoon cornstarch and 2 tablespoons rice wine. Reserve. In another bowl, blend together soy sauce, vinegar and sesame oil.

Heat 1 cup peanut oil in a wok until very hot. Add half of chicken and cook, stirring, for 1 minute, or until chicken turns white. Using a Chinese strainer, transfer chicken to a large mixing bowl. Adding oil if needed, fry remaining chicken. When second batch is ready, transfer it to mixing bowl. Add peanuts and bell peppers to chicken.

Discard all but 1 tablespoon oil and heat wok until hot. Stir-fry chiles in hot oil until they smoke, about 30 seconds. Add garlic and ginger; stir for another 30 seconds. Quickly add soy-sauce mixture, followed by chicken mixture. Toss over high heat until bell peppers begin to soften, 2 to 3 minutes.

Quickly whisk together rice wine and cornstarch mixture again, then add to chicken. Cook for 1 more minute, stirring constantly. Sprinkle with scallions and cilantro and serve.

Wine: Harpersfield Vineyards Gewürztraminer
(Ohio: Lake Erie) or a Gewürztraminer from Alsace

Hazelnut-Crusted Chicken Breasts with Garlic Lemon Mustard

THESE MELT-IN-YOUR-MOUTH bone-less chicken breasts have a crisp coating of hazelnuts and are served with a lemony garlic mustard sauce. The crowd-pleasing recipe can easily be multiplied for a buffet. Hazelnuts, aka filberts, may come with their (bitter) skins still on. To remove skin and toast nuts simultaneously: soak for 1 minute in cold water. Then drain (not dry) them and bake for 7 to 10 minutes at 400°F, or until skins darken and begin to flake. Dump nuts onto a large towel. Wrap and rub to flake off as much of the skins as possible.

SERVES 8

7 tablespoons (⅞ stick) unsalted butter
3 plump garlic cloves, pressed
Minced zest of 2 lemons
⅓ cup fresh lemon juice
¼ teaspoon Tabasco
⅓ cup Dijon mustard
1¼ cups finely chopped toasted hazelnuts
⅔ cup fine dry bread crumbs
1 teaspoon dried tarragon
½ teaspoon dried thyme
2 teaspoons kosher salt
1¼ teaspoons freshly ground white pepper
4 chicken breasts, skin and bones removed, split
8 thin slices lemon

Preheat oven to 375°F. Lightly butter a shallow baking pan just large enough to hold chicken breasts in a single layer.

In a small saucepan, combine remaining butter, garlic and lemon zest. Place over low heat until butter has melted and aromas of lemon and garlic are released. Set aside.

Combine lemon juice, Tabasco and mustard in a shallow soup plate and blend thoroughly. In another soup plate, combine nuts, crumbs, herbs, salt and white pepper.

Preheat oven to 375°F.

Dip each chicken breast half into mustard mixture, then coat evenly with hazelnut mixture. Place each piece, skin side down, in prepared pan without touching.

Pour butter mixture evenly over chicken. (If you wish, pan can be covered and refrigerated for up to 6 hours. Bring to room temperature 1 hour before baking.)

Bake for 20 minutes, then turn very gently. Place a lemon slice over each breast. Spoon pan juices over top and continue baking until chicken is browned and firm to the touch, about 30 minutes more. Serve immediately.

Wine: Shafer Vineyards Chardonnay "Red Shoulder Ranch" Napa Valley Carneros (California: Napa Valley) or another rich Chardonnay

When plague hit Marseilles in the early eighteenth century, there were four thieves who picked the pockets and purses of the dead with complete immunity and impunity. Their secret for avoiding what had laid their victims low was "four thieves vinegar," loaded with garlic.

Chinese Five-Spice Chicken

WE'VE BEEN DELIGHTING GUESTS with this dish for years. The small pieces of crackling-coated chicken tickle your taste buds with the blended flavors of spices, ginger and garlic. The chicken is garnished with salt, scallions and cilantro.

SERVES 4

1   3½-to-4½-pound frying chicken, backbone removed
1   tablespoon Chinese five-spice powder
1   tablespoon minced fresh gingerroot
3   plump garlic cloves, smashed and minced
3   plump scallions, smashed with cleaver
2   tablespoons dark soy sauce
1   tablespoon rice wine or vermouth
2   teaspoons dark sesame oil
1   tablespoon Sichuan peppercorns
1   cup kosher salt
1   cup cornstarch
    Up to 3 cups peanut oil

4   scallions, trimmed with 1 inch green, minced
1   tablespoon minced fresh cilantro

Cut chicken into quarters and remove wings and drumsticks, discarding wing tips. Separate drumettes from wings. Cut each breast into 3 pieces and each thigh in half. Place chicken pieces in large mixing bowl. Add five-spice powder, ginger, garlic, scallions, soy sauce, rice wine and sesame oil. Toss chicken with seasonings to coat evenly. Marinate 2 hours at room temperature.

While chicken is marinating, prepare Sichuan salt: Toast peppercorns in a small dry skillet over medium-high heat, stirring and tossing until darkened and fragrance is released. Remove from heat and grind in a pepper mill or spice mill or with a mortar and pestle. Pour into a small jar with a tight-fitting cap. Add salt and stir to blend. (Store with cap tightly in place. This salt will keep for years.)

Pour cornstarch into a paper or plastic bag. Remove chicken from marinade, a few pieces at a time, and place in bag. Shake to coat well. Transfer chicken to a metal cake rack. Repeat until all pieces are coated.

Pour oil into a wok and heat until a cube of bread tossed in turns golden (350° on a deep-frying thermometer). Being careful not to overcrowd, place chicken, 4 to 6 pieces at a time, into oil. Turning often, fry until pieces are golden brown, 5 to 8 minutes. Transfer chicken pieces to paper toweling and keep warm until entire chicken is fried.

Transfer chicken to a heated serving bowl. Sprinkle with scallions, cilantro and a generous amount of Sichuan salt. Toss and serve.

Wine: Arrowwood Vineyards & Winery Pinot Blanc Russian River Valley "Saralee's Vineyard" (California: Sonoma County) or a Pinot Blanc from Alsace

Sweet & Spicy Butterflied Hens

GARLIC, CHILES, GINGER and lemongrass work together to bring out the best in this Asian-style sauce, which becomes the marinade for our butterflied hens. These crispy birds, with their intensely flavored sauce, are a show-stopper. Poussins run ¾ to 1 pound; Cornish hens are about 1¼ pounds.

SERVES 4

4   1-to-1¼-pound Cornish hens
      or poussins
1   ½-inch-thick slice fresh gingerroot
2   small dried chiles
1   plump shallot, peeled
4   plump garlic cloves
1   bulb lemongrass
      Zest and juice of 1 lime
⅓   cup fresh orange juice, preferably
      blood or honey orange
2   tablespoons dark soy sauce
¼   cup sweet soy sauce, or hoisin sauce
      plus 1 tablespoon more soy
2   tablespoons dry sherry
2   teaspoons dark sesame oil
1   teaspoon ground cardamom
1   teaspoon dried mint or 2 teaspoons
      chopped fresh mint
1   teaspoon freshly ground white pepper
¼   teaspoon grated nutmeg

Stock

2   tablespoons olive oil
1   carrot, quartered
1   small onion, quartered
1   clove
5   cups water

4   scallions, trimmed with 1 inch
      green, minced
1   tablespoon minced fresh cilantro

Rinse hens and pat dry. Set giblets aside (reserve livers for another use). Using a sharp knife, carefully butterfly hen by cutting through backbone without cutting bird in half. Once cut is made, use your hand to pound bird open. Remove backbone and wing tips and set aside with giblets. Butterfly remaining hens. Place in a large, shallow roasting or broiling pan.

In the bowl of a food processor, combine ginger, chiles, shallot, garlic and lemongrass. Pulse until very fine. Add lime zest and juice, orange juice, soy sauces, sherry, sesame oil, cardamom, mint, white pepper and nutmeg. Pulse until mixture forms a thick sauce. Pour marinade over hens and coat evenly. Cover and let marinate in refrigerator for at least 2 and up to 6 hours, turning occasionally. Bring to room temperature before roasting.

Meanwhile, make stock: Heat olive oil until hot in a medium-sized skillet. Add reserved giblets, wing tips and backbones, as well as carrot and onion stuck with clove. Stir over medium-high heat until browned, 5 to 8 minutes. Transfer mixture to a saucepan and add water. Cook over high heat until liquid boils; reduce heat and simmer for 1¼ hours. Using a slotted spoon, remove and discard solids. Increase heat under saucepan and briskly simmer stock until reduced to ¾ cup. Chill until needed. Skim off fat before using.

Preheat oven to 425°F.

Pour all excess marinade into a small bowl. Carefully arrange hens skin side up. Roast for 15 minutes, then baste with some marinade. Continue roasting for 15 to 25 minutes more, until hens are fork-tender and crisp.

Transfer hens to heated serving plates. Add stock to pan and deglaze over high heat, scraping loose all browned bits. Cook briskly until sauce has reduced and thickened, about 5 minutes. Spoon sauce over hens, sprinkle with scallions and cilantro and serve.

Wine: Château Tahbilk Shiraz Gouldburn Valley
(Australia: Gouldburn Valley) or another rich and chewy
California Pinot Noir or Australian Shiraz

Piquant Roasted Capon with Corn Bread Stuffing

CAPONS ARE EXCEPTIONALLY MOIST and tasty. Larger than the average chicken, they're perfect for a small holiday gathering, especially when stuffed. We begin by seasoning our capon both under and on the skin with a garlicky minted citrus glaze. While most of the stuffing will fit in the cavity, there will be some extra to bake on the side. Doubled, this recipe makes enough stuffing for a 14-pound turkey.

SERVES 6

¼ cup orange juice

1 tablespoon fresh lime juice

1 tablespoon fresh lemon juice

2 plump shallots, minced

4 plump garlic cloves, pressed

2 tablespoons minced fresh mint

1 teaspoon kosher salt

1 teaspoon freshly ground white pepper

½ small serrano or jalapeño chile, seeded and minced

2 tablespoons honey

1 7-to-8½-pound capon

Corn Bread Stuffing

2 teaspoons kosher salt

2 teaspoons freshly ground white pepper

2 teaspoons freshly ground black pepper

1 teaspoon ground red pepper (cayenne)

1 teaspoon dried oregano

1 teaspoon dried thyme

½ teaspoon dried sage

4 tablespoons (½ stick) unsalted butter

½ cup finely chopped white or yellow onions

½ cup finely chopped scallions, including some green

½ cup finely chopped red bell pepper

3 plump garlic cloves, pressed

8 cups crumbled Three-Peppers Under-Cover Corn Bread (page 106)

3 large eggs

1 teaspoon Tabasco

½ cup evaporated milk

¾ cup rich chicken stock
Kosher salt and freshly ground black pepper

One hour before roasting, combine citrus juices, shallots, garlic, mint, salt, white pepper, chile and honey. Blend thoroughly either in a food processor or by hand.

Place capon on a platter and gently loosen skin around neck opening. Carefully move your fingers underneath skin to loosen skin covering breast and at the top of thighs. Using a spoon, pour some marinade under skin so it will directly moisten breast and run into thigh. Baste outside of capon as well as cavity.

Meanwhile, make stuffing: In a small bowl, combine salt, ground peppers, oregano, thyme and sage and set aside. Melt butter in a small skillet over medium heat. Add seasonings and cook, stirring constantly, for 1 minute. Pour mixture into a large bowl. Add onions, scallions, bell pepper and garlic. Stir to blend well, then add corn bread. Mix thoroughly. Beat eggs with Tabasco and evaporated milk and stir in. Blend well and reserve.

Preheat oven to 450°F.

Just before roasting, spoon stuffing loosely into neck opening and body cavity of capon, then use small skewers to securely close openings. Spoon leftover stuffing into a 2-to-4-cup ovenproof baking dish and reserve.

Place stuffed capon, breast side up, in a very large cast-iron skillet or a shallow roasting pan. Brush with remaining marinade. Roast for 45 minutes, basting once with pan juices.

Place baking dish with extra stuffing in oven with capon. Reduce temperature to 400°F and continue roasting capon for 1¼ to 2 hours more, or until thigh juices run clear when pricked with a knife (final temperature after roasting should be 165°F). Extra stuffing should be browned on top and piping hot.

Transfer capon to a carving platter and let rest in a warm place. Place roasting pan on stove, skimming off obvious surface fat. Add stock to pan and cook over high heat, scraping up browned particles. Whisk sauce vigorously, reducing somewhat to thicken. Adjust seasonings, adding salt and pepper if necessary. Transfer pan sauce to a gravy boat.

Carve capon. Serve stuffing from both cavity and baking dish in a large heated serving bowl. Serve with sauce on the side.

Wine: Paul Hobbs Cellars Pinot Noir
"Hyde Vineyard" Carneros (California: Napa Valley)
or a red Burgundy from France

Sicilian Roast Turkey with a Surprising Stuffing

THERE'S NOTHING QUITE LIKE this herbed and garlicky bread crumb custard stuffing. It's amazingly light and delicious, especially when made with fresh herbs. Our friend Diann Yambor told us, "My Sicilian grandfather always made this for holidays." Cooking the turkey is simple; we baste it to have some good pan drippings for the gravy—you don't have to. If you start with a really good bird, the juices will stay inside. Calculate roasting time by multiplying 11 minutes times the weight of the unstuffed bird.

SERVES 12 TO 14

Garlic & Herb Bread-Crumb Custard Stuffing

14 large eggs
4 plump shallots, minced
6 plump garlic cloves, smashed
   and minced
½ cup minced fresh flat-leaf parsley
¼ cup minced fresh basil
   (2 tablespoons dried)
2 tablespoons fresh thyme leaves
   (1 tablespoon dried)
3 tablespoons minced fresh tarragon
   (1½ tablespoons dried)

1 tablespoon minced fresh rosemary
   (2 teaspoons dried)
1 tablespoon minced fresh oregano
   (1 teaspoon ground)
1 tablespoon minced fresh sage
   (1 teaspoon ground)
1 tablespoon kosher salt
2 teaspoons freshly ground black pepper
½ cup grated Parmesan cheese
5 cups fine dry bread crumbs,
   plus more if needed

Turkey Gravy

1 package turkey giblets and neck
1 pound chicken backs
3½ quarts water
2 carrots, scrubbed
2 large yellow onions, studded
   with 1 clove each
1 bay leaf
4 branches fresh flat-leaf parsley
6 black peppercorns, bruised
½ cup vegetable oil
⅔ cup unbleached flour
2 cups dry red wine

Turkey

1 **18-to-24-pound turkey**
2 **tablespoons olive oil**
 Kosher salt and freshly ground
  black pepper to taste
 Garlic powder
2 **large yellow onions, unpeeled,**
  cut in half
2 **carrots, scrubbed**
2 **cups chicken stock**

To make stuffing: In a large mixing bowl, thoroughly beat eggs. Then beat in shallots, garlic, herbs, salt, pepper and cheese. Add bread crumbs and beat again. Mixture should be very thick and heavy. If too runny, add more crumbs. Reserve.

To make gravy: Combine turkey neck, heart and gizzard with chicken backs and water in a 6-quart soup pot. (Reserve liver for another use, or add, if desired, to stock for last 10 minutes of cooking.) Bring to a boil, reduce heat and simmer briskly for 30 minutes, skimming off any scum that forms on surface. Add carrots, onions, bay leaf, parsley and peppercorns, and continue to simmer, covered, for 2 hours. (This can be done ahead.) Remove giblets, slice or mince and set aside. Strain stock and measure; there should be 10 cups. If there is more, uncover and continue simmering until reduced. Discard remaining solids. Reserve and reheat just before finishing gravy.

In a 10-inch cast-iron skillet, heat oil, add flour and whisk over medium heat until flour is very dark brown, 4 to 6 minutes. Reduce heat to very low and gradually add wine. Whisk thoroughly until mixture is smooth and well blended. Then whisk in 1 cup stock. Slowly, over 1½ hours, add remaining stock, always cooking mixture over lowest heat possible and whisking frequently. When all stock is incorporated, add sliced or minced giblets and set aside.

To prepare turkey: Preheat oven to 450°F. Pat turkey dry. Lightly season neck and body cavities and loosely stuff with dressing. Skewer and lace cavities shut with string. Rub bird with some olive oil and lightly season with salt, pepper and garlic powder. Truss turkey, if you like, and place on a rack in a roasting pan. Add onions and carrots to roasting pan.

Roast turkey uncovered for 45 minutes. Reduce heat to 400°F and baste with some chicken stock. Turn roasting pan (cover turkey with foil if it is getting too brown) back to front. Baste at least three times more, rotating pan at least one more time.

Insert instant-read thermometer into fleshy part of breast; when it reads 165°F, remove turkey from oven and place bird on a heated platter in a warm place for 30 to 45 minutes. Do not cover bird during this time or it will steam.

While bird is resting, degrease drippings in roasting pan; discard onion and carrots. Add prepared gravy to drippings and cook over medium-high heat, stirring vigorously, until all particles adhering to pan have been loosened and gravy has come to a boil.

Carefully scoop stuffing from turkey cavity and place in a heated serving bowl. Carve turkey and place on heated serving platter. Serve with gravy on the side.

Wine: Taurino Notarpanaro Rosso del Salento (Italy: Puglia) or another richly flavored, earthy red wine from southern Italy

What's in Garlic?

Here are the nutrients you get from 100 grams, or about 3½ ounces, of garlic according to *Garlic Press*:

Composition	Minerals	Vitamins
61.3% moisture	390-460 mg phosphorus	15 mg vitamin C
30.8% carbohydrate	100-120 mg potassium	0.5 mg nicotinic acid
6.2% protein	50-90 mg calcium	0.25 mg thiamin
1.5% ash	43-77 mg magnesium	0.08 mg riboflavin
0.2% fat	10-22 mg sodium	
	2.8-3.9 mg iron	
	0.5-1 mg aluminum	
	0.2-1 mg barium	

(*Garlic Press* cited the 1985 work of G. R. Fenwick and A. B. Hanley in "CRC Critical Review in Food Science and Nutrition.")

Pennington and Church, in the 13th edition of *Food Values of Portions Commonly Used*, agree that except for taste, there isn't much to garlic. It's about 60 percent water and 30 percent carbohydrate. The rest is protein, fat and traces of minerals and vitamins. Thiamin is the only vitamin present beyond trace amounts. There is some potassium and phosphorus (in proportions that are the reverse of the figures cited by Fenwick and Hanley) and traces of sodium, calcium and iron. Although some alternative-medicine gurus cite selenium as a key element in garlic, it is not listed in any nutrition workups we have seen, nor is sulfur. Neither substance is a nutrient. As to calories, a 3-gram clove has four. If you're dieting, garlic is your friend.

Grilled Marinated Duck Breasts with Peppered Pineapple Sauce

THIS FESTIVE DISH offers lots of flavor for little work. Soy sauce, walnut oil and a very fruity port wine make a great background for garlic-and-ginger-marinated duck breasts. The peppery pineapple sauce, piqued with garlic, onions and Asian seasonings, gets a touch of heat from Chinese chili paste.

SERVES 6

3 duck breasts, boned and split
½ cup medium soy sauce
¼ cup Gramm's Six Grape Porto, or another good-quality red port
¼ cup pineapple juice
3 plump garlic cloves, pressed
1 tablespoon minced fresh gingerroot
2 teaspoons freshly ground black pepper
3 tablespoons walnut oil

Peppered Pineapple Sauce

2 tablespoons olive oil
¾ cup finely diced sweet onions
3 plump garlic cloves, smashed and minced
1 tablespoon minced fresh lemongrass or zest of 1 lemon

2 cups finely diced fresh pineapple or 2 cups canned crushed pineapple, drained
¼ cup fruit vinegar
2 tablespoons dark brown sugar
2 tablespoons minced fresh gingerroot
2 tablespoons fresh lime juice
2 tablespoons dark soy sauce
3 tablespoons Chinese plum sauce or plum preserves
2 teaspoons coarsely ground black peppercorns
1 teaspoon Chinese chili paste

¼ cup chopped fresh cilantro leaves

At least 4 and up to 6 hours ahead, prepare duck breasts. Carefully trim and discard excess fat. With a sharp knife, score through skin and part of underlying fat layer by making two or three lengthwise slashes across top of each piece. In a mixing bowl, combine soy sauce, port, pineapple juice, garlic, ginger and pepper. Whisk in walnut oil to make a thick emulsion. Put breasts and marinade in a large zipperlock plastic bag. Seal tightly and marinate in refrigerator for at least 2½ hours, turning occasionally. Bring breasts to room temperature 1 hour before grilling.

To make sauce: Heat olive oil in a medium-sized nonreactive saucepan over medium heat. Add onions, garlic and lemongrass; stir until onions are softened, 2 to 4 minutes. Add pineapple, vinegar, sugar, ginger, lime juice, soy sauce, plum sauce or preserves, pepper and chili paste. Bring to a simmer over low heat and cook, stirring, until pineapple is tender and sauce has thickened, 8 to 12 minutes. Let cool slightly before serving.

Thoroughly clean the surface of a gas or charcoal grill with a metal brush; then coat surface evenly with vegetable spray. Heat grill on high heat until hot.

Place duck breasts on grill rack, skin side down, and grill over high heat for 6 minutes (if very thick, grill 2 minutes more); turn and grill 2 minutes. Place breasts on a carving platter and allow to rest for 5 minutes. If cooking on top of stove, heat a large cast-iron skillet over high heat. Place breasts, skin side down, in skillet, reduce heat to low and cook until skin is brown and crisp and fat is rendered, about 20 minutes. Turn over and cook for 3 minutes for medium-rare. Let meat rest in a warm place for 10 minutes.

Carve each breast across grain into about 6 slices. Spoon some sauce onto each heated serving plate. Arrange duck breasts on sauce in overlapping slices. Serve with more sauce over top. Sprinkle generously with cilantro.

Robert Sinskey Winery Carneros Pinot Noir
(California: Napa Valley) or a French Beaujolais

Sauerkraut-Stuffed Duck with Candied Garlic & Apples

OUR FRIEND JOHN SCHUMACHER serves extraordinary food at Schumacher's, the charming inn in New Prague, Minnesota, that he and his wife Kathleen own. Years ago he graciously shared his recipe for a terrific sauerkraut-and-potato-stuffed duck. We've embellished the stuffing with garlic and mellow leeks, and added a sweet garlic-apple sauce.

SERVES 6 TO 8

2 tablespoons vegetable oil

3 plump garlic cloves, pressed

3 cups thinly sliced leeks, white and tender green

2 cups sauerkraut, rinsed and drained

2 tablespoons sugar

2 tablespoons unbleached flour

½ teaspoon caraway seeds

½ teaspoon dried thyme

¾ cup drained grated baking potato (1 large)
   Freshly ground white pepper

2 4½-to-5-pound ducks, surface fat removed
   Kosher salt

3 tablespoons unsalted butter

4 plump garlic cloves, thinly sliced

6 tart apples, cored and sliced into ¼-inch-thick wedges

⅔ cup firmly packed dark brown sugar

Preheat oven to 450°F. Place a large rack inside a large, shallow roasting pan.

Heat oil in a small skillet over medium heat. Stir in garlic and leeks. Cover skillet and reduce heat to low. Cook until leeks are very soft, 8 to 10 minutes, stirring occasionally.

Meanwhile, in a large mixing bowl, combine sauerkraut, sugar, flour, caraway, thyme, potato and white pepper; blend thoroughly. When leeks are done, mix well with sauerkraut.

Stuff cavity of each duck with half of stuffing mixture. Close cavities with skewers and string. Prick ducks all over with skewer to release fat.

Place ducks, back side up, on rack in pan. Roast for 35 minutes.

Pour off all fat from pan. Prick fatty areas of ducks again and turn breast side up. Roast for 40 minutes.

Drain off accumulated fat again. Reduce heat to 350°F and roast for 30 minutes more, or until skin is dark and crisp. Transfer ducks to a carving board.

During final 20 minutes of roasting, prepare apples. Melt butter in a medium-sized cast-iron skillet. Add garlic and apples. Stir over medium heat for 5 minutes. Sprinkle evenly with brown sugar. Reduce heat to low and cook, stirring often, for 10 minutes. Increase heat to high and cook, stirring often, until sauce is thick and apples are tender.

Carve ducks into halves or quarters. Distribute among heated serving plates along with stuffing. Serve with garlic-apple sauce.

Wine: Lockwood Vineyard Merlot
(California: Monterey County)
or another rich and fruity California Merlot

GARLIC & HEALTH

AT A SUPERMARKET CHECKOUT COUNTER we saw this tabloid headline: "Nature's most powerful weapon in the war against disease and aging!" The weapon was garlic, of course. The article promised garlic would cure everything: sore muscles, bladder infections, high cholesterol, a weak immune system, high blood pressure, arthritis and even cancer. No more colds, fatigue, indigestion or itchy skin. Your hearing will stop deteriorating. The free radicals that have been pillaging your organs will be routed by sword-brandishing sulfur compounds from your garlicky dinner. And perhaps best of all, impotence will be a dim memory!

That's the kind of press garlic has been getting lately. And for good reason: garlic *is* good for you.

Garlic's power to heal has long been celebrated. In ancient Coptic medicine, oil and garlic were taken to purge the intestines, clear the head and enhance lactation in nursing mothers. (We wonder how the babies liked that!) One treatise listed this prescription for a healthy life: Abstain from sex, fish, vegetables and milk. Eat instead a dish of garlic, pomegranate, raisins, honey, vinegar, herbs and spices.

The Roman writer Aulus Cornelius Celsus wrote that garlic was good for a fever. Hippocrates, who continues to inspire physicians, was himself inspired by garlic. Galen, a Greek doctor, celebrated what farmers called *theriac*, a garlic cure-all. And Pliny, the peripatetic Roman naturalist, thought garlic was good for almost every known affliction.

This tradition is now part of popular culture. The *Times* of London calls the garlic phenomenon "a new age stew . . . of health awareness, environmental concern and all-around political correctness." Ask an Internet search engine to look up "garlic and health" and you'll find tens of thousands of references.

It's everywhere. On Broadway, in *Having Our Say*, Bessie and Sadie Delaney talked about eating garlic for their health. The sisters were both over 100 when the play about their lives was produced, and they were there watching it, still lucid, strong and sophisticated, and giving some credit to garlic.

This old-fashioned folk wisdom about garlic's healing powers has recently come under the scrutiny of modern medical researchers. There are hundreds of studies of the relationship between garlic and cholesterol, high blood pressure and certain cancers and of the antioxidants that combat those tumor-causing "free radicals" that subject us to peril. One scientist says garlic is as good an anticoagulant as aspirin; another says it can clear up the congestion of colds. (Garlic has been shown to increase body heat, which may explain how it got a reputation as an aphrodisiac.)

Botanist James A. Duke has sought out every modern scientific study of the traditional uses of all herbal medicines, including garlic. Most of what Pliny claimed for garlic two millennia ago can now be defended scientifically, according to Dr. Duke. In his latest book, *The Green Pharmacy*, he makes a case for garlic's ability not only to prevent cancer and heart disease, but to effectively treat a host of conditions, including high blood pressure, high cholesterol, angina, cardiac arrhythmia, and a score of other conditions. And it's generally agreed that garlic is antibacterial, retarding spoilage in food.

In *The Healing Foods*, Patricia Hausman and Judith Hurly cite the work of Dr. Arun Bordia of the Tagore Medical College in India, showing that garlic can reduce cholesterol levels and that it is an effective cancer-fighting antioxidant. Other investigators have found that compounds in garlic may help lower blood pressure by affecting the processes in the blood that create platelets.

Some experts hold that garlic may also slow the growth of cancers. Dr. Richard Rivlin of the Sloan-Kettering Institute appeared on NBC's *Dateline* to make the case for eating a couple of cloves each day to reduce your risk of developing cancer. Sujatha Sundaram and Dr. John Milner at Penn State believe that garlic consumption can lead to a lower risk of colon cancer. One potent garlic component (known as SAC, or S-allylcysteine) seems to inhibit a carcinogen that binds itself to breast tissue in rats. Even the American Institute for Cancer Research has weighed in, with studies suggesting that garlic may ward off cancer of the esophagus, as well as conferring a range of benefits worthy of Pliny, including reducing cholesterol, lowering triglycerides, thinning the blood and reducing the threat of heart attack.

But many medical experts are more cautious. Stephen Warshafsky, an internist at the New York Medical College at Valhalla, says that a review of the data indicates garlic *may* reduce cholesterol but is not a panacea. In 1997 the *Annals of Internal Medicine* said that a half or whole clove of garlic a day can help lower cholesterol by inhibiting an enzyme that is involved with cholesterol production in the liver. But the article cautioned that garlic is not a substitute for a diet that is consistently low in fat. And although an Oxford study reported by *Miracle Magazine* showed that a group of men with high cholesterol achieved an 8 percent reduction in cholesterol by taking 600 to 900 mg of dried garlic each day for a month, a group that used prescription medicines did better, achieving a 20 to 40 percent reduction.

Stephen Fulder, in his book *Garlic*, makes the case for garlic in general health care, but with a caveat: "Readers should not take suggestions concerning its use as prescriptions for specific health problems. . . . Those with health problems should always seek professional assistance."

The *University of California at Berkeley Wellness Letter*, published by the university's School of Public Health, is well regarded in academic medicine circles as well as among New Age and holistic medicine practitioners. In 1996, after months of study, the folks at Berkeley headlined an article: "Garlic: great for cooking, but not much else." Granting that garlic "has been part of humanity's medicine kit for thousands of years," the newsletter took a look at the health claims made over the years by promoters. Their conclusion: despite the huge number of studies that have been conducted, "there is no evidence one way or another" to support any of the health claims made on garlic's behalf.

The definitive answers aren't in yet, but there's enough evidence for us to say that garlic is good for you. And, just as important, it can make you a better cook and make your dinner more enjoyable. So just eat garlic!

RED MEAT

Rumanian Garlic-Smothered Rib Steak with Hungarian Onions   289

Grilled Hanger Steak with Citrus Garlic Marinade   290

Flank Steak with Balsamic Vinegar Marinade   291

Skirt Steak with Many-Pepper Garlic Sauté   292

Braised Short Ribs in Barbecue Sauce   294

Asian-Style Oven-Braised Short Ribs with Garlic, Hoisin & Beer   296

Many-Peppers Meat Loaf   298

Glazed Corned Beef with Roasted Shallots, Carrots & Parsnips   300

Heavenly Hash   302

Barbecued Brisket   304

Veal Brisket Roasted with Garlic, Onions & Plums   306

Roasted Rack of Veal with Garlic & Sage   308

Grilled Veal Tenderloin in Asian Orange Marinade   309

Cast-Iron-Skillet Veal Chops with Tapenade Vinaigrette   310

Veal Scaloppine with Lemon Garlic Anchovy Sauce   311

Sicilian Veal Braciole   312

Fragrant Veal Loaf with Garlic Custard Sauce   314

Orange & Fennel-Laced Veal Stew with Vegetables   316

(continued)

Rumanian Garlic-Smothered Rib Steak with Hungarian Onions

THIS IS ONE OF OUR all-time favorite summer indulgences—thick rib steaks, preferably USDA Prime, cooked over a hot grill until black on the outside and marvelously pink within. Before slicing the steaks, we slather them first with a barely cooked coating of chopped garlic, then with darkly sautéed sweet onions seasoned with good Hungarian paprika. This dish comes from our friend Sanford Herskovitz, who says that the garlic topping is Rumanian and the onions Hungarian.

SERVES 4

5   tablespoons olive oil, plus more
      if needed
2   large sweet onions, cut in half and
      thinly sliced
1   tablespoon sweet Hungarian paprika
8   plump garlic cloves, smashed and
      chopped finely, but not quite minced
2   2-inch-thick rib steaks,
      about 2 pounds each
      Kosher salt and freshly ground
      black pepper

Heat 3 tablespoons olive oil in a large skillet over medium-high heat. Add onions, lower heat, and sauté, stirring often and adding more oil if needed, until golden brown, about 30 minutes. Stir in paprika and set aside.

Pour remaining 2 tablespoons olive oil into a small saucepan. Add garlic and reserve.

Shortly before grilling, thoroughly clean surface of a gas or charcoal grill with a metal brush, then coat surface evenly with a vegetable spray. Heat grill until hot.

Season steaks with salt and pepper. Grill for 8 minutes, turn and grill for 6 minutes more, or until an instant-read thermometer inserted into middle of side of steak reads 125°F for rare or 135°F for medium.

Let steaks rest for 5 to 7 minutes. At the same time, heat garlic until oil is bubbling hot, then remove from heat. Reheat onions and season with salt.

With slotted spoons, spread garlic, then onions, evenly over steaks. Carve into thick slices. Serve on heated plates.

Wine: Lorinon Rioja (Spain) or another rich Rioja

Grilled Hanger Steak with Citrus Garlic Marinade

OUR PREFERENCE in beef is for cuts that may require a bit more chewing but are rich in flavor. Hanger steak, also known by its French name of *onglet*, or butcher's tenderloin, has historically been the cut saved by the butcher for himself, and there's just one per animal. Marinated and grilled, this cut of meat is sublime. Our orange juice marinade, with lots of onion and garlic, is further enriched with pepper and vinegar.

SERVES 6

1   medium-sized sweet onion, quartered
4   plump garlic cloves
1   medium-sized green bell pepper
1   dried chile, crumbled
1   1-inch slice fresh gingerroot, peeled
10 fresh mint leaves
3   long sprigs fresh thyme
1   cup fresh orange juice
½   cup canola oil
¼   cup white wine vinegar
    Juice of 1 lime
1   teaspoon finely ground black pepper
3   pounds hanger steak
    Kosher salt and freshly ground black pepper

In the bowl of a food processor, combine onion, garlic, bell pepper, chile, ginger, mint, thyme and orange juice. Pulse until mixture is pureed. Add oil, vinegar, lime juice and ground pepper. Blend thoroughly.

Place meat in a jumbo zipperlock bag. Pour marinade over meat, seal and refrigerate, turning several times, for a minimum of 4 hours and up to 10. Let stand at room temperature for 1 hour before grilling.

Coat surface of a gas or charcoal grill with vegetable oil spray. Heat grill until hot.

Remove meat from marinade and season with salt and more pepper. Grill steaks for 3 minutes on one side. Turn and grill for 2 minutes on second side for medium-rare. Transfer meat to carving board and let rest for 5 minutes.

Slice hanger steaks on an angle and serve. For a special indulgence, serve Lemon Pepper Aioli (see page 153) on the side.

Wine: Howell Mountain Vineyards "Old Vines"
Zinfandel (California: Napa Valley) or
an Australian Shiraz

Flank Steak
with Balsamic Vinegar Marinade

BROWN MUSTARD and horseradish make a great background for garlic in this marinade. We add some balsamic vinegar for a slightly sweet dark richness. You can use this delicious marinade on virtually any meat or chicken, but we especially enjoy it with flank steaks cooked on the grill.

SERVES 6

¼ teaspoon ground red pepper (cayenne)
1 teaspoon freshly ground black pepper
5 plump garlic cloves, pressed
3 tablespoons prepared brown mustard
1 tablespoon horseradish
3 tablespoons balsamic vinegar
¼ cup canola oil
2 flank steaks, about 2 pounds each
Kosher salt

In a mixing bowl, combine cayenne, black pepper, garlic, mustard and horseradish. Blend thoroughly, then whisk in vinegar. Slowly whisk in oil, beating vigorously to make a thick emulsion.

Place flank steaks in a large zipperlock bag. Add marinade and seal bag tightly. Massage bag to coat meat with marinade. Refrigerate, turning occasionally, for at least 2 hours or up to 8. Bring meat to room temperature before grilling.

Evenly coat a clean grill rack with vegetable oil spray. Heat grill until hot. Remove flank steaks from marinade and place on a large platter. Season generously with salt. Grill for 4 minutes on each side for rare. If meat is thick, grill 1 more minute on second side. Let steaks rest on a carving board for 5 minutes.

Carve into thin slices on an angle across grain and serve with natural juices.

Wine: Wild Horse Winery Central Coast Syrah
(California: Santa Barbara County)
or a Côtes-du-Rhône from France

Skirt Steak
with Many-Pepper Garlic Sauté

ALTHOUGH THEY'RE THOROUGHLY delicious, skirt steaks are not one of those melt-in-your-mouth cuts. But if you marinate them in a garlic-rich vinaigrette and put them on the grill, you'll have big flavor and near-tenderness. This recipe is one of our summer favorites, especially when the melange of peppers for the sauté comes from a nearby farm garden. Be flexible with the peppers, basing your selection on color and degrees of heat, so that the dish is right for your palate. Fresh cilantro and lime juice add a pleasing contrast.

SERVES 6

Marinade

- ½ cup rich red wine vinegar
- 1 teaspoon Colman's dry mustard
- 5 plump garlic cloves, smashed
- ¼ cup olive oil
- ½ cup canola oil
- 1 large yellow onion, coarsely chopped
- ¼ cup chopped fresh cilantro

- 3 pounds skirt steak, cut into 6-inch-long pieces

Pepper Sauté

- 1 large red bell pepper
- 1 yellow or orange bell pepper
- 3-4 mild chiles
- 1 poblano chile
- 2 New Mexico red chiles, or another hot chile, cut into thin rings and seeded
- 1 large, sweet onion, thinly sliced
- 3 tablespoons olive oil
- 4 plump garlic cloves, thinly sliced and julienned
- 2 tablespoons fresh lime juice
  Kosher salt and freshly ground white pepper
- ¼ cup minced fresh cilantro

To make marinade: Combine vinegar, mustard and garlic in a large nonreactive baking dish. Blend thoroughly, then whisk in oils to make a thick emulsion. Add onions and cilantro. Then add meat, turning in marinade to coat on both sides. Cover dish with plastic wrap and refrigerate for at least 4 hours and up to 8, turning the meat several times.

To make pepper sauté: Seed peppers and cut lengthwise into ¾-inch-wide strips. Combine all peppers and onions in a large mixing bowl.

Heat oil in a wok until hot. Add pepper mixture to hot oil and stir-fry over high heat until peppers and onions are nearly tender, about 3 minutes. Add garlic and toss until slivers are somewhat softened. Transfer pepper mixture to a serving bowl and toss with lime juice. Season with salt and pepper. Stir in cilantro. Set aside in a shallow serving bowl.

Thoroughly clean the surface of a gas or charcoal grill with a metal brush, then coat surface evenly with vegetable spray.

Heat grill on high heat. Remove skirt steaks from marinade and place on hot grill. Turn after 2 minutes and grill for another 2 minutes for rare, 3 minutes for medium. Transfer to a carving board and let rest for 2 minutes. Slice meat crosswise into 2-inch-wide pieces. Serve meat on heated plates generously garnished with warm pepper sauté.

Wine: Daniel Brusset Gigondas (France: Rhône Valley) or a very rich and complex Côtes-du-Rhône from France

Braised Short Ribs in Barbecue Sauce

THESE SHORT RIBS ARE SO GOOD, slowly braised in a pleasingly sweet and tangy barbecue sauce. Serve the ribs with Spoonbread with Jalapeño, Cheddar and Garlic (page 368) or Fried Polenta Triangles with Garlic and Shallots (page 370).

SERVES 4

½ cup unbleached flour
5 pounds beef short ribs cut
    from the plate
7 plump garlic cloves, unpeeled
¼ cup plus 1 tablespoon vegetable oil
1 large yellow onion, finely diced
    Zest of 2 lemons, minced
2 teaspoons ground cumin
1 tablespoon medium-hot chile powder,
    preferably ground pasilla
    (see page 414)
2 teaspoons kosher salt
1 teaspoon freshly ground white pepper
2 tablespoons dark molasses
¼ packed cup dark brown sugar
½ cup ketchup
½ cup prepared brown mustard
½ cup vodka

Juice of 2 lemons
1 bay leaf
1 teaspoon freshly ground black pepper

Preheat oven to 325°F.

Pour flour into a soup plate. Carefully coat short ribs in flour; set aside on a rack.

Heat a large cast-iron skillet over medium heat until hot. Cook garlic cloves in dry skillet, turning often, until soft to the touch and somewhat blackened in spots, about 15 minutes. Set aside until cool, then peel and mince. Reserve.

Heat ¼ cup oil in same skillet until hot. Working in batches, brown short ribs on all sides over medium-high heat, about 5 minutes. Transfer to a large platter when browned.

Add remaining 1 tablespoon oil and onions to skillet and stir over medium-low heat until all browned particles adhering to skillet are loosened. Cook onions, stirring occasionally, until soft and golden, 10 to 15 minutes. Stir in reserved garlic, lemon zest, cumin, chile powder, salt and pepper; stir for 1 minute to release flavors. Then add molasses, brown sugar, ketchup, mustard, vodka, lemon juice and bay leaf. Blend thoroughly. When liquids begin to bubble, stir in black pepper and slip browned short ribs back into the pan.

Cover skillet tightly with foil, place a lid over foil and braise in preheated oven for 2 hours, or until meat is fork-tender. Carefully skim off surface fat and remove bay leaf before serving.

Wine: Peachy Canyon Paso Robles Zinfandel (California: Paso Robles) or a Crozes-Hermitage from France's Rhône Valley

"The taste of garlic at its most intense, chopped and uncooked, is detectable on the skin for up to seventy-two hours after ingestion."

— A warning from John Lanchester's *The Debt to Pleasure*, in which the protagonist's dark and malevolent side emerges between insightful culinary observations

Asian-Style Oven-Braised Short Ribs with Garlic, Hoisin & Beer

A CLUTCH OF SPICES—STAR ANISE, Sichuan peppercorns, five-spice powder, ginger, lemongrass and garlic—blend together to make an exotic sauce with soy and hoisin. Inspired by the flavors at the funky San Francisco restaurant BetelNut, which has been described as an Asian beer hall, we add dark beer and caramelized onions to make a ravishing braising medium for our short ribs. And for a final fresh-flavor touch, a generous blast of fresh lime juice, roasted peanuts and cilantro. Serve these ribs with a rice dish.

SERVES 4

2   teaspoons Sichuan peppercorns

½   cup unbleached flour

5   pounds beef short ribs cut
    from the plate

¼   cup plus 2 tablespoons vegetable oil

2   cups finely diced white onions

¼   cup water

5   plump garlic cloves, smashed
    and minced

2   tablespoons minced fresh gingerroot

3   dried chiles, crumbled

2   tablespoons minced fresh lemongrass
    (or minced zest of 2 lemons)

1   star anise

1   tablespoon sugar

2   teaspoons five-spice powder

½   cup dry sherry

½   cup hoisin sauce

¼   cup soy sauce

1   12-ounce bottle dark beer

2   limes, quartered

½   cup roasted peanuts

4   scallions, trimmed with 1 inch
    green, minced

Preheat oven to 325°F.

Place Sichuan peppercorns in a small skillet and cook over medium-high heat, stirring constantly, until toasted, 2 to 3 minutes. Transfer to a mortar and crush with a pestle.

Pour flour into a soup plate. Carefully coat short ribs in flour; set aside on a rack.

Heat ¼ cup oil in a large cast-iron skillet until hot. Working in batches, brown short ribs on all sides over medium-high heat, about 5 minutes. Transfer to a large platter when browned.

Add 2 tablespoons oil and heat. Add onions and cook, stirring, over medium-high heat until soft and beginning to stick to skillet, 6 to 10 minutes. Stir in water, garlic, ginger, chiles and lemongrass. Continue to cook 2 to 3 minutes to soften garlic and lemongrass. Add crushed peppercorns, anise, sugar and five-spice powder and cook, stirring, for 1 minute to release flavors.

Add sherry, hoisin and soy. Stir over high heat until mixture bubbles. Add beer and bring to a second boil. Stir bubbling sauce for 1 to 2 minutes to thicken somewhat.

Slip browned short ribs into sauce and spoon sauce over each. Cover tightly and transfer to oven.

Bake for 2¼ hours, or until meat is fork-tender. Transfer short ribs to a heated platter. Skim surface fat. Bring liquid to a boil over high heat and cook until sauce thickens, 3 to 5 minutes.

Divide short ribs among heated serving plates. Spoon sauce over meat. Spritz with lime. Sprinkle with peanuts and scallions.

Wine: Domaine Richeaume Rosé de Provence
(France: Côtes de Provence) or a lusty rosé from California

Many-Peppers Meat Loaf

THIS LUSTY, GARLICKY MEAT LOAF combines pork, veal and beef with a mixture of minced fresh peppers and dried ground peppers. Generous quantities of onions and celery give additional deep flavors. A newly streamlined version of one of our most popular dishes, this exceptionally tender, colorful meat loaf is worth making just for sandwiches, especially on homemade bread. Our friends and family request it often. In fact, we think Linda's sons would prefer this to all her other dishes, even lobster.

SERVES 8 TO 10

1   tablespoon kosher salt
1   teaspoon freshly ground black pepper
1   teaspoon freshly ground white pepper
1   teaspoon ground red pepper (cayenne)
1   teaspoon ground cumin
1   teaspoon ground dried oregano
1   teaspoon dried thyme
4   tablespoons (½ stick) unsalted butter
5   plump garlic cloves, smashed
    and minced
1   cup finely chopped yellow onions
½   cup minced celery, including
    some tops
¼   cup minced scallions, including
    tender green
1   medium red bell pepper, seeded
    and finely chopped
1   hot fresh chile, minced
½   cup evaporated milk
3   large eggs
2   tablespoons Worcestershire sauce
1   tablespoon Tabasco
2   pounds lean ground pork
1½ pounds lean ground beef
1½ pounds lean ground veal
1½ cups fine dry bread crumbs
2   bay leaves

In a small bowl, combine salt, black and white pepper, cayenne, cumin, oregano and thyme. Blend well.

Melt butter in a small skillet. Add seasoning mixture and stir over medium-high heat for 2 minutes, or until mixture becomes very fragrant. Pour into a large mixing bowl.

Add garlic, onions, celery, scallions and peppers to bowl with spices. Blend in milk, eggs, Worcestershire and Tabasco. Add meats and bread crumbs. Mix vigorously with your hands until seasonings and meats are thoroughly blended.

Turn mixture into a large roasting pan. Firmly shape it into a long loaf that is 4 to 6 inches wide and 4 to 5 inches high. Place bay leaves on top. Cover and chill for at least 2 hours or up to 4. Remove from refrigerator 1 hour before cooking.

Preheat oven to 400°F.

Bake meat loaf for 1 hour 15 minutes, or until it is nicely browned. To test for doneness, insert a knife into center; if knife feels hot to your lip, meat loaf is done.

Let pan stand at room temperature for 10 minutes before slicing. Cut into slices at least 1 inch thick. Serve with a zesty sauce on the side, such as Fresh Caramelized Tomato Sauce (see page 158).

Wine: Bruno Giacosa Barbera d'Alba (Italy: Piedmont) or another Barbera from Piedmont

Glazed Corned Beef with Roasted Shallots, Carrots & Parsnips

GARLIC IS ABSOLUTELY ESSENTIAL IN the pickling process for corned beef. We add still more garlic for the lengthy boiling. To enhance the special flavors of this dish, we like to finish cooking it in the oven under a somewhat sweet and piquant glaze of cider, maple syrup, mustard and horseradish. Instead of the usual rather bland boiled vegetables, we accompany this with sweetly caramelized roasted ones.

SERVES 8

2   tablespoons black and white peppercorns
1   8-to-10-pound cured whole beef brisket, preferably kosher
8   garlic cloves
4   small dried chiles
2   bay leaves
1   tablespoon Dijon mustard
1   tablespoon grated white horseradish
½   cup apple cider
½   cup maple syrup
10   whole cloves
    Freshly grated nutmeg
10   plump shallots, peeled and cut in half

12   medium carrots, trimmed, scrubbed and quartered
12   small parsnips, trimmed, scrubbed and quartered
2   tablespoons olive oil
1   tablespoon minced fresh herbs (parsley, thyme, tarragon, dill)
    Kosher salt and freshly ground black pepper
    Grated white horseradish and Dijon mustard

Put peppercorns in a single layer on a kitchen towel and press down with a heavy skillet just enough to bruise them.

In a large soup pot, combine brisket, peppercorns, garlic, chiles and bay leaves. Add water to cover and place over high heat. Cover pot tightly and bring to a boil. Reduce heat to low and simmer until meat is fork-tender, 3½ to 4½ hours.

Carefully remove meat from pot and place, fat side up, in a large, shallow pan. (If you wish, you can hold corned beef in refrigerator until you are ready to make glaze. Just bring to room temperature before glazing.)

Preheat oven to 400°F.

In a small saucepan, blend together mustard and horseradish. Slowly blend in cider and maple syrup. Bring to a boil, then simmer for 2 minutes.

Meanwhile, score top of meat and stud with cloves. Pour glaze over top. Sprinkle with nutmeg. Bake for 30 minutes, or until shiny and hot, basting once.

When meat is done, transfer to a carving board. Discard any juices in pan. Increase oven temperature to 500°F and place a rack in upper third of oven.

Add shallots, carrots and parsnips to roasting pan. Drizzle with olive oil and toss to coat well. Place pan on top rack in oven and roast until vegetables are fork-tender, 10 to 14 minutes. Sprinkle with herbs, salt and pepper.

As vegetables are cooking, trim all visible fat from top of meat. Then carve across grain into thin slices. Overlap meat slices slightly at one end of a large heated serving platter. Add vegetables at the other end.

Serve with bowls of horseradish and mustard on the side.

Wine: Rosenblum Cellars Zinfandel "Vintner's Cuvée" (California) or another medium-bodied Zinfandel

Heavenly Hash

ALONG WITH THE GARLIC used in cooking the corned beef, we include some dry roasted cloves in the hash itself. After baking, the hash is served with poached eggs and a zesty tomato sauce on top. While a dish this rich is a special indulgence, it's our all-time favorite for brunch.

SERVES 8 TO 10

5 large Yukon gold or red-skin potatoes, peeled

5 plump garlic cloves, dry-roasted (see page 34) and minced

5 pounds leftover Glazed Corned Beef (see page 300), cut into large chunks

1 large white onion

8 scallions, trimmed with 1 inch of green, chopped

½ medium-sized green bell pepper

12 branches fresh flat-leaf parsley, chopped

1 tablespoon minced fresh oregano or marjoram (1 teaspoon dried)

2 teaspoons minced fresh thyme (1 teaspoon dried)

Kosher salt and freshly ground black pepper

¼ cup Worcestershire sauce

2 teaspoons Tabasco

7 tablespoons butter

8-10 large eggs

2 tablespoons cider or fruit vinegar

1½ cups Barbecue Sauce with Roasted Tomatoes, Horseradish & Bourbon (page 156), or another spicy tomato sauce

Combine potatoes with cold water to cover in a large saucepan. Cover and bring to a boil. Cook until potatoes are somewhat tender, 25 to 35 minutes. Drain. Chop fine and place in a large bowl. Add garlic.

Working in batches, mince beef in the bowl of a food processor. Add beef to potatoes. Finely chop onion and add to mixture. Then add scallions, pepper, parsley and herbs. Add Worcestershire and Tabasco.

In a large skillet, preferably cast-iron, melt butter. Carefully cook until butter begins to brown, about 1 minute. Tilt skillet to coat sides, then pour browned butter into bowl with meat mixture.

Blend mixture thoroughly. Spoon into skillet and press to pack down evenly. (Hash can be prepared to this point up to 24 hours ahead; cover, refrigerate and bring to room temperature before proceeding.)

Preheat oven to 425°F. Bake hash until piping hot and crusty on top, 35 to 40 minutes.

Shortly before hash is done, prepare to poach eggs. Fill a large sauté pan with water. Add vinegar and some salt. Bring to a softly rolling boil. When hash is ready, transfer pan to stove top. Have heated plates nearby.

Working in batches of four, poach eggs: Break eggs one at a time into a small cup and slip into bubbling water. Using a slotted spoon, quickly flip whites around yolk, trying to keep each egg in an oval shape. Cook each egg for 2½ minutes. In the last moments, spoon hash onto each plate. Place an egg in center and sprinkle with a few grindings of pepper. Serve with sauce on the side.

Wine: Martinelli Vineyards Zinfandel Russian River Valley "Jackass Vineyard" (California: Sonoma County) or full-bodied Côtes-du-Rhône

Barbecued Brisket

WHEN WE HAVE LARGE, casual gatherings of friends, we often serve platters of hearty dishes, some made ahead so their flavors ripen and intensify. To save time, we prevail upon our butcher friend, Mr. Brisket (Sanford Herskovitz), to prepare his famous smoky barbecued brisket. (Ours is delicious, but his is so easy.) Thankfully, he has shared his "recipe," allowing us to make adjustments, such as rubbing the meat with a spicy combination of seasonings. The rest of the recipe is mostly Sanford's, although we did have to make a few subtle interpretations:

Linda: *What do you season it with?*
Sanford: *Whatever I have, if I have anything.*
Linda: *Sanford, how long do you give it on the grill?*
Sanford: *Oh, about an hour or two—or until I remember it's out there.*
Linda: *How often do you turn it?*
Sanford: *Turn it? Say, I run a meat business, not a restaurant; I haven't got time to run outside and turn it!*

SERVES 10

2   tablespoons dark brown sugar
1   tablespoon fennel seeds, lightly crushed
2   tablespoons garlic powder
1   teaspoon ground red pepper (cayenne)
1   teaspoon freshly ground white pepper
¼   teaspoon ground cloves
1   whole beef brisket (9-12 pounds)
24 thin slices of garlic (3-4 plump cloves)
    Kosher salt and freshly ground black pepper
1   jumbo Spanish or white onion, thinly sliced
3   cups Barbecue Sauce with Roasted Tomatoes, Horseradish & Bourbon (page 156), plus more if desired

Two days before serving: In a small bowl, blend together brown sugar, fennel seeds, garlic powder, cayenne, white pepper and cloves. Reserve.

Using a sharp knife, make 12 slits on top of brisket and 12 on underside. Insert a garlic slice into each. Place brisket in a large nonreactive pan and coat thoroughly with seasoning rub, salt and pepper. Cover with plastic wrap and refrigerate for at least 12 hours.

One day before serving: Prepare a charcoal fire in one half of your grill. (This is called an "indirect" fire.) Spray surface of rack with vegetable oil spray. When coals are moderately hot, place brisket, fat side up, on rack away from fire. Cover grill and cook meat for 1½ hours, turning after 40 minutes.

Meanwhile, preheat oven to 325°F.

Place brisket, fat side up, in a heavy roasting pan with a tight-fitting cover. Distribute onions over and around meat. Pour 1 cup barbecue sauce over meat. Cover tightly and braise for 2 to 3 hours, or until thin part of brisket is fork-tender.

When done, let meat cool. Remove from roasting pan and wrap thoroughly, first in plastic wrap and then in foil. Pour liquid from pan into a large bowl and cover. Chill meat and gravy overnight.

To carve: Trim all excess fat from top of brisket; discard. Carefully separate top (called the point) piece from bottom (the flat) with a sharp knife. With a sharp carving knife, beginning with top, slice each piece on a slight angle, cutting across grain. Arrange overlapping slices in an ovenproof casserole, placing slices from top of brisket on bottom of casserole, followed by slices from bottom of brisket (flat).

Preheat oven to 350°F.

Remove fat from gravy and discard. Spoon remaining barbecue sauce into gravy. Pour about half of gravy over meat. Cover casserole tightly and bake until meat is fork-tender, 1 to 1½ hours. Reheat remaining gravy and serve on the side.

Wine: Bodegas Berberana D'Avalos Tinto
(Spain: Rioja Alta) or a medium-bodied, fruity
Cabernet Sauvignon from California

Veal Brisket Roasted with Garlic, Onions & Plums

VEAL BRISKET, leaner than its beef counterpart, has a more delicate flavor. This fruited preparation is enlivened by garlic and ginger. We use the Chilean plums available in the spring to make a delicious dish for either Easter or Passover. Made with ripe native plums on a cold early-autumn night, the tangy fruit sauce is more assertive.

SERVES 6 TO 8

4 cups chopped white onions
2 large carrots, finely chopped
7 ripe dark plums, pitted and chopped
8 plump garlic cloves, smashed
    and minced
2 teaspoons ground gingerroot
2 veal briskets, about 5 pounds total
    Kosher salt and freshly ground
    black pepper
1 tablespoon hot Hungarian paprika
1 cup plum preserves
1 cup Bennett's chili sauce or
    another spicy chili sauce
½ cup plum wine (available in
    Oriental markets) or apple juice
2 bay leaves

The day before serving, preheat oven to 325°F. Combine onions, carrots, plums and garlic in a large bowl. Sprinkle with ginger and toss well to blend. Spread half of mixture in a heavy roasting pan fitted with a tight-fitting cover. Place briskets, fat side up, on onion mixture. Rub meat evenly with salt, pepper and paprika. Scatter remaining onion mixture over briskets.

Blend together plum preserves, chili sauce and plum wine. Pour evenly over meat. Place a bay leaf on each brisket. Cover tightly and roast, basting occasionally, until fork-tender, about 2¼ hours.

Remove from oven and place briskets on a large platter to cool. Discard bay leaves, wrap briskets in foil and refrigerate. Spoon solids into the bowl of a food processor. Pulse to puree. Combine with gravy remaining in pan and pour into a container. Cover and chill overnight.

A few hours before serving, remove briskets from refrigerator and slice thinly across grain. Arrange slices in an ovenproof dish. Preheat oven to 325°F.

Remove congealed fat from surface of gravy and pour gravy over sliced meat. Cover with foil or a lid and place in oven for 1 hour, or until hot. Serve meat on heated plates with a generous portion of gravy. Serve more gravy on the side.

Wine: Franus Winery Zinfandel Mt. Veeder "Brandlin Vineyard" (California: Napa Valley) or another rich Zinfandel from California

IN OUR GARDEN

IN THE MIDDLE OF OCTOBER 1996, we, garlic virgins, planted 60 cloves of six different varieties in our organic back yard. Then came one of our coldest winters ever. Garlic cloves need some cool weather after planting, but this was too much. We feared for their lives. But we needn't have; we now know how tough garlic can be.

By the middle of June, the hardnecks had started growing their scapes, which within a week became wonderful curving spirals. Bob Zimmerman, an Ohio grower, urged us not to cut the scapes.

"They're fun to watch and they won't hurt the size of the head all that much. Enjoy what's happening." So we watched the scapes curve and twist and finally stand straight up, five feet high.

In late July, we harvested. Not a single plant was lost. We tasted the garlic immediately. It was the best we'd ever had. "Of course it was great," said our garlic guru, Chester Aaron. "But we'll make it better. After you harvest them, hang them up to dry for two weeks. If you thought they were good right out of the garden, just wait until they've cured a little."

As always, Chester was exactly right.

Roasted Rack of Veal with Garlic & Sage

LOOKING LIKE A SMALL BEEF RIB ROAST, this luxury cut of meat is perfect for a special occasion. Seasoned with mustard, garlic and sage, then topped with herbed bread crumbs, it is quickly roasted at a high temperature. Finally, we slice it into succulent chops. We prefer to serve this roast without a sauce, but if you want one, try the Garlic Custard Sauce on page 314.

SERVES 6 TO 8

4 plump garlic cloves, smashed
   and minced

8 fresh sage leaves, plus 4 sage flowers,
   if available, minced

1 tablespoon Dijon mustard

1 whole (7-bone) veal rack, chine bones,
   feather bones and cap removed,
   weighing 6½-7 pounds when
   trimmed
   Kosher salt and freshly ground
   black pepper

½ cup fine dry bread crumbs

2 tablespoons minced fresh chives

1 tablespoon minced fresh parsley

2 tablespoons olive oil

In a small bowl, mix together garlic, sage (reserve 1 teaspoon) and mustard. Using a sharp knife, make about 20 small slits on top of roast. Use knife to insert some seasoning paste into each slit. Season underside of roast with salt and pepper. Place meat on a rack in a shallow roasting pan. Rub remaining paste over fat side of meat.

In another small bowl, blend together bread crumbs, chives, parsley and remaining 1 teaspoon sage. Coat top of roast with this mixture, then drizzle with olive oil. Let stand for 30 minutes.

Preheat oven to 450°F. Roast until thermometer reads 125°F for rare, 45 to 55 minutes, or 130°F for medium.

Carefully transfer roast to a carving board and let rest for 5 minutes. Slice into chops and serve.

Wine: Château Fourcas-Loubaney Listrac
(France: Bordeaux) or another red wine from
the easternmost part of Bordeaux's Médoc region

Grilled Veal Tenderloin in Asian Orange Marinade

WE GROW VAST AMOUNTS of basil in the summer. One of our favorite kinds is the wonderfully aromatic Thai basil, which blends perfectly with garlic, ginger and lemongrass (which we also have in the garden). To these herbs we add orange and lime juices, soy and sesame oil to make a complexly flavored Asian-style marinade for veal tenderloins. These seasonings caramelize, yielding delicious pan juices when the tenderloins are sliced.

SERVES 6

- 2 plump shallots
- 1 1-inch-thick slice fresh gingerroot
- 5 plump garlic cloves
- 1 bulb fresh lemongrass
- 10 stalks cilantro
- 8 leaves fresh basil, preferably Thai
  Juice of 3 medium-sized oranges
- 2 tablespoons soy sauce
- 1 tablespoon fresh lime juice
- 2 teaspoons dark sesame oil
- 1 teaspoon freshly cracked black pepper
- ⅓ cup canola oil
- 5 veal tenderloins, about ¾ pound each
  Kosher salt

In the bowl of a food processor, combine shallots, ginger, garlic, lemongrass, cilantro, basil, orange juice, soy sauce, lime juice, sesame oil and black pepper. Pulse until mixture is pureed, scraping sides at least once. Add canola oil and blend.

In a zipperlock plastic bag, combine marinade and meat. Seal and refrigerate, turning occasionally, for at least 2 hours and up to 6. Bring to room temperature 1 hour before grilling.

Shortly before serving, thoroughly clean surface of a gas or charcoal grill with a metal brush, then coat surface evenly with vegetable oil spray. Heat grill until hot. Remove tenderloins from marinade and sprinkle with salt. Tuck thin, tapered end of tenderloin underneath thick part to make an evenly sized piece and secure with a toothpick. Place on hot grill and cook 3 minutes on each side for rare. Let meat rest for 10 minutes on a warm platter.

Carve on an angle into ½-inch-thick slices. Overlap slices on heated serving plates. Serve with pan juices.

Wine: Williams & Selyem Winery Pinot Noir Sonoma Coast "Hirsch Vineyard" (California: Sonoma County) or a red Burgundy from France

Cast-Iron-Skillet Veal Chops with Tapenade Vinaigrette

A SIMPLE TAPENADE laced with balsamic vinegar makes a sumptuous topping for oven-finished long-bone, frenched eye-of-the-rib veal chops, among the most extravagant cuts of meat.

SERVES 4

Vinaigrette

3 tablespoons balsamic vinegar

¼ cup extra-virgin olive oil

3 anchovies, drained and minced

3 plump garlic cloves, smashed and minced

½ cup finely diced peeled and seeded tomato

⅓ cup minced pitted Kalamata olives

Minced zest of 1 lemon

Freshly ground black pepper

10 fresh basil leaves, rolled and julienned

4 12-ounce eye-of-the-rib veal chops, 1½ inches thick, frenched

Kosher salt and freshly ground black pepper

3 tablespoons unbleached flour

3 tablespoons canola oil

1 plump garlic clove, smashed

To make vinaigrette: Two to three hours before serving, whisk together vinegar and olive oil in a small bowl. Blend in remaining ingredients except basil. Set aside at room temperature, stirring occasionally. Just before serving, blend in basil.

Preheat oven to 450°F.

Season veal chops with salt and pepper. Lightly dust with flour.

Heat oil and garlic in a large cast-iron skillet over high heat. Remove garlic and discard. Add chops and brown on both sides, 1 to 2 minutes a side. Transfer skillet to oven. Bake for 12 minutes or less, depending upon thickness of meat.

Remove skillet from oven. Carefully transfer chops to heated plates and let rest 5 minutes.

Spoon vinaigrette over each chop and serve.

Wine: Carfaro Cellars Napa Valley Merlot
(California: Napa Valley) or a red Bordeaux from France

Veal Scaloppine with Lemon Garlic Anchovy Sauce

THESE TENDER VEAL SLICES are served with a fresh butter sauce with mellow overtones. It's a wonderfully pleasing dish and one in which garlic is an equal player with the other elements.

SERVES 2 TO 4

⅓ cup unbleached flour
1 pound veal scaloppine,
   sliced very thin and pounded
3 tablespoons olive oil,
   plus more if needed
3 tablespoons unsalted butter
6 anchovy fillets, minced
2 plump garlic cloves, pressed
1 tablespoon fresh lemon juice,
   plus more if preferred
   Kosher salt and freshly ground
   black pepper
2 tablespoons minced fresh
   flat-leaf parsley

Pour flour onto a large plate. Dredge veal slices, coating lightly but evenly. Heat oil in a large skillet over medium-high heat. When hot, add veal slices, without crowding, in batches if necessary. Brown on both sides, 2 to 3 minutes total, and transfer to a heated plate when done.

When all veal is browned, pour off oil and put butter in skillet. Melt over medium heat, then add anchovies, stirring until melted. Quickly add garlic and lemon juice. Whisk for 1 minute, or until butter sauce is bubbly. Pour sauce over veal. Season with salt and lots of pepper. Sprinkle with parsley and serve.

Wine: Oakville Ranch Vineyards Napa Valley Chardonnay
"ORV" (California: Napa Valley)
or another rich California Chardonnay

Sicilian Veal Braciole

THESE TENDER ROLLED stuffed veal slices grew out of a Sicilian recipe that was part of Cleveland chef Paul Minnillo's childhood. In those days the braciole would be made with beef cooked in a tomato sauce. Paul made the adaptation because, as he says, "veal is so much more delicately flavored. And since it is so much lighter, why overwhelm it with tomato sauce?" Traditionally the garlic would be incorporated into the stuffing raw. Paul prefers the more mellow flavor of caramelized garlic, so we begin this recipe by roasting a whole head. What you don't use can be added to mashed potatoes or a root vegetable puree.

SERVES 6

1   large head garlic, roasted
     (see page 34)
6   5-ounce slices veal top round
⅓   cup olive oil
     Finely minced zest of 2 lemons
3   large hard-boiled eggs, peeled
8-10 sprigs fresh flat-leaf parsley
4   ounces pancetta (available at
       Italian markets), finely diced
     Kosher salt and freshly ground
       white pepper

½   cup grated Parmesan cheese
¾   cup Pinot Noir, or other
       dry red wine

Cut twelve 6-inch lengths of thin kitchen twine and set aside.

Place veal slices on a work surface and pound until thin, each measuring about 10 by 4 inches.

Squeeze six plump garlic cloves out of their skins into a shallow wooden bowl. Add lemon zest, eggs and parsley. Chop together until fine. Reserve.

Place pancetta in a small nonstick skillet and sauté until all fat is released. Pour fat from skillet and reserve cooked pancetta.

Season both sides of pounded veal with salt and pepper. Distribute egg mixture among veal slices, spreading evenly over surface of meat. Sprinkle with pancetta, then with Parmesan.

Roll each slice tightly and tie in two places with twine. Repeat until all are rolled and tied.

Heat olive oil in a large skillet with a tight-fitting lid.

Over medium heat, sauté rolls until brown on all sides, 10 to 15 minutes, adding more oil if needed. Add wine, cover, and cook over low heat until wine is evaporated, about 15 minutes.

Remove skillet from heat and let braciole cool. Remove string. Cut rolls into ¾-inch-thick slices and serve.

Wine: Patz & Hall Pinot Noir "Hyde Vineyard" (California: Carneros) or a red Burgundy from France

BEYOND VAMPIRES

♣ University of Washington scientists have saved young trees from rabbits and deer by scattering garlic-smelling pellets around the trees.

♣ Garlic and eucalyptus can control cotton pests, according to a study made at an Indian university.

♣ Environmentally aware officials in Avon Lake, Ohio, announced in December of 1996 that they might use a repellent containing garlic to ward off mosquitoes.

Fragrant Veal Loaf
with Garlic Custard Sauce

GROUND VEAL mixed with a bit of smoky bacon makes a splendidly delicate meat loaf; a generous amount of fresh arugula or watercress adds color and tang. Although five cloves of garlic may sound like a lot, the flavor is perfectly balanced by the shallots, mint and tarragon. The garlic custard sauce, which is simple to make, enhances the meat loaf. This sauce is also delicious with grilled fish.

SERVES 4 TO 6

Meat Loaf

2 pounds ground veal

2 thick slices bacon, minced

½ cup minced shallots

5 plump garlic cloves, smashed
   and minced
   Kosher salt and freshly ground
   black pepper

1 teaspoon dried mint

½ teaspoon dried thyme

½ teaspoon dried tarragon

¼ teaspoon freshly grated nutmeg

1 cup coarsely chopped arugula
   or watercress

¾ cup fine dry bread crumbs

2 large eggs, beaten

½ cup evaporated milk

1 bay leaf

Garlic Custard Sauce

2 large eggs

2 plump garlic cloves, pressed
   Minced zest and juice of 1 lemon

1 cup chicken stock, very hot

1 tablespoon minced fresh chives

To make meat loaf: In a large bowl, blend together veal, bacon, shallots, garlic, 2 teaspoons salt, 1 teaspoon pepper, mint, thyme, tarragon, nutmeg and arugula or watercress. Mix in bread crumbs and eggs. Then blend in milk and mix with your hands until thoroughly blended. Form into a 2½-inch-high loaf that is 4 inches by 9 inches.

Preheat oven to 375°F.

Place loaf in a shallow roasting pan. Press bay leaf on top. Roast for 1 hour 15 minutes, or until nicely browned. To be certain meat loaf is done, insert a knife into center and touch to lower lip. When very hot, meat loaf is done.

Transfer loaf to a warm platter. Allow to rest for 10 minutes before slicing.

Meanwhile, make sauce: Beat eggs until very light and thick, preferably in a mixer with a whisk attachment. Beat in garlic, zest and lemon juice. Very, very slowly, with motor running constantly, add hot stock. Transfer to a heavy-bottomed saucepan and whisk over medium heat until mixture thickens enough to coat a wooden spoon, 3 to 4 minutes. Remove sauce from heat and whisk in chives; season with salt and pepper.

Pour half of sauce over meat loaf and slice. Serve meat on heated plates with more sauce.

Wine: Calera Wine Co. Chardonnay Mt. Harlan (California: Mt. Harlan) or another full-bodied Chardonnay from California

Orange & Fennel-Laced Veal Stew with Vegetables

WE LOVE THE COMBINATION of fennel and garlic, especially in this veal stew. Using orange juice makes the stew especially fresh-tasting. A touch of smoky bacon at the beginning, carrots and pearl onions in the middle, and escarole near the end—all work together to make this a truly memorable dish.

SERVES 6 TO 8

⅔ cup unbleached flour

3½-4 pounds veal stew meat, cut into 2-inch cubes

3 thick strips bacon, cut into matchsticks

Up to 7 tablespoons olive oil

1 cup minced shallots

4 plump garlic cloves, pressed

1 tablespoon water

2 cups fresh orange juice (blood oranges are superb)

3 cups dark brown veal or beef stock

2 teaspoons kosher salt

1 teaspoon freshly ground black pepper

2 teaspoons ground fennel seeds

½ teaspoon dried thyme

1 bay leaf

Minced zest of 1 orange

20-22 pearl onions, blanched, peeled and trimmed

6 medium-sized carrots, scrubbed and quartered

2 cups coarsely chopped escarole

Preheat oven to 325°F.

Place flour in a plastic bag. Add meat and shake to coat meat evenly but lightly with flour. Reserve remaining flour.

Place a 5½-quart Dutch oven, preferably cast-iron, over medium-high heat. Cook bacon until most of fat is rendered, stirring often. With a slotted spoon, transfer bacon strips to a small bowl and reserve. Add 2 tablespoons olive oil to bacon fat and heat until hot. Working in batches, brown meat cubes on all sides, adding oil as needed and transferring meat to a bowl as it browns.

When all veal is browned, add 1 tablespoon oil, shallots and garlic to pan. Stir vigorously over medium heat to loosen browned bits adhering to pot. Add water and stir until shallots are softened, 2 to 3 minutes. Sprinkle 2 tablespoons flour over mixture and stir for 1 minute. Then add orange juice and whisk over high heat to loosen any more particles adhering to pot. Blend in stock, salt, pepper, fennel, thyme, bay leaf and orange zest. Return veal and bacon to pot and add onions and carrots. When mixture begins to bubble, cover tightly.

Place in oven and bake for 1¼ hours. Stir in escarole. Continue to cook, covered, for ½ hour more. Meat will be fork-tender and sauce will be flavorful. Skim off any surface fat, remove bay leaf and adjust seasonings.

Serve in heated soup plates.

Wine: Albert Belle Crozes-Hermitage
(France: Rhône Valley) or another Crozes-Hermitage

Veal Shanks
with Garlic, Kalamata Olives & Wine

THERE'S A LOT OF GARLIC IN THIS DISH, but when slowly cooked with the browned shanks and caramelized onions, the garlic becomes warmly mellow, making a luxurious base for a simple white wine sauce. Serve our braised veal shanks with mashed potatoes and lots of sauce.

SERVES 4

⅓ cup unbleached flour
4 2½-inch-long veal shanks
¼ cup olive oil
2 cups dry white wine
3 tablespoons unsalted butter
4 cups finely chopped Spanish onion
5 plump garlic cloves, smashed
   and minced
1 teaspoon dried thyme
½ teaspoon dried sage
   Minced zest of 1 lemon
   Minced zest of 1 orange
1 cup chicken stock
⅔ cup coarsely chopped pitted
   Kalamata olives
   Kosher salt and freshly ground
   black pepper

Generous pinch of freshly
   grated nutmeg
⅓ cup minced fresh flat-leaf parsley

Place flour in a shallow soup plate; carefully coat shanks with flour. Heat oil in a large, heavy, nonreactive sauté pan with a tight-fitting lid. Add shanks and brown on all sides, 14 to 20 minutes. Transfer shanks to a large platter. De-glaze pan by pouring in wine and whisking over high heat until browned particles are loosened. Pour wine sauce into a large bowl and reserve.

Preheat oven to 350°F.

In same sauté pan, over medium heat, melt butter. Add onions and stir over medium heat until caramelized, 15 to 20 minutes. Stir in garlic, thyme, sage, lemon zest and orange zest. Cook briefly, just to release flavors. Add reserved wine sauce, stock, olives, salt, pepper and nutmeg. Increase heat and cook until liquids bubble.

Slip shanks into bubbling sauce, making certain to spoon some sauce over each shank; cover tightly.

Transfer pan to oven and braise, basting occasionally, until meat is fork-tender, 1½ to 2 hours.

Serve 1 shank per person on a heated plate. Nap lavishly with sauce and sprinkle with parsley.

Wine: Falesco Merlot di Aprilia (Italy: Umbria) or a medium-bodied red wine

Some jockeys in Hungary put garlic cloves on their horses' bits to repel other horses. Any race horse thus equipped would be certain to win by at least a nose.

Garlic & Herb-Crusted Rack of Lamb with Mustard

NOTHING COULD BE EASIER than coating lamb with Dijon mustard and covering it with this tasty mixture of garlic, bread crumbs and herbs. Not only does the lamb have a superb flavor, it is both simple and festive. Try this recipe when you are having dinner guests after a busy work day. This dish is fine without a sauce, but if you really want to splurge, serve a béarnaise sauce on the side.

SERVES 4

¾ cup fine dry bread crumbs

3 plump garlic cloves, smashed and minced

1 tablespoon herbes de Provence, or a mixture of dried rosemary, thyme, basil and savory

2 racks of lamb (2 pieces), 6-8 chops each, cap and chine bones removed

3 tablespoons extra-virgin olive oil Kosher salt and freshly ground black pepper

½ cup Dijon mustard

In a small bowl, blend together crumbs, garlic and herbs. Set aside.

Lightly rub underside of meat with some olive oil. Sprinkle meat generously on both sides with salt and pepper. Place fat side up in a shallow roasting pan. Using a spatula, evenly coat top of meat with mustard. Sprinkle evenly with crumb mixture to make a thick coating. Drizzle remaining olive oil over top. Let stand 1 to 2 hours at room temperature.

Preheat oven to 475°F.

Place meat in oven and reduce temperature to 450°F.

Roast for 22 minutes, or until an instant-read thermometer reads 125°F for rare. Remove meat from oven and let stand for 5 minutes. Carefully slice and arrange chops on heated plates. Garnish with fresh herbs, if you wish.

Wine: Duckhorn Vineyards Merlot Napa Valley (California: Napa Valley) or another rich and complex, somewhat earthy Merlot

Grilled Garlicky Rack of Lamb

LAMB AND GARLIC are famous companions. Red wine, olive oil, rosemary and garlic are the essentials in this marinade. If you have lavender, use that as well. This lamb will taste as good as it smells while marinating. As long as the weather is not so cold that the grill won't stay lit, we prepare rack of lamb outdoors in this fashion.

SERVES 4

3 plump garlic cloves, smashed
    and minced
2 tablespoons minced fresh rosemary
1 scant tablespoon minced fresh
    lavender (optional)
2 teaspoons fresh thyme leaves
    Coarsely ground black pepper
1 tablespoon Dijon mustard
½ cup dry red wine
⅓ cup olive oil
⅓ cup canola oil
2 racks of lamb (2 pieces),
    6-8 chops each, cap and
    chine bones removed
    Kosher salt
    Sprigs of rosemary, thyme
    and lavender for garnish

Combine garlic, herbs and 2 teaspoons pepper in a mixing bowl. Blend in mustard, then wine. Slowly whisk in oils to make a thick emulsion. Place lamb in a shallow nonreactive dish just large enough to hold it. Pour marinade over lamb, being certain to coat thoroughly. Allow to marinate in refrigerator for 4 to 8 hours. Turn several times. Bring to room temperature before grilling.

Shortly before serving, thoroughly clean the surface of a gas or charcoal grill with a metal brush, then coat surface evenly with vegetable oil spray. Heat grill until hot.

Remove lamb from marinade. Season with salt and lots of pepper. Protecting bones with foil, grill racks for 6 minutes on each side for rare. Let rest for 10 minutes, then carve into chops.

Arrange 3 to 4 chops per person on heated plates. Garnish with fresh rosemary, thyme and lavender flowers.

Wine: Colgin Cabernet Sauvignon Napa Valley
"Herb Lamb Vineyard" (California: Napa Valley)
or a rich and complex red Bordeaux from France

Fragrant Roast Leg of Lamb with Garlic & Rosemary

WE MAKE TINY SLITS all over the lamb and push a fragrant mixture of herbs and garlic into each one. For added flavor, the leg is roasted over a bed of mixed herbs. The flavors and aromas are outstanding. Finally, we deglaze the roasting pan with a little red wine to make a simple pan sauce for the meat. We thank Barbara Kafka's stellar book *Roasting: A Simple Art* for giving us the inspiration to roast lamb legs at a high temperature—as we have done for years with turkey.

SERVES 8 TO 12

Mixed Herb Bed

- 1   large bunch fresh flat-leaf parsley
- 2   long branches fresh rosemary, broken in half
- ½   cup fresh winter savory (or 1 tablespoon dried)
- 3   plump garlic cloves, coarsely chopped

- 1   7-to-8-pound trimmed (pelvic bone removed) leg of lamb
- 4   plump garlic cloves
- 1   tablespoon fresh rosemary
- ¼   cup loosely packed fresh flat-leaf parsley

Kosher salt and freshly ground black pepper
- 2   teaspoons olive oil
- 2   tablespoons plus 2 teaspoons Dijon mustard
- ¾   cup dry red wine

Preheat oven to 500°F.

To prepare herb bed: Distribute parsley evenly in a shallow roasting pan. Distribute rosemary and savory over parsley. Sprinkle with chopped garlic.

Make 20 to 30 slits on each side of lamb. Mince together garlic, rosemary and parsley. Carefully insert some of garlic mixture into each slit. Season bottom side of meat with salt and pepper. Place lamb fat side up on herb bed in roasting pan. Rub top with olive oil, then season generously with salt and lots of pepper. Spread 2 tablespoons mustard evenly over surface.

Place pan in preheated oven and roast for 1 hour 10 minutes, or until internal temperature in center of thickest part of meat reaches 125°F for medium-rare. Transfer lamb to a carving board and let rest in a warm place for 15 minutes before carving.

Discard blackened herbs in roasting pan. Whisk in remaining 2 teaspoons mustard, then add wine. Place pan over high heat and deglaze, scraping loose any browned particles adhering to pan. Blend sauce and adjust salt and pepper, if necessary.

Carve meat and serve. Blend any meat juices into pan sauce, skim off surface fat and serve on the side.

Wine: De Lorimier Winery Meritage Red Alexander Valley Mosaic (California: Sonoma County) or a rich and earthy California Cabernet Sauvignon

Oven-Barbecued Lamb

THE MERE MENTION of Kentucky barbecued lamb made Linda salivate. She tore into her research and, thanks to a quick response from authors Cheryl and Bob Jamison, she eagerly planned a trip to Owensboro to sample that town's unusual barbecue—mutton cooked to tenderness deep inside a covered barbecue pit. Even though this recipe bears little resemblance to the Owensboro lamb—except for some Southern roots—we do love it. It was adapted from an old recipe in Marion Flexner's *Dixie Dishes*, in which the lamb is browned and braised in a tangy barbecue sauce that has a special richness from charred onions.

SERVES 8 TO 12

3 jumbo Spanish onions, trimmed
  and quartered
¼ cup olive oil
1 6-to-8-pound leg of lamb,
  boned, rolled and tied
3 plump garlic cloves, thinly sliced,
  plus 4 plump garlic cloves,
  smashed and minced
3 tablespoons unbleached flour
  Kosher salt and freshly ground
  black pepper
1 tablespoon Colman's dry mustard
2 cups water
1½ cups tomato sauce
⅓ cup red wine vinegar
1 tablespoon Worcestershire sauce
1 tablespoon sugar
1 bay leaf

Preheat oven to 500°F. Place onions in a large, shallow baking dish and toss with 1½ tablespoons olive oil. Roast, stirring several times, until onions are darkly caramelized with charred edges, about 1 hour. Scrape onions, and any caramelized juices adhering to pan, into a wooden bowl. Using an old-fashioned chopping blade, chop thoroughly, but not too fine, and set aside.

Using a sharp knife, make about 30 slits all over lamb. Insert garlic slices in slits. Rub meat on all sides with flour, salt and pepper. Pour remaining 2½ tablespoons olive oil into a large cast-iron skillet and heat over medium-high heat. Carefully brown lamb on all sides, 10 to 15 minutes.

Preheat oven to 350°F.

Transfer browned roast to a large, heavy roasting pan. Drain fat from skillet and add onion mixture. Add minced garlic and dry mustard to chopped onions. Blend well. Stir in remaining ingredients. Cook over high heat, stirring often, until sauce is bubbling. Pour over meat. Cover roaster tightly and place in oven.

Braise lamb, basting occasionally, until meat is fork-tender, about 3 hours. Transfer lamb to a carving board and let rest for 10 minutes. Skim off any surface fat from pan sauce. Adjust seasonings and keep warm.

Carve lamb and serve on heated plates with lots of sauce.

Wine: Silver Oak Cellars Cabernet Sauvignon, Alexander Valley (California: Sonoma County) or another complex Cabernet Sauvignon

Out-of-India Grilled Butterflied Leg of Lamb with Spicy Mint Sauce

SUMMERTIME DINNER PARTIES call for early-morning cooking and meat prepared on the grill. This delectable leg of lamb is marinated in a garlicky citrus sauce piqued by a blend of Indian spices. Because of the variations in thickness of this cut, you will have lamb in degrees of doneness—from medium-rare to well done—when you finish. If your grill is intensely hot, check the second side of lamb after 10 minutes.

SERVES 6 TO 10

Marinade

½   cup canola oil

½   cup extra-virgin olive oil

1   cup fresh orange juice

½   cup fresh lime juice

¼   cup fresh lemon juice

3   tablespoons raspberry vinegar

5   plump garlic cloves, smashed and minced

1   rounded tablespoon minced fresh gingerroot

½   cup minced shallots

½   cup minced sweet onions

1   tablespoon minced fresh cilantro

2   teaspoons ground coriander

2   teaspoons turmeric

2   teaspoons good-quality Madras curry powder

1   teaspoon ground cardamom

1   teaspoon ground red pepper (cayenne)

1   teaspoon freshly ground white pepper, plus more to taste

1   7½-to-8½-pound leg of lamb, boned and butterflied
    Kosher salt

Sauce

2   bunches fresh cilantro, stems discarded (about 2 cups)

1   packed cup fresh mint leaves, preferably a fruit mint

3   tablespoons raspberry vinegar

¼   cup extra-virgin olive oil

¼   teaspoon Tabasco

1   teaspoon kosher salt

½   teaspoon freshly ground white pepper

To marinate meat: The day before serving, combine marinade ingredients in a large mixing bowl and whisk vigorously. Open meat and place in a large nonreactive shallow pan or large zipperlock bag. Pour marinade over meat and turn to coat both sides. Cover and refrigerate, turning several times. Bring meat to room temperature several hours before grilling.

To make sauce: Combine cilantro and mint in the bowl of a food processor. Pulse to chop fine. Add remaining sauce ingredients. Puree thoroughly, scraping down sides of bowl several times. Scrape into a small serving bowl and refrigerate.

To grill meat: Thoroughly clean the surface of a gas or charcoal grill and spray with vegetable oil spray. Heat until hot.

Remove meat from marinade but do not wipe off. Grill over hot coals, covered, for 12 minutes a side, or until thickest part of meat is 125°F when checked with an instant-read thermometer.

Let meat rest for 5 minutes before carving. Arrange slices on a heated platter. Serve with sauce on the side.

Wine: E. Guigal Côte Rôtie "La Turque" (France: Rhône Valley) or a rich Australian Shiraz

Cheese-Crusted Lamb Chops Perfumed with Garlic, Rosemary & Lemon

THESE MELT-IN-YOUR-MOUTH lamb chops are one of the stars on the menu of Cleveland's most celebrated restaurant. Under the watchful eye of Vid Lutz, executive chef of Johnny's Bar on Fulton and of Johnny's Downtown, the chops are pounded to about ¼ inch in thickness, dipped into three different coatings and flash-sautéed to golden crispness on the outside while cooked to perfect pinkness inside. Vid's simple pan sauce adds just the right perfume—blended notes of garlic, rosemary and lemon—to balance the chops' richness. We like to spoon Minted Sauce of Garlic & Cilantro (page 148) on the side.

If your butcher cannot pound the chops for you, it's easy enough to do it yourself. Using the flat side of your mallet, pound and slide it rather than pounding straight down. Repeat the motion around the chop until the meat is an even thickness. Also, keep in mind that domestic chops usually have larger eyes (more meat) than New Zealand lamb.

SERVES 4 TO 6

2 large eggs
½ cup heavy cream
1 plump garlic clove, smashed, plus 2 garlic cloves, smashed and minced
12-14 rib lamb chops, about 1 inch thick, frenched, trimmed of excess fat
Kosher salt and freshly ground black pepper
¾ cup grated imported Romano cheese
1 cup fine dry bread crumbs
¼ cup olive oil, plus more if needed
2½ teaspoons minced fresh rosemary
¼ cup dry white wine
1 tablespoon fresh lemon juice
2 tablespoons unsalted butter

In a shallow soup plate, beat eggs together with cream. Add smashed garlic clove and set aside.

Place each chop flat on cutting board and carefully pound meat, sliding the mallet as it hits. Pound until chop is ⅓ to ¼ inch thick. (This takes about four pounds per chop.) Repeat until all chops are pounded. Sprinkle with salt and pepper.

Pour cheese into a shallow soup plate and bread crumbs into another. Set next to beaten egg mixture.

One at a time, dredge chops in cheese, then dip into egg wash, shaking off excess, and finally coat lightly with crumbs. Place chops on a rack until ready to cook. They can stand for 1 hour.

Over medium-high heat, heat a very large skillet, preferably cast-iron. Or you may find it easier to use 2 large skillets. Pour in enough oil to generously coat bottom. When oil is hot, add chops in a single layer. Sauté until golden brown, then turn and finish. Chops should require about 1 to 2 minutes per side for medium-rare—do not overcook.

When done, transfer chops to a heated platter. Pour off all but 2 tablespoons oil from skillet. Over medium heat, add minced garlic and rosemary. Stir until garlic begins to soften, about 30 seconds. Add wine and cook over high heat until reduced by half, about 1 minute. Whisk in lemon juice; remove from heat and whisk in butter. Season with salt and pepper.

Divide chops among 4 or 6 heated dinner plates, overlapping them somewhat on the plate. Dress with a little pan sauce.

Wine: Château Lynch-Bages, Pauillac (France: Bordeaux)
or another lush and complex red Bordeaux from France

Skewered Lamb
with Chiles, Cumin & Garlic

GROUND DRIED RED CHILES, freshly toasted and ground cumin and garlic form the seasoning base for these fire-grilled skewers of lamb. We first came upon meat prepared with these spices a decade ago in the great bazaar of Ürümqi, a doorway to China's Xinjiang Province. Much of the population in this far northwestern part of China is Muslim, so lamb is a favored part of their diet. This amazing market, packed with food, camels, rugs, clothing and hardware supplies, is also a superlative culinary adventure. All around, food vendors cook their treats over small charcoal braziers. Our favorites were these lamb kabobs. The best vendors were those who continued to sprinkle the meat with a powdered seasoning mixture throughout the cooking. Our changes are minimal: We marinate the meat in olive oil, lime juice and garlic, then we add a final spritz of fresh lime for a contrast to the spicy seasoning. Freshly ground cumin makes a big difference in the taste here, but ordinary ground cumin works well too.

SERVES 4

½ cup olive oil
Juice of 2 limes, plus 3 limes
    cut in half
3 plump garlic cloves, pressed
2½ pounds boneless leg of lamb,
    cut into 1½-to-2-inch cubes
2 tablespoons cumin seeds
2 tablespoons medium-hot chile powder
1 tablespoon garlic powder
1 tablespoon kosher salt
Yogurt mixed with chopped mint
    for topping (optional)

Between 3 and 6 hours before serving, combine olive oil, lime juice and garlic in a large mixing bowl. Blend vigorously, then toss with meat to coat thoroughly.

Heat a small skillet over high heat until hot. Add cumin seeds and stir until seeds are dark brown and quite fragrant. Remove from heat and transfer to a plate to cool. Grind toasted cumin in a spice grinder or with a mortar and pestle. (If using ground cumin, do not toast or grind.) Pour freshly made cumin powder into a small bowl. Stir in chile powder, garlic powder and salt.

Remove meat from marinade and dry gently with paper towels. Divide lamb among 8 skewers and sprinkle evenly with spice mixture. Let stand for 1 hour.

Thoroughly clean surface of a gas or charcoal grill with a metal brush; then coat surface evenly with vegetable oil spray. Heat grill on high heat. Place skewers on rack and grill for 4 minutes a side, sprinkling meat generously with spice mixture several times while grilling.

Transfer skewers to a large platter. Squeeze lime juice over meat and serve. Top with minted yogurt.

Wine: Sausalito Canyon Zinfandel Arroyo Grande
(California: Central Coast)
or a rich Cabernet Sauvignon from Chile

Lamb Shanks & Flageolets with Tomato Orange Sauce

OUR FRIENDS AT KINGSFIELD GARDEN sent us a winter care package of heavenly dried beans from their farm. Being especially partial to the combination of flageolets and lamb, we were inspired. A trip to the market, which was featuring California blood oranges, completed the idea for this lively dish. As it happens, lamb, beans, garlic and oranges have an affinity for one another. Extra flavor comes from dried mint and sliced green olives. If blood oranges are not available, regular ones will also produce a delicious dish.

SERVES 4

2 cups dried flageolets or dried baby lima beans

¼ cup unbleached flour

4 lamb shanks (¾-1 pound each)

3 tablespoons olive oil, plus more if needed

2 large yellow onions, finely diced

5 plump garlic cloves, smashed and minced

2 large carrots, finely chopped

2 cups fresh orange juice, preferably from blood oranges

1 cup tomato puree

1 teaspoon kosher salt

1 scant teaspoon freshly ground black pepper

1 teaspoon dried mint

½ cup coarsely diced pitted green olives, preferably from Italy

In a deep saucepan, combine flageolets or lima beans with enough water to cover by 3 inches. Bring to a boil, reduce heat, cover and simmer until beans are tender and skins plump up, 50 minutes to 1¼ hours. Drain and reserve.

Preheat oven to 325°F.

Place flour on a plate and dredge shanks, coating evenly. Pour oil into a 10-inch cast-iron or other ovenproof skillet and heat over medium-high heat. Quickly sear shanks, browning on all sides, 6 to 8 minutes. Remove from skillet.

Add more oil, if needed, and add onions. Stir over medium heat until somewhat golden, 5 to 8 minutes. Add garlic and carrots; stir over medium heat for 4 to 5 minutes, until carrots begin to cook. Stir in orange juice, scraping skillet to loosen any browned particles that adhere to bottom. Stir in tomato puree, salt, pepper, mint and olives. Bring sauce to a boil.

Return shanks to skillet, basting generously with sauce. Cover skillet with a tight-fitting lid.

Place skillet in oven and braise shanks until very tender, about 2¼ hours. Uncover skillet, baste with pan sauce and turn on broiler. Glaze shanks under broiler for 3 to 5 minutes. Carefully remove skillet from oven and place on stove.

Transfer shanks to a heated platter. Bring sauce to a rolling boil over high heat. Cook, stirring constantly, until sauce thickens a bit, 3 to 5 minutes. Stir cooked beans into sauce and simmer until heated through.

Divide shanks among heated serving plates and serve with beans and sauce.

Wine: Forman Vineyard Cabernet Sauvignon
(California: Napa Valley) or another rich
and complex Cabernet Sauvignon

Mustard-Crusted Roast Pork with Peppered Garlic & Pear Compote

THIS IS A FESTIVE WAY to serve roast pork. We order the rib section of the loin and ask to have it chined (backbone sawed away) to facilitate carving into individual chops. The roast will look like a miniature rib roast. Stud the meat with a garlic-and-onion herb paste, then roast it with a thin mustard coating, and you'll have a fragrant and flavorful dish. Instead of a traditional sauce, we accompany our meat with a somewhat peppery gingered pear and garlic compote with a sweet citrus sauce. This compote is also terrific with a good smoked ham, or even with turkey. Finally, we should mention that pork no longer has to be cooked well done; trichina is killed at temperatures above 137°F.

SERVES 6

Pork

4 plump garlic cloves
1 small yellow onion
8 fresh sage leaves (½ teaspoon ground dried)
1 bone-in rib section of pork loin (7-8 ribs), chined (see note above)
⅓ cup Dijon mustard

Kosher salt and freshly ground black pepper

Compote

1½-2 pounds pears, preferably Bosc, peeled, cored and cut into ¾-inch chunks
2 tablespoons fresh lime juice
¼ cup orange juice
⅓ cup firmly packed dark brown sugar
3 plump garlic cloves, smashed and minced
1 plump shallot, minced
1 tablespoon minced fresh gingerroot
1 teaspoon freshly ground black pepper, or more to taste
2 tablespoons minced fresh cilantro

To prepare pork: In a small food processor, or with a chef's knife, mince together garlic, onion and sage to make a paste.

With a sharp knife, make 20 to 40 small slits all over pork roast. Using the knife, push small amounts of garlic paste into slits.

Rub bone side of meat with salt and pepper. Place roast, bone side down, on a shallow roasting pan. Carefully spread mustard in a thin coating over top, or fat side, of meat. Season generously with salt and pepper. Let rest for 1 to 2 hours.

Meanwhile, make compote: Combine all ingredients except cilantro in a medium-sized nonreactive heavy saucepan. Place over medium heat until mixture begins to boil. Reduce heat, partially cover, and simmer until pears are quite tender, 30 to 40 minutes. Then, using a slotted spoon, carefully transfer pears to a bowl. Turn up heat under saucepan and boil until liquid is thick, 3 to 5 minutes. Add to pears, stir and cool.

When compote has cooled somewhat, stir in cilantro.

Place rack in lower third of oven. Preheat oven to 500°F.

Place pork in oven and roast until thermometer reads 140°F for medium, 45 to 50 minutes. Transfer roast to a carving board. Let rest for 10 minutes before carving.

While meat is resting, reheat compote until warm but not hot.

Serve pork roast on heated plates garnished with compote.

Wine: Domaine Zind-Humbrecht Riesling Herrenweg
Turckheim Vielles Vignes (France: Alsace)
or another rich Alsatian Riesling

ARISTA
THE ULTIMATE GARLIC ROAST

FIFTEENTH-CENTURY TUSCANS knew a good thing when they tasted it, as we're told by the fabled Florentine silk merchant and gastronome Pellegrino Artusi, in his collection of historic Italian recipes in 1891. So popular is *The Art of Eating Well* that the book continues to be in print more than 100 years later. In a marvelous English translation by Kyle M. Phillips III (Random House, 1996), we Americans are able to experience for ourselves the extraordinary recipes and culinary stories written by this delightful man of the world.

And so we learn about a Florence gathering—the Council of 1430, which was called to resolve ecclesiastical differences between the Roman and Greek churches. The assembled bishops and their staffs were served a fabulous pork loin studded lavishly with garlic and rosemary and roasted on a spit. The luscious dish was well received: *"Arista, arista!"* rang out across the dining hall.

Today *arista* comes in many variations. Artusi's recipe was for a bone-in pork loin weighing between 7 and 9 pounds, roasted on a spit. But some contemporary cooks bone out the loin. Once roasted, *arista* can be served hot or at room temperature—Tuscans prefer to serve it cool.

Phillips suggests adding peeled and cubed potatoes to the roast 40 minutes before it is done. "They'll absorb the drippings from the *arista* and taste heavenly." Italians call potatoes cooked with a roast *patate alla ghiotta* (glutton's potatoes). Our recipe follows.

Arista

(FLORENTINE BONELESS PORK ROAST)

THIS ROAST CAN BE SERVED either hot or at room temperature.

SERVES 8 TO 12

1   8-to-9-pound pork loin roast
     (5½-6 pounds after boning)

18 plump garlic cloves

⅓   packed cup fresh flat-leaf
     parsley leaves

2   tablespoons fennel seed

2   tablespoons fresh rosemary

1   tablespoon kosher salt,
     plus more as needed

2   teaspoons freshly ground black
     pepper, plus more as needed

½   cup extra-virgin olive oil, or as needed

Open meat on a hard surface, fat side down. Using a meat mallet, evenly pound loin to make it thinner to facilitate rolling. Keep long side parallel to your body.

Combine garlic, herbs, salt, pepper and oil in a small food processor. (Or mince garlic, grind herbs in a spice grinder and combine with oil in a small bowl.) Using three-fourths of paste, coat the open pork loin. Then, rolling with long side facing you, firmly roll up meat as for a jellyroll. Tie together with kitchen twine about every 1½ inches.

Make 12 to 14 slits around outside of roast. Push bits of paste into slits. Rub remaining paste over outside of roast. Sprinkle with more salt and pepper. Refrigerate for several hours. Bring to room temperature before roasting.

Preheat oven to 500°F. Generously oil a shallow roasting pan. Place roast on pan.

Roast meat for 45 minutes, or until internal temperature reaches 140°F.

Transfer roast to a heated platter and let rest for 10 minutes. (Internal temperature will reach about 150°F.)

Discarding twine, slice roast and drizzle with more olive oil.

Roasted Pork Loin
with Tomato, Plum & Garlic Chutney

A FINE IOWA RESTAURANT OWNER and cook, Kay Owen, introduced us to the combination of pork and chutney when we visited Lacorsette in Newton, Iowa, many years ago. In our current variation on her dish, we cook tomatoes, plums or prunes and garlic into a thick puree jazzed up with a tangy combination of ginger, vinegar and brown sugar. This chutney keeps for weeks in the refrigerator—just take it out well before serving, since it's best at room temperature. Mix a little into the pan drippings for an added touch.

SERVES 6 TO 8

Tomato, Plum & Garlic Chutney

- 3 cups diced fresh pitted plums, dried prunes or a mixture of both
- 3 large tomatoes, peeled, seeded, and coarsely chopped, juice reserved
- 1 cup firmly packed dark brown sugar
- 1 cup sugar
- ¾ cup red wine vinegar
- 1 teaspoon mustard seed
- 1½ teaspoons kosher salt
- ¼ teaspoon ground red pepper (cayenne)
- 1 small yellow onion, thinly sliced
- 5 plump garlic cloves, cut into slivers

- 2 tablespoons minced fresh gingerroot
- 2 rounded tablespoons golden raisins

Pork

- 6 plums, preferably prune plums, pitted and thinly sliced
- 4 plump garlic cloves, smashed and minced
- 1 plump shallot, minced
- 1 boneless pork loin, 3½-4½ pounds
  Kosher salt and freshly ground white pepper
- 1 cup Madeira wine or tawny port

To make chutney: At least half a day before serving, combine all ingredients except raisins in a heavy saucepan. Bring just to a boil, then reduce heat to a simmer. Cover and cook over very low heat for 1½ hours. Stir in raisins and continue cooking until mixture is very thick, about ½ hour more. Let cool, then adjust seasonings.

To prepare roast: Bring roast to room temperature. Preheat oven to 500°F. In a shallow roasting pan, toss together plums, garlic and shallots. Pat mixture into a bed for pork. Season pork with salt and pepper and place on plum mixture. Pour ½ cup Madeira or port around bottom of meat. Roast for 45 minutes or until internal temperature reaches 140°F.

Transfer roast to a heated platter and let rest for 10 minutes (internal temperature will reach about 150°F). Add remaining ½ cup Madeira to browned fruit, whisking briskly to loosen any bits adhering to pan. Stir 1 to 2 tablespoons of chutney into pan sauce and heat thoroughly.

Carve roast into thin slices, overlapping several on each heated dinner plate. Spoon some pan sauce over each serving and place generous serving of chutney on one side.

Wine: Hidden Cellars Winery Zinfandel "Old Vines" (California: Mendocino) or a medium-bodied, fruity Zinfandel

Adobo-Rubbed Grilled Pork Tenderloin with Pineapple Citrus Salsa

OUR ADOBO PASTE, very loosely inspired by other such Caribbean seasoning mixtures, is a complex mixture of garlic, lime, ginger, mint, sage and mace. It adds a warm, rather exotic flavor to the tenderloins. The pineapple and citrus salsa is flavored by garlic and mint and enlivened by honey, crystallized ginger and crunchy toasted pecans.

SERVES 4

- 6 plump garlic cloves
- ¼ cup fresh lime juice
- 1 tablespoon olive oil
- 1 ½-inch-thick slice fresh gingerroot, peeled
- 2 teaspoons minced fresh mint leaves
- 1 teaspoon minced fresh sage leaves
- 1 teaspoon kosher salt
- 1 teaspoon freshly ground black pepper
- ½ teaspoon ground mace
- 1 dried chile, crumbled
- 2 pork tenderloins

Pineapple Citrus Salsa

- 1½ cups diced fresh pineapple
- 1½ cups coarsely cut orange segments (about 2 oranges)
- ⅓ cup chopped fresh mint leaves, preferably a fruit mint
- 3 plump garlic cloves, smashed and minced
- 1 small sweet onion, finely diced
- 1 tablespoon minced hot fresh chile (optional)
- 3 tablespoons sherry vinegar
- 2 tablespoons good-quality honey
- 1 rounded tablespoon minced crystallized ginger
- Juice of 1 lime
- Kosher salt and freshly ground black pepper
- ¼ cup minced fresh cilantro
- 2 tablespoons finely chopped garlic chives (optional)
- ½ cup toasted pecans, chopped

In the bowl of a food processor, combine garlic, lime juice, olive oil, ginger, mint, sage, salt, pepper, mace and chile. Pulse until mixed into a paste.

Thoroughly coat tenderloins with paste. Place on a platter, cover and refrigerate for at least 3 hours, or up to 6. Bring to room temperature 2 hours before grilling.

Meanwhile, make salsa: In a medium-sized bowl, combine pineapple, orange segments, mint, garlic, onion, chile, vinegar, honey, crystallized ginger, lime juice, salt and pepper. Blend thoroughly and refrigerate for several hours. Just before serving, spoon salsa into a serving bowl. Add cilantro, garlic chives, if using, and pecans.

Shortly before serving, thoroughly clean surface of a gas or charcoal grill with a metal brush; then coat surface evenly with vegetable oil spray. Heat grill until hot.

Place tenderloins on grill, cover, and cook for 6 minutes. Turn meat and grill 5 minutes more for medium. Remove tenderloins from heat and let rest 5 minutes in a warm place. Slice on a slight angle and spread out in a fan shape on heated serving plates. Spoon salsa over some of slices and serve remaining salsa on the side.

Wine: Robert Biale Zinfandel Napa Valley Aldo's
Vineyard Proprietor's Series (California)
or another concentrated Zinfandel

Chinese Sweet and Sour Pork

ONIONS AND GARLIC play an important role in the yin and yang of any good sweet and sour sauce, especially in this Cantonese-inspired dish. A special twist is using pork tenderloin instead of butt; we also brown the meat without deep-frying it. Tenderloin cooks quickly and has a pleasing texture; butt takes a long time to cook and is usually quite stringy.

SERVE 4

Marinade and Pork

1½ pounds pork tenderloin, cut into slices ⅓ inch thick
2 large egg whites, beaten until thick and frothy
1 plump garlic clove, smashed
1 scallion, smashed with flat side of a cleaver
1 thin slice gingerroot, smashed with flat side of a cleaver
1 tablespoon soy sauce
1 tablespoon rice wine
⅓ cup cornstarch

Seasonings

4 scallions, with 1 inch tender green, cut into 1-inch pieces
¼ cup medium-diced white onion
5 plump garlic cloves, smashed and minced
2 tablespoons minced fresh gingerroot
1 small fresh hot chile, preferably red, finely diced
1 medium-sized green bell pepper, in medium-sized dice
⅔ cup medium-diced fresh pineapple (optional)

Sauce

1 tablespoon cornstarch
½ cup chicken stock
⅓ cup red wine vinegar
⅓ cup ketchup
⅓ cup sugar
2 tablespoons soy sauce
1 teaspoon dark sesame oil

Up to ½ cup peanut oil
⅓ cup minced scallions with tender green
2 tablespoons minced fresh cilantro

To marinate pork: Cut each circular slice lengthwise into three strips, then cut each strip in half crosswise. Place in a large bowl and add egg whites. Toss meat to blend well. Add garlic, scallion and ginger, then soy sauce and rice wine. Marinate for 30 minutes. Drain liquid and remove garlic, scallion and ginger. Add cornstarch to meat and toss to blend thoroughly.

While meat is marinating, prepare seasonings and sauce.

To prepare seasonings: In a small bowl, combine all ingredients. Set aside within easy reach of stove.

To make sauce: In another bowl, whisk together cornstarch and stock. Whisk in vinegar, then remaining sauce ingredients. Reserve with seasonings.

To assemble: Pour 3 tablespoons oil into a wok and set over high heat until hot. Working in batches and adding more oil as needed, transfer pork slices to wok and toss over high heat until golden brown, 2 to 4 minutes. Transfer cooked pork to a warm platter.

When all pork is cooked, drain all but 1 tablespoon oil from wok and heat. Quickly add seasonings and toss over high heat until peppers begin to wilt, about 1 minute. Quickly whisk sauce mixture to blend; add to wok. Toss over high heat for 30 seconds. Return pork slices to wok and toss briskly until mixture is thoroughly hot and sauce has thickened, 1 to 2 minutes.

Transfer pork mixture to a heated serving bowl and garnish with scallions and cilantro. Serve immediately.

Wine: Domaine Tempier Bandol Rosé
(France: Bandol) or Étude Napa Valley Rosé (California)
or another rich rosé from France or California

Pork Loin Strips Roasted in Plum Barbecue Sauce

WE HAVE ALWAYS FOUND PLUMS and garlic to be an especially pleasing combination. Here they're enhanced by a host of Asian ingredients to make a spicy, fruited barbecue sauce that shines with pork loin. Best of all, you can put this dish together a day ahead and just pop it into the oven for 45 minutes before serving.

SERVES 6 TO 8

Plum Barbecue Sauce

½   cup plum jam, or 4 ripe plums, pureed

1   cup fresh orange juice

¼   cup crème de cassis

¼   cup black soy sauce

3   tablespoons Chinese chili sauce

¼   cup hoisin sauce

¼   cup tomato sauce

3   plump garlic cloves, smashed
     and minced

2   shallots, finely minced

2   tablespoons minced gingerroot

1   tablespoon minced lemongrass bulb
     (or zest of 1 lemon, minced)

2   tablespoons dark sesame oil

Roast

4 ½   pounds boneless pork loin,
         silverskin removed

3   tablespoons fresh cilantro leaves

To make sauce: In a large mixing bowl, blend together all sauce ingredients.

To prepare roast: Remove any fat and gristle from pork loin; cut with grain (lengthwise) into strips about 3 inches thick. Place meat in a shallow nonreactive baking dish. Pour sauce over meat and toss to coat evenly. Marinate in refrigerator for 4 hours, or overnight. Turn from time to time.

Preheat oven to 375°F. Remove pork strips from marinade and arrange on a rack in a roasting pan. Roast for 45 minutes, basting from time to time with marinade. Let cool slightly and slice each strip crosswise into thin slices. Arrange on a serving platter and sprinkle with cilantro.

Wine: Ridge Vineyards Petite Sirah Napa County "York Creek" (California: Napa Valley) or another ruggedly intense and peppery Petite Sirah from California

Cornmeal-Crusted Pork Chops with Garlic

THIN PORK CHOPS are first dipped in a garlicky egg bath and rolled in an herbed cornmeal coating. The chops are then fried on top of the stove in a small amount of oil for a crispy exterior with a very tender interior. Cornmeal-crusted pork chops go back to Fred's West Virginia roots—good, basic comfort food. They're great in winter served with spoonbread or pan-fried potatoes. But we especially love them in late summer with some fried green tomatoes.

SERVES 2

    2 large eggs
 1½ teaspoons garlic powder
    1 plump garlic clove, pressed
   ¼ teaspoon Tabasco
   ¾ cup medium-ground cornmeal
   ½ teaspoon dried thyme
    1 teaspoon kosher salt
    1 teaspoon freshly ground white pepper
    6 ½-inch-thick loin pork chops
       Up to ¼ cup canola oil,
         plus more if needed

Combine eggs, garlic powder, garlic and Tabasco in a shallow soup plate and beat thoroughly. Combine cornmeal, thyme, salt and white pepper in another shallow soup plate and blend.

Dip chops in egg mixture, then dredge to coat evenly in cornmeal mixture, transferring coated chops to a cooling rack.

In a large cast-iron skillet, pour enough oil to generously coat bottom, 3 to 4 tablespoons. Heat over high heat until hot. Add chops, reduce heat to medium and fry for 5 minutes, or until golden. Adding more oil if needed, turn and fry 5 minutes, or until golden on both sides. Drain chops on paper towels, then serve on heated plates.

Wine: André Brunel Côtes-du-Rhône
(France: Rhône Valley) or another peppery
Côtes-du-Rhône

Braised Butterflied Pork Chops with Garlic & Herb Stuffing

THERE'S SOMETHING very comforting about the melding of the smoky stuffing flavors—bacon lardons, shallots and garlic—with a simple wine sauce. It's a dish we make often in the winter; it can be completely prepared in advance, then popped into the oven just in time for dinner. Sometimes we serve it with spoon bread or grits, other times with pureed winter squash or braised cabbage.

SERVES 4

4   1½-to-2-inch-thick center-cut
    loin pork chops
2   thick strips smoked bacon,
    cut into matchsticks
1   plump shallot, finely diced
3   plump garlic cloves, smashed
    and minced
1   tablespoon unsalted butter
2   tablespoons mixed fresh herbs:
    rosemary, thyme, basil, savory, or
    2 teaspoons dried herbes de Provençe
1   tablespoon minced fresh
    flat-leaf parsley
½   cup fine dry bread crumbs
    Kosher salt and freshly ground
    black pepper
¼   cup unbleached flour
2   tablespoons olive oil
1½ cups dry red wine,
    plus more if needed
1   bay leaf

Preheat oven to 325°F.

Holding a knife parallel to work surface, cut horizontally through meaty part of each chop toward bone to create a pocket.

Place a large cast-iron or stamped-steel skillet with a tight-fitting cover over medium heat until hot. Sauté bacon until it is soft and brown but not quite crisp. Stir in shallots and garlic; cook until softened, 2 to 3 minutes. Add butter and herbs; stir until butter has melted. Remove from heat and stir in crumbs, salt and pepper. Divide stuffing among chops, firmly packing it into each pocket. Wipe skillet clean and reserve.

Pour flour into a soup plate. Carefully coat chops in flour, keeping one hand on pocket opening to hold in stuffing. Set chops aside on a rack. Season generously with salt and pepper.

Lightly coat skillet with olive oil and heat over medium-high heat. Brown chops on both sides, 2 to 3 minutes.

Pour wine over chops, add bay leaf and heat until wine is bubbling. Cover tightly and transfer to oven.

Braise chops until meat is fork-tender, 1¼ to 1½ hours.

To serve, divide chops among four heated plates. Return skillet to high heat and cook until sauce is slightly reduced. Remove bay leaf, spoon sauce over chops and serve.

Wine: Domaine Carneros Pinot Noir Carneros (California: Napa Valley) or a red Burgundy from France

Cider-Braised Pork Chops with Roasted Garlic Mustard Sauce

WHETHER IT'S CIDER or the whole apple itself, apples and pork always make a great team. Here we braise thick chops in cider, apples, onions and garlic. When the chops are tender, we finish the sauce with some roasted garlic puree, mustard and sour cream. To make things a bit easier for yourself, start roasting the garlic about 30 minutes before you put the chops into the oven. Or even better, do as we do, and make sure you always have some roasted garlic puree right in the refrigerator!

SERVES 2

2 loin pork chops, 1½ inches thick
2 tablespoons unbleached flour
3 tablespoons olive oil
1½ cups finely diced yellow onions
2 plump garlic cloves, pressed
1 large tart apple, peeled, cored
   and finely chopped
¾ cup apple cider
   Kosher salt and freshly ground
   black pepper
2 teaspoons minced fresh tarragon
   (1 teaspoon dried)
1 large head garlic, roasted and
   pureed (page 47)

1 rounded tablespoon Dijon mustard
⅓ cup low-fat sour cream

Preheat oven to 325°F.

Sprinkle pork chops evenly with 1 tablespoon flour. Rub to coat, then repeat on second side.

Heat oil in a medium-sized ovenproof skillet over high heat. Brown chops on both sides, 3 to 4 minutes. Transfer chops to a plate.

Reduce heat to medium and add onions, garlic and apple. Stir until onions soften, 2 to 3 minutes. Stir in cider, salt, pepper and tarragon. Increase heat and stir to loosen any browned particles adhering to pan. When liquid begins to bubble, add pork chops and baste well.

Cover skillet with a tight-fitting lid and braise in oven until chops are fork-tender, 1¼ to 1½ hours. Transfer chops to a heated plate and keep warm. Return skillet to stovetop. Whisk in garlic puree, mustard and sour cream. Whisk over medium heat until sauce is evenly blended and hot (do not boil). Add more pepper, if you wish.

Serve chops generously napped with sauce.

Wine: Truchard Pinot Noir Carneros
(California: Napa Valley) or a red Burgundy from France

Garlic & Lemon Roasted Pork Ribs with Black Pepper

THESE SPARERIBS ARE CUT Chinese-style (crosswise) so that they're small and easy to handle. Rubbed with a garlic-lemon oil and lots of pepper, they are quickly baked until crisply delicious. All that's left to add is a dash of lemon juice. This is our hearty version of a recipe of James Beard's. The ribs make a simple main course when served with some creamy mashed potatoes. But we often serve them as a zesty appetizer.

SERVES 2 TO 4

- 3 tablespoons olive oil
  Zest of 2 lemons, minced
- 3 plump garlic cloves, pressed
- 1 tablespoon finely ground black pepper
- 1 tablespoon finely ground white pepper
- 3 3½-pound slabs whole spareribs, brisket, clip and skirt removed (also called a trimmed 2-pound St. Louis rib), cut in half crosswise
  Kosher salt
- 2 lemons, cut in half

Preheat oven to 375°F.

Combine oil, lemon zest and garlic in a small bowl and blend thoroughly. In another bowl, blend together black and white pepper.

Rub ribs thoroughly with oil mixture. Sprinkle pepper mixture over both sides of ribs and rub to coat evenly. Salt generously.

Arrange ribs in a single layer in shallow baking pans. Bake for 30 minutes, then pour off any liquid accumulated, turn, and bake another 30 minutes, or until ribs are crisp around edges. Spritz generously with lemon juice.

Cut into individual ribs and serve right away.

Wine: Bodega Weinert Malbec (Argentina) or Blackstone Merlot Napa County Reserve (California: Napa Valley) or another medium-bodied California Merlot

Chinese Baked Spareribs with Shredded Vegetables

THESE SLIGHTLY SWEET BUT SPICY Chinese spareribs are simple to make and a real pleasure to eat. The shredded raw vegetables with their sugared rice vinegar dressing make a pleasing counterpoint. In each part of this dish, the garlic plays a somewhat different role. Combined with the soy sauce and bean paste coating for the ribs, it becomes very mellow. Uncooked as part of a vinaigrette in the salad, it plays a more pronounced and pungent role.

SERVES 2 TO 4

Ribs

⅓ cup black soy sauce
⅓ cup rice wine
3 tablespoons sugar
2 crushed dried chiles
3 rounded tablespoons sweet bean paste
2 tablespoons minced fresh gingerroot
4 plump garlic cloves, smashed and minced
3 scallions, minced
2-3 3½-pound slabs whole spareribs, brisket, clip and skirt removed (also called a trimmed 2-pound St. Louis rib)

Shredded Vegetables

2 cups shredded napa cabbage
1 large sweet onion, grated
4 medium-sized carrots, grated
1 tablespoon kosher salt
2 plump garlic cloves, pressed
¼ cup sugar
1 teaspoon ground toasted peppercorns (see page 296)
⅓ cup rice vinegar
2 tablespoons dark sesame oil

To prepare ribs: In a medium nonreactive bowl, thoroughly blend together soy sauce, rice wine, sugar, chiles, bean paste, ginger, garlic and scallions. Evenly coat ribs on all sides with mixture and marinate for 3 hours in refrigerator.

To prepare vegetables: Combine cabbage, onion and carrots in a large bowl and sprinkle with salt. Let stand for 15 minutes, then drain thoroughly of excess liquid. Add garlic, sugar, peppercorns, vinegar and sesame oil; stir thoroughly. Let stand for at least 1 hour or up to 2.

Preheat oven to 375°F. Place ribs, top side down, on racks in a shallow roasting pan and roast for 30 minutes. Carefully turn and roast 25 minutes more. Ribs should be well browned.

Cut ribs into individual pieces and pile in center of a platter. Using a slotted spoon, surround ribs with salad.

Wine: Jean-Paul Thévenet Morgon "Vielles Vignes" Beaujolais (France: Burgundy) or California Pinot Noir

GROWING GARLIC

HERE ARE SOME BASICS for the home gardener
planning to grow garlic:

A patch of dirt. It doesn't have to be big—you can grow a winter's supply in a 3-by-5-foot bed or in some flowerpots. The soil must be reasonably fertile and in the sun for a good part of the day.

Climate. Garlic grows almost everywhere. To find out what varieties will do best in your climate and latitude, check with the county agricultural agent or a local grower or a seed company.

Soil. Garlic does well in all kinds of soil conditions, but some are better than others. The best advice is to use a rich, loose soil loaded with organic matter. It should drain easily; garlic doesn't like to be too wet.

Fertilizer. Garlic gobbles up the nutrients even in a rich patch. It especially needs phosphorus and nitrogen. Some growers will not use the same soil again until it has been replenished by a cover crop—buckwheat, for example—for two or three years after garlic has been harvested. (Some growers give a field five years to get ready for the next garlic planting.) If you want to use the same plot two years in a row, add compost or an appropriate fertilizer from your garden store.

Seed cloves. Some big growers buy planting stock from other growers; some set aside a part of their own crop for the next season. The home gardener can either order heads of favorite varieties from seed catalogs or save some heads through the summer until fall planting time. Be sure to get varieties that are appropriate for your climate and day length. Garlic heads being kept for planting should not be broken down into cloves until time to plant.

Prepare the bed. In the early fall, clear the patch you intend to use and work in fertilizer.

Plant the garlic. Generally speaking garlic should be planted in late October or early November. After planting, it needs six to eight weeks of cool weather (below 40°F) before the cloves are ready to sprout. When you are ready to plant, break the heads down to free the cloves. Then plant the cloves about 2 inches deep and 4 inches apart, making sure that the leaf end of the clove is up and the root end down. (It saves the plant's energy if the leaf doesn't have to do a 180 to grow up.) If the patch is big, configure the planting in rows 8 to 12 inches apart. If you live in a particularly cold area, mulch the bed to protect it from really deep frosts.

Tend the growth. As spring approaches, the green tips will start to appear. Don't worry; like crocuses, they can deal with harsh weather. But it's important to keep down weed growth; garlics don't like the competition. If you see something coming up that shouldn't be there, yank it out. Garlic is not water-greedy, but in dry times, give the patch an occasional watering.

Topsets. In most regions, if you are growing hardnecks, by mid-June the stiff central stems, or scapes, will appear. They will go through a number of gyrations, curling and uncurling as they develop. Most growers cut off the scapes so that more energy will go to the development of the heads. (The topsets can be eaten when young and green, used as you might use any mature garlic, or tossed into a stir-fry.) If you decide to let the topsets mature, you can use them for planting, although it will take three years or so before they produce significant bulbs. (Allium scientist John Swenson points out that even so-called softneck garlics can bolt, or grow a topset, under stress.)

Harvest. In most parts of the country, the garlic will be ready for harvest in mid to late July. Watch the leaves, and when they start dying back, turning brown and drooping, get ready. When about half of the leaves have turned brown, it's time to dig. The root development is extensive, so it's hard to just pull the heads out. You may want to undercut the plant with a tool to cut the roots so that the head will come up more easily. Take care not to cut or otherwise hurt the head as you do this.

Dry or cure. After you have taken up your garlic heads, tie them in bundles of six or eight, and hang them up in a cool, dry place, such as the garage, for curing. If you have grown several varieties, label them. Leave them there for about three weeks before you

trim off their stems and roots in preparation for storage. If you intend to grow more, you can set aside about 10 percent of the bigger, better heads for your fall planting.

Storage. Garlic has a long shelf life. The softnecks, stored in a cool, dry place, may last for nine months before they start to deteriorate; the hardnecks will not last quite so long. There are a number of ways to keep them longer. On the Internet, a woman suggested slicing garlic thin, spreading it on parchment and drying it in a low oven. Some people crush garlic and mix it with oil, then freeze the mixture in small plastic bags. Others put peeled cloves into olive oil for long-term storage. But harmful bacteria can thrive in such a setting; oil, contrary to popular belief, is not a preservative. Major outbreaks of botulism have been traced to garlic stored in oil. So if you are planning to put garlic (or other plant matter) in oil, it should first be cooked or soaked for 12 hours in vinegar or some other acidic medium. Even then, research shows, it should be refrigerated to increase the margin of safety.

Marketing. If you have grown more garlic than you and your neighbors, family and friends can possibly eat, and if there is no immediate vampire threat, you might decide to go commercial, brushing the heads sparkling clean and selling them to a specialty food store. You will not make enough money to send your kids to college, but you might earn enough for dinner out with your spouse—maybe without garlic.

STARCHY SIDES
POTATOES, CORNMEAL, RICE & BEANS

(Where the dish might be the feature of a vegetarian main meal, we offer wine suggestions.)

Mashed Potatoes with Roasted Garlic & Olive Oil   356

Pureed Parsnips & Potatoes with Garlic Chips   357

Savory Potato Wedges with Garlic Oil & Herbs   358

Oven-Roasted Potatoes with Gremolata   359

Ballpark Oven-Baked Garlic Potato Chips   361

Cheddar Potato Gratin with Garlic & Onions   362

Simple Gratin of Potatoes, Garlic & Fennel   363

New Potatoes with Basil & Garlic Vinaigrette   364

Latkes with Dry-Roasted Garlic   366

Simple Yellow Grits with Roasted Garlic Butter   367

Spoonbread with Jalapeño, Cheddar & Garlic   368

Fried Polenta Triangles with Garlic & Shallots   370

Spicy Baked Beans with Smoked Sausage & Lots of Garlic   372

Oven Risotto with Garlic, Radicchio & Saffron   374

Mashed Potatoes with Roasted Garlic & Olive Oil

WE MASH THESE SMALL POTATOES with their skins to give them extra texture and flavor. Then we add the roasted garlic and its oil for a mild and delicate caramelized sweetness. These are sinfully delicious.

SERVES 6

12 plump garlic cloves, peeled
½ cup extra-virgin olive oil,
     plus more if needed
2 pounds small Yukon gold potatoes
     or any small, thin-skinned
     potato, scrubbed
     Kosher salt
     Freshly ground black pepper

Preheat oven to 350°F.

Combine garlic and olive oil in a small ovenproof dish. Cover tightly with foil. Bake for 45 minutes, or until garlic is golden and very tender. Puree with oil in a food processor fitted with the metal blade or in a blender. Reserve and keep warm.

Meanwhile, place potatoes in a large saucepan and cover with cold water and a pinch of salt. Cover pot and bring to a boil over high heat. Reduce heat and simmer until potatoes are tender, about 20 minutes. Drain thoroughly. Using a potato masher, mash potatoes as smooth as possible. Return to pan and, over very low heat, slowly incorporate pureed garlic and oil a bit at a time, stirring all the while, adding more oil if necessary. Season with salt and pepper and serve.

Pureed Parsnips & Potatoes
with Garlic Chips

BECAUSE WE TRY HARD to cook seasonally and regionally, we use a lot of root vegetables throughout Ohio's long winters. Parsnips have become one of our favorites because of their mellow, slightly sweet taste. We enjoy them combined with potatoes, especially the delicate Yukon gold. We brown garlic chips in butter, then mix the browned garlicky butter right into the puree. A crisp sprinkling of garlic chips takes this humble dish to new flavor heights.

SERVES 6

2½ pounds Yukon gold potatoes,
      peeled and cut into ½-inch dice

3 medium parsnips, peeled and
      cut into ½-inch dice

6 tablespoons unsalted butter,
      cut into small pieces

6 plump garlic cloves, thinly sliced

⅓ cup hot milk, plus more if needed
      Kosher salt and freshly ground
      white pepper

Combine potatoes and parsnips in a large saucepan filled with water. Cover tightly and bring to a boil over high heat. Reduce heat and simmer briskly until potatoes and parsnips are tender, 15 to 20 minutes.

Meanwhile, melt butter in a small saucepan over medium heat. Add garlic slices and cook, stirring often, until slices are browned, 3 to 5 minutes. When the somewhat foaming butter browns, the garlic is ready. Quickly remove garlic from heat, transfer to paper toweling and cool. Reserve butter for potatoes.

When potatoes and parsnips are tender, drain well. Place in saucepan and return to low heat. Mash potato mixture until smooth with a potato masher, then stir in hot milk. Blend well, then stir in browned garlic butter and mash until smooth. If mixture seems too dry, gradually stir in more milk. Season with salt and white pepper. Cover and keep warm.

Quickly mince garlic chips. Serve puree sprinkled with minced toasted garlic.

Savory Potato Wedges with Garlic Oil and Herbs

THESE CRISP POTATO WEDGES with a luscious garlic-and-herb coating have been a regular part of our family dinners for years. But we're often embarrassed when people ask us for the recipe, since they think we've slaved for hours to make something so good. The potatoes are wonderful with anything grilled, from poultry to meat to fish.

SERVES 4 TO 6

⅓ cup olive oil
2 plump garlic cloves, smashed and minced
1½ tablespoons minced fresh parsley
1½ tablespoons minced fresh sage (1¼ teaspoons dried)
1½ tablespoons fresh thyme leaves (2¼ teaspoons dried)
1½ tablespoons minced fresh tarragon (2¼ teaspoons dried)
1½ tablespoons minced fresh rosemary (2¼ teaspoons dried)
4 large russet potatoes, scrubbed
1½ teaspoons freshly ground black pepper
Kosher salt

At least 1 or up to 4 hours ahead, blend olive oil and garlic in a small bowl and reserve.

Preheat oven to 450°F.

Blend together parsley, sage, thyme, tarragon and rosemary in another bowl.

Lightly brush a shallow baking pan large enough to hold potatoes in a single layer with garlic oil. Cut each potato in half and cut each half lengthwise into six wedges. Distribute wedges evenly in prepared pan. Drizzle with remaining garlic oil and toss in pan to coat more evenly. Sprinkle with herbs and pepper.

Bake, stirring twice, for 1 hour, or until potatoes are very crisp on the exterior. Season generously with salt and serve.

Oven-Roasted Potatoes with Gremolata

WHEN NEW POTATOES are quartered and slowly roasted, they become tender and buttery inside. A few minutes at high heat gives them a marvelous crisp and tasty exterior. This agreeable contrast is further enhanced by a touch of gremolata—an Italian dry "sauce" of parsley, lemon zest and garlic.

Linda enjoyed a similar dish, cooked in goose fat, when she first visited southwest France more than 20 years ago. Besides its picturesque walled villages and Romanesque churches and monasteries, the region is celebrated for a robust and luscious cuisine that celebrates duck, goose and foie gras. This same region is the home of the healthiest people in France. For a real treat, try these potatoes cooked with duck or goose fat.

SERVES 6 TO 8

24-30 small new potatoes, preferably
     Yukon gold, scrubbed
     Up to ⅓ cup olive oil or duck
     or goose fat

½ cup minced fresh flat-leaf parsley
4 plump garlic cloves, smashed
   and minced
   Zest of 2 lemons, minced
   Kosher salt and freshly ground
   black pepper

Preheat oven to 300°F.

Leaving skins on potatoes, cut into quarters. Place on a large, shallow-sided baking sheet. Drizzle with 3 tablespoons oil or fat and toss to coat well.

Bake potatoes for 2 hours, stirring several times and adding more oil if needed. Potatoes will be tender and lightly browned.

While potatoes are roasting, combine parsley, garlic and lemon zest and blend thoroughly.

Increase oven temperature to 450°F and bake potatoes until very brown, about 15 minutes.

Remove potatoes from oven. Sprinkle with salt and pepper. Toss with gremolata to coat evenly and serve.

GARLIC COMES
TO THE BALLPARK

NOT LONG AGO AT CLEVELAND'S JACOBS FIELD, a young peanut vendor, fabled for his ability to throw a bag of peanuts to a customer three sections away, found himself in trouble with the management when he knocked the hat off a fan's head. No harm was done, and no peanut was broken.

But what if this young man were working San Francisco's Candlestick Park (now officially known as 3COM) or the Oakland-Alameda Coliseum? And what if his errant product were a garlic sandwich or a packet of garlic fries? A bad toss might not cause physical harm, but no one would want to get too close to the victim for the rest of the day.

It could happen. Because out in California, garlic has come to the ballpark.

"Fancy park fare dares fans," announced a headline in a trade publication. The story went on to concede that while garlic fries are unlikely to usurp hot dogs, there is a good trade in niche items. San Francisco's ballpark boasts a Stinking Rose concession stand, a corporate cousin of the restaurant of that name, which sells a 40-clove garlic sandwich. And on the other side of the bay, the Coliseum offers garlic fries—steak fries dipped into a sauce of olive oil, fresh garlic and chopped parsley. No hot dogs. Hold the mustard.

Ballpark Oven-Baked Garlic Potato Chips

BITE INTO THESE CRUNCHY CHIPS and you will be amazed. Baseball fans that we are, even we were astonished to read that the ballpark in Oakland, California, serves garlic French fries. That news inspired us to create some oven-roasted garlic chips—a little lower in fat and higher in crunch than their deep-fried cousins.

SERVES 8

1 cup plus ¼ cup olive oil
4 plump garlic cloves, slivered,
    plus 3 more, smashed and minced
2 sprigs fresh rosemary
1 dried red chile
4 large baking potatoes, peeled
    Kosher salt and freshly ground
     black pepper
2 tablespoons minced fresh flat-leaf
    parsley

At least 4 hours ahead, combine 1 cup olive oil, slivered garlic, rosemary and chile in a small bowl and set aside. Remove garlic, rosemary and chile with a slotted spoon before using.

Preheat oven to 425°F. Generously brush a large baking sheet with garlic oil.

Using a mandoline or a food processor fitted with the slicing blade, carefully cut potatoes into ⅛-inch-thick slices. Place slices in a large bowl. Add remaining garlic oil and generous amounts of salt and pepper. Toss thoroughly to coat potato slices.

Arrange potatoes in a single layer on baking sheet. (You may have to do this in two batches.) Bake until most of each chip is golden brown, 20 to 30 minutes. Drain on paper towels.

Just before serving, combine ¼ cup olive oil, minced garlic and parsley in a large mixing bowl; add chips and toss. Sprinkle chips with more salt and pepper if you wish.

Serve warm or at room temperature.

Cheddar Potato Gratin with Garlic & Onions

THESE SLICES OF TENDER potatoes and onions baked in a milky bath generously laced with garlic and Cheddar are hearty enough to make a meatless main dish. Serve a tomato soup first, then finish with a salad. Choose a starchy potato for this dish.

SERVES 6 TO 8

- 3 plump garlic cloves, pressed
- ½ pound sharp Cheddar cheese, shredded (2 cups)
- 3 pounds starchy white potatoes, peeled and thinly sliced
- 2 cups whole milk
- 1 large white onion, thinly sliced
  Kosher salt and freshly ground white pepper
  Freshly grated nutmeg
- ½ cup heavy cream
- ¼ cup bread crumbs
- 2 tablespoons unsalted butter, melted

Preheat oven to 350°F. Generously butter a shallow 3-quart baking dish.

In a small bowl blend together garlic and cheese. Reserve.

Combine potatoes and milk in a heavy-bottomed saucepan and bring to a boil. Cover and reduce heat to low. Simmer briskly for 30 minutes.

Spoon one-third of potato mixture into baking dish. Sprinkle with half of onions. Sprinkle with salt and white pepper, then one-third of cheese mixture. Repeat, making two more layers of potato mixture and ending with garlic and cheese.

Sprinkle with nutmeg. Pour cream over top. Sprinkle evenly with bread crumbs, then melted butter. Bake uncovered for 1½ hours, or until crust is brown and potatoes are very tender when pierced with a skewer. Serve.

Wine: Girard Winery Chenin Blanc Napa Valley Dry (California: Napa Valley) or an Alsatian Pinot Blanc from France

Simple Gratin of Potatoes, Garlic & Fennel

IN YEARS PAST we used to make this dish with heavy cream. Now we use milk, adding a small amount of flour for thickening. The resulting combination of potatoes slowly cooked to creamy tenderness with thin-sliced fennel and garlic loses nothing except some extra fat. The gratin complements a host of roasted meats and chicken dishes. This recipe requires a starchy potato, so any of the so-called baking potatoes, or russets, will do. Do not slice potatoes in advance and hold them in water, since this would remove much of the starch.

SERVES 6 TO 8

- 4 tablespoons (½ stick) butter
- 3 pounds russet potatoes, peeled and thinly sliced
- 1 quart whole milk
- 1½ cups very thinly sliced fresh fennel bulb, hard core removed
- 2 tablespoons minced fresh garlic
- 2 tablespoons unbleached flour
    Kosher salt and freshly ground black pepper
    Freshly grated nutmeg

Preheat oven to 350°F. Thoroughly coat a shallow 3-quart baking dish, preferably ceramic, with 1 tablespoon butter.

Combine sliced potatoes and milk in a heavy-bottomed saucepan and bring to a boil. Reduce heat to low, cover and simmer for 15 minutes; be careful not to let pot scorch.

Using a slotted spoon, transfer one-third of potatoes to prepared dish. Sprinkle with half of fennel and half of garlic. Sprinkle evenly with half of flour and dot with 1 tablespoon butter. Season with salt and pepper. Repeat with one-third of potatoes and remaining fennel and garlic. Sprinkle with remaining flour; dot with remaining 1 tablespoon butter. Season with more salt and pepper.

Arrange remaining potatoes on top. Pour milk over potatoes. Sprinkle with more salt and pepper, as well as some gratings of nutmeg.

Bake uncovered for 1 hour 15 minutes, or until potatoes are tender and top is very brown.

Wine: Selene Sauvignon Blanc Carneros
"Hyde Vineyard" (California: Napa Valley)
or another rich and aromatic Sauvignon Blanc

New Potatoes
with Basil & Garlic Vinaigrette

COOKING SMALL POTATOES in chicken stock gives them a superlative flavor from the start. If you choose young potatoes, the skin adds another layer of flavor. We especially like this salad in late summer made with "marble" potatoes, the very small ones that slip through the farmer's sizing machines because they're so tiny. Marbles will cook in about 15 minutes; the larger ones take up to 25.

SERVES 8 TO 10

3 pounds small red, yellow or white potatoes, scrubbed and unpeeled
4 peppercorns, smashed
4 cups chicken stock
¼ cup sherry vinegar

Vinaigrette

1 dried red chile, crushed
4 plump garlic cloves, smashed and minced
¼ cup sherry vinegar
1 tablespoon Dijon mustard
¼ cup vegetable oil
¼ cup extra-virgin olive oil
Kosher salt and freshly ground black pepper to taste

1 medium-sized red bell pepper, finely diced
1 green bell pepper, finely diced
½ cup finely diced red onion
½ cup finely diced celery
¼ cup minced fresh basil

Combine potatoes, crushed peppercorns, and stock in a heavy saucepan. Bring to a boil over high heat; reduce heat and cover. Simmer slowly until potatoes are tender (time depends upon their size).

Drain, reserving stock, if you wish, for a soup. Carefully slice potatoes in ¼-to-½-inch-thick slices. Put into a large bowl, sprinkle with vinegar and cool.

To make vinaigrette: Combine chile, garlic and mustard in a medium-sized bowl. Whisk in vinegar. Slowly add oils, whisking vigorously to make a thick emulsion. Season generously with salt and pepper.

When potatoes are cool, add peppers, onion and celery.

Pour vinaigrette over mixture and toss very gently. Add basil and toss again. Let stand for 1 hour before serving. If you store this dish in refrigerator, be sure to let it come to room temperature before serving.

> The English have finally embraced garlic, it seems. Britain's first garlic shop is now open and, among other things, it sells garlic condoms.
>
>

Latkes with Dry-Roasted Garlic

POTATO PANCAKES, Jewish soul food traditionally served at Hanukkah, are lifted to ethereal heights by the addition of mellow dry-roasted garlic. Our lacy pancakes, or latkes, are best served immediately. But you can reheat them in a hot oven just before serving, or you can make them ahead and store in the freezer. To reheat frozen pancakes, place them frozen on a cookie sheet; bake for 8 to 10 minutes in a 500°F oven. If you grate potatoes in a food processor, alternate with onion to help reduce darkening of the potatoes.

SERVES 4 TO 6
(ABOUT 16 3½-INCH LATKES)

- 10 plump garlic cloves, unpeeled
- 4 large russet (Idaho) potatoes, peeled and coarsely grated
- 1 medium-sized white onion, coarsely grated
- 1 large egg
- 2 tablespoons unbleached flour
   Salt and freshly ground black pepper to taste
   Up to ¾ cup vegetable oil for frying
   Sour cream for garnish

Preheat oven to 250°F.

Heat a small cast-iron skillet or griddle over medium-high heat until hot. Cook garlic cloves, turning often, until soft to the touch and somewhat blackened in spots, 10 to 15 minutes. Set aside until cool, then peel and mince. Reserve.

Drain liquid from grated potatoes. Mix well with onion, egg and flour. Blend in garlic, then add salt and pepper.

Pour enough oil into a large cast-iron skillet to generously coat bottom. Heat over medium-high heat until smoking. Using a slotted spoon to permit excess liquid to drain, drop potato mixture into fat according to size preferred. We use a very full slotted spoon and, once latkes are in skillet, use a spatula to press mixture into fairly thin cakes about 3½ to 4 inches in diameter.

Fry latkes until golden on bottom, about 4 minutes. Turn and brown on other side. Remove with a slotted spatula and drain on paper towels. Transfer to a paper-towel-lined cookie sheet and keep warm in oven. Continue making latkes, adding more oil as needed.

Serve 2 to 3 per person, garnished with dollops of sour cream.

Simple Yellow Grits with Roasted Garlic Butter

ALONG WITH FRIED GREEN TOMATOES and pork chops, Fred brought grits into Linda's life. Often served as a side dish with breakfast, grits are a coarser grind than cornmeal. In the South, grits are usually white (as is the cornmeal). In the North, grits are usually yellow. We buy our grits locally from the Fowler's Milling Company (see Sources, page 415) but they are available from a number of other mail-order sources as well.

SERVES 4

- 1 large head garlic, roasted
     (see page 34)
- 2 tablespoons unsalted butter
- 4 cups degreased chicken or
     vegetable stock
- 1 teaspoon kosher salt
- 1 cup stone-ground yellow grits
     Freshly ground white pepper

Remove garlic head from baking dish and let cool. Then squeeze garlic flesh from papery skin and chop thoroughly. Melt butter in a small saucepan or in a microwave in a small dish. Blend garlic and butter together and reserve.

Combine stock and salt in a heavy-bottomed saucepan and bring to a boil. Very slowly stir in grits. Stir over medium-low heat until mixture begins to boil. Cover and reduce heat to very low. Cook, stirring from time to time, for 12 minutes. Remove cover and stir thoroughly, being certain to scrape bottom and sides of pot. Cover and cook for 3 more minutes, or until very thick.

Stir in garlic butter and white pepper. Serve.

Spoonbread with Jalapeño, Cheddar & Garlic

ACCORDING TO JOHN MARIANI'S *Dictionary of American Food & Drink*, spoonbread is "a soft, custardlike dish usually made with cornmeal. The term may come from an Indian word for porridge, *suppawn*, or from the fact that the dish is usually eaten with a spoon." Spoonbread can be a simple mixture of cornmeal, milk and eggs. Or it can be thoroughly gussied up, as in this recipe, which includes the flavors of the Southwest as well as a generous amount of Cheddar cheese. Any kind of leftover spoonbread makes a satisfying breakfast. Cut it into thick slices and fry it until browned on both sides. Serve a poached egg on top.

SERVES 8

2¼ cups buttermilk

4 large eggs, separated

3 tablespoons unsalted butter

6 plump roasted garlic cloves, roasted (see page 34), minced

1 rounded tablespoon minced hot fresh chile, preferably a red one

1 teaspoon coarsely ground black pepper

1 teaspoon medium-hot chili powder

1½ cups yellow cornmeal

1 teaspoon baking powder

½ teaspoon baking soda

2 teaspoons sugar

2 teaspoons salt

⅔ cup grated sharp Cheddar cheese

1 cup boiling water

Minced fresh chives and cilantro for garnish

Place rack in upper third of oven. Preheat oven to 375°F.

Butter a 2-quart soufflé dish and dust with cornmeal.

In a medium-sized mixing bowl, beat together buttermilk and egg yolks. Reserve.

Melt butter in a small skillet over medium heat. Add garlic, minced chile, ground black pepper and chili powder. Stir for 30 seconds, to just slightly cook peppers and release oils. Reserve.

In a large mixing bowl, combine cornmeal, baking powder, baking soda, sugar, salt and cheese. Add boiling water and garlic mixture.

Blend thoroughly. Gradually whisk in buttermilk mixture. Stir until well combined.

Beat egg whites until they form firm peaks. Lighten cornmeal batter by blending with a large spoonful of beaten whites. Then add remaining whites to batter and fold quickly until whites are well incorporated.

Pour batter into prepared soufflé dish and bake uncovered 35 to 40 minutes, or until center is very soft but not runny.

Spoon onto heated plates. If you wish, serve with a bit of unsalted butter on top and garnish with chives and cilantro.

Fried Polenta Triangles with Garlic & Shallots

As FRED IS QUICK to remind Linda, polenta is really just cornmeal mush. For him it is soul food and should be fried in butter and served for breakfast with sugar. We also like it the Italian way—fried in a very good olive oil and served as a savory dish. This version is especially tasty because of the shallots and garlic.

We make the polenta in a double boiler so that it doesn't have to be stirred constantly. Also the frying is begun under a cover so that the triangles heat through.

While we especially enjoy these triangles with any saucy veal dish, they are also delicious when served as a brunch dish topped by a poached egg and sautéed mushrooms in red wine sauce.

SERVES 6

6   cups boiling chicken or
      vegetable stock
1   teaspoon kosher salt
⅛   teaspoon freshly ground white pepper

1⅔ cups medium-grind cornmeal
3   plump garlic cloves, pressed
1   plump shallot, minced
1   tablespoon unsalted butter
3   tablespoons extra-virgin olive oil
⅔   cup freshly grated Parmesan cheese

Fill bottom part of a large double boiler with just enough water so it does not touch bottom of top part (you may have to experiment a little). Bring water to a boil over high heat. Reduce heat to low, so that water simmers very slowly. Pour boiling stock into top part of double boiler and stir in salt and pepper. Slowly stir in cornmeal, whisking vigorously to avoid lumps. Whisk in garlic and shallot. Cover tightly and cook, whisking vigorously about every 15 minutes, until polenta is very creamy and tender, 1 to 1¼ hours. Stir in butter.

Pour polenta onto a cold surface, preferably a marble pastry board. Using a pastry blade or spatula, form polenta into a large square. As it cools, keep pushing the edges in and up so that it forms a 6- or 7-inch square at least 1 inch thick. When polenta is cold, about 1 hour, cut it into 4 squares, then 8 triangles.

Just before serving, heat olive oil in a large cast-iron skillet. Add triangles, cover and cook over medium heat until browned on bottom, about 4 minutes. Turn and fry, uncovered, until other side is browned, 3 to 4 minutes more.

Serve polenta triangles either on top of or underneath a sauce.

Sprinkle with cheese.

Wine: Badia a Coltibuono Centamura Bianco
(Italy: Tuscany) or, if serving with a mushroom sauce,
a medium-bodied red wine from Italy

Spicy Baked Beans
with Smoked Sausage & Lots of Garlic

WHILE WE HAVE MANY RECIPES FOR baked beans, the consensus of our friends is that this is their favorite. Start this dish in the morning and it will be ready in time for your dinner barbecue. Instead of presoaking the beans, we cook them right out of the package, along with layers of finely chopped onions, lots of garlic and bacon. As the beans slowly simmer in a gingered tomato sauce laced with bourbon, the garlic and onions caramelize, adding their flavors to the generous slices of smoked sausage. The beans soak up all the juices until they are plump and tender and the sauce is thick and velvety. You can experiment with all types of smoked sausages and bacon. Our personal favorite continues to be the outstanding smoked links from S. Wallace Edwards in Surry, Virginia (see Sources, page 415).

SERVES 12 TO 16

- 2 tablespoons unsalted butter, melted
- 10 plump garlic cloves, smashed
- 1½ pounds sweet onions
- 1 loosely packed cup fresh flat-leaf parsley, thick stems removed
- 2 tablespoons fresh thyme leaves (1 tablespoon dried)
- 2 pounds Great Northern beans, rinsed and picked over
- ¾ pound bacon, cut into small pieces
- 1 pound smoked sausage, cut into ¼-inch-thick slices
- 4 whole allspice
- ⅔ cup firmly packed dark brown sugar
- 8 cups boiling water, plus more as needed
- 2 teaspoons coarsely ground black pepper
- ⅔ cup dark molasses, preferably unsulfured
- 2 cups tomato sauce
- 1 tablespoon chili powder
- 1 tablespoon ground ginger
- 1 tablespoon Colman's dry mustard
- ¾ cup bourbon whiskey
- 2 bay leaves
- 1 tablespoon kosher salt

Preheat oven to 275°F. Coat sides of a 6½- to-7½-quart bean pot or cast-iron Dutch oven with melted butter.

Finely chop together garlic, onions, parsley and thyme. Place one-fourth of beans in pot and scatter with one-fourth of onion mixture and one-fourth of bacon and sausage. Place one allspice in layer. Repeat layers, ending with a layer of bacon and remaining allspice.

In a large mixing bowl combine brown sugar, 3 cups boiling water and remaining ingredients except bay leaves and salt. Pour mixture over beans. Place bay leaves on top.

Cover pot and bake for 2 hours. Add 2 cups water, cover and continue baking for 2 more hours. Add 2 cups more water. Cover and continue to bake for 3 hours, or until beans are tender. Stir in salt. (Beans will have cooked 7 hours by this point.)

If liquids seem well absorbed, add 1 cup more water. Remove cover and bake 1 hour more or until sauce is very thick and a thin crust forms on top. Remove bay leaves and serve.

Wine: Château Routas Rouge "Traditional" (France: Provence) or a rich and spicy Zinfandel from California

Oven Risotto
with Garlic, Radicchio & Saffron

THIS DELICIOUS, CREAMY golden risotto is enriched by a generous addition of good Parmesan cheese. The best part of this dish is that you can do all the preparation in advance and assemble the dish just before baking. Oven-baked risotto is almost carefree.

**SERVES 4 AS A MAIN DISH,
8 AS A FIRST COURSE**

 5   cups chicken stock
 3   tablespoons olive oil
 3   plump garlic cloves, smashed
        and minced
 1   dried chile, crumbled
 1   medium yellow onion, finely diced
 1½   cups Arborio rice
 ¼   teaspoon crushed saffron
 ½   teaspoon kosher salt
 ½   teaspoon freshly ground white pepper
 1   cup julienned radicchio
 1   cup freshly grated Parmesan cheese
 ¼   teaspoon freshly grated nutmeg

Julienned fresh basil for garnish

Preheat oven to 400°F. Thoroughly oil a deep 2-quart ovenproof baking dish.

Heat stock in a small saucepan until hot. Cover and set aside.

Combine olive oil, garlic and chile in a heavy saucepan. Place over medium heat until hot; stir in onions. Reduce heat, cover and sauté until onions are tender, about 5 minutes. Add rice and stir for 2 minutes. Stir in saffron, salt and white pepper. Add hot stock and cook over high heat until mixture begins to boil, 3 to 4 minutes. Remove from heat; stir in radicchio and half of cheese.

Pour into prepared baking dish; sprinkle evenly with remaining cheese and nutmeg. Cover tightly with foil and bake in preheated oven until rice is cooked through and has absorbed most of liquid, 35 to 40 minutes. Risotto will be quite moist. Serve in heated soup plates with more cheese and a sprinkling of basil.

Wine: Vietti Barbera d'Alba Pian Romualdo (Italy: Piedmont) or Altesino Rosso di Altesino (Italy: Tuscany)

VEGETABLES

(Where the dish might be the feature of a vegetarian main meal, or make a pleasing first course, we offer wine suggestions)

Stuffed Shiitake Mushroom Caps with Garlic & Lemon   378

Kentucky "Fried" Corn   379

Oaxacan-Style Spicy Corn with Garlic Mayonnaise   380

Amazing Creamed Corn & Roasted Garlic   381

Hearty Corn Cakes with Dry-Roasted Garlic   382

Dolmas Warda (Assyrian Grape Leaves Stuffed with Mushrooms, Garlic, Rice & Walnuts)   384

Golden Harvard Beets with Leeks & Garlic   386

Freddie's Fabled Fried Green Tomatoes   387

Summertime Stuffed Tomatoes   388

Stir-Fried Rapini with Garlic   389

Tangy Glazed Swiss Chard   390

Chinese-Style Fried Eggplant with Garlic & Chile   391

A Garlic Lover's Eggplant Parmesan   392

Madeiran Braised Carrots, Squash & Potatoes with Fresh Garlic   393

Cheesy Cabbage Gratin   394

Mediterranean Zucchini Stuffed with Garlic & Parsley   395

Zucchini Pancakes   396

Puree of Root Vegetables with Apple & Roasted Garlic   397

Autumn Gratin of Turnips, Sweet Potatoes & Garlic   398

Thanksgiving Winter Squash with Roasted Garlic   399

Spicy Mushroom-Stuffed Braised Tofu with Garlic, Ginger & Soy Sauce   400

COOKS TALK GARLIC

Marcella Hazan: "I love fresh green garlic, which appears in the market in Venice at the beginning of May. It is so sweet." She feels that "the best garlic dish is one in which you are all but unaware of its presence, yet if it were missing, the flavor would fall apart."

Paul Bertolli, who became famous for his work at Chez Panisse, has moved on to his own restaurant, Oliveto in Oakland. He loves rocambole and Carpathian red garlic, which he gets from writer-farmer Chester Aaron. He is also fond of spring garlic, harvested before it starts to bulb. And he uses garlic only in its season.

When **Paula Wolfert,** our premier expert on Mediterranean cuisines, thinks of garlic, she also thinks of olive oil. No one writes better than she about garlic and olive oil: "When the two are combined in a creamy suspension, something sublime is born. It is, I think, one of the greatest discoveries in culinary history."

Another favorite technique involves crushing the garlic in a mortar with parsley, something she learned from Richard Olney. "He used the combination on top of coq au vin," she told us, "really a revelation at the time."

If she is using raw garlic in the autumn or winter, she splits the cloves to remove the green shoots. But her absolute favorite is fresh green garlic, pulled and used before the plant has even had time to think about bulbing.

Gray Kunz dazzled the customers at New York's Lespinasse Restaurant. He is another who loves the fresh green garlic of the springtime. "Not too pungent," he says. "The size is small and it peels well." His favorite garlic dish is "roasted peeled garlic sautéed with olive oil, deglazed with pastis liqueur with chopped fennel seeds and saffron added, and, at the end, a tad of butter." It's just a little snack, enough to tingle the taste buds.

Ken Hom says, "I especially love young spring garlic, as shoots and as young green garlic. It has a sweet fragrance and freshness like no other." He never puts garlic through a press because it makes the taste too strong and sometimes bitter. As for his favorite garlic dish, he waxes rhapsodic over "fried thinly sliced garlic with fresh chili and squid, salt and pepper."

Odessa Piper, chef-owner of L'Etoile in Madison, Wisconsin, says, "Garlic can make or break a dish. Is the cook handling it with proper understanding of how to use it?" Garlic "has the ability to infuse itself into other ingredients, making a higher synthesis of flavor."

Her husband is a wine importer, and Piper says raw or undercooked garlic makes him skittish. She warns that the serious food and wine lover "has to be careful with garlic. Poorly handled, it can wreck a wine."

"One of my favorite uses of garlic," she writes, "is to put it with fresh gingerroot and Riesling, caramelized sugar and a bit of soy sauce. Reduce it all down to a syrup and use it to glaze pork." But the hands-down winner in her opinion is this preparation for garlic mashed potatoes: "Boil garlic cloves in milk to remove the harsh notes. Then roast the garlic in olive oil. Add the roast garlic to mashed potatoes thinned with a little of the garlic milk."

Christopher Kimball's *Cook's Illustrated* magazine is admired by serious cooks everywhere. His main concern is avoiding the bitterness that often comes from overcooking garlic. "If you cook crushed cloves in hot oil until golden and then let them steep for 10 minutes, you can use the oil and discard the cloves. It's a good way to get the flavor without the bitterness." If a recipe calls for sautéing garlic for two or three minutes, he recommends doing it for just one minute. And "to avoid the deadly, heavy, bitter taste of garlic that often results after long cooking, you can add a small amount of garlic near the end of cooking instead."

When you chop garlic, it always seems to stick to the knife. Kimball's advice: "When using herbs and garlic in a recipe, mince them together. The garlic will stick to the herbs and not so much to your knife. If you're chopping only garlic, wet the knife before you begin."

Stuffed Shiitake Mushroom Caps with Garlic & Lemon

GARLIC, BUTTER AND LEMON are the ultimate flavorings for the warm, woodsy flavor of fresh shiitakes.

SERVES 4

4   very large (4-6 inches in diameter) shiitake mushrooms
5   tablespoons unsalted butter
2   plump garlic cloves, smashed and minced, plus 1 thinly sliced
1   plump shallot, minced
1   teaspoon minced fresh oregano (½ teaspoon dried)
⅓   cup fine dry bread crumbs
3   thin slices prosciutto, chopped
1   tablespoon minced fresh chives
    Kosher salt and freshly ground black pepper
1   tablespoon medium soy sauce
1   lemon, cut in half
1   tablespoon olive oil
⅓   cup chicken stock

Preheat oven to 425°F. Remove and discard mushroom stems.

Melt 1 tablespoon butter over medium heat in a small skillet. Stir in minced garlic and shallot. Stir until wilted, 3 to 4 minutes. Stir in oregano, bread crumbs and prosciutto. Cook for 1 minute, then remove from heat. Stir in chives, salt and pepper.

Gently mound stuffing mixture over bottom (gill side) of mushroom caps. Melt remaining 4 tablespoons butter over medium heat in an ovenproof skillet just large enough to hold mushroom caps. Add garlic slices and soy sauce. Arrange mushroom caps in skillet, stuffed side up. Cover and cook over low heat for 10 minutes, or until mushroom caps appear to have softened slightly.

Uncover, spritz tops with juice of half a lemon and drizzle with olive oil. Pour chicken stock into skillet. Place in oven and bake until tops are browned and mushrooms are tender in center, 10 to 15 minutes.

Transfer mushrooms to heated serving plates. Stir juice of remaining lemon half into skillet. Baste mushrooms with pan juices and serve.

Wine: Domaine Lucien Albrecht Riesling (France: Alsace) or Schug Carneros Estate Chardonnay Carneros (California: Sonoma County)

Kentucky "Fried" Corn

E FOUND THE INSPIRATION FOR this recipe in *The Kentucky Housewife*, written in 1839. Although it's called "fried" corn, there's no frying in the recipe. Cut the kernels off the cobs and scrape off all the tasty milk. Cook them covered, with garlic, shallots and a smidgen of hot pepper. It's simple and delicious. As in Lettice Bryan's day, the freshest corn is always the best, bursting with milk and fresh flavor.

SERVES 4 TO 6

7 very fresh ears of corn, shucked
3 tablespoons unsalted butter
3 plump garlic cloves, smashed
   and minced
1 small fresh hot chile pepper, minced
1 plump shallot, minced
1 tablespoon water or milk
   Kosher salt and freshly ground
      white pepper
2 tablespoons minced fresh chives,
   preferably garlic chives

Using a sharp knife, carefully slice tops of corn kernels into a large pan. Then scrape off remaining part of kernel down to cob, along with any milky juice, into same pan. Reserve.

Melt butter in a nonstick skillet over medium heat. Add garlic, chile and shallot. Stir until softened, 1 to 2 minutes. Add corn mixture, water or milk, salt and white pepper. Cover skillet tightly and cook over low heat, stirring several times, until corn is very tender, about 15 minutes. Adjust seasonings, sprinkle with chives and serve.

Oaxacan-Style Spicy Corn with Garlic Mayonnaise

A COATING OF GARLIC MAYONNAISE and a lavish sprinkling of peppery seasonings make this boiled corn an irresistible treat. It's inspired by the ears of field corn sold by street vendors in the remarkable Mexican colonial town of Oaxaca, where we often go for Christmas celebrations. During the days before the holiday, the *zocalo,* or town square, is a hubbub of activity. Among the food vendors are those with little carts complete with heat for boiling corn. The hot corn is slathered with mayonnaise and coated with an amazing pepper-and-cumin mixture. We walk around the *zocalo,* happily gnawing the ear, juices dribbling down our chins, groaning with pleasure at every bite!

SERVES 2 TO 4

1 tablespoon kosher salt

1 tablespoon ground cumin

2 teaspoons ground red pepper (cayenne)

1½ teaspoons freshly ground white pepper

1½ teaspoons freshly ground black pepper

1 teaspoon ground oregano

⅔ cup mayonnaise

2 plump garlic cloves, pressed

4 ears corn, husks and silk removed

In a small bowl, blend together salt, cumin, cayenne, white and black pepper and oregano. Reserve.

Blend together mayonnaise and garlic.

In a large soup pot, bring 4 to 5 quarts of salted water to a vigorous boil. Add corn, cover pot and reduce heat to a rapid simmer. Cook corn until tender, 2 to 3 minutes.

Remove corn from pot and shake off water. Spear bottom of each ear with a corn holder. With a pastry brush, liberally paint ears with mayonnaise. Then generously sprinkle on all sides with seasoning mixture. Serve immediately.

Amazing Creamed Corn & Roasted Garlic

THE FRENCH MIGHT CALL THIS A *"pechez mignon,"* a small indulgence. Vid Lutz, executive chef of Cleveland's celebrated restaurants Johnny's Bar on Fulton and Johnny's Downtown, blew us away with this addictively decadent dish. While we love to serve it as an accompaniment to something from the grill, we've also served it as a first course with Silken Garlic Custards (page 74). From a color and texture standpoint, large yellow corn kernels are best.

SERVES 4 TO 6

2 tablespoons unsalted butter

8 plump garlic cloves, roasted
   (see page 34) and finely chopped
   Corn cut from 6 large ears
   (2-2½ cups)

1 medium-sized red bell pepper,
   finely diced
   Kosher salt and freshly ground
   white pepper

⅓ cup heavy cream

½ cup finely grated Romano cheese

In a medium-sized saucepan, melt butter over medium-high heat. Add garlic and stir vigorously until butter foams and garlic fragrance is very sweet, about 1 minute. Add corn and stir for 2 minutes. Reduce heat to medium and add bell pepper. Stir for 1 to 2 minutes, or until pepper begins to soften. Add salt and white pepper.

Add cream and cheese. Stir often until mixture begins to bubble. Simmer slowly until sauce thickens, 1 to 2 minutes. Serve.

Wine: Maculan Chardonnay (Italy: Veneto)
or another aromatic medium-bodied Chardonnay

Hearty Corn Cakes
with Dry-Roasted Garlic

CORNMEAL AND FRESH CORN KERNELS add a nutty quality to the sweetness of the dry-roasted garlic in these corn cakes. Buttermilk and basil make them big in flavor but nonetheless light. We serve them as a side dish with anything from the grill or with roasted pork dishes. Corn cakes also make a great treat for Sunday breakfast with warm maple syrup. For dinners, we like to garnish them with Minted Sauce of Garlic & Cilantro (page 148), Chimichurri (page 151) or simply bottled salsa.

SERVES 8 AS A SIDE DISH

8	plump garlic cloves, unpeeled
1	cup unbleached flour
¾	cup yellow cornmeal
2	teaspoons baking powder
½	teaspoon baking soda
1	tablespoon sugar
1	teaspoon freshly ground white pepper
1	teaspoon kosher salt
2	tablespoons extra-virgin olive oil
3	large eggs, lightly beaten
1¼	cups buttermilk, plus more if needed
¼	cup minced shallots
1½	cups fresh corn kernels
¼	cup minced fresh basil
½	cup olive oil

Heat a small cast-iron skillet or griddle over medium-high heat until hot. Cook garlic cloves, turning often, until soft to the touch and somewhat blackened in spots, 10 to 15 minutes. Set aside until cool, then peel and mince. Reserve.

Combine flour, cornmeal, baking powder, baking soda, sugar, white pepper and salt in a large mixing bowl. Whisk until mixed.

In a small mixing bowl, combine olive oil, eggs and buttermilk. Beat vigorously to blend. Pour over dry ingredients and blend thoroughly.

Add roasted garlic, shallots, corn and basil. Fold lightly to blend. Mixture should be thick enough to make a pancake. If it's too thick, stir in a bit more buttermilk. If too thin, add cornmeal, 1 tablespoon at a time, and blend carefully.

Preheat oven to 250°F.

Lightly coat a large skillet with oil. Heat over medium-high heat until oil begins to sizzle. Pour enough batter to make 3-inch round cakes; do not crowd. Fry until bubbles begin to appear on surface, about 2 minutes. Turn and brown on other side. Transfer cakes to a cookie sheet lined with paper towels and hold in a warm oven until all are made.

Serve with a relish or sweet sauce on the side.

When not served with a sweet sauce:

Wine: Flora Springs Wine Co. Soliloquy (California: Napa Valley) or another lush and aromatic Sauvignon Blanc

Dolmas Warda

(ASSYRIAN GRAPE LEAVES STUFFED WITH MUSHROOMS, GARLIC, RICE & WALNUTS)

WHILE STUFFED GRAPE LEAVES ARE basic to virtually every Middle Eastern culture, this recipe is distinctive. The unusual mixture of fresh mushrooms, lots of garlic, rice and chopped walnuts is seasoned with coriander, dill, mint and cayenne. The cooking medium is a richly flavored sauce of lemon and caramelized onions. And the stuffed leaves are cooked in the oven, rather than on the stovetop.

Assyrian cooking is especially rich in its use of complex flavors. Nowhere is this cuisine better presented than in David Benjamin Warda's self-published *Assyrian Cookery: Exotic Foods That Outlasted a Civilization* (1997), a beautifully produced book rich in recipes from a family culinary tradition that goes back through 3,000 years of Persian history and lore. We thank Warda for allowing us to use this recipe, just one of dozens that stimulate the senses and satisfy the soul. (For Warda's cookbook, call toll free: (888) 277-4742.)

MAKES 40 GRAPE LEAVES

1 16-ounce jar grape leaves
1 cup short-grain rice, soaked in water overnight
6 tablespoons olive oil
1 pound fresh mushrooms (hearty brown kinds such as portobello, shiitake or porcini), cleaned and coarsely chopped
8-10 plump garlic cloves, chopped
½ cup chopped walnuts

1 tablespoon coriander seeds (or ground coriander)
1 tablespoon dried dill weed
1 tablespoon dried mint
1 teaspoon crushed dried red chiles
Kosher salt and freshly ground black pepper
2 large Spanish onions, peeled and chopped
1 tablespoon paprika
4 cups water
Juice of 2 lemons
Lemon wedges

Drain grape leaves and carefully unroll. Discard any stems and soak leaves for several hours in warm water, changing water several times.

Drain thoroughly.

While grape leaves are soaking, make filling: Rinse and drain rice, then transfer to a large mixing bowl.

Heat 4 tablespoons olive oil in a skillet over medium heat. Add mushrooms and cook, stirring often, until excess liquid disappears, about 6 minutes. Add mushrooms to rice. Reserve skillet. Add garlic and walnuts to rice mixture and set aside.

In a small skillet over medium heat, roast coriander seeds, stirring constantly, until golden brown, 1 to 2 minutes. Grind in a spice mill or mortar with pestle. Add coriander, dill, mint and chiles to rice mixture. Add salt and pepper to taste. Reserve.

In reserved skillet, heat remaining 2 tablespoons olive oil. Add onions and cook over very low heat, stirring often, until onions are golden brown, 1 to 1½ hours. (This will give onions a very sweet flavor.) When onions are caramelized, remove from heat. Stir in paprika, water and lemon juice. Add salt to taste. Reserve.

While onions are cooking, prepare rolls: In a 4-to-5-quart nonreactive casserole, arrange a layer of grape leaves to cover bottom.

Working with about 10 grape leaves at a time, lay them out, vein side up, on a work surface. Spoon about a tablespoon of rice filling in center of each. Fold sides in toward center. Fold top down, then roll stem end up, rolling somewhat loosely, leaving room for rice to expand. Place filled leaves, seam side down, in lined dish. Repeat until all but 6 to 8 leaves are filled.

Preheat oven to 325°F.

Pour onion sauce over rolls. Cover with reserved grape leaves. Lay an inverted ovenproof dish over leaves to keep filled rolls from moving during baking.

Cover casserole and bake for 2 hours, or until most of liquid is absorbed. Turn off heat and allow *dolmas* to steep until they reach serving temperature. If you wish, store in refrigerator, bringing to room temperature before serving.

Serve with wedges of lemons.

Wine: Domain Zind-Humbrecht Old Vines Pinot Gris (France: Alsace) or another Alsatian Pinot Gris

Golden Harvard Beets with Leeks and Garlic

A COMBINATION OF SUGAR and vinegar gives Harvard beets their characteristic sweet and sour flavor. We've modified the traditional recipe by building our sauce on a richly mellow base of softened garlic and leeks. While we enjoy all kinds of beets, golden ones fresh from the garden are the absolute best. Keep in mind that freshly pulled beets cook more rapidly than old ones.

SERVES 4

2	pounds fresh beets, preferably golden
2	tablespoons unsalted butter
⅔	cup thinly sliced young leeks, including tender green
2	plump garlic cloves, slivered
½	cup sugar
2½	teaspoons cornstarch
¼	cup fruit vinegar (raspberry, pear or peach)
¼	cup water, plus 2 tablespoons if needed Kosher salt and freshly ground white pepper
1	tablespoon minced fresh chives for garnish

Trim beets, leaving tap root and 1 inch of top. Clean well. Place in large saucepan and cover with water. Bring to a boil over high heat, reduce heat, cover and simmer briskly until beets are tender when pierced with a knife, about 20 minutes or longer, depending on age and size of beets. Drain and rinse with cold water. Remove taproot and stem. Slip off skins with your fingers and discard. Cut beets into thin slices and set aside in a large mixing bowl.

In a small saucepan, melt butter over medium heat. Add leeks and garlic; cook, stirring often, until leeks have softened, 3 to 4 minutes. Sprinkle with sugar and cornstarch and blend. Stir in vinegar and water. Cook over medium heat until mixture begins to boil, 3 to 4 minutes. Reduce heat to low and simmer until thickened, about 2 minutes. If sauce seems too thick, thin with hot water, 1 tablespoon at a time.

Pour hot sauce over beets. Season with salt and white pepper. Blend thoroughly. Store beets in refrigerator. Serve hot or at room temperature, sprinkled with chives.

Stir-Fried Rapini with Garlic

THE BITTERNESS OF RAPINI (broccoli rabe) is beautifully tamed by the sweet and mellow flavors of our beloved stinking rose. Add some soy sauce and a touch of chicken stock to be certain that the somewhat tough ends of this green vegetable are momentarily braised. But don't worry if they're still a bit crisp; they are better that way.

SERVES 4

2   teaspoons cornstarch
⅓   cup chicken stock
2   teaspoons soy sauce
1   teaspoon dark sesame oil
2   tablespoons canola oil
1   dried chile, crumbled
2   plump shallots, finely diced
4   plump garlic cloves, smashed
       and minced
1   bunch rapini (broccoli rabe), about
       1 pound, cleaned, dried, tough
       ends discarded, coarsely chopped
2   tablespoons minced fresh chives,
       preferably garlic chives

In a small bowl, blend together cornstarch and stock. Stir in soy sauce and sesame oil. Set aside.

Heat canola oil in a wok over high heat. Stir in chile, then shallots and garlic. Cook for 20 seconds, stirring constantly. Add rapini and stir until it wilts, about 2 minutes.

Stir cornstarch mixture, then pour over rapini. Continue to cook, stirring constantly, until rapini is thoroughly coated with sauce and somewhat tender, 1 to 2 minutes.

Sprinkle with chives and serve.

Tangy Glazed Swiss Chard

WE HAVE TWO SMALL PATCHES of chard in our garden. We toss the young leaves into salad (the red chard is very pretty that way). The larger leaves we save for braising. A carefully watched sauté pan will yield tender, slightly tangy chard covered in a light glaze of reduced stock and vinegar. This makes a great side dish with lamb or chicken. Or it can be blended with bow-tie noodles and some pine nuts browned in a bit more olive oil for a hearty pasta supper. Finally, if you grow oregano, add some of the little seed heads that appear at summer's end. The flavor is glorious.

SERVES 2 TO 3

1   pound large Swiss chard leaves,
    cleaned and dried
2   tablespoons fruity extra-virgin olive oil
1   plump garlic clove, minced
1   plump shallot, minced
⅓   cup chicken or vegetable stock
1   teaspoon minced fresh oregano
1   tablespoon fruit vinegar
    (pear, peach, berry)
    Kosher salt and freshly ground
    white pepper

Carefully run a knife along edges of thick chard stems and cut away. Cut stems into 1-inch pieces and set aside in a bowl.

Coarsely chop leaves and place in another bowl.

In a large nonstick sauté pan, heat olive oil over low heat. Add garlic and shallots. Cover and cook until softened, about 3 minutes. Add chard stems. Stir to coat with oil. Add all but 2 tablespoons stock. Cover and cook over very low heat for 10 minutes, stirring occasionally.

Add chard leaves, remaining 2 tablespoons stock, oregano and vinegar. Stir well and cover. Cook another 10 minutes. Chard should be tender and liquids reduced to a light glaze. Season with salt and white pepper and serve.

Chinese-Style Fried Eggplant with Garlic & Chile

CRUNCHY ON THE OUTSIDE, creamy on the inside. A spicy sprinkling of garlic, cilantro and chile pepper makes this delicious eggplant dish perfect. Don't be too frugal with the oil; add some as you go along, allowing it to heat each time so that the batter browns consistently. This dish was inspired by San Francisco's Yank Sing, perhaps our favorite dim sum restaurant in this country.

SERVES 4

1 cup unbleached flour
2 teaspoons baking powder
1 teaspoon kosher salt
1 cup ice-cold sparkling water
4 plump garlic cloves, smashed
    and minced
1 fresh hot chile, preferably red, minced
3 tablespoons minced fresh cilantro
½ teaspoon Sichuan peppercorns
    (see page 296)
1 teaspoon kosher salt
    Peanut oil for deep-frying
1½ pounds baby eggplant, preferably
    Japanese, cut crosswise into
    1-inch-thick slices
    Lime wedges

Into a large mixing bowl, sift together flour, baking powder and salt. Add sparkling water and mix vigorously. Let batter rest for a few minutes.

Meanwhile, combine garlic, chile, cilantro, peppercorns and salt in a small bowl. Preheat oven to 250°F.

Pour oil into a wok about 1½ inches deep. Heat until hot (365°F on a deep-frying thermometer). Working quickly, dip eggplant pieces into batter and drain excess. Drop eggplant into hot oil, a few pieces at a time, and cook until golden on each side, about 1½ minutes a side. Drain on paper towels, then keep warm on a towel-covered cookie sheet in oven. Add oil as needed; when oil is hot, repeat until all pieces are fried.

Serve on heated plates, sprinkled with garlic mixture and garnished with lime wedges.

Wine: Domaine Fondreche Ventoux Rouge

(France: Côtes-du-Ventoux)

or a spicy red wine from France's Languedoc region

A Garlic Lover's Eggplant Parmesan

EGGPLANT LAVISHLY SEASONED with cheese, garlic and herbs is wonderful enough. But bathed in tomato sauce and baked, this old standby is absolutely delicious. Broiling the eggplant is much simpler than frying and uses a lot less oil.

SERVES 8 TO 10

5	cups Special Marinara Sauce (page 155)
3½- 4	pounds eggplant, peeled and cut crosswise into ½-inch slices
	Up to ⅔ cup olive oil
	Kosher salt and freshly ground black pepper
8	plump garlic cloves
⅓	cup fresh flat-leaf parsley leaves
⅓	cup fresh basil leaves
1	pound fresh mozzarella, thinly sliced
1	cup freshly grated Parmesan cheese

Pour marinara sauce into a small saucepan and bring to a boil over medium heat. Reduce heat and simmer briskly until sauce is reduced to 4 cups. Set aside.

Place oven or broiler rack just below broiling element. Heat broiler until hot.

Lightly brush eggplant slices with olive oil and season generously with salt and pepper.

Place slices close together directly on rack. Grill or broil eggplant until lightly browned on one side, 6 to 8 minutes. Turn, brush with oil and brown. Transfer browned eggplant to cooling racks. Repeat until all slices are browned.

While eggplant is broiling, mince together garlic, parsley and basil. Reserve.

Preheat oven to 400°F.

Generously oil a 3-to-4-quart casserole, preferably one that is wide and not too deep. Ladle ½ cup sauce into bottom.

Divide eggplant into thirds. Using one-third of slices, cover bottom of pan. Sprinkle with one-third of garlic mixture, then one-third each of mozzarella and Parmesan. Cover with 1 cup sauce. Repeat layers. Then, for last layer, cover with remaining garlic mixture, then mozzarella. Finally, add remaining 1½ cups sauce, then remaining Parmesan.

Bake eggplant uncovered for 50 minutes, until top is browned and sauce is bubbling. Let stand for 10 minutes before cutting into squares and serving.

Wine: Eberle Winery Zinfandel Paso Robles
Sauret Vineyard (California: Paso Robles)
or a rich Chianti Classico from Italy

Madeiran Braised Carrots, Squash & Potatoes with Fresh Garlic

WE FIRST ENJOYED THIS well-cooked mélange of potatoes (we prefer small new ones), chunks of fat carrots and summer squash in a tiny seafood restaurant, Jaquet, in the Old City of Funchal, Madeira. Jaquet, a tiny, cavelike room with 24 stools at small tables, serves some of the best fish and shellfish we have ever tasted. The refrigerator and cooler are at the entrance. At the back, up one step, is a minuscule open kitchen. There is no menu; *Senhora* Jaquet calls out what's available as she glides from stovetop to fryer to windowsill (her handy prep station). Her husband, Luis, darts about the front, simultaneously bringing fish from the cooler while serving more cold beer to the guests at the tables. *Senhora* uses chopped fresh garlic as most Americans use parsley—as a generous garnish for everything. It's especially delicious on her two side dishes: crisply deep-fried potatoes and this vegetable compote.

SERVES 4 TO 6

2 large, fat carrots, scrubbed

4 small yellow squash, scrubbed

1 pound small, uniformly sized new potatoes, scrubbed
  Kosher salt and freshly ground black pepper

2 tablespoons olive oil

4 plump garlic cloves, smashed and minced

Cut the carrots into chunks—plump ends into ¾-inch lengths, thinner ends about 1¼ inches. Cut squash into large chunks. In a large, heavy saucepan, combine potatoes, carrots and squash. Add water to cover. Season generously with salt and pepper. Add olive oil and cover tightly.

Place over high heat until water begins to boil. Reduce heat and simmer briskly until potatoes are fork-tender. (Potatoes 1¼ inches in diameter cook in about 20 minutes.)

Drain vegetables instantly. Season with more salt and pepper.

Sprinkle with garlic and serve.

Wine: Domaine Lucien Thomas Sancerre Clos de la Crèle (France: Loire Valley) or a crisp, fruity Sauvignon Blanc

Cheesy Cabbage Gratin

THIS SIMPLE DISH of cabbage in a garlicky, creamy cheese sauce, with just a suggestion of heat from some Tabasco, is a great addition to a winter buffet.

SERVES 6

8   cups finely shredded Savoy cabbage
    (1 head)
2   tablespoons unsalted butter
2   tablespoons unbleached flour
1½ cups milk
10 drops Tabasco
    Kosher salt and freshly ground
      white pepper
1   cup shredded sharp Cheddar cheese
3   ounces low-fat cream cheese
3   plump garlic cloves, pressed

Preheat oven to 500°F.

Generously oil a shallow 3-quart gratin dish. Place cabbage in dish and set aside.

In a medium-sized saucepan, melt butter over medium heat. Whisk in flour and blend thoroughly. Slowly add milk, whisking until mixture is a smooth, somewhat thick, white sauce. Reduce heat and stir in Tabasco, salt and pepper. Then add cheeses, stirring until melted. Whisk in garlic.

Pour cheese sauce over cabbage and blend together.

Bake uncovered for 15 to 18 minutes. Sauce should be thick and creamy; cabbage will be cooked through and crusty on top. Serve hot.

Wine: Château Potelle Sauvignon Blanc Napa Valley
(California: Napa Valley) or another crisp Sauvignon Blanc

Mediterranean Zucchini Stuffed with Garlic and Parsley

SWEET YOUNG ZUCCHINI are just perfect when lightly stuffed with a pungent combination of garlic, parsley and olive oil. If you travel through France's Côte d'Azur in summer, you are bound to find these in seaside bistros.

SERVES 4

8 small zucchini, about 4 inches long
5 plump garlic cloves, smashed
  and minced
⅔ cup minced fresh flat-leaf parsley
½ cup extra-virgin olive oil
  Kosher salt and freshly ground
  black pepper

With a sharp knife, make a long, ½-inch-deep and slightly angled slice along top of each zucchini. Make a second, slightly angled slice ¾ inch from first to create a shallow cavity in zucchini. Remove wedge.

In a small bowl, blend together garlic, parsley, half of olive oil, salt and pepper. Distribute mixture among prepared zucchini, packing stuffing well.

Arrange zucchini in a shallow baking dish just large enough to hold them. Drizzle with remaining ¼ cup olive oil.

When ready to bake, preheat oven to 450°F. Bake until zucchini are tender and stuffing is brown on top, 15 to 20 minutes. Serve.

Wine: Joseph Phelps Vineyards Grenache Rosé Vin du Mistral (California) or a French Tavel Rosé from Provence

Zucchini Pancakes

GRATED ZUCCHINI, minced garlic, shallots and basil are bound together with eggs, flour and buttermilk to make delicate pancakes that are flavorful yet very light in texture. These make a terrific side dish or a light summer supper along with soup and good bread.

MAKES EIGHT 3½-TO-4-INCH PANCAKES

2   packed cups grated young zucchini, lightly salted and drained for 1 hour
4   plump garlic cloves, smashed and minced
1   plump shallot, minced
2   large eggs
7   large basil leaves, opal if possible, finely julienned
⅓   cup unbleached flour, plus more if needed
3   tablespoons buttermilk, plus more if needed
1   tablespoon extra-virgin olive oil
    Kosher salt and freshly ground white pepper
6   gratings fresh nutmeg or ⅛ teaspoon grated nutmeg
    Up to ½ cup olive oil

Yogurt with minced garlic chives for garnish

Place zucchini in a colander and press to make certain it is well drained. In a large mixing bowl, beat together garlic, shallot, eggs and basil. Add flour and stir until blended. Whisk in buttermilk, extra-virgin olive oil, salt, white pepper and nutmeg. Fold in zucchini. Let rest for 30 minutes.

When ready to cook, check mixture. If it seems too thick, add a bit of buttermilk. If batter is too runny, add a bit more flour.

Heat 3 tablespoons oil in a large skillet over high heat. When sizzling, drop in enough batter to make thin, 3-inch pancakes. Do not crowd. Fry until brown, turn and fry on other side, about 3 minutes total. Transfer to paper towels to drain. Repeat until all pancakes are made, adding more oil as needed.

Serve with a dollop of yogurt and a sprinkling of chives.

Wine: Jepson Vineyards Chardonnay
(California: Mendocino County)
or another medium-bodied Chardonnay

Puree of Root Vegetables with Apple & Roasted Garlic

IN OHIO'S LONG WINTER, we eat a lot of root vegetables. This sublimely simple puree combines mellow roasted garlic with sweet parsnips, crisp celery root and pungent rutabaga. This is a flexible dish; you can always substitute more of one vegetable in place of another. You can also include potatoes and use fewer root vegetables. For a silky texture, rub the puree through a *chinois*, or drum sieve, as the French do. And finally, thin any leftovers with a good stock and enjoy this puree as a soup.

SERVES 6 TO 8

1   jumbo rutabaga (1½ pounds), peeled
1   large celery root (1 pound), peeled
2   large parsnips, peeled
2   plump garlic cloves, peeled
1   large tart apple, peeled, cored
     and quartered
4   tablespoons (½ stick) unsalted butter
1   large head garlic, roasted
     (see page 34)
½   cup milk
⅓   cup heavy cream

Kosher salt and freshly ground
  white pepper to taste

Cut vegetables into 1-inch cubes. Place rutabaga in a 3-to-4-quart saucepan nearly filled with salted water. Cover and bring to a boil over high heat. Reduce heat and simmer for 10 minutes. Add celery root, parsnips and garlic. Increase heat to boil, then reduce to a simmer. Cook for 15 minutes. Add apple and continue to simmer, covered, until vegetables are tender, about 15 minutes more.

Drain thoroughly. Using a slotted spoon, place half of solids in the bowl of a food processor fitted with the metal blade. Add half of butter, roasted garlic flesh and milk. Puree until smooth. Spoon into a bowl. Puree remaining solids with remaining butter, garlic and milk. Add to bowl. Beat in cream, salt and white pepper.

Reheat in a microwave or covered in a very heavy saucepan over very low heat before serving.

Autumn Gratin of Turnips, Sweet Potatoes & Garlic

OUR GRANDDAUGHTER MADISON accompanied Linda to Silver Creek Farm one glorious autumn day. Armed with a pitchfork, the two trudged into the fields, where they dug handsome turnips, beets, carrots and assorted other treasures. Madison enjoyed an ambulatory salad as she toured the rows, sampling the small fronds of kale, bronze lettuce and mizuna. While she loved eating the turnip tops, the glistening bulbs did not appeal to her. Hoping to tempt her, we created this creamy and savory gratin. (She still preferred the turnip tops!)

SERVES 6

4   tablespoons (½ stick) unsalted butter
1   pound turnips, scrubbed and
      thinly sliced
2   medium-large sweet potatoes,
      peeled and thinly sliced
4   plump garlic cloves, smashed
      and minced
1½ cups milk
1   cup grated semisoft cheese,
      such as raclette or fontina

Kosher salt and freshly ground
   white pepper
Freshly grated nutmeg
2   tablespoons fine dry bread crumbs

Preheat oven to 375°F. Generously oil a shallow 3-quart gratin dish.

Melt butter in a large skillet. Add turnips, sweet potatoes and garlic. Toss several times to coat with butter. Cover and cook over very low heat for 10 minutes, just to begin cooking process. Add milk and cook over high heat until liquids bubble. Stir in cheese, salt and pepper. Blend until cheese is evenly distributed.

Transfer mixture to gratin dish. Grate some nutmeg over top, then sprinkle evenly with bread crumbs.

Bake uncovered for 1 hour, or until top is golden brown and vegetables are exceptionally tender. Serve.

Wine: Qupé Cellars "Bien Nacido" Cuvée White Santa Barbara County (California: Santa Barbara County) or a French Chardonnay from the Macon

Thanksgiving Winter Squash with Roasted Garlic

A GLORIOUS SHINY ORANGE-GOLD, this squash puree has been part of our Thanksgiving buffet table for years. Long ago we began to roast our winter squash rather than steam it, so that the juices would caramelize. Now we always prepare too much for the meal, just so we'll have leftovers to turn into soup.

SERVES 8

5   pounds mixed winter squash, such as Hubbard, butternut, acorn and red kuri, split and seeded

3   large heads of garlic, roasted (see page 34), pan juices reserved

8   tablespoons (1 stick) unsalted butter, cut into small pieces
    Kosher salt

1   teaspoon freshly ground white pepper, plus more if needed

6   gratings fresh nutmeg

Preheat oven to 425°F.

Cut squash in half and place, skin side up, in a large roasting pan. Add enough water to generously cover bottom of pan. Roast until flesh is fork-tender. Remove from oven and allow to cool until easily handled.

While squash is cooling, squeeze garlic flesh from skins into a food processor. Add garlic pan juices.

Spoon squash flesh and butter into food processor, working in batches if needed. Pulse until thoroughly pureed. Add salt, pepper and nutmeg.

Pour squash into a buttered ovenproof casserole. If making ahead, cover with plastic wrap and store in refrigerator. Bring to room temperature several hours ahead of serving.

Preheat oven to 350°F and bake, loosely covered with foil, until hot, about 30 minutes.

Spicy Mushroom-Stuffed Braised Tofu with Garlic, Ginger & Soy Sauce

THIS DELICIOUS, HEALTHFUL DISH can be served as a side dish, but it also makes a satisfying first course to a vegetarian dinner. Our shiitake mushroom and garlic stuffing is richly flavored with scallions, ginger and mushroom soy sauce. Blocks of tofu are readily available in supermarkets everywhere.

SERVES 6

3	tablespoons peanut oil
1	dried chile, crumbled
3	plump garlic cloves, smashed and minced, plus 1 pressed
3	teaspoons minced gingerroot
2-3	ounces shiitake mushroom caps, finely chopped
⅓	cup minced scallions
3	teaspoons mushroom soy sauce
2	teaspoons dark sesame oil
3	rectangular blocks firm tofu
½	cup unbleached flour
2	tablespoons dry sherry
⅓	cup chicken or vegetable stock
2	tablespoons minced fresh cilantro
1	tablespoon minced fresh chives

Heat 1 tablespoon peanut oil in a small skillet over medium heat. Add chile, minced garlic and 2 teaspoons ginger. Stir for 30 seconds to release flavors. Add chopped mushrooms, 1 tablespoon scallions and 1 teaspoon mushroom soy sauce; cover and reduce heat. Cook, stirring occasionally, until mushrooms are tender, about 5 minutes. Uncover, increase heat and cook until liquid is almost evaporated, 1 to 2 minutes. Stir in 1 teaspoon sesame oil.

Cut tofu into 1-inch-thick slices. Dredge thoroughly in flour and arrange on a flat, lightly floured platter. Using a very narrow spoon or a vegetable peeler, make an opening in center of each piece about ¾ inch in diameter. Spoon some mushroom filling into each center.

Combine remaining 1 teaspoon ginger and 4 tablespoons scallions in a small bowl; blend in pressed garlic. In another bowl, blend together remaining 2 teaspoons soy sauce and 1 teaspoon sesame oil, then add sherry and stock.

Heat remaining 2 tablespoons oil in a large, heavy skillet over medium-high heat. Using a spatula, gently transfer tofu squares to skillet and sauté until bottom is golden, 3 to 4 minutes. Gently prick unbrowned side with a fork. Very carefully turn tofu.

Sprinkle evenly with stock mixture, then with scallion mixture. Cover and braise until liquid is somewhat absorbed by tofu, 4 to 6 minutes. Uncover and cook until liquid is further reduced, 2 to 3 minutes.

Transfer to serving plates. Spoon remaining liquid over top; sprinkle with cilantro and chives.

Wine: San Quirico Vernaccia (Italy: Tuscany) or a crisp and citrusy Sauvignon Blanc

BOBBA-MIKE'S GARLIC FESTIVAL

ONE DAY IN LATE WINTER, we got a small box of garlic in the mail. There were 24 heads, small, pearly-white softnecks, weighing about an ounce each. They were solid and had not started to sprout, although they had been harvested six months earlier. We cracked a head and ate a clove or two. The flavor was subtle and complex, challenging our descriptive powers.

Our friends Bob Zimmerman and Wendy Douglas knew we were taste-testing garlic and figured correctly that we were running low on the fresh stuff. We called them at Bobba-Mike's Garlic Farm in Marshallville, Ohio, to thank them and ask the name of the garlic.

"We don't know," they told us. "It's just an Italian white. We got it a few years ago from an 86-year-old Italian man in Pennsylvania. For him it was just the garlic that his parents brought from Italy early in the century. It has no special name—just Italian. We've tried to make it grow larger over the past years, but it just won't do it. It is what it is."

Since botanists can't develop new strains of garlic, farmers have to accept what nature does as a line accommodates itself to a specific climate and latitude. Somewhere in southern Italy generations ago, this particular garlic just happened, and it continued to develop and change in garden patches in western Pennsylvania and northern Ohio.

Our suppliers of the unusual cloves are typical of the energetic and curious farmers who grow specialty garlic. Their partnership has had a high profile in northern Ohio for several years. Business was so good that Douglas quit her full-time job to give their little farm all of her attention. And Zimmerman, a longtime world-traveling employee of the Swedish car maker Volvo, has cut back his commitment to the company to have more time for marketing their gourmet garlic, as well as creating a brand-new festival.

We saw them on a beautiful September day at the Lorain County fairgrounds, where the first-ever Ohio Garlic Festival was under way, produced by Bob and Wendy, working with some other small growers and garlic aficionados.

Gilroy it wasn't. But a lot of passionate people wanted to embrace the stinking rose, talk propagation with garlic growers who came to share their wares, listen to lectures on health, nutrition and cookery and eat heavily garlicked potatoes, steak and chicken.

DESSERTS

Honey-Poached Garlic Sauce for Ice Cream   **405**

Caramelized Garlic French Ice Cream with Lavender   **406**

Apple Spice Cake with Roasted Garlic   **408**

BOLDLY GO—
BUT NOT TOO FAR

A RETIRED DIPLOMAT AND AUTHOR of numerous monographs on diplomatic subjects, Nicholas Roosevelt published two intriguing books on cookery during the 1950s. In *Creative Cooking*, published in 1956, he urged cooks to experiment boldly with seasonings, but with one caveat:

> *If you will bear in mind the oft-repeated principle, "Don't overdo," you will be on the road to the acquisition of culinary wisdom. But be bold. Try combining flavors. Make tests to determine how much of a particular seasoning you find agreeable. And on those off days when every dish seems stale, flat and unprofitable, reach for your garlic press and begin by adding a half drop of garlic juice. Garlic fanatics insist that garlic is even good in ice cream. But members of the American Garlic Society, of which I am one, are of the opinion that one should draw the line somewhere. If I can have garlic in hors d'oeuvres, soup, the main course and salad, I'm prepared to pass it up in ice cream.*

Honey-Poached Garlic Sauce for Ice Cream

THIS CINNAMON-PERFUMED honey garlic sauce is worth taking a trip to New Orleans to taste. We thank Upperline Restaurant's owner JoAnn Clevenger for sharing it with us.

SERVES 4 TO 6

1   cup good-quality honey
1   cup water, plus more if needed
10 plump garlic cloves, peeled
1   long piece lemon peel
1   6-inch stick cinnamon

Combine all ingredients in a heavy saucepan and bring to a boil. Reduce heat and simmer slowly until water has evaporated and garlic is tender and golden (caramelized), 40 to 50 minutes. If water boils away before garlic has caramelized, add more water, 1 tablespoon at a time, until garlic is golden and very soft.

Remove sauce from heat and let cool. Discard lemon peel and cinnamon. If you wish, mash garlic cloves before serving.

Serve garlic sauce at room temperature. Ladle over good-quality vanilla or honey ice cream.

Caramelized Garlic French Ice Cream with Lavender

CRAZY AS IT FIRST SOUNDS, a creamy, custard-based ice cream with mellow, sweet roasted garlic is absolutely delicious, especially when we add hints of vanilla and cinnamon—and a subtle but arresting suggestion of lavender. (For lavender, see Sources, page 414.) This great ice cream will be a hit with everyone, even those who would normally eschew our much-loved stinking rose. Start this recipe a day ahead.

SERVES 8 TO 10

Crème Fraîche

1   cup heavy cream
     (not ultra-pasteurized)
3   tablespoons buttermilk

3   cups milk
2   3-inch branches fresh lavender
3   plump garlic cloves, smashed,
     plus 5 large heads roasted garlic
     (page 34), at room temperature
1   vanilla bean, slit lengthwise
1   stick cinnamon
7   large egg yolks
1   cup sugar
¼   teaspoon freshly grated nutmeg

Lavender flowers or candied
    violets for garnish
Caramel sauce, milk-chocolate
    shavings or raspberries (optional)

The night before, make *crème fraîche*: In a small bowl, blend together heavy cream and buttermilk. Cover loosely and let stand at room temperature overnight. The next morning, blend well, cover and set aside in refrigerator.

In a small saucepan, combine milk, lavender, smashed garlic cloves, vanilla bean and cinnamon. Bring to a boil, cover and remove from heat. Let stand for 30 minutes.

While milk mixture cools, squeeze roasted garlic from skins. Chop until finely minced, then set aside.

Combine egg yolks and sugar in the bowl of an electric mixer fitted with a whip (if mixing by hand, use a large-bulbed whisk). Beat at high speed until yolks are pale and form a ribbon when dropped from beater. Beat in nutmeg.

Remove vanilla bean from milk and scrape seeds back into pot. Discard bean, lavender branch, smashed garlic cloves and cinnamon stick.

With motor running, gradually pour milk

into egg and sugar mixture. Then pour into a heavy-bottomed saucepan. Fill a large mixing bowl with ice cubes and set aside. Cook egg mixture over low heat, stirring constantly, until it forms a very thick custard that will thickly coat a wooden spoon (about 180°F on a candy thermometer). Add minced roasted garlic and blend thoroughly. Remove custard from heat and place pan on bed of ice. Stir in *crème fraîche*. Keep stirring until mixture cools, about 5 minutes. Chill in refrigerator, about 45 minutes.

Freeze in an ice-cream maker according to manufacturer's instructions. Spoon into a plastic container and store in freezer until serving time.

Serve ice cream garnished with lavender flowers or candied violets. You might also serve with some caramel sauce, milk-chocolate shavings or raspberries.

Wine: Blandy's Madeira 5-Year-Old Bual
(Portugal: Madeira)

Apple Spice Cake with Roasted Garlic

GARLIC CAKE? Even we were skeptical. But we'd heard tales of the several different, delectable garlic cakes served at New Orleans's Upperline Restaurant during their annual garlic festival. We think we've done the idea justice with our recipe, because after one bite, we were hooked on this rustic, apple-studded version with smoky garlic overtones.

SERVES 8 TO 10

1½ cups plus 2 tablespoons
     unbleached flour

1 teaspoon baking soda

¼ teaspoon salt

½ teaspoon ground cinnamon

¼ teaspoon ground ginger

⅛ teaspoon freshly grated nutmeg
  Grated zest of 1 large lemon
  Juice of 1 large lemon

3 large, tart apples, peeled, cored and
  chopped medium-fine

8 tablespoons (1 stick) unsalted
  butter, softened

⅔ cup sugar
  Flesh of 2 heads roasted
  garlic (see page 34)

2 tablespoons ruby port wine
  or applejack

1 large egg

½ cup milk

⅔ cup finely chopped pecans

2 tablespoons confectioners' sugar

Preheat oven to 350°F. Thoroughly butter a 9-inch round cake pan.

Sift together flour, baking soda, salt and spices. Set aside.

Combine lemon zest, lemon juice and apple pieces in a medium-sized bowl. Mix with your hands to thoroughly coat apples. Set aside.

In the bowl of an electric mixer, cream butter thoroughly. Gradually add sugar, beating vigorously and scraping sides several times. Beat in garlic and port, scraping sides several times. Add egg and beat until mixture is smooth.

Gradually add flour mixture to butter mixture, alternating with milk. Blend at low speed, scraping sides of mixing bowl several times. Remove bowl from mixer and stir in apple mixture. Stir in pecans. Blend thoroughly.

Pour batter into prepared cake pan, smoothing top with a spatula. Bake until cake shrinks from sides of pan and a toothpick inserted into center comes out clean, 60 to 75 minutes.

Transfer cake to rack and cool. Cover cake pan with a large plate or another rack and invert to release cake. Remove baking pan. Place a serving plate over cake bottom and flip cake over, top side up. Sift confectioners' sugar over cake.

Serve plain, or with whipped cream or Honey-Poached Garlic Sauce.

Eleanor Roosevelt ate three chocolate-covered cloves of garlic every day to keep her memory sharp.

Garlic Festivals

Adams Garlic Festival
August
Pawcatuck, Connecticut
Adams Family Farm
(860) 599-4241

Canadian Field Day
June
Lasallete, Ontario, Canada
Joe Ondusko, Garlic Growers
Association of Ontario

Canadian Garlic Festival
August
Sudbury, Ontario, Canada
(705) 693-3072

Celebrated Clove Garlic Festival
Fall
Boston, Massachusetts
Bruce Bickford
(508) 369-5329

Chez Panisse Garlic Festival
July 14
Berkeley, California
Chez Panisse Restaurant

Fox Run Winery Garlic Festival
August
Penn Yan, New York
(315) 536-4616 or
(800) 636-9786

Garlic Fest
May
Fairfield, Connecticut
Notre Dame Catholic School
(203) 372-6521

Gilroy Garlic Festival
July
Gilroy, California
(408) 842-1625

Glorious Garlic Festival
August
Perth, Ontario, Canada
(613) 273-5683

Great Northern Garlic Lovers Festival
August
Simcoe, Ontario, Canada
(519) 294-0523

Hudson Valley Garlic Festival
September
Saugerties, New York
Rod Wilson
(914) 246-3090
or (518) 677-3544

Israel Family Village Festival
August
Arlington, Washington
(360) 435-2270

Los Angeles Garlic Festival
July
Westwood, California
(800) 96-GARLIC

Ohio Garlic Festival
September
Wellington, Ohio
Bob Zimmerman and
Wendy Douglas
(330) 855-1141

**Peconic River Herb Farm
Garlic Day**
September
Calverton, New York
(516) 364-0058

**Southern Vermont Garlic and
Herb Festival**
September
Whitingham, Vermont
Steve Wrathll
(802) 368-7147

**Virginia Wine and Garlic
Festival**
October
Amherst, Virginia
Richard Hanson
(804) 946-5169

**Washington, D.C., Garlic
Festival**
June
Montgomery County, Maryland
Margaret Leitch
(301) 417-6698

**Western N.Y. Garlic Harvest
Fest**
August
Batavia, New York
Gary Skoog
(716) 637-6586

Sources

Garlic and Other Alliums by Mail

The Allium Connection
1339 Swainwood Drive
Glenview, IL 60025
(847) 729-4823
John F. Swenson
One of the world's leading allium experts, Mr. Swenson imports a variety of French shallots for retail sales. And he manages to locate a large variety of fine garlic for both seed and culinary purposes.

Bobba-Mike's Garlic Farm
P.O. Box 261
Orrville, OH 44667
(330) 855-1141
Bob Zimmerman and Wendy Douglas grow high-quality culinary garlic, including more than a dozen hardneck varieties. They sell gift packages, braids and seed cloves.

Chester Aaron
P.O. Box 388
Occidental, CA 95465
(707) 874-3114
Aaron grows a small amount of interesting garlic, most of which is sold to chefs in the Bay area.

His books on garlic are in bookstores everywhere.

Christopher Ranch
305 Bloomfield Avenue
Gilroy, CA 95020
(408) 847-1100
Probably the world's largest garlic producer, Christopher Ranch markets several lines and sizes of garlic and produces sauces, salsas and peeled cloves for restaurant and institutional use.

Filaree Farm
182 Conconully Highway
Okanogan, WA 98840
(509) 422-6940
Maya Watershine Woods
Over 450 varieties of garlic have been grown on this organic farm. An excellent source for seed cloves, hardneck and softneck culinary garlics and an excellent dehydrated garlic powder. Gift boxes can be shipped nationwide. They sell the book *Growing Great Garlic*, essential for all who would like to grow the stinking rose.

Garlic Valley Farms
Glendale, CA 91201
(800) 424-7990

William Anderson
Products include Garlic Juice Spray, an 8-ounce pump bottle containing the juice of 150 cloves, and Juicy Garlic Puree, an 8-ounce squeeze bottle of finely pureed raw garlic. Anderson also manufactures a garlic-based insect repellent called Victor Mosquito Barrier, available at Walmart, Home, Ace and Lowes stores. ("We are tree huggers here," Anderson says. "We are using too many poisons. We want to use natural methods to control pests.")

Kingsfield Gardens
Blue Mounds, WI 53517
(608) 924-9341
Richard Abernathy and Erica Koenigsaecker
These Wisconsin organic farmers grow both the hard-to-find French gray shallots and the large, better-known red shallots. They are also an excellent source for Red Bottle onions and Cipollini onions. They grow a variety of exceptionally clean and flavorful leeks. Their season is late summer through late autumn.

Robison Ranch
P.O. Box 1018
Walla Walla, WA 99362
(509) 525-8807
Jim Robison
This is an excellent source for very plump, richly flavored shallots and garlic (late summer through early winter), as well as Walla Walla onions (July and August).

Garlic for the Garden

These are sources for everything you need for growing garlic, from seed cloves of various varieties to information about how to do it.

The Cook's Garden
P.O. Box 535
Londonderry, VT 05148
(800) 457-9703

Garlic Seed Foundation
Rose Valley Farm
Rose, NY 14542-0149

Johnny's Selected Seeds
Foss Hill Road
Albion, ME 04910
(207) 437-9294

Seed Savers Exchange
Rural Route 3
P.O. Box 339
Decorah, IA 52101
(319) 382-5990

Seeds of Change Organic Seeds
P.O. Box 15700
Santa Fe, NM 87506-5700
(505) 438-8080

Shepherd's Garden Seeds
6116 Highway 9
Felton, CA 95018
(860) 482-3638

Southern Exposure Seed Exchange
P.O. Box 158
North Garden, VA 22959

Garlic and Health

Garlic Information Center Hotline
Cornell University Medical College
(800) 330-5922
To check ongoing research into garlic's power, call this number.

Swanson Health Products
P.O. Box 2803
Fargo, ND 58108
This company produces and distributes an enormous range of natural and herbal medicines, including scores of products involving garlic. The company catalog is available upon request.

Garlic Paraphernalia, Products and Publications

Clove-n-Vine
17500 SW Oldsville Road
McMinnville, OR 97128
Besides the usual garlic paraphernalia, Clove-n-Vine publishes and sells a booklet, "How to Make a Garlic Braid."

Everything Garlic
P.O. Box 91104
West Vancouver, BC
V7V3N3 Canada
(800) 668-6299
This retail operation specializes in everything garlic.

Flower Films
10341 San Pablo Avenue
El Cerrito, CA 94530
Garlic Is as Good as Ten Mothers is a documentary made in the early '80s by Les Blank. The 52-minute film is available on videotape.

Garlic Seed Foundation
Rose Valley Farm
Rose, NY 14542-0149
David Stern
The Garlic Press is published periodically by the Foundation for garlic growers and garlic lovers. It contains current thinking and some really good writing on garlic.

General Housewares
Terra Haute, IN
(812) 232-1000
Their Good Grips Garlic Press
is self-cleaning and is the winner
of the Tylenol/Arthritis
Foundation Design Award.

The House of Garlic
63 East State Street
Doylestown, PA 18901
This store sells everything a
garlic lover might enjoy.

Mostly Garlic Magazine
Doug Urig
19 E. Church Street
Milan, OH 44846
Write to the above address for a
subscription to this publication.

**Progressive International
Corporation**
P.O. Box 97046
Kent, WA 98064-9746
This company produces and
distributes all kinds of house-
wares, including scores of items
for dealing with garlic.

Vermont Garlic Company
P.O. Box 12
Whetstone Road
Marlboro, VT 05344
(802) 254-2527
Fax: (802) 258-4767
This company produces a variety
of dried garlic mixes as well as
fresh bottled preparations.

Specialty Food Products

Dean & DeLuca
560 Broadway
New York, NY 10012
(800) 221-7714
Now with locations outside of
New York City, this company is
among the finest sources for all
specialty products, including
cheeses, vinegars, imported olive
oils, exotic grains, dried mushrooms, fresh mushrooms, fruits,
chiles, Mediterranean olives such
as Kalamata and Niçoise, anchovies, polenta and Arborio rice.

El Paso Chile Company
909 Texas Avenue
El Paso, TX 79901-1524
(800)27-IS-HOT
This is our preferred source for
high-quality hot sauces, salsas
and chiles. It also offers tins of
dried chile powders, including
red jalapeño and pasilla.

**Matanzas Creek Winery
Tasting Room**
6097 Bennett Valley Road
Santa Rosa, CA 95404-9583
(707) 528-6464
This celebrated winery has become equally famous for its organically grown lavender. What
began as a lush entrance-to-the-
winery garden has developed
into a serious business. If you
want dried lavender for culinary
purposes, get it here.

Orlando Casados
P.O. Box 1149
San Juan Pueblo, NM 87566
(505) 852-4482
This is an excellent source for
dried chiles.

The West Point Market
1711 West Market Street
Akron, OH 44313
(800) 838-2156
Well known in the specialty food
industry, this market is a fine
source for hard-to find-products
such as Mediterranean olives,
high-quality olive oils, walnut
oils, fruit vinegars, exotic grains,
dried beans, flours and a wide
variety of imported cheeses and
chocolate.

Zingerman's Delicatessen
422 Detroit Street
Ann Arbor, MI 48104
(734) 663-DELI
Fax: (313) 769-1235
Besides making the best deli
sandwiches in the cosmos, this
Ann Arbor institution is nation-
ally celebrated for its extensive
collection of olive oils, vinegars,
imported and domestic cheeses,
salt-packed anchovies and capers
and other specialty products. A
mail-order catalog makes it possible for the entire country to enjoy Ari Weinzweig's great store.

Meats, Poultry, Shellfish

Mr. Brisket
2156 South Taylor Road
Cleveland Heights, OH 44118
(216) 932-8620
Accustomed to shipping prime meats and kosher-style-killed, hormone-free poultry around the world, owner Sanford Herskovitz is also an enthusiastic source for information about beef, veal, lamb, pork and poultry.

S. Wallace Edwards & Sons, Inc.
P.O. Box 25
Surry, VA 23883
(800) 222-4267
This family-owned Virginia ham company has produced cured and smoked hams, sausages and bacon since the early 1920s. They use as little nitrate and salt as possible, hickory-smoke their products at high temperatures and age them in climate-controlled rooms. The Wigwam hams age for one full year. Edwards's remarkable bacon is lightly cured, never injected with water or chemicals and hickory smoked for 18 hours. When you cook it, the slices stay virtually the same size, rather than shrinking.

Taylor United
SE 130 Lynch Road
Shelton, WA 98584
(360) 426-6178
The Taylor family is a popular West Coast source for farmed oysters. Now Taylor is farming the less common "Mediterranean" mussels, which are especially meaty and tender. They spawn at a different season from other varieties, so they are available in summer when the others are not especially desirable. Taylor ships mussels all over the country.

Grains, Beans, Flours

Arrowhead Mills
P.O. Box 2059
Hereford, TX 79045
(806) 364-0730
This company is one of the best producers of certified organic flours and beans. It will ship directly to your home and can also advise you about where to purchase its products in your region.

The Fowler's Milling Company
12500 Fowlers Mill Road
Chardon, OH 44022
(800) 321-2024 or
(216) 286-2024
Rick Erickson
This is an excellent source for stone-ground flours, medium-grind yellow cornmeal and grits. Fowler's also produces a fine line of dry mixes for pancakes, muffins and cornbreads.

King Arthur Flour Baker's Catalogue
P.O. Box 876
Norwich, VT 05055
(800) 827-6836
An excellent source for high-quality flours and cornmeal, as well as for other products related to home baking. We especially like the large, very heavy baking tile, as well as the lightweight metal paddle.

Lowell Farms
4 N. Washington
El Campo, TX 77437
(888) 484-9213
Fax: (409) 541-5655
Lowell and Linda Raun
These Texas rice farmers grow and sell certified organic white jasmine and brown jasmine rice.

Pans

The Pan Man
P.O. Box B
Perrysburg, NY 14129
(716) 532-5154
A good source for cast-iron skillets.

Garlic on the Internet

Any of the internet search engines will yield tens of thousands of references to garlic. Here are a few popular sites that can provide a lot of information.

www.gilroy.org
(Gilroy Chamber of Commerce)

www.garlicfest.com
(Gilroy Garlic Festival)

www.hopefarm.com/garlic.htm
(Hudson Valley Garlic Festival)

www.garliclovers.com
(Washington, D.C., Garlic Festival)

e-mail: garlic8@aol.com

e-mail: garlic@mistral.co.uk
(Garlic Information Center, Catsfield, East Sussex, England)

e-mail: garlik@earthlink.net
(Garlic Research Labs, Glendale, Calif.)

BIBLIOGRAPHY

Aaron, Chester. *Garlic Is Life*. Berkeley: Ten Speed Press, 1996.

Airola, Paavo. *The Miracle of Garlic*. Sherwood, Ore.: Health Plus Publishers, 1978.

Anderson, Burton. *The Wine Atlas of Italy*. London: Reed International Books, 1996.

Anderson, Jean, and Barbara Deskins. *The Nutrition Bible*. New York: William Morrow, 1995.

Artusi, Pellegrino. *The Art of Eating Well*. (translated by Kyle M. Phillips III). New York: Random House, 1996.

Beard, James, and Sam Aaron. *How to Eat Better for Less Money*. New York: Simon & Schuster, 1954.

Byler, Emma. *Plain and Happy Living*. Cleveland, Ohio: Goosefoot Acres Press, 1991.

Corriher, Shirley O. *CookWise*. New York: William Morrow, 1997.

Crawford, Stanley. *A Garlic Testament*. New York: HarperCollins, 1992.

Culpeper, Nicholas. *Culpeper's Complete Herbal*. Sonoma, CA: Foulsham & Co., 1995. Originally published as *The English Physician*. 1652.

Damrosch, Barbara. *The Garden Primer*. New York: Workman, 1988.

Dal Bozzo, Jerry. *The Stinking Rose Cookbook*. Berkeley, Calif.: Celestial Arts, 1994.

Duke, James A. *The Green Pharmacy*. Emmaus, Pa.: Rodale, 1997.

Engeland, Ron L. *Growing Great Garlic*. Okanogan, Wash.: Filaree Productions, 1991.

Fulder, Stephen, and John Blackwood. *Garlic*. Rochester, Vt.: Healing Arts Press, 1991.

Goldstein, Darra. *The Georgian Feast*. New York: HarperCollins, 1993.

Harris, Lloyd J. *The Book of Garlic*. New York: Holt Rinehart Winston, 1975.

Hausman, Patricia, and Judith Benn Hurley. *The Healing Foods*. New York: Dell, 1989.

Heinerman, John. *The Healing Benefits of Garlic*. New Canaan, Conn.: Keats Publishing, 1994.

Jones, Henry A., and Louis K. Mann. *Onions and Their Allies*. New York: Interscience Publishers, 1963.

Lang, Jenifer Harvey, ed. *Larousse Gastronomique*. New York: Crown, 1988.

Laube, James. *The Wine Spectator's California Wine*. New York: Wine Spectator Press, 1995.

Luard, Elisabeth. *The Old World Kitchen*. New York: Bantam, 1987.

McGee, Harold. *On Food and Cooking: The Science and Lore of the Kitchen*. New York: Charles Scribner's Sons, 1984.

Manniche, Lise. *An Ancient Egyptian Herbal*. Austin: University of Texas Press, 1989.

Ody, Penelope. *The Complete Medicinal Herbal*. London: Dorling Kindersley, 1993.

Oldmeadow, Ernest. *The Lilies of the Kitchen*. London: Wine and Food Society, 1943.

Parker, Robert M., Jr. *The Wines of the Rhône Valley*. New York: Simon & Schuster, 1987.

———. *Parker's Wine Buyer's Guide*. New York: Simon & Schuster (a Fireside Book), 1993.

Pennington, Jean A.T., and Helen Nichols Church. *Food Values of Portions Commonly Used*. Philadelphia: J.B. Lippincott,1980.

Pliny. *Natural History* (translated by W.H.S. Jones). Cambridge, Mass.: Harvard University Press, 1969.

Roosevelt, Nicholas. *Creative Cooking*. New York: Harper & Brothers, 1956.

———. *Good Cooking*. New York: Harper & Brothers, 1959.

Robinson, Jancis. *The Oxford Companion to Wine*. New York: Oxford University Press, 1994.

Root, Waverley. *Food*. New York: Simon & Schuster, 1980.

Selko, Adrienne. *Do I Have to Wear Garlic Around My Neck?* Cleveland, Ohio: Interex, 1996.

Simmons, Amelia. *American Cookery* (facsimile of 1796 work). Toronto: Oxford University Press, 1958.

Simonds, Nina. *Classic Chinese Cuisine* (revised edition). Boston, Mass.: Houghton Mifflin, 1994.

Stoker, Bram. *Dracula*. New York: Oxford University Press, 1983.

Sunshine Research. *All About Garlic*. Medford, Ore., 1987.

Thorne, John. *Outlaw Cook*. New York: Farrar Straus Giroux, 1992.

Thornton, Phineas, The *Southern Gardener and Receipt Book*. Newark, N.J.: A. L. Dennis, 1845; Facsimile: Birmingham, Ala.: Oxmoor House, 1984.

Trenhaile, Diane. *How to Make a Garlic Braid*. McMinnville, Ore.: Clove-n-Vine, 1995.

Truax, Carol, ed. *Ladies' Home Journal Cookbook*. Garden City, N.Y.: Doubleday, 1960.

Tschirky, Oscar. *"Oscar" of the Waldorf's Cook Book* (facsimile of 1896 work). New York: Dover Publications, 1973.

Wine Spectator's Ultimate Guide to Buying Wine, 5th edition. New York: Wine Spectator Press, 1996.

Wolf, Leonard. *Dracula: The Connoisseur's Guide*. New York: Broadway, 1997.

INDEX